S0-AVC-687

Dedicated to:

Dave Addie

Neal Allen

Jakob Ambrosius

Manuel Balsa

Ed Bean

Gordon Buchanan

Paul Burke

Bill Butler

Dick Colf

Mike Dalton

Ernie Elko

Gary Gregg

Don Hamilton

Ron Hodgson

Jim Hole

Linda Hughes

Gerald Knoll

Walter Kuchar

Larry Makelki

Tim Melton

Art Mikalcheon

Cal Nichols

Al Owen

Dick Paine

Marcel Roberge

Roger Roberge

Harold Roozen

Bruce Saville

Simon Sochatsky

Rusty Stalwick

Barry Weaver

Keith Weaver

Jim Woods

Jim Zanello

and

Anonymous

Edmonton's Hockey Knights is a publication of the Edmonton Sun and is not associated with, endorsed by or sponsored by the Edmonton Oilers Hockey Club and Edmonton Investors Group Limited Partnership or any of their affiliates, the National Hockey League or any of its member teams or other affiliates, or the National Hockey League Players' Association.

Acknowledgments

Publisher
Craig Martin

Creative Director
Terry Cowan

Photo Editors
Perry Mah
Terry Cowan

Editors
Laurie MacFayden
Shirley Taylor

Photo Reproduction
Brad Ray
Alex Wylie

Production
Will Stephani
Dru Warwick

Research
Darcy Anderson
John Sinclair

Graphics
Gary Logie

Marketing and Promotions
Bonnie Lopushinsky

A special thank you to all the Edmonton Sun writers
and photographers past and present whose words and
images help capture the special history
of hockey in Edmonton.
Thank you to Jack Manson, Mick Poliak
and the Edmonton Archives for access
to their hockey memorabilia.

Cover Photograph
Perry Mah

Cover Design
Terry Cowan

Table of Contents

Copyright The Edmonton Sun, 1998

All rights reserved. The use of any part of this publication reproduced, transmitted in any form or by any means, electronic, mechanical, recording or otherwise, or stored in a retrieval system, without the prior consent of the publisher, is an infringement of the copyright law. In the case of photocopying or other reprographic copying of the material, a licence must be obtained from the Canadian Copyright Licensing Agency (CANCOPY) before proceeding.

Printed by Quality Color Press
Printed in Canada

Canadian Cataloguing in Publication Data

Jones, Terry, 1948-
Edmonton's Hockey Knights, 79-99

ISBN 0-9684526-0-4

1. Edmonton Oilers (Hockey team)--History. I. Title.

GV848.E35J66 1998   796.962'64   C98-901292-1

About The Author

Terry Jones is *The Edmonton Sun*'s exceptionally versatile and well-travelled sports columnist. With a list of coverage credits which include 10 Olympic Games and another dozen major international Games, Jones has covered 26 Grey Cups, 18 Super Bowls, more than 100 World Series games, eight World Figure Skating Championships and a long list of other major national and international sports events including World Cups of soccer.

But to be a sports columnist in Edmonton, first you have to be a hockey writer. A native of Lacombe, with 31 years covering sport in Edmonton beginning at The *Journal* and on to his happy home at *The Sun*, Jones has covered most major moments of Oilers history including all 206 playoff games. Our man has also covered all of the Canada Cups and similar events since the '74 Canada-Russia Series and this spring will cover his 400th Stanley Cup playoff game.

Jones, whose work also appears in the *Toronto Sun*, *Calgary Sun*, *Ottawa Sun* and on the CANOE Internet site, has written several other books. They include *The Great Gretzky* and two updated *Yearbook* versions of the book. He also wrote books on the Edmonton Oilers and Calgary Flames for the Creative Education series in the U.S. Co-author of a book on the Eskimos of the '70s, *Decade of Excellence*, he also wrote five CFL yearbooks and is a veteran radio and TV commentator.

A resident of Sherwood Park with his wife Linda, Terry has a son, Shane, and twin daughters, Nicole and Trina.

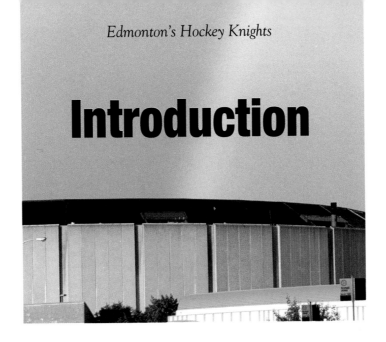

Introduction

Journalism is history on the run. And what a run it's been covering the Edmonton Oilers as a sports columnist. Never in the entire history of the NHL has there been a story like the first 20 years of Edmonton Oilers hockey in the City of Champions. And to take on a project which would also celebrate the 20th anniversary of *The Edmonton Sun*, a newspaper which has always been about sports and photography, was a joy. So much has happened, I found the years began to run into each other. To rewrite myself and the history I wrote on the run, and to try to bring back to life *Sun* coverage of the Oilers served another purpose which I hope hits home as you take the trip with the words and the pictures on these pages. My hope is that it reminds you of how incredibly fortunate we have been living here in Edmonton. And, more than anything, I hope this book serves to remind us all of what we almost lost.

Never has there been so much success so soon. A Stanley Cup within the first five years. Five Stanley Cups in a span of seven years. A score is 20 years and this book celebrates scoring – the 6,065 goals the Oilers have scored – more than any other team in the league over the same span. It celebrates the greats who scored them. It celebrates the management which built and rebuilt the team. And it celebrates the city which refused to lose its team every time all looked lost.

From the beginning to a new beginning with a new young team forging forward to the future with a unique multi-owner community concept, this book celebrates a small-market team also attempting to defy the odds on the ice where the object remains to excite and entertain in an era of neutral-zone traps and left-wing locks.

Terry Jones

Chapter 1

You've Come A Long Way, Baby

The National Hockey League was a million miles away.

It was a voice on the radio — the voice of Foster Hewitt as you scrubbed in a tub in the middle of the kitchen floor on Saturday night, bath night on the Prairies, your mother pouring the hot water from a kettle while your grandfather danced a jig in the living room with a broom, the Toronto Maple Leafs having just scored.

It was still a million miles away when you rode your bicycle to your grandfather's house and gaped in awe at his brand new black and white television screen, waiting for *Hockey Night In Canada* to come on the air with play well under way.

And it was still a million miles away when your dad took you to watch Gordie Howe, Alex Delvecchio, Terry Sawchuk and the Detroit Red Wings, who were holding their training camp in Edmonton and playing an exhibition game against the Western Hockey League Flyers.

It was still a million miles away when you watched Glen Sather win a Memorial Cup with the Edmonton Oil Kings, and when Wild Bill Hunter introduced the idea of the World Hockey Association.

And for a while there, in 1998 – in the heart of hockey but on the extremities of most maps – it looked as if it might, sometime soon, be a million miles away again.

To understand what the NHL and the five-time Stanley Cup-winning Edmonton Oilers mean to a city and a sport, balancing the will to win with the will to survive as the league's modern day small-market minor miracle, you have to know Edmonton's hockey history.

The Edmonton Eskimos hockey club, 1920-21

1

What might a hockey player from 1894, able to fast-forward through time to Edmonton for one game in 1998 think as the Oilers embark on their 20th season in the NHL?

The first recorded hockey game in Edmonton was on Christmas Day, 1894. Thistle beat Strathcona 3-2. Nobody wore No. 99, but give Edmonton a team and the next thing you know they're playing for the Stanley Cup.

By December 14, 1908, hockey in Edmonton was already big time. That was the year the Edmonton Eskimos challenged the Montreal Wanderers for the Stanley Cup.

That's what you did back then. Challenge. There was no NHL as such yet. But the Stanley Cup was the Stanley Cup, even though it was supposed to be called the Dominion Hockey Challenge Cup. It didn't exactly *look* like the Stanley Cup, the one victorious players carry over their heads today. But it was the beginning of North America's oldest and grandest trophy. And it was, indeed, the exact trophy that Lord Frederick Arthur Stanley, Governor General of Canada, paid $48.67 to have a British silversmith design. It was seven-and-a-half inches tall and 11½ inches wide. And in 1908, Edmonton was playing for it.

Considering what would happen 80 and 90 years later – with free-agency becoming an enemy of small-market teams – maybe there

was some justice in Edmonton playing for that first Stanley Cup way back then.

The Edmonton Eskimos were champions of Alberta in the spring of 1908 and issued the challenge. But the Edmonton team that showed up to play for Lord Stanley's silverware in December wasn't the team that had won the province. In fact, the only two players from that team retained by player/manager Fred Whitcroft were forwards Jack Miller and Harold Deeton. And Deeton

Top to bottom: Edmonton Eskimos hockey club, 1920-21; Edmonton Superiors, 1930-31; Edmonton Waterloo Mercurys, 1949.

was the only home-grown hero, Miller being an import from Peterborough, Ont.

Professionalism was just coming into hockey at the time. And there were no rules. It was no problem for Edmonton to sign up a hockey superstar like the legendary Lester Patrick and a lesser star like Tom Phillips, for example. They were among hockey's original free agents.

While some of the ringer recruits like Ted Lindsay's father Bert, a goalie, actually showed up in Edmonton to train with the team and play three games locally before heading to Montreal, Patrick and Phillips met the team in Winnipeg and never did actually set foot on Jasper Avenue or make it into the team picture.

The team lost its first game 7-4 and won the second 7-6. At the time the Stanley Cup championship was a two-game total-goal series, so Montreal won the Cup 13 goals to Edmonton's 11. Several hockey historians would later write that the two best players on the team turned out to be the two genuine Eskimos, Deeton and Miller. Whitcroft hadn't played them in the first game. He'd admit, later in life, that if he'd played them in both games, Edmonton would probably have won the Stanley Cup.

A year later Edmonton challenged for the Cup again. This time it was against the Ottawa Senators, in Ottawa, in January of 1910 and Albert Henry George Grey, the next Governor General of Canada – who had donated the Grey Cup for football in 1904 – dropped the puck for the ceremonial faceoffs.

That series is remembered in Stanley Cup history because the first game had to be stopped after Edmonton's third goal, which gave

2

Jim (the Chief) Christiansen, left, and Jack Manson, with Dusty.

the Prairie challengers a 3-2 lead. It seems one of the Edmonton players "lost his trousers" and had to go to the dressing room. Later, the game was delayed for another 10 minutes because cigar and cigarette smoke from the 5,000 fans had filled the rink.

After the smoke had cleared, Edmonton lost the game 8-4. They also lost the second game, 13-7.

In 1923, the team now coached by Deacon White and starring Duke Keats went to the Stanley Cup as Western Canada Professional Hockey League champions, defeating the Regina Capitals in Edmonton before 7,000 fans – with ticket prices of $1.25, $1 and 75 cents.

Once again Edmonton's Stanley Cup opponents were the Ottawa Senators, starring a 21-year-old kid by the name of Frank (King) Clancy and featuring the likes of Cy Denneny, Sprague Cleghorn and goalie Clint Benedict. The Eskimos, featuring Bullet Joe Simpson, allegedly then the fastest man on skates, lost again – this time by soccer scores of 2-1 (overtime) and 1-0. The series is best remembered in Stanley Cup history for Clancy playing in goal for two minutes after Benedict took a two-minute penalty. Clancy didn't allow a goal, and ended up playing all six positions for Ottawa in that series.

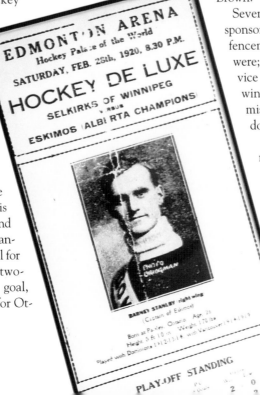

That was the last appearance Edmonton made in the Stanley Cup finals until 1983. But there was a lot of Edmonton hockey history in between.

In 1932 the Edmonton Superiors, sponsored by Gainers, travelled to St. Moritz, Switzerland, and won the world championship.

"There were no Russians involved back then, but that's what they called it when we played it," remembers Buster Brown, the spry 89-year-old grandfather of current Edmonton Eskimos defensive back Trent Brown.

Seven players actually worked at the Gainers plant which sponsored the Superiors. Only left-winger Brown and defenceman John Lammie are still alive. Team Tuxedo they were; the entire team was outfitted with tuxedos on the advice of a Winnipeg team which had taken on the world the winter before and had come home complaining that they missed a lot of functions because they didn't have tuxedos.

The "Soops," as they were known, were on a first-name basis with figure skater Sonja Henie in St. Moritz.

"She was living in St. Moritz with her mother and she dropped the puck for most of our games. We talked to her a lot around the hotel. She was a nice girl," Brown would remember 66 years later.

The team played games in Great Britain, Norway, Poland, Belgium, Czechoslovakia, Germany and Italy before heading to Paris for a warm-up tournament with three games against France.

"We played 38 games on our tour and won

34, tied three and only lost one. We played two games against France and lost one. That team was made up entirely of French-Canadians. But that was a highlight. We played before 18,000 fans in the Palais des Sports," said Brown. "We also played before crowds like we never saw before. It was a wonderful three months."

The actual championships were the easiest games the team played.

"Some were awful easy," remembers Brown.

The toughest games were played when the team returned home. "That year they put in a rule to allow the forward pass in Canada and we'd never played that way. We lost a few until we got on to it."

The Superiors somehow managed to get lost in Edmonton's hockey history.

"You know, nobody ever mentions us any more," says Brown today. "They haven't mentioned us for a long time. It's funny people never heard more about us over the years. We were the going team back then."

Along for the ride on that trip, representing the Edmonton Hockey Association, was a young Clarence Campbell who, a year earlier, had to be escorted off the ice in Trail, B.C., between Edmonton players after he officiated the game against the Trail Smoke Eaters which helped qualify Edmonton for the trip. That's the same Clarence Campbell who went on to become the legendary and long-time president of the NHL during the days now referred to as the Original Six. For 31 years, 1946-77, he ruled the NHL, the longest run for the head of any professional sports league in North America.

Campbell started many of the amateur sports associations that exist in Edmonton today.

"There was a time he ran everything in this town," remembers Cecil (Tiger) Goldstick, who was the trainer and equipment manager for most of the teams in town for years.

Despite the fact he was a Rhodes Scholar and represented Canada as a lawyer at the Nuremberg trials, Campbell's greatest joy was in refereeing hockey games.

"He was colourful," remembers Goldstick. "When he was dishing out penalties, he'd first point to the player, then he'd point to the penalty box and if a player wanted to argue, that was OK, but Campbell wouldn't listen to him until after he was in the box. That's the way he worked."

Campbell explained his officiating style.

"I thought I was a darned good referee," Campbell told me way back when. "Referees were like Spitfire pilots in those days. All of us ran our machines differently. We all called the games by the seat of our pants."

Campbell, in that long-ago interview, said he did two things in Edmonton of which he was particularly proud.

"I built Renfrew Park," he said of the baseball field that

was later known as John Ducey Park and now, rebuilt as Telus Field, is home to the Triple-A Trappers. "And in the mid-'30s I owned the Eskimos football team by the simple procedure of using all my winter referee money to pay for the team debts."

In addition to Campbell, the Hockey Hall of Fame has inducted many Edmonton stars, one of the most famous of which was the legendary Eddie Shore. An Edmonton Eskimo in 1925-26, Shore went on to the Boston Bruins where he became the only defenceman to win four Hart Trophies. He was known throughout his career as "The Edmonton Express."

But it wasn't until 1948 that Edmonton again had a team to turn on the town. The Flyers became the first team to really get Edmonton's blood boiling since J. Percy Page and the Edmonton Grads owned the world of women's basketball between wars. The Flyers won the Allan Cup – donated by Sir Hugh Montagu Allan in 1908 – as Canadian senior hockey champions.

Gordie Watt was captain of the team. They named Watt honourary mayor of Edmonton when the Flyers won (bad boy Pug Young was named honourary police chief). And that week Watt became a father. In honour of the trophy he'd just won, he named his kid Allan. Allan Watt. Today he's the Oilers vice-president of sponsorships, sales and services.

Frank Currie coached the club. Al Rollins, who would go on to win the Vezina and Hart trophies with the Chicago Blackhawks in 1954, was the goalie. And the team featured the "receding hairline" of follicly challenged Elmer Kreller, Alex Pringle and Fred Smitten.

It was the Ottawa Senators, the team of the same name that defeated Edmonton in the 1923 Stanley Cup, providing the opposition for the series. It opened with a game in Regina, followed by two in Edmonton, and concluded with two in Calgary where the Flyers won the series, four games to one.

The team was the toast of the town. They came home to a parade down Jasper Avenue witnessed by an estimated 60,000 people, more than a quarter of the population of the city. The players were given the keys to the city and gifts galore.

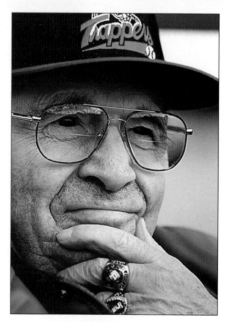

Clockwise from top left: Eddie Shore, Clarence Campbell, Cecil (Tiger) Goldstick.

"I still have a set of silverware I was given," says Louis Holmes, a player on that team who four years later would coach an Olympic gold medal-winning team. "We went over big. We were all shocked how big. In hockey back then, the Allan Cup was the next biggest thing to the Stanley Cup. It sure faded out over the years, but that's the way it was then."

Members of the 1947-48 Edmonton Flyers on a visit to city hall, back row, from left: Andy Clovechok, Doug Lane, Fred Smitten, Gordon Buttrey, Jack Manson, John Black, Billy Morrissey (stick boy). Front row: Louis Holmes, Edmonton Mayor Bill Smith, Councillor Terry Cavanagh.

The most famous of all the Edmonton hockey teams, after the Oilers, is the 1952 Edmonton Mercurys. But that's now, not then. Funny how history works.

When Canada took the NHL stars to the Olympics in Nagano, Japan, in 1998, an old, predominantly red, woollen jersey borrowed from the Hockey Hall of Fame was hung in prime position in the Team Canada dressing room. It was Al Purves's Edmonton Waterloo Mercurys 1952 Olympic sweater with the white Maple Leaf on the front and "Canada" stitched above his No. 4 on the back. It was there to provide motivation.

Back home, the former Mercs wanted Canada's multimillionaire pros to know they were cheering for them.

"We wanted to see Canada win the gold medal again before we die," said Purves. "We've had that last-team-to-win-an-Olympic-gold story long enough. It's time another batch of those gold medals were brought home where they belong.

"We wanted to be an inspiration. We're all flag-wavers, that's one thing old Mr. Christiansen taught us," he said of the owner of the Waterloo Mercury dealership who financed the trip after having taken the team to London in 1950, where they won the world championship – an event which would remain forgotten when the nation started recognizing the team as the last Canadian Olympic hockey champions. Other Canadian teams would win world championships after them; the Olympics would become the Mercurys' claim to fame. But they'd been ignored all those years.

Without their sponsor, Jim Christiansen, the Mercs wouldn't have been the team that won Canada's last gold in hockey. They wouldn't have been able to take the trip.

Christiansen, who died in 1953 from the pneumonia he caught during the Olympics, bankrolled the entire team, feeding them when their Canadian Amateur Hockey Association pittance ran out.

"If it wasn't for Mr. Christiansen we would have gone hungry a lot of nights," said Holmes of the man who spent $30,000 – a fortune in those days – to fund the world championship trip of 1950 and as much and more for the Olympic trip in 1952.

It's too bad Christiansen didn't live to see the day his squad would be Edmonton's most famous hockey team – after the one that ended up winning Stanley Cups.

It felt good, finally, to be celebrated. And the fact is, they were celebrated more in 1988, 1992, 1994 and 1998 than they had been when they actually won the Olympic gold medal in hockey, the last one Canada would win in some – possibly all – of their lifetimes. Just to be invited to centre ice to be introduced at the start of an Oilers game before the NHL pros headed to Nagano was a kick for the old Mercs.

Until the organizers of the Calgary '88 Olympics did something special to honour them, they were indeed a forgotten team. After a while, their noses were out of joint.

"Sure, we were mad," Dave Miller admitted to me about four Olympics ago. "We were a part of history. We were the last Canadian team to win a gold medal. That's not a bad claim to fame."

Miller died in 1996. Thomas Pollock and George Abel passed away between Olympics, too. There are seven of them, plus their coach and their trainer, still left. Billy Gibson lives in Lethbridge. Ralph Hansch, Billy Dawe, Eric Patterson, Jack Davies, Don Gauf and Purves all live in Edmonton. Coach Louis Holmes and trainer Monty Ford are still in Edmonton as well. Before the Nagano Olympics, they were introduced at a Coliseum full of Oiler fans and, as would be the case with the '48 Flyers team that was honoured in the same way a month or so later, a special-edition sweater was created and made available for sale.

The 1954-55 Edmonton Flyers.

Glenn Hall, above, tended goal for the 1952-53 Flyers before starring with the NHL's Chicago Blackhawks. Left, Zane Feldman. Right, Leo LeClerc.

They're all in their 70s now and coach Holmes is in his 80s. And while there was a time, during the prime of their lives, when they resented the fact that world-championship teams like the Penticton Vees and Trail Smoke Eaters seemed to own a special place in Canada's sports history and they didn't, they certainly got over it.

In a book published prior to the '98 Winter Olympics, celebrating Canada's gold medal-winning teams, there was a picture of the parade in Edmonton after the Mercs returned with their Olympic gold medals in '52.

Maybe that's how they should be remembered – in the greater glory of that afternoon, as seen in that picture – instead of the way it really was.

They played 51 games in 85 days on a European tour leading to the Olympic gold that year. But the truth is that when they returned home, much like the Edmonton Superiors before them, they were greeted by only family and friends. Eventually a downtown

Johnny Bucyk

motorcade was put together for the Mercs.

"People turned out for the parade only because they were given a half-day holiday," remembers Purves. "I could see it on their faces. They were saying, 'Who the hell are they?'"

• • •

Fame and remembrance are not the same things. Remembered by more of the over-50 crowd of today was Edmonton's first real professional hockey team, the Western Hockey League farm team of the Detroit Red Wings.

The Edmonton Flyers of the 1950s had some particularly powerful lineups.

In 1952-53, Al Arbour and Glenn Hall were the stars for Bud Poile's Flyers as they won their first President's Cup in the WHL. But the best team was the 1954-55 club, which included future

Hall of Famers Hall and Arbour, Edmonton natives Normie Ullman and Johnny Bucyk, Keith Allen, Bronco Horvath, Vic Stasiuk, Jerry Melnyk, Hugh Coflin, Don Poile, Eddie Stankiewicz, Ray Hannigan and Larry Zeidel. That team swept the Calgary Stampeders in four games to win the President's Cup and become the first team in WHL history to win both the President's Cup and the Director's Cup for finishing first in league play.

"It was before Detroit brought us all up to the NHL and made the trades to send Bucyk, Horvath and Stasiuk to Boston," Glenn Hall said of the so-called "Uke line."

"The thing is that we were all young players except a guy like Keith Allen, who was a little older. It was a pretty good hockey team. But if you could have kept it together another two or three years, it would have been an unbelievably good hockey team," the Stony Plain farmer who would go on to become Mr. Goalie, arguably the greatest goalie in

the game with the Chicago Blackhawks, said looking back 43 years after the fact.

"We just had a bunch of good, hard-working hockey players. Horvath, Stasiuk and Bucyk was a real good line. Ullman, Melnyk and McNeill were really young kids. Arbour was a real solid defenceman.

"We were all just thrilled to be playing together in Edmonton with the Flyers and had no idea if we'd make it to the NHL or not. I don't remember spending a whole lot of time worrying about it. I didn't really care. I loved to play hockey. We weren't getting paid much money. I think I made $4,500 and the minimum in the NHL was $6,000. We had a great team and we were having a great time. The Gardens was generally full. We had a great rivalry with Calgary. The two cities hated each other back then, too. The atmosphere was great. Everybody on that team really liked each other. It was a terrific time in our lives."

That was a great time in Edmonton's sports history overall. Jackie Parker, Johnny Bright, Normie Kwong, Rollie Miles and the Edmonton Eskimos football team were winning Grey Cups in 1954-55-56, and curler Matt Baldwin was winning Briers.

In 1961-62, Poile's Flyers would win the WHL title again. Mark Messier's dad Doug played for that team. Famed bad boy Howie Young, Billy McNeill, Eddie Joyal, Len Lunde, Roger Dejordy, Chuck Holmes and Don Poile also played for that club.

At that time, the American Hockey League was taking over from the WHL as the developmental league. And times were getting tough. The 1962-63 season would be the last for pro hockey in Edmonton for a while. But the Flyers name would live on in the NHL.

In 1966 Keith Allen and Bud Poile would go to Philadelphia to start an NHL expansion franchise together.

"We named the Philadelphia Flyers after the Edmonton Flyers," said Poile.

In the Edmonton hockey era that followed, junior hockey was king and junior hockey was the Oil Kings.

The Kings were in existence before the pro Flyers skated in the old Western league. In fact, many of the stars of the Flyers started with the team formed in 1950-51 under the sponsorship of Edmonton Waterloo Mercurys' famed patron Jim Christiansen. On the Oil Kings team in 1951-52 were Bucyk, Ullman, Melnyk and McNeill. The team was coached by Ken McAuley. And the manager was Leo LeClerc.

Ah, Leo (The Lip) LeClerc.

At the age of two he lost an eye because of ashes from his grandfather's pipe. But there was no damage done to his mouth. For 14 years

Top: Edmonton Eskimos game at Edmonton Gardens, 1920-21 season; middle: Edmonton Oil Kings owner Bill Hunter and coach Bill Gadsby; bottom, Memorial Cup-champion Oil Kings, 1965-66.

he referred to himself as the "only unpaid professional in hockey" as he directed the Oil Kings to an amazing run of success. He always refused to be paid for the job, said his former assistant GM Fred Windwick quoting The Lip as saying, 'If you pay me, you're going to try to tell me what to do.' "

With a team that included Bucyk, Ullman, Melnyk, Holmes, McNeill, Ray Kinasewich, Ron Tookey, Ed Diachuk and Jack Lamb, the Oil Kings made it to the Memorial Cup final on a 34-game winning streak. But they lost to the Rudy Pilous-coached St. Catharines Tee Pees.

In 1960 it was Edmonton-St. Catharines again with an Edmonton team that included Bruce MacGregor, Eddie Joyal, Larry Lund, Lorne Braithwaite and Don Passutto with Dale Gaume and Russ Gillow in goal. Again the Oil Kings lost.

Buster Brayshaw became coach of the Oil Kings for the trip to the 1960-61 Memorial Cup, which was no trip at all. It was the first time the event was staged in Edmonton.

Newcomers to the team included Butch Barber, Vince Downey, Larry Hale and Roger Bourbonnais. The stick boy was a kid by the name of Swede Knox, who would hold the position for several more years before going on to a long career as an NHL linesman.

Father Bauer's Toronto St. Michaels team won that series in six.

The next year the Oil Kings recruited a young man by the name of Glen Sather to play on the "kid line" with Butch Paul and Max Mestinsek. From Wainwright, Sather was an 18-year-old whose future career goal was to become a recreational director.

Again the Oil Kings made it to the Memorial Cup and again they lost, this time in five games to the Hamilton Red Wings, who had on their roster a young man who would become Canada's hero in the 1972 Canada-Russia Series – Paul Henderson.

The next year, Edmonton finally won the Memorial Cup.

The final was again played in the Gardens. This time it was against the Niagara Falls Flyers, coached by Hap Emms. Niagara Falls won the first game 8-0 but ended up losing the series, which turned on a hit by Pat Quinn that saw Niagara Falls star Gary Dornhoefer carried off the ice with a broken leg. Also injured for Niagara Falls in the series were Terry Crisp, Bill Goldsworthy, Don Awrey, Wayne Maxner and goalie George Gardiner.

Sather, Quinn and Bert Marshall, all members of that team, ended up as NHL coaches. Bob Falkenberg, Gregg Pilling, Ron Anderson, Dave Rochefort, Russ Kirk, Bourbonnais, Mestinsek, Paul, Barber, Doug Fox and Reg Taschuk also played on that squad.

Back again the following year, the Oil Kings lost to the Toronto Marlies in what became known in Edmonton as "the silent series." Wes Montgomery was the play-by-play broadcaster but Maple Leaf Gardens owner Harold Ballard refused to allow him to broadcast the games unless CHED Radio paid $500 a game for the privilege. The Marlies won in four straight games and no word was heard on local radio.

In 1964-65 the Memorial Cup final was back in Edmonton and if it had been rough in the Gardens two years earlier, that was nothing compared to this one.

The Oil Kings lost the first two games to the Niagara Falls Flyers but were up 5-1 in Game 3 with three minutes to play. Rosaire Paiment high-sticked Oil Kings defenceman Al Hamilton. A Flyer punched Kings rookie Ace Bailey. Bob Falkenberg was an on-ice spectator when Derek Sanderson sucker-punched him on the temple and then jumped on the unconscious Oil King defenceman and punched him five more times while he was on the ice. Another Flyer started pounding little Fran Huck, a "pickup" from Regina that teams were allowed in those days. It was at that point that the referee called 25 Edmonton police officers onto the ice.

It was the only game the Oil Kings won in a series in which Bernie Parent was the star in goal for Niagara Falls.

Leo LeClerc stepped down after that season. His Oil King teams had won six Abbott Cup championships to earn the trips to the Memorial Cups, one of which they won. One of the things that made those teams great was that they competed against clubs like the Lacombe Rockets, Drumheller Miners and Red Deer Rustlers in a regular-season schedule in the Central Alberta Hockey League, which became the Alberta Senior Hockey League.

LeClerc and Brayshaw and the Oil Kings of that era, famous for playing Sunday afternoon games at the Gardens featuring silver collections, were sponsored by the Detroit Red Wings. And the scouting of players by Clarence Moher played a big part in their success.

All that would change as a new Oil King era began – the Bill Hunter era.

Wild Bill Hunter may go down as the most memorable character in Edmonton sports history. His press conferences were legendary. He once called a press conference to announce that he was calling a press conference for the following day.

At a press conference to introduce a new head coach, Hunter was in mid-introduction when he noticed late-arriving radio man Wes

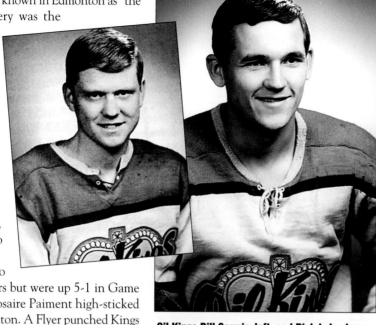

Oil Kings Bill Comrie, left, and Rick LeLacheur (1968-69 season).

Montgomery. "Come in, you asshole," said Hunter. And the new coach, Ken Hodge, figuring that must be his cue, came out from behind the curtain. Hunter's usually staged controversies with Calgary's Scotty Munro provided excellent entertainment. He was forever firing his coaches, including Bill Gadsby in the middle of a playoff series, to replace them with himself. And he organized several of his own Bill Hunter testimonial dinners.

In 1965-66, when the Fiery Red Leader era began in Edmonton, times were changing. The Oil Kings were still playing in the Alberta Senior Hockey League. And that was the year of years. The Oil Kings would win their second Memorial Cup. The Drumheller Miners would win the Allan Cup. The Lacombe Rockets would travel to Europe and win the Ahearne Cup. And the Red Deer Rustlers would win the Canadian Intermediate A title.

Hunter hired Billy Warwick as his first Oil Kings coach, but it was Ray Kinasewich who ended up taking over and coaching the club to the Memorial Cup title over Bep Guidolin's Oshawa Generals, a team which featured a kid named Bobby Orr.

Falkenberg was the captain of that club with Al Hamilton, Dave Rochefort and Ross Perkins as assistant captains. Don (Smoky) McLeod was the goalie. Other members of the team included Red Simpson, Jim Knox, Doug Barrie, Ross Lonsberry, Ace Bailey, Ron Walters, Jim Harrison (a pickup from Estevan, Sask.), Ted Rogers, Jim Schraefel, Kerry Ketter, Ron Anderson and Craig Cameron.

That summer the top junior teams in Canada formed the Canadian Major Junior Hockey League and raised the age limit to 21, broke away from the CAHA and lost the right to play in the Memorial Cup.

But the Oil Kings were involved in one of the wildest playoff series ever that spring against Brian Shaw's Moose Jaw Canucks, featuring a young Edmonton goalie by the name of Ken Brown playing out of his head in the Moose Jaw nets to upset the Oil Kings in a best-of-nine series which included three ties.

The next year the Tier 1 teams were legal and in 1968-69 the Oil Kings finally had a rival. Scotty Munro's Calgary Centennials were born. Edmonton lost the final three years in a row to Bobby Clarke, Reggie Leach and the Flin Flon Bombers. Finally, in 1970-71, Edmonton, now coached by Brian Shaw, beat the Patty Ginnell-coached Bombers

8

1962-63 Memorial Cup champion Edmonton Oil Kings included Glen Sather (back row, fifth from left).

in the final. And it was decided to take the team to Quebec City to play the Ramparts in a best-of-three series for the Memorial Cup. Led by Guy Lafleur, the Ramparts won 5-1 and 5-2.

Edmonton's last trip to the Memorial Cup was in 1971-72. Picking up Calgary goalie John Davidson, the Shaw-coached Oil Kings went to Ottawa for the national championship, which had switched to the tournament format still used today. Both the Cornwall Royals, coached by Orval Tessier, and the Peterborough Petes, coached by Roger Neilson, beat the Oil Kings.

Oil Kings playing at the beginning in the Bill Hunter era included Rick LeLacheur, Bill Comrie, Billy Moores, Bob and Ted McAneely, Bob Birdsell, Greg Boddy, Ian Wilkie, Frank Spring, Al Cameron, Ron Jones, Randy Wyrosub and Doug Kerslake.

Oil Kings of the back end in the Bill Hunter era included Phil Russell, Tom Bladon, Doug Soetaert, Darcy Rota, Don Kozak, John Rogers, Larry Hendrick, Fred Comrie, Randy Smith, Dave Inkpen, Terry Smith, Brian Ogilvie, Harold Snepts, Ted Olsen and Mike Will.

Ah, what it was like to be an Oil King.

"We were sort of like the Oilers are today," says Bill Comrie. "It was the Eskimos and us. It was a wonderful

Oil Kings alumni game, 1986: Top row, from left: Gord Garbutt, Lyle (Sparky) Kulchisky, Barry Debenham. Bottom row: Bill Comrie, Glen (Slats) Sather, Jim Knox.

From left, Oil Kings director Jim Pelehos, WCHL president Ed Chynoweth, WCHL chairman Brian Shaw, Oil Kings president Bill Hunter.

time. The games were all sold out, and to be as young as we were and recognized by everybody everywhere we went was really something. When you were growing up in Edmonton, you went to all the Oil King games. When I was young I went and watched Glen Sather and all those guys. And to actually put that jersey on ... it was like putting the Montreal Canadiens jersey on, to us."

Rick LeLacheur says that's the thing that may be hard to fathom in this day and age.

"It was an honour to play for that team."

Comrie, owner of the Brick Warehouse, and LeLacheur, recently retired as head of Economic Development Edmonton, both look back and say they owe a lot to Bill Hunter.

"Bill Hunter was a great inspiration for all of us," says Comrie. "He was always talking positive and his little sayings are still with all of us. What he taught us as young men, we were able to carry on into our future lives."

LeLacheur also swears by Hunter.

"He always put on an external show. But he had a heart of gold. And I feel very fortunate that he made me the captain of that team. He really helped me to develop leadership skills."

The Edmonton Oil Kings era was over soon enough. But Wild Bill Hunter was bringing a new era to Edmonton. And the National Hockey League wouldn't be a million miles away any more.

Chapter 2

Bring On The World

The flowers of the Edmonton sports media, skeptics all, had been invited to the back room of a Jasper Avenue restaurant called the Steak Loft by Bill Hunter, Gary Davidson and Dennis Murphy. They had a new hockey league to sell. And the selling started in that room, that night.

Davidson and Murphy had been founding fathers once before, giving birth to the American Basketball Association which took on the established National Basketball Association. Now it was hockey's turn.

The WHA began with Murphy and Davidson, not Hunter. But that's a technicality.

Murphy and Davidson had a problem. They needed a hockey man. And who better than Wild Bill Hunter?

"We didn't know a damned thing about hockey," Murphy laughs 25 years later.

But Murphy knew a born-in-Alberta Los Angeles sportswriter by the name of Walt Marlow. And Marlow knew Bill Hunter. All of a sudden Hunter was flying to California, and before long he was flying to California again with Ben Hatskin and Scotty Munro, the men who had broken away and formed an outlaw junior league and knew how to be hockey rebels.

Shortly after, a story broke in the *New York Times* naming Edmonton as one of 12 cities awarded a franchise in a new league to be known as the World Hockey Association.

WHA rookie Wayne Gretzky is sandwiched between Birmingham Bulls Craig Hartsburg, left, and Jim Turkiewicz. Opposite: New Oilers Eddie Mio, Peter Driscoll and Gretzky arrive from Indianapolis.

11

"This is no fly-by-night operation," said Hunter, starting the sales job when the steaks had been consumed and the wine and drinks were still being poured.

"It's major league all the way. It will operate next year. There is no question of that. I plan to hold a press conference next week with the founders of the new league right here in Edmonton."

Hunter laid it out.

"This is a one-shot opportunity for Edmonton to go major league. We don't have a building to go major league. But I'm confident the World Hockey Association will stimulate action."

It is impossible to celebrate the Oilers' 20th NHL season without celebrating the World Hockey Association.

If there hadn't been a WHA, there wouldn't have been an Edmonton Oilers franchise to merge with the NHL, or to save and secure for the future. And who knew that the Oilers would one day be the sole survivors of the WHA?

"If it hadn't been for the WHA there would be no Coliseum, no Edmonton Oilers in the National Hockey League and no Stanley Cups in Edmonton," Hunter said 25 years later.

"From the day we made the first announcement to the day we hired a local artist to design the logo, I always believed the Oilers would be in the NHL and that one day there would be a Stanley Cup for Edmonton, Alberta and Western Canada to celebrate."

Hunter wouldn't make it all the way to the merger. The man whose press conferences were legend would eventually have to call his last one, in which he'd tearfully tell the media,

Oilers goaltender Ken Brown, 1979.

"When they write my obituary, it'll be a positive one."

We haven't had to write it yet. But when we do, it *will* be a positive one.

The population of Edmonton, when the first hockey game was played in 1894, was 1,165. By 1908, when the Eskimos became the first team to play for the Stanley Cup, it was 18,500. In 1932, when the Superiors won the world championship, it was 78,387. By 1948, when the Flyers won the Allan Cup, the city had grown to 126,609. The population reached 169,196 in 1952 when the Mercurys won their Olympic gold medal. It was up to 209,353 in 1955 when the Edmonton Flyers had

their best pro team. And there were 303,756 citizens when Glen Sather and his Oil Kings teammates won Edmonton's first Memorial Cup in the spring of 1963.

Now it was 1972 and Edmonton was more than a pimple on the prairie. It had 441,530 citizens and the surrounding towns had grown up, too, giving Edmonton a "metro" population of half a million.

Problem was, almost all of Edmonton's hockey history had happened in the same place – the barn that was the Edmonton Gardens, a facility that was actually condemned as a fire hazard in 1966 before it was refurbished. And the Oilers had to begin play in the WHA in the Gardens.

In February of '72 the WHA held its inaugural draft. Much fun was made of the fact it was held in Anaheim, California – near Disneyland. The league frequently had to endure Mickey Mouse references because of that unwise choice of venues.

In all, 1,037 players were selected in 121 rounds, 97 of them by Wild Bill Hunter and the Edmonton franchise. Thirty-three of those were players currently in the employ of the National Hockey League. One was Russian Rags Ragulin.

Hunter was ahead of his time with that one.

"We took Ragulin because he's a great player and you have to be prepared for the possibility that one day the entire Soviet team might defect," he said at the time.

Hunter wasn't just setting up an Edmonton team. He was flying all over the map, helping Murphy set up a league.

Hunter had Zane Feldman and then Dr. Charles Allard as owners in Edmonton. But owners had to be found around the rest of the league. Ben Hatskin was in charge of signing Bobby Hull. Once that was accomplished it was onward and upward.

Originally, Hunter was going to call his team the Edmonton Oil Kings and give his junior team another name. But when Calgary opted out, along with the Miami Screaming Eagles, Hunter decided to call his club the Alberta Oilers.

As Hunter predicted – although he had to play poker by announcing he'd found private money to build an arena – the Edmonton Exhibition Association (later Edmonton Northlands) set about building an arena. On June 19, 1972, city council approved expenditures for the $15-million Northlands Coliseum.

Larry Gordon welcomes the new troops, Peter Driscoll, Wayne Gretzky and Eddie Mio.

Hunter didn't exactly put together the greatest team in the history of hockey for the Gardens that first year. In a lot of ways, it looked like an Oil Kings reunion. He tipped his hand at that draft by picking Al Hamilton, Doug Barrie, Eddie Joyal and Ross Perkins as four of his first six picks.

Hamilton was half amazed and half amused with the way it worked with him and Wild Bill.

"He kept pestering me and pestering me," said the player who would become the last of the original WHA Oilers.

"I came so close to telling him to sell the refrigerator to some other Eskimo. And there were a few days, in the beginning, when I wish I had.

"Our first game was in that barn against the Los Angeles Sharks," he said of the old Gardens, which looked like the Taj Mahal to him when he first came to town. "That game seemed to go until almost 2 a.m. and had a hundred brawls. I had some serious doubts about what I'd gone and done. But looking back, I can't help but be thankful that I let Bill Hunter talk me into coming home."

Original WHA Oilers included goalies Jack Norris and Ken Brown, Hamilton, Falkenberg, Barrie, Perkins, Joyal, Bob Wall, John Fisher, Ken Baird, Ron Walters, Bernie Blanchette, Ron Anderson, Steve Carlyle, Roger Cote, Rusty Patenaude, Bob McAneeley, Bill Hicke, Brian Carlin, Dennis Kassian and star Jim Harrison – who allowed himself to be photographed with a shopping cart full of money when he signed for $75,000.

Goalie Ken Brown, who today heads up *The Edmonton Sun*'s 50-person advertising department, was an original Alberta Oiler.

"It was wonderful. It was an incredible experience. Ninety-five per cent of the guys Hunter signed for the team that first year were local guys. There was a definite kinship built in. We were all

back home from all those different places we'd been playing," said Brown.

"The best part of it was that it was like being a pioneer. There were days in that first year in the Gardens that were pretty depressing, but when they built the new Coliseum, wow. The feeling of pioneering, of overcoming everything, that was the most spectacular thing of all. Going to Quebec City, a place where most of us had never been before, and staying at the Chateau Frontenac and eating the pre-game meal in one of the great dining rooms in the world ... that was all a part of it. So were those incredibly long travel days with the weird routes you had to take to get from Hartford to Quebec City and so on. But there was real adventure there. It was so much fun and such an adventure that we got used to the inconveniences that cropped up.

"And Wild Bill was amazing. His enthusiasm. His zest. Just his bounce. I can imagine what he was going through in that first year. I can imagine the axe handles that were hanging out of the bag at that point. I remember once, at an airport, Hunter was pacing around like a caged tiger burning off all his energy when our goalie coach that first year, Glenn Hall, with his great sense of humour, said, 'Quick, Bill, organize something.' "

That sense of being a pioneer grew with Brown when he became the radio colour commentator for Oilers broadcasts for 10 years, including the final year of the WHA and the Stanley Cup years in the NHL.

Looking back on that first day he was an Alberta Oiler, could he see the days ahead?

"Not a chance," he said.

The Oilers won the first WHA game ever played, 7-4 against the Nationals in Ottawa. The Oilers' Ron Anderson scored the first goal in WHA history and Billy Hicke scored on

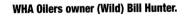

WHA Oilers owner (Wild) Bill Hunter.

Peter Pocklington, left, and Nelson Skalbania, 1984.

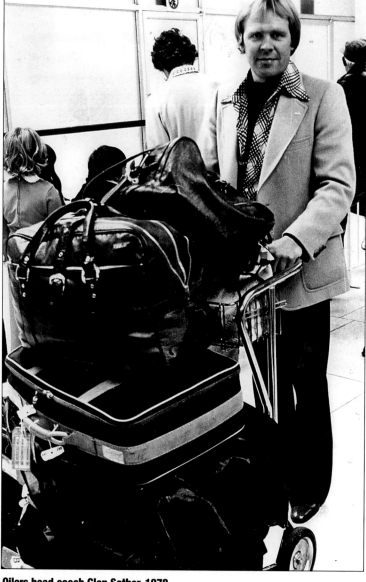

Oilers head coach Glen Sather, 1978.

the first WHA penalty shot. Both had two-goal nights.

Jim Harrison had a game that first season that would have been called Gretzky-like if it had been played today.

It happened on Jan. 30, 1974. In an 11-3 win over the New York Raiders, Harrison registered 10 points. The accomplishment won him a place in the *Guinness Book of Records*. And he swears, because he missed three breakaways and set up several teammates who were wide open, "I shoulda had 15."

Normie Ullman scored his 500th major-league goal as a WHA Oiler. He said he wished he had scored it in the NHL. But linemate Rusty Patenaude, who set him up, called it the highlight of his career.

Off to a blazing start one season, Brian Shaw said, "We may never lose again" and promptly started a losing streak that went on so long it looked as if the Oilers might never win again.

Then there was the time Oilers tough guy Frank (Seldom) Beaton

Oilers jerseys including Paul Shmyr's captain 'K' from the WHA.

was smuggled out of a Cincinnati dressing room in an equipment bag and driven to a remote location outside of town, where he flagged down the team bus, narrowly escaping a summons – for allegedly punching a service-station attendant – which earlier in the day had wrongly been served on the voice of the Oilers, Rod Phillips.

Two of the Hansen brothers from the movie *Slap Shot*, starring Paul Newman – Jack and Steve Carlson – were WHA Oilers.

And there was Jacques Plante.

The first goalie to wear a mask, and a true hockey legend, Plante ended his career as an Oiler. Signed for two years at $150,000 a season, Plante played in goal for the Oilers in the very first game in Northlands Coliseum in 1974.

For a while there, it looked as if Edmonton was going to watch something special when Plante posted an 8-1 win-loss record and a 2.53 goals-against average. But then he started having equilibrium problems and played only

The Edmonton Oilers vs. Gordie Howe and the Hartford Whalers.

home games. He finished with a 15-14-1 record and called it a career.

Ken Brown played mostly in the road games — and he'd go for the deal all over again.

"I considered myself the most fortunate guy in the world," said Brown. "I was coached by Glenn Hall, my all-time idol, in my first year in the WHA. And I played as a teammate with Jacques Plante when he was 46 years old, almost twice my age, in the last year of his pro career. I sat on the bench having goosebumps watching Jacques Plante play. He was so good it was amazing."

The original Oilers coach was Ray Kinasewich, who had coached Hunter's 1966 Oil Kings Memorial Cup junior team. Kinasewich gave himself a leave of absence from his company, Stork Diaper Service, to take the job. Brian Shaw, Clare Drake, Bep Guidolin and Glen Sather would follow in succession – thrice interrupted by Hunter himself taking over as coach, of course.

The Oilers managed a winning record (barely) in each of their first two years with identical 38-37-3 seasons. Two games under .500 in their third year the team hit the skids, going 27-49-5 in 1975-76, during which they set the WHA record for most road losses (32) in a single season. Not much better (34-43-4) a year later, the team made it within one game of .500 before recording a league-leading 98-point season in the WHA's final year of operation.

In seven seasons the Oilers managed to win only one playoff series, winning just nine of 33 playoff games. But they paid their dues.

They didn't win much, but they were a rock-solid franchise by WHA standards. In the 1977-78 season the Oilers set a WHA attendance record with 431,006 fans, despite being one game under .500. And the Edmonton franchise was the all-time WHA leader in attendance.

While the Oilers really weren't much of a WHA team on the ice, their timing was terrific. The Winnipeg Jets, on the other hand, had an exceptional WHA team, winning three of the seven Avco Cups, but their timing was terrible.

Things were coming together for the Oilers in what

would turn out to be the final year of the WHA. And it would have a huge impact on the NHL years that would follow.

For starters, there was the hiring of Barry Fraser as chief scout during the off-season. He's the guy who selected Kevin Lowe in the first round, Mark Messier in the second and Glenn Anderson in the third round of the 1979 NHL entry draft; Paul Coffey in the first, Jari Kurri in the third and Andy Moog in the sixth round in 1980; and Grant Fuhr in the first and Steve Smith in the fifth round in 1991.

Many things and many people were falling into place. But if there was a most important day in Oilers' WHA history, that day would be Nov. 1, 1978.

That was the day new owner Peter Pocklington announced he'd purchased three players from his former co-owner Nelson Skalbania, who by that time was the owner of the Indianapolis Racers.

The three acquisitions were en route to a press conference in Edmonton later that evening. They were goalie Eddie Mio, journeyman Peter Driscoll, and a skinny 17-year-old kid by the name of Wayne Gretzky.

Only a couple of months earlier, Skalbania had landed his plane in Edmonton and held a two-member-of-the-media press conference to announce the signing, at 35,000 feet over the Rocky Mountains in a private plane, of that 17-year-old kid to a contract with the Racers.

Skalbania stopped in Edmonton because he had owned the Oilers before he sold the team to Pocklington. He knew the reporters. He also knew the National Hockey League meetings were just getting under way at that hour and he wanted them to swallow their cigars all around the table.

"It was really wild," Gretzky, whose first nickname was "Brinks," remembered 20 years later.

"I didn't know where I was going but I went to Vancouver. I was told by my agent, Gus Badali, that 'the guy owns a team and wants to sign you.'

"But at the time, believe it or not, it was Houston or Indianapolis," Gretzky revealed. "When I wrote the

Teammates help Wayne Gretzky celebrate his 18th birthday, Jan. 24, 1979.

contract out on the plane, it had 'Houston or Indianapolis' on the contract. At the time, Nelson was negotiating to buy Houston. Gus was pushing big time for it to be Houston."

Gretzky wrote it all out himself on a crumpled piece of paper. But before the flight, Skalbania tried to figure out what this young man he was going to spend all that money to sign was all about.

"He asked me, 'Do you think you can play pro hockey?' Gretzky recalled. "I told him, 'If I didn't think I could, I wouldn't be here.'

"Nelson was a big burner and liked to run. He made me run six miles with him. He was surprised I was able to run the whole six miles. The rest is kind of history."

Looking back, there's one part Gretzky laughs at now.

"We're going from his place to the airport and his Rolls-Royce breaks down. So he gets another Rolls-Royce sent out, and it breaks down, too.

"The most my dad ever made was $32,000 a year and Nelson says to him, 'Walter, never buy a Rolls-Royce.' "

Gretzky treasures the memory of his first two WHA goals as an Indianapolis Racer, when he was flanked by wingers Kevin Nugent and Angie Moretto.

"They were both against Edmonton," he said. "They were both on Dave Dryden. Twenty years later someone sent me a tape of my first two goals against Edmonton, and I'm looking at them with my kids and my young boys were laughing at me. They said I looked like I was a little kid."

And he remembers the day Skalbania sold him to Pocklington, the day he flew to Edmonton with Mio and Driscoll and went directly to the Edmonton Inn for the press conference.

It was a chartered Learjet which cost Pocklington $7,900.

"He told me I could go to Winnipeg or Edmonton," Gretzky said of Skalbania, who had decided the kid wasn't going to make him any money in Indianapolis. "He told me I had my choice, Winnipeg or Edmonton.

"Gus Badali was a real big believer in Edmonton. He told me if anybody in the WHA makes it

into the NHL, Edmonton would have the best chance."

Gretzky, at the time, said, "Nelson should have left me here in June."

Might he have become a Winnipeg Jet instead?

"Crazy Nelson wanted to play backgammon for Gretzky against one-third ownership of the Jets. It was one day before Nelson sold him to Edmonton," said Winnipeg Jets' owner Michael Gobuty.

A forgotten footnote to the deal was that the player Indianapolis chose to replace Gretzky was another 17-year-old. A kid from St. Albert by the name of Mark Messier.

Mio, who more or less made himself travelling secretary on the three-man trip to Edmonton, ended up as one of Gretzky's best friends after that.

"Eddie always jokes that I was a throw-in on that deal," laughed Gretzky, who would one day take a group of locked-out NHL stars on a trip to Europe and put Mio in charge of travel arrangements.

"I had $100 on me. Eddie had a credit card with a $600 limit. Pocklington had to phone ahead to pay for the plane."

Gretzky remembers Glen Sather coming up to him, and one of the first things Sather said was that he'd be living with him for a month.

"I remember living with Sather and one night him telling me that one day real soon Edmonton would be in the NHL, that one day I'd be captain of the team in the NHL and one day we'd win the

Walter Gretzky watches his son Wayne sign his long-term Oilers contract.

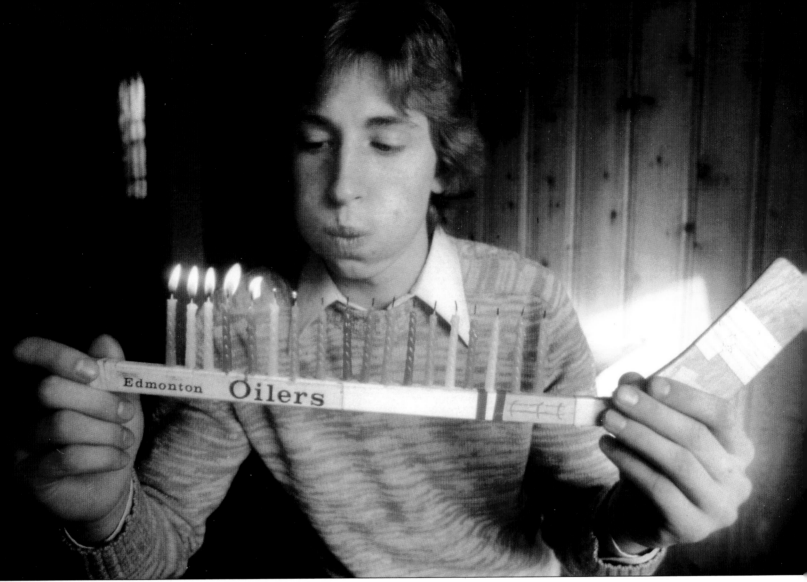

Birthday boy wonder Wayne Gretzky blows out 18 candles on a miniature hockey stick.

Stanley Cup. And I believed him, too."

He remembers how he almost let Sather convince him to wear No. 14 for the Oilers, since his idol Gordie Howe's number, 9, was already taken.

"That's the number he had made up for me. He said it would put a lot less pressure on me than if I wore No. 99. I told him it doesn't matter what number I'm wearing, I'm going to have a lot of pressure and I'd like No. 99. By game time I had No. 99 again."

Gretzky also looks back and laughs at the day he signed at centre ice, with his kid brothers dressed up in Oiler jerseys and all wearing alpine hats with "Gretzky" stencilled on the front.

From that point on, Gretzky was pretty much the best thing that had happened to Edmonton since the discovery of oil at Leduc No. 1. If the Oilers hadn't really been worth watching in their first six seasons in the WHA, they were more than worth the price of admission now.

Before his 18th birthday Gretzky had 23 goals and 46 points in 39 games and was leading the Oilers in scoring by a large margin.

And then there was his birthday.

"I signed until 1999. This is the year. The 1998-99 season," Gretzky laughs with delight now.

On Jan. 26, 1978, with a cake in the shape of "99" and a bottle of sparkling "baby" champagne from his teammates, the Oilers held an advertised pre-game birthday party with his parents and his three brothers and sister.

> ## ' I signed until 1999. This is the year. The 1998-99 season.'
>
> *– Wayne Gretzky on signing the 21-year contract in 1978*

But there was no notice that part of the ceremony at centre ice would be the signing of a 21-year contract that would allegedly keep Gretzky as an Oiler until 1999 (albeit with a 10-year renegotiation clause).

"Looks like I'm here for life," said Gretzky at the time, in what would be filed under the category of "Famous Last Words."

"I've played in four different cities in the last three years. I don't need to move again. Everything is great here. There's no sense in leaving."

For the first 10 minutes that night it looked as if Pocklington had made a major mistake. Gretzky couldn't have played any worse.

"I couldn't make a pass. I could barely write my name on the contract."

Looking back two decades later, Gretzky smiles.

"My dad told me I should sign it. He said you never know if you're going to get injured. He said, 'You love it here, sign it.' I had a lot of people telling me it was for too long and not to sign it. But my dad said, 'Take the security.' It worked out."

Gretzky's favourite memory of his WHA year was when he was chosen to play against the Soviets in the WHA all-star game and he ended up on the same line as the old fellow they were referring to as Father Time. A guy by the name of Gordie Howe.

"At the time that was the highlight of my life," Gretzky said. "Gordie told me just to get the puck to him and he'd get it in. And on our first shift, about 10 seconds in, that's what happened.

"I'm saying, 'This guy IS pretty good,' " he said of his boyhood idol.

"I remember leaning over to Gordie on the bench and telling him,

17

'I'm so nervous.'

"He looked back at me and said, 'So am I.'

"I didn't believe him then. I thought he was kidding. But now I'm not the young kid. I'm playing with the young kids. And they tell me they're nervous. And I tell them I'm nervous, too. And I'm not kidding. It never goes away. Now I know Gordie wasn't kidding."

Howe also had his son Mark on the line.

"We're still the oldest line on the ice," was Gramps' one-liner back then.

Howe's evaluation of Gretzky after the experience? "He'll never make it," he laughed.

Today, Gretzky says people may not believe it but he owes a lot to his WHA year.

"I don't know where my career would have gone if I hadn't gone to the WHA," he said.

"I'd still have been in junior. I could have been hurt. I could have got messed up or gone to the NHL in a bad situation ...

"I'm very grateful the WHA was around and that I became a part of it."

Gretzky only played the one year in the WHA. And he finished 15th in all-time Oilers WHA scoring.

Ahead of him, in order, were Al Hamilton, Rusty Patenaude, Blair MacDonald, Bill (Cowboy) Flett, Ken Baird, Doug Barrie, Jim Harrison, Ron Chipperfield, Brett Callighen, Ross Perkins, Norm Ullman, Tim Sheehy, Eddie Joyal and Mike Rogers.

Behind him in the Top 50 were Barry Long, Paul Shmyr, Joe Micheletti, Bob Wall, Dave Langevin, Bruce MacGregor, Ron Climie, Bryan Campbell, Tom Gilmore, Dennis Sobchuk, Steve Carlyle, Rick Morris, Bob McAneeley, Bobby Sheehan, Stan Weir, Val Fonteyne, Mike Zuke, Ron Walters, Glen Sather, Len Lunde, Norm Ferguson, Bob Falkenberg, Randy Rota, Bob Russell, Juha Widing, Steve Carlson, Peter Driscoll, Brian McKenzie, Billy Hicke, Ron Anderson, Dave Semenko, Gavin Kirk, Brian Carlin, Pierre Guite and Ray McKay.

To the younger generation, most of those listed may be just names. But to the people who were there, every name presents a picture and recalls a memory.

1979 WHA all-star Wayne Gretzky lines up beside his hero, Gordie Howe.

Sather is the one who hits with all generations. He played 81 games and scored 19 goals with 34 assists for 53 points before he moved from captain to coach and replaced Guidolin, a former Boston Bruins coach who was under tremendous pressure and couldn't handle his hockey hot seat.

"Bep told me if I didn't take the job, I'd sit in the stands," Sather tells the story 20 years later.

Under Sather's direction, and with Gretzky's scoring ability, the Oilers put together a 13-game unbeaten streak in the second half of the schedule to finish first in the regular season with a 48-30-2 record.

Pocklington dangled a carrot for them, too. He told the players if the team finished first he'd provide one-way tickets to holiday resorts in either Tahiti or Morocco. And if they won the Avco Cup, he'd change them to round-trip tickets, plus hotel and meal expenses and $1,000 in spending money.

A few years earlier, when Pocklington co-owned the team with Nelson Skalbania, they tried the same routine. The Oilers were battling for a playoff berth and rewards were promised for making it. When they did, Skalbania called the team to attention in the dressing room and actually passed around one-way tickets to Hawaii, telling the team they'd get the return tickets if they won a playoff series. (He even had one for the local sports columnist – me – an actual, paid-for, legitimate airline ticket. To Tuktoyaktuk. One-way; no return ticket if the Oilers won a playoff round.)

It turned out to be one-way tickets only – for everybody. The Oilers finally won a playoff series and made it to the Avco Cup final, where they lost to the Winnipeg Jets.

It was the last Avco Cup and, if nothing else, left the hockey world with one wonderful trivia question.

Who scored the last goal in WHA history?

Answer: Dave Semenko.

The Oilers had scored a 10-2 win at home in Game 5, but lost Game 6 and the series 7-3 in Winnipeg.

Sather listed "mental preparation" and "mental discipline" as the miss-

ing links. A lack of playoff experience. And not knowing what it takes to win.

"All I can say is that, hopefully, we all learned a lot of things."

A total of 3,394 games after the World Hockey Association began, the Seven Years War was over.

And in the end Ben Hatskin, the WHA executive and Jets owner who signed Bobby Hull to get the league launched, presented the trophy to Winnipeg but said he wished Edmonton had won it.

"Quebec won it. New England won it. And Winnipeg won it. It would have been perfect if Edmonton had won it, too," Hatskin said. "After everything Edmonton had been through and the way the fans made Edmonton the backbone franchise of the league, it's too bad there wasn't one Cup for Edmonton."

For weeks during the playoffs Edmonton had one eye on the Oilers and the other on the other league. The Oilers, you see, were officially in the NHL before the business of ending the WHA was done.

On April 9, the fans started lining up at 4:30 in the morning outside the Coliseum for Oilers' NHL season tickets which would go on sale at 9. When the doors opened there were more than 1,000 current WHA season ticket-holders in line to put in their orders. Twelve hours later the team had taken in more than $1 million from the first day for the 7,200 season ticket-holders who had two weeks to renew and double up if they so chose.

The New England Whalers and Edmonton Oilers had finished up a playoff game one night when the crowd refused to leave the Coliseum. Fans waited around overnight for the 1,400 remaining season tickets available on a first-come, first-served basis at 9 a.m. the following day.

It was an amazing month in boom-town Edmonton. The Oilers sold over $5 million in season tickets, the Canadian Football League's Eskimos had 39,000 more fans signed up for another $3.5 million at Commonwealth Stadium and Pocklington's Edmonton Drillers of the North American Soccer League opened play with crowds of 13,537 and 16,122. And the Oilers were still playing and selling tickets in the WHA playoffs.

Coach Glen Sather with director of player development Bruce MacGregor.

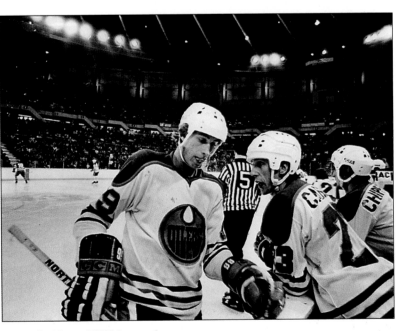

Wayne Gretzky and WHA teammates.

In one month, Edmontonians had spent $10 million on sports tickets. In 1979 dollars.

Most of the talk was about next year. But there were still the last games and the eulogies to be delivered for the WHA.

Edmonton, Quebec, Winnipeg and Hartford survived. But they left behind a considerable graveyard.

There were 35 different ownerships in WHA history. And the teams ...

The Miami Screaming Eagles. The Dayton Gems. They never saw the light of day. San Francisco became Quebec City before a game was played. The Birmingham Bulls, Cincinnati Stingers, Indianapolis Racers, Vancouver Blazers, Jersey Knights, New York Golden Blades, New York Raiders, Ottawa Civics, Ottawa Nationals, Toronto Toros, Houston Aeros, San Diego Mariners, Phoenix Roadrunners, Los Angeles Sharks, Michigan Stags, Baltimore Blades, Calgary Cowboys, Denver Spurs, Cleveland Crusaders and Chicago Cougars. And who will ever forget the Minnesota Folding Saints I and II?

Anyone covering the WHA couldn't possibly fail a geography exam. One two-game Oilers road trip to Phoenix and Cincinnati involved takeoffs and landings at 13 different airports. Ullman announced his retirement to me, effective the end of the season, over fish and chips at a layover at the Kansas City airport.

The WHA, throughout all those years, stood for a lot of things. Wishful Hockey Association. Weekend Hockey Association. World Home for the Aged. Won't Hit Anybody. But in the end it was Wayne's Hockey Association.

There were so many memories, a lot of them bad ones of players who wore Oilers uniforms. But in the end, with admission to the NHL, they suddenly became warmer memories. Why, there were even moments when Edmonton almost felt sorry for all those stuffy old NHL cities. Gad, what they missed out on!

On the other hand, nostalgia wasn't exactly running rampant. The WHA was history. But this was the beginning of history for the Edmonton Oilers in the world's ultimate hockey league.

Chapter 3

New Kids On The Block

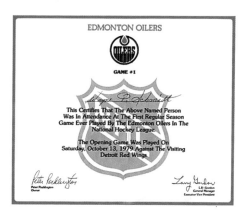

MEDIA
GUIDE
79-80

T he destination read Chicago, O'Hare. But you only had to be on Northwest Airlines Flight 458 for about 10 minutes to figure out that the destination was more like Disneyland.

The Edmonton Oilers were en route to their first game in NHL history. And it was as if they were all kids. Some of them had spent five and six seasons in the World Hockey Association. Even some of the older players, going back to the NHL where they'd previously played, were like kids again. Owner Peter Pockling-ton had just predicted that the Oilers would win the Stanley Cup in five years. But for the players on that plane, the only future they could see was that first game.

"You could see it back on the long weekend in Edmonton," said 38-year-old netminder Dave Dryden on that plane. "In the pre-season games against Toronto and New York, we were the same way we were that first night a couple of years ago when we played the Russians. Really ex-cited. I guess it might seem amazing how excited all these guys are. But that's not the way it works."

Glen Sather had his own thoughts as he sat on that flight into the unknown.

NHL Oilers vs. Atlanta Flames, 1979-80 season. Opposite: Studio shot of Wayne Gretzky modelling GWG jeans.

Oilers centre Ron Chipperfield vs. Minnesota North Stars.

"There's more to it. All these guys are trying to prove they are good hockey players. They want to show these guys in the NHL that they're good hockey players. Like Brett Callighen. Everybody who has seen him in pre-season play wonders where in heaven we found him. Brett Callighen came to us three years ago with very few skills. He's gone from run-of-the-mill to become a fine player. Blair MacDonald has improved immensely over the last few years. They're excited. Now they have a chance to go and show it where everybody is going to notice."

Ron Chipperfield, who was named team captain on that flight at 35,000 feet somewhere over Saskatchewan, laughed about the feeling.

"The NHL is the place to play," he said. "I guess I can admit that now.

"It's sort of strange," he said of the feeling on that flight. "I honestly do feel like a rookie. I don't think I will three weeks from now. I certainly hope not. But right now, I'm sure as hell excited. And it's great to have this happening with a team like this. We have a lot of young players on this team. Usually you only have a rookie or two on a team and everybody kind of makes examples out of them. But the whole club, from the 18-year-olds to the older guys, all feel like we're in the same boat."

It made everybody giddy.

Kevin Lowe put it best, as he would on so many subjects over the years to follow.

"Sometimes I think a rookie would feel embarrassed. I mean, it's a thrill for a rookie. It was a thrill against Toronto and New York on the weekend. I mean, when I ran into Phil Esposito on the ice, he turned to me and said, 'Watch out, Kevin.' That was kind of neat. If it wasn't for the way everybody feels on this team, I don't think I'd tell anybody that."

Wayne Gretzky was flying high on the way to that game, too.

"You've got to be a man to play hockey, but you have to have a lot of boy in you, too," said the already mature-beyond-his-years star of the team. "The boy is really coming out in everybody right now. I was really pumped going into last year in the WHA. But I could feel it in those exhibition

games. The crowds seemed more excited. This may sound dumb, but every time you score a goal, it's more exciting in the NHL."

The Oilers had been able to protect Gretzky as part of the merger arrangements between the WHA and the NHL. They dazzled at the draft, selecting Lowe, Mark Messier and Glenn Anderson that first year. And while the following year, in 1980, they picked Paul Coffey, Jari Kurri and Andy Moog, and a year after that Grant Fuhr, those Johnny-come-latelies missed the treasured experience of being a Day Oner and wearing the Oilers uniform for their first NHL game.

"Hoo boy, I can't believe this is happening," said Gretzky in the bowels of the old Chicago Stadium two hours before they played the Blackhawks in Game 1, Year 1.

When it was over, the player Gordie Howe would come to call "the best" and Bobby Hull would say "did more for hockey than any person who ever played or likely ever will," said it was a knee-knocking experience.

"I'd never been that nervous before in my life," said Gretzky.

Messier, the other 18-year-old on the team that had 12 players with no previous NHL experience, said that if Gretzky was nervous, he was petrified.

Oilers defencemen Pat Price (26) and Kevin Lowe vs. Chicago Blackhawks.

"All I could think about was, 'We're in the NHL.' It got to me," he admitted. "It really hit me in the afternoon. Until I sat there at about 3 p.m., I hadn't really let it get to me. But I sat in my hotel room and all I could think about was, 'Hey, we're in the NHL.' It got to me."

An hour before game time, Callighen and Dave Semenko tossed around a softball in a corridor to try to unwind. You don't see many NHL players tossing around a softball an hour before game time. Then again, you don't see many players having a hotdog an hour before game time – and Gretzky would do that with regularity.

On that night of Oct. 10, 1979, the Oilers lost their first NHL game, 4-2 to the veteran Chicago club. But they won instant respect.

"They were a good-skating, hard-working

team," said about-to-retire Hall of Famer Stan Mikita of the kids on the other side of the ice that night. "They were trying to prove something and, as far as I'm concerned, they did."

Goaltender Tony Esposito said it was no normal night.

"It was nerveracking," he said. "I was happy when it was over. I've never played against most of them. They did a tremendous job. If they continue to play like that, they're going to surprise a lot of teams."

Bobby Hull, the former Chicago Blackhawk who felt a tad attached to this team from its WHA roots, watched the opening game and called the Oilers "the most incredible expansion team I've ever seen."

The Oilers won that praise over 60 minutes. But the first five minutes were something else again. They might have been the most pathetic five minutes the team played all year. The Oilers, for the first few shifts, had everybody in the rink thinking, "Oh my Lord, are these WHA teams going to be THAT bad?"

"I knew that would happen," said Sather. "There was no way to prevent it. Not in my wildest dreams did I expect them to be relaxed."

But there they were in the NHL. There were times when it looked as if it would never happen. And the way it turned out, despite the jitters and the 2-0 lead the Oilers gave the Blackhawks by 2:33 of the first period, the Oilers looked very much as if they belonged in the NHL.

Lowe scored the Oilers' first goal, a fact every Edmonton fan could still tell you 20 years later. It came at 9:49 of the first period. It was a 15-foot backhand. Gretzky and Callighen drew assists on the memorable marker.

Five minutes later, left-winger Dave Hunter tipped in Stan Weir's goal-mouth pass for the second goal in Oilers history. But history only remembers the first goal.

The Oilers lineup and summary sheet of that first game is now a collector's item:

Chief scout Barry Fraser.

28	Dave Dryden	G
31	Eddie Mio	G
2	Lee Fogolin	D
4	Kevin Lowe	D
5	Doug Hicks	D
6	Colin Campbell	D
7	Ron Chipperfield	F
8	Risto Siltanen	D
11	Mark Messier	F
12	Dave Hunter	F
14	Blair MacDonald	F
18	Brett Callighen	F
19	Bill Flett	F
20	Dave Lumley	F
21	Stan Weir	F
24	Peter Driscoll	F
26	Pat Price	D
27	Dave Semenko	F
99	Wayne Gretzky	F

On the return flight to Edmonton for the home opener, Sather pulled out his pocket calculator. The idea was to determine the average age of the lineup the Oilers iced for openers. It worked out to 24.5. Minus 33-year-old Al Hamilton, it worked out to 23 years on the nose.

• • •

The Oilers had spent seven years in the WHA waiting for the game they'd play next, so they didn't much mind waiting a little longer for their first NHL home game. Fog in Vancouver delayed the arrival of the Detroit Red Wings.

This night it wasn't the first goal that mattered most, it was the last goal, scored by Mark Messier, which gave the Oilers a 3-3 tie.

The next time out the Oilers tied Vancouver 4-4 and Gretzky scored his first goal, a backhand through the pads of Canucks goalie Glen Hanlon with 1:09 left, to secure Edmonton's second point in the standings.

"That's five years in a row that I've scored my first goal on a backhand. Last year it was on Dave," No. 99 said of Dryden, reminding everybody of the now legendary trivia question about which team Gretzky scored his first professional goal against: the Oilers.

It took until Oct. 21 for the Oilers to register their first NHL win. The fact it came against another WHA merger team, the Quebec Nordiques, took something away from the occasion. Blair MacDonald scored his first NHL hat trick in the 6-3 win.

The great adventure had begun.

But like most hockey seasons, it began long before the team hit the ice. While Larry Gordon was the general manager in the Oilers' first year in the league, Sather was doing the deals on the hockey side. And he didn't wait long to telegraph that he had an ability in that area. By early June he had managed to keep at least four of his WHA regulars from the grasp of the NHL teams. He worked out deals with the Los Angeles Kings to lay off Mac-Donald, the Montreal Canadiens to stay away from Hunter and

Program from Oilers' first NHL home game, opening night vs. Detroit.

Joe Micheletti and the Philadelphia Flyers to pass on centre Ron Chipperfield. But when the NHL sat down to reclaim players on June 8, the Oilers had been hit the hardest. They'd lost 17, Winnipeg 11 and Quebec and Hartford seven each.

When it came time for the expansion draft, the WHA boys saw through what the NHL was trying to do – dumping bad contracts and washed-up players. The Oilers picked four free-agent players – Doug Favell, John Gould, Inge Hammarstrom and Tom Edur – to whom they had no intention of offering contracts.

The Oilers also picked off a few guys guys who would prove to be players. Dave Lumley and Cam Connor came in a prearranged deal with the Canadiens.

With their first pick the Oilers took Lee Fogolin from Buffalo. Then

Colin Campbell

Brett Callighen

Dave Hunter

Dave Lumley

Blair MacDonald

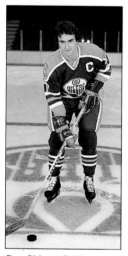

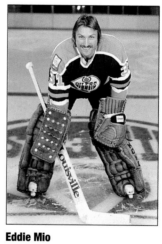

Dave Dryden

Ron Chipperfield

Eddie Mio

Doug Hicks

Risto Siltanen

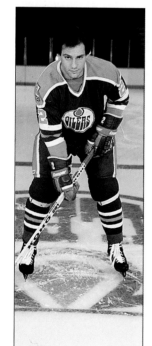

Lee Fogolin

Peter Driscoll

Pat Price

Dave Semenko

Stan Weir

Wayne Gretzky

Kevin Lowe, above, and Mark Messier.

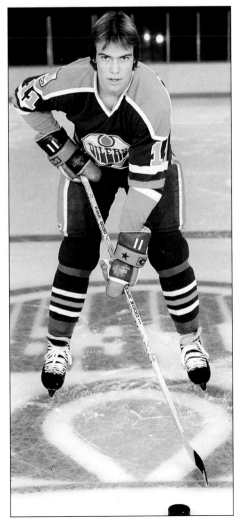

they plucked Pat Price from the New York Islanders and Colin Campbell from the Pittsburgh Penguins, followed later by Doug Hicks from the Chicago Blackhawks.

"I was sweating for a while there in the beginning, hoping Fogolin would be available when it came around to our turn," said Sather after the telephone draft.

Scotty Bowman, who had just been hired as Buffalo's new GM, wondered out loud why Fogolin had been left available by the Sabres in the first place.

At the entry draft, the Oilers picked dead last, 21st overall. And, of course, they picked Lowe.

"I had him rated anywhere from 10th to 13th overall," said scout Barry Fraser. "He was the best player available."

There was also the signing of Sather himself.

"Glen is on a five-year contract and maybe an option for life," said owner Pocklington.

Sather had other options that first year. But he decided to stay.

"I guess I like the fact I'm responsible for what happens," said Sather. "Five years from now maybe they'll say I blew it, but at least I've got some years to go to build a club. I like a team that's a big family, from the owner down. I thought we did pretty well putting this team together because of the six Ps: Proper Planning Prevents Piss Poor Performance. We did our homework and everything seemed to fall into place when it came time to pick players off other teams. None of the other WHA teams threw a monkey wrench into proceedings to screw us up. We needed defencemen badly. And we got them, four young ones in Fogolin, Price, Campbell and Hicks."

Sather's biggest asset in that first year, in fact the first 20 years, was his patience.

Not that there weren't some twists and turns. As in late October, when he demoted Messier to the Houston Apollos of the Central Hockey League and assessed him a substantial fine for disciplinary reasons. Messier had missed a plane.

Earlier he'd missed a bus and had also once been late for practice.

"I think he'll make an excellent pro once he learns how to catch buses on time, be at the airport and discipline himself," said Sather. "He's got to learn hockey is the most important thing in his life right now and he must make the sacrifices."

Messier learned. He learned so well people would later call him the greatest leader in the history of hockey.

Pocklington never learned. While his "we'll win the Stanley Cup in five years" quote became legend, he started early his habit of saying the wrong things.

The Oilers, by early December, were 20th in a 21-team league despite having two players in the top 10 in scoring. And the publicity-loving Pocklington, through the friendly local sports columnist he'd one day spray with an entire bottle of champagne following an Oilers' Stanley Cup win, made the following public pronouncement:

"The only way to get a strong team for the future, to one day win a Stanley Cup, is to finish down around last and get all the draft choices. Quite frankly, I'd not be the slightest bit embarrassed if we finished last this year. That way we'd get the No. 1 first-round draft pick," he told me.

There was more.

"It's obvious. We've got half a team here. We're going to find the other half in the next two or three years."

The 18-year-old kid with the 28-year-old head on his shoulders saw it otherwise.

"There should be an Avco Cup ring on this finger," said Wayne Gretzky. "Last year we had the better team. But we ended up losers. And that's been in the back of my mind ever since. This year we have the best team of the ones in the race for the final few playoff spots. If we don't make the playoffs, we've wasted the year. If we don't make the playoffs, we'll go to camp next year and be more or less starting from scratch again.

"The whole thing about this year is to gain experience. To develop character as a team. If we don't make the playoffs, we'll go to camp and we'll be starting all over again. But if we do make the playoffs, we'd go into our future with a winning attitude. That's what we need. That attitude is everything. A lot is riding on this."

There were few experiences that first year which could match the one on Dec. 14.

It was the day Edmonton had most lusted after, the dream day when an Edmonton team would skate on the same ice as the most storied squad in the history of hockey. In the National Hockey League. This was the day the fans would stand and thunder their approval. They even cheered during the warm-up. But it wasn't supposed to turn out the way it did in this game against the Montreal Canadiens.

The Oilers won their Stanley Cup that mid-December night. That's how it was for the players. And that's how it was for the fans.

The Oilers, that night, did something you just DON'T do. You just don't beat the Habs the first time you play them.

It had never happened before. Not once. Never in the legends of Les Rouge, Blanc et Bleu had a first-year team won its first game against the Canadiens. It took the Vancouver Canucks a decade to win one against Montreal at home. To that point, the Washington Capitals had never done it.

It was mind-boggling. The fans were able to walk away from the Coliseum that night saying they'd just watched the team which, to that point, had won 22 Stanley Cups but had NEVER beaten the Edmonton Oilers.

Almost for certain, to that point in Edmonton hockey history, there had never been such a crescendo of sound from start to finish, even on those memorable nights against the Soviet nationals.

When it was over and a 5-3 victory belonged to an "expansion team" fighting to stay out of last place in a 21-team league, it was difficult not to get too carried away.

"How can you help but get yourself more up than for any game you've ever played?" asked Gretzky. "The fans were cheering for us in warm-up!"

A thousand fans showed up at the Coliseum to watch the Canadiens' morning skate. Executive vice-president Larry Gordon swore he received a phone call offering $500 for standing-room tickets for the game.

Out in Fort Saskatchewan they were playing an Alberta Junior Hockey League game, and every time the Oilers scored, *that* place went nuts. And when the final score was announced, the Oilers received a standing ovation there, too.

It was –25 C outside, but it was warm and fuzzy everywhere in Edmonton.

Gretzky had never before played a two-way hockey game like he did that night.

Eddie Mio was spectacular in goal. The dumb thing was that he got caught up in traffic before the

Oiler goaltender Ron Low.

was one of the best forechecking clubs I've seen all year."

Wonderful as that night was, most nights weren't like that at all. By Jan. 11 the Oilers arrived. Last place was theirs.

"This team is too tight at home. And the kids aren't the problem," said Sather.

It was somewhere in there that I wrote them off. And, ahem, I went just a little bit too far ...

"Realizing the media have been known to both unite and inspire this team on occasion this year when others have failed, I'm willing to make the following once-in-a-lifetime offer. If the Oilers make the playoffs, I'll eat this column in a sauce of bitter lemon, sour grapes and sauerkraut topped with sour cream."

That was my last paragraph of a they-won't-make-the-playoffs-now column on Feb. 25.

When the trade deadline came, the Oilers had won but one of their previous 11 games and it looked even more hopeless than the picture I'd painted in print.

Sather made a trade on that first-year deadline day that to this day he says was the toughest decision he ever had to make. His captain, Chipperfield, was in Winnipeg at the deathbed of his mother.

"I didn't want to do it. But he was the only player Quebec really wanted. It was a hard decision to make but I've got to stress how important it is for us to try and make the playoffs," Sather said as he announced his first major deadline deal.

The guy he got in exchange was goalie Ron Low.

While breaking the news to Chipperfield in his situation was gut-wrenching for Sather, Quebec coach Jacques Demers was calling the $75,000-a-year journeyman Low into his office to deliver the news on the other end.

"Ron," he said, "I'm afraid I've got some bad news for you. We've traded you to Edmonton ..."

"Bleeping great!" enthused Low before Demers could go on.

He was thrilled.

"All my life I've wanted to play out west," Low said of becoming

game and showed up at the rink when everybody else was already in uniform. He was somewhat rattled by the thought that he might miss the biggest game of his career – and miss it in a Capilano freeway traffic jam.

The Oilers, who had taken five of a possible six points from the New York Islanders at this stage of the season despite their lowly lot in the overall standings, proved again that they could rise to the occasion.

"We got beat by a team that showed a lot of poise," said Canadiens coach Claude Ruel. "They worked hard all night. They didn't quit. That

the Oilers' sixth seasonal goaltender. Born in Birtle, Man., but raised in nearby Foxwarren, Low continued, "It'll be great to play instead of worrying about all this BS."

It was one of those trades where Low didn't even have to catch a plane to catch up with the team. The Oilers' next game was in Quebec the following night – and he was starting.

"I'm not sure it's a good idea," said Low upon hearing that news. "I could have a helluva game or I could let in five goals. I'll be awfully ner-

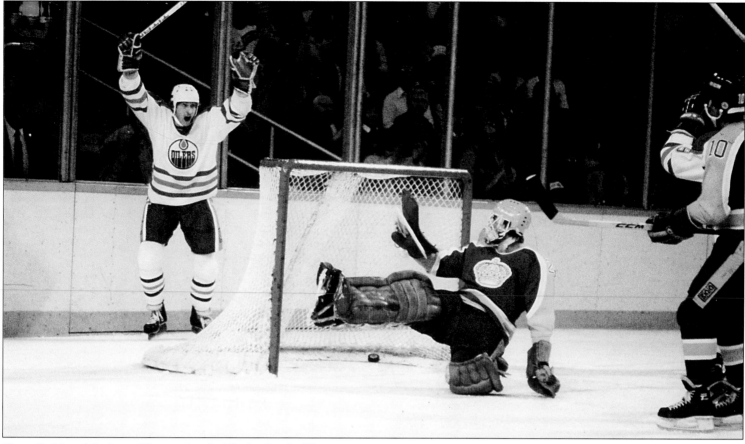

Wayne Gretzky celebrates an Oilers goal against the Los Angeles Kings.

vous."

He had a helluva game.

The Oilers won 6-3. Low stopped 42 shots.

Sather, it had been made clear, would become the team's actual, 100 per cent, general manager the next year. But one night in late March, during a post-game TV interview discussing Sather's projected role with the hockey team in the second season, Pocklington blurted out the following:

"He'll hire a super coach next year," he said of Slats.

Pocklington made the statement with about 20 seconds left in the show, just long enough to ask one more question to make absolutely certain he had said – and meant – what we thought we'd heard him say.

What followed in the moments after we went off the air was almost slapstick.

Pocklington, who moved pretty well for an owner, and your agent, who moves pretty slow for a sportswriter, raced each other for Sather's office. Sather had been watching the show and when we reached his office, he didn't seem to be amused. He did admit, though, with Pocklington in his presence, that there would be some changes coming.

"There are a lot of possibilities for next year. But we have six games to play before the end of this season. Listen, I don't want to be saying things to the guys like that I'm not going to be coach next season. I don't want to say anything to upset this club right now. We're fighting for our lives to get into the playoffs."

And get in they did.

Ending with a standing ovation in the final minute of a 6-2 win over the Colorado Rockies in their final home game, the Oilers, with a desperate finishing kick, had sprinted into the playoffs through the front door after having spent most of the season in the back alley.

The now 19-year-old Gretzky became the NHL scoring leader by adding his 51st goal and two assists. He wound up with a remarkable 137 points, tied for first in the league with Marcel Dionne. But he didn't get to share the Art Ross Trophy as top scorer because Dionne had two more goals. And he didn't win the Calder Trophy as rookie of the year because, while they refused to admit that the WHA was a major league for every minute of its existence, the NHL decided that playing one year with the competition made him ineligible for consideration as a rookie.

Whatever the story of the team that first year, Gretzky's individual achievements were the story of the entire season in the NHL.

No. 99 had his first Great Gretzky game in the NHL on a November night which was the anniversary of his joining the Oilers in the WHA a year earlier. That night he was coming off three games out of the lineup with tonsillitis.

By Jan. 24, preparing for a game against the Toronto Maple Leafs on the first anniversary of signing the 21-year deal at centre ice, Gretzky was asked if he thought he could win the scoring championship.

"You mean, beat Jesus and God?" he asked.

He meant Marcel Dionne and Guy Lafleur.

"I'm as good as they are," Gretzky had decided. "The key is to keep telling myself that I'm as good as they are."

Gretzky kept climbing the ladder, passing Charlie Simmer and Dave Taylor until Jesus and God were the only two in his sights.

"At the start of the season there were a lot of people who were still saying I couldn't play in the NHL," said Gretzky of coming from the WHA, where a 51-year-old man had been playing.

Gretzky confessed his individual goal for the season was to finish third in scoring because he'd been inspired by a story in the Toronto program

Vermilion, Alberta's Bill (Cowboy) Flett.

Two of the greatest: Montreal's Guy (The Flower) Lafleur and Edmonton's Wayne Gretzky.

before the game in Maple Leaf Gardens.

"It predicted I'd probably do OK in the NHL, but the last line of the article said I'd finished third in scoring in the WHA but, of course, there was no way I'd finish third in the NHL."

On Feb. 15 Gretzky took up official residence on page 136 of the NHL record book. He had seven assists in a game against the Washington Capitals.

All the praise and adulation that was being heaped on Gretzky didn't spoil him. In fact, he was clearly more driven by the desire to help the team into the playoffs than to win any scoring title.

After the final regular-season win, Gretzky could hardly talk. Weak from the tonsillitis he'd battled to overcome all year, he'd scored 12 goals and 12 assists in the final 11 games to more than play his part.

But it was Low who led the Oilers to their incredible finish, with eight wins, one tie and only two losses since his arrival. The Oilers needed leadership, heart and goaltending more than anything during the year. And they found it all in one guy when they needed it the most.

"The script is over," said Low after winning that last game. "The other day I said this was the biggest thrill of my life. I wasn't kidding. I can't believe it's happened to me. But the script was there, wasn't it?"

The Oilers, if the results of the remaining weekend of the schedule turned out right, could actually end up 15th. But Low, for his part, said he was hoping they'd be 16th.

"Why not? If we're 16th we play the first-place team," he said of the two-at-home, two-away schedule against each team and the 1 vs. 16, 2 vs. 15, 3 vs. 14, etc., playoff format used in the first two seasons after the merger.

"The Philadelphia Flyers are first. We might as well play the best team. And who knows, the way we're going now and with a short, best-of-five series ... well, who knows?"

And, gulp, swallow, there I was, local sports columnist, sitting at a table at centre ice surrounded by a crowd of booster club members, photographers and television cameras, eating my column with sauerkraut, sour cream and bitter lemon.

I love sauerkraut. The Coliseum chef did a nice job shredding up the column. But there was too little sauerkraut and too much sour cream. And I went directly from that embarrassing little ceremony to the airport to catch the plane to Philadelphia and the Oilers' first Stanley Cup playoff game.

It was the only time I've ever used one of those airplane barf bags.

History would record a Philadelphia Flyers sweep in the Oilers' first Stanley Cup playoff series. One. Two. Three. No runs. No hits. No errors. Nobody left on base. A first-place team wiping out a 16th-place team in straight games. History unfolding as it should.

Except it wasn't really like that.

Low got his wish. The Oilers finished 16th. They were playing the team which had recorded a 35-game streak without a loss that season. And he almost made it happen in Game 1.

It was the game of his life. And he lost.

He faced 51 shots, 17 more than his mates could volley at Flyers netminder Pete Peeters, an Edmonton native, at the other end.

For 80 games, Gretzky was on the receiving end of 90 per cent of the praise involving the Oilers. But when it came to this one, even though he scored two goals to bring the Oilers back from 2-0 in a game that would end up in overtime, Gretzky wasn't going to take any credit until, first, he gave credit.

"That's the greatest game of goaltending I've ever seen a guy play," said No. 99.

"Right now Ron Low is the best goaltender in the NHL. He's so hot, it's unbelievable. He's been absolutely amazing.

28

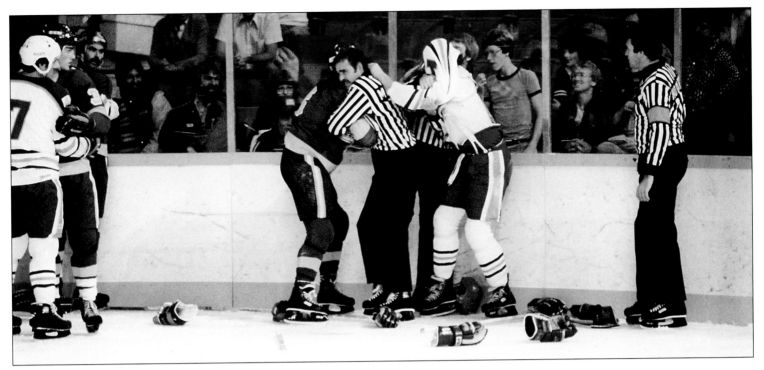

Boys will be boys: Oilers drop the gloves vs. Los Angeles Kings.

"We could have won tonight. And that's not reality. They're a first-place club and we're a 16th-place club. They've probably got more than 500 games of playoff experience if you add up the years of Bobby Clarke, Reggie Leach, Rick MacLeish, Bill Barber, Andre Dupont, Jimmy Watson, Bob Kelly and all those other guys. And we've only got two or three guys who've even been *in* the playoffs before.

"If we win this series, it'll be because of goaltending. And the way Ron Low is playing, I still think we've got a chance. Heck, tonight was our first Stanley Cup playoff game. With all our youth and inexperience, I think we did pretty well. But we know we can come up with a heck of a lot more offence than *that*."

Low, for his part, said he figured his new teammates were "a little star-struck" in their first Stanley Cup game.

The Oilers learned one of many playoff lessons in losing 5-1 in Game 2. In a word, "discipline," said the man who would one day go on to become the Oilers head coach.

"That's turned out to be the biggest difference in this series so far. The Flyers are beating us with play-off discipline."

Joe Watson, the Flyers scout who'd followed the Oilers down the stretch, agreed with Low.

"I couldn't believe the way the Oilers would take two-minute shifts. Sometimes they seemed to come off the ice when they felt like it."

So they headed home, but hardly as a down-and-out team. They were about to play the first Stanley Cup playoff game in Northlands Coliseum.

They lost 3-2 in double overtime.

"It's a damned shame," said Fogolin when it was over. "Just when it's beginning to be fun, it's over."

Future Oiler Ken Linseman scored the winner for the Flyers at 3:56 of the second overtime period.

Wayne Gretzky surrounded by young fans.

"They should be damned proud of themselves in that other dressing room," said Flyers coach and ex-Edmonton Oil King Pat Quinn when it was over. "They showed us their mettle. They showed us what they're made of and what they're going to do in the future."

Clarke said it really wasn't fair to the Oilers, who were leading Game 1 with 79 seconds to go when he scored a fluke goal to take that one to overtime.

"Let's face it, the whole series could have gone either way. We could just as easily be down 2-1 today as series winners in three straight. With two games in overtime and this one in double overtime ... and that 5-1 game wasn't a 5-1 game.

"The only thing that beat them in this series was our experience," said Clarke, who said no way would Edmonton finish 16th in its second season.

"Not with this experience. Not with Low playing like that for them. And certainly not with Wayne Gretzky and Mark Messier. They are both, obviously, outstanding."

Messier had stepped forward in the playoffs and, more so than even Gretzky and Low, drawn rave reviews.

"That Messier," said Bill Barber. "Well, he convinced me that he's going to turn out to be just super."

The Flyers didn't have to be asked for their thoughts on the Oilers in their dressing room that night. They were volunteering. And then there was Jacques Plante, the Hall-of-Fame Montreal Canadiens goalie who finished up his career with the Oilers in the WHA and was goalie coach for the Flyers that year.

"All they need is a couple of key drafts and a trade or two and, I'll tell you what, they're going to be there," said Plante. "In five years, they could be playing for the Stanley Cup in the final series. And when they get there, with the talented youth they have, they'll be around for a long, long time."

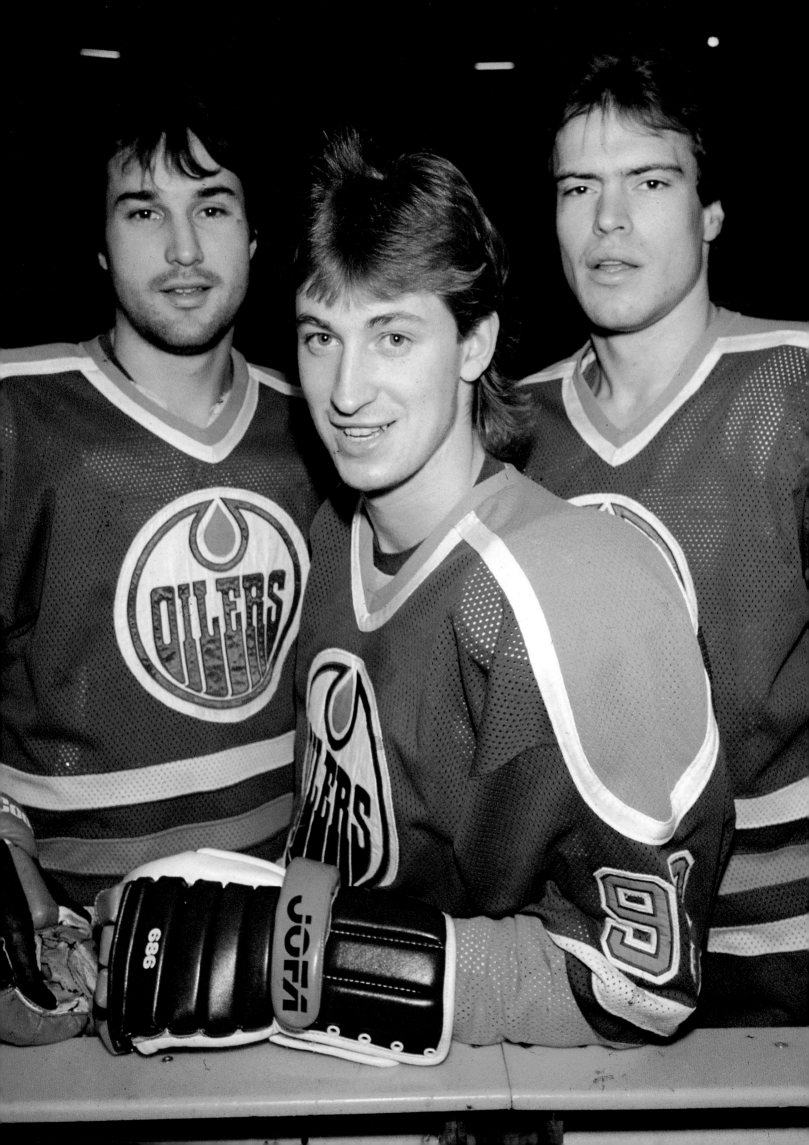

Chapter 4

Here We Go, Oilers, Here We Go

Bill Hunter should have been there.

And there wasn't anywhere he'd rather have been that night, in Edmonton's expanded-to-17,334-seat Northlands Coliseum, where the largest seated hockey crowd in the history of Canada sat on the opening night of the Oilers' second NHL season.

It was Al Hamilton Night. It turned into Bill Hunter Night. But the man who gave birth to the team in the WHA, in his role as a fund-raiser for the late Father Athol Murray's Notre Dame College in Wilcox, Sask., was in charge of the premiere of the movie *The Hounds of Notre Dame* there in Saskatchewan that same night.

It was the night they handed Hamilton his Oilers jersey and officially retired his No. 3.

"One gentleman isn't here," an emotional Hamilton, a former junior Oil King when Hunter ran the club in Edmonton, told the crowd. "Bill Hunter is the man who talked me into coming here. He said this would become the greatest major-league hockey town in Canada. I'm not sure that I believed him. But wherever you are tonight, Bill, thank you."

Hamilton went out with a sense of humour when he talked to reporters during the game up in the press box.

"I know why they retired the number. They wanted to make sure nobody ever wore it again – because that number was injury prone. I was worried I would trip up the stairs, wearing the sweater, when I left the ice."

Intensity on the Oilers bench. Opposite: Paul Coffey, Wayne Gretzky, Mark Messier.

Hamilton, after he left the media laughing, surveyed the Coliseum crowd on his way out and mentioned Hunter again.

"Everybody's dream came true," he said.

It was, unintentionally, a night to honour the Oilers' WHA roots and then move forward to the future.

One of the reasons Hamilton was calling it a career was to make room for youth.

"If I was in the same position as Glen Sather, I'd go with a young team, too," said the 34-year-old Hamilton. "This is going to be an excellent young team."

More pieces were falling into place, not the least of which was the Oilers' No. 1 draft pick that year – Paul Douglas Coffey.

The Montreal Canadiens picked first in the draft. They selected Doug Wickenheiser. The Oilers picked sixth. Paul Coffey.

"Wayne Gretzky really likes him," laughed Sather of his selection. "And whatever Wayne wants, he gets . . . Gretz says Paul can skate faster sideways than he can skate forward."

The Oilers, who also picked a kid from Finland by the name of Jari Kurri in the fourth round and a goalie named Andy Moog in the seventh, thought they had something special in Coffey with or without Gretzky's scouting report (they'd played Junior B hockey together four years earlier).

"He's the guy we wanted all year long," said Sather. "He can control the tempo of a game the way he wheels out of his own end with the puck. He's a great skater."

Coffey said he was hoping the Oilers would pick him.

"Edmonton was my first choice," he said. "When Edmonton drafted me, it was a feeling of relief, not surprise. I met a lot of the guys and Edmonton sounds like a great place to play. It's a great sports town."

The Oilers also signed Glenn Anderson to a three-year contract for $250,000 a year after he'd played for peanuts and lived in a trailer behind the Calgary Corral while playing for the Canadian Olympic team.

Oh, yes. They also hired a new coach to replace Sather: Bryan Watson.

It was Watson, who had played on the same WHA team with Mark Messier, who had convinced the Oilers to pick Messier in Round 3 of the merger draft.

It is traditional, of course, to write a column on the coach prior to the start of each hockey season. But with Watson there was nothing normal about it. One had to determine a thing or two.

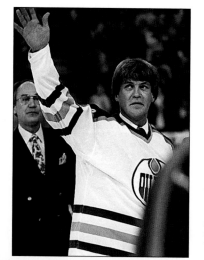

Al Hamilton's retirement party, Northlands Coliseum, October 1980.

"If the Oilers win their first 20 games as a result of coaching genius, who do I credit as the genius?" I found myself asking the coach.

"Or, conversely ..."

"I think I understand the question," said Watson.

"Glen Sather is the general manager.

"I am the coach.

"And Billy Harris is the assistant coach."

That's not how the media guide had it.

Sather's bio began: "Five years ago, if you took a poll of the general managers in the NHL and asked them who was the craftiest GM in the business, there is little doubt that Sam Pollock of the Montreal Canadiens would have been the unanimous choice. His heir apparent is Glen Sather. In just three years, the 36-year-old Sather has risen from the playing ranks to the position of president and general manager of the team while maintaining his position as coach. He has accomplished that feat with an incredible combination of skill, street smarts and positive thinking."

Note the wording, "maintaining his position as coach."

The Watson bio began: "Some people have such an incredible zest for living that their enthusiasm rubs off on people around them. In a large part that's why Bryan Watson was hired as a coach with the Edmonton Oilers."

Note the wording, "a coach."

"There has been some confusion," Watson admitted on the eve of the opener. He admitted that most people around the league thought Sather was still the coach and he was an assistant who worked behind the bench.

"The most important thing is that the players recognize that I am the coach," said Watson.

That said, coach Watson did point out that Sather "may or may not" exercise his option to become *the* coach now and again. But he said he didn't think that would happen.

The team Watson put on the ice for the first game of the 1980-81 season was even younger than the one from the Oilers' first season. The oldest player was 28-year-old Stan Weir. Gretzky, Messier and Coffey were all 19. Kurri and Anderson were both 20. Kevin Lowe was 21. Risto Siltanen and Dave Hunter were 22. The average age of the team was 23.5 years.

The first task of Watson's team was to win the Battle of Alberta. In the off-season, inspired by the success of the Oilers franchise in Edmonton, a Calgary group, which in the beginning included ex-WHA Oiler owner Nelson Skalbania, relocated the Atlanta Flames. And Game

Mark Messier relaxes in the Coliseum bleachers.

1 of what would quickly become one of the fiercest rivalries in the game was in the Coliseum on Oct. 22.

The Oilers won it 5-3. And the star was Dave Semenko.

Placed on a line with Gretzky a week earlier, Semenko already had six goals, including two against the Flames.

"You guys are using keys on your typewriters you've never used before," said Watson of the sportswriters who, to this point, had seen Semenko mostly in a role as the new heavyweight champion of hockey.

"It's an enjoyable habit to get into," said Semenko after the game. "I've got enough bad habits, like smoking. It'll be nice to get a few good ones."

"You can put Gretzky with just about anyone and the guy will look good," said Flames coach Al MacNeil.

Down in Section M, the new rivalry was most definitely brewing.

Two fans had bet $2,000 on the game.

"Just a friendly little wager," said a Mr. N. Skalbania of Calgary.

"That's just what you saw," said a Mr. P. Pocklington of Edmonton of the

Paul Coffey chats with Bryan Watson.

cash which changed hands.

"I never knew Semenko could put the puck in the net," said Skalbania, who owned the Oilers when Semenko broke into pro hockey in the WHA. "I especially didn't know he could put the puck in the net with a goalie in front of it."

Pocklington went into the dressing room before the game and said he figured the bet was a cinch because the Flames still saw themselves as Atlanta, but his team was looking at this as something special.

"When I went into the room before the game, there was an air of electricity," said Pocklington. "We've just seen the start of the greatest rivalry the NHL has ever seen."

Pocklington gave every player on the team a side of beef after the game, pointing out that would absolve him "in case there was some sort of NHL rule against owners betting on games."

At least Watson had that game.

A couple of weeks later he was given the gate.

"With friends like this, Bryan Watson must wonder if he needs any en-

Glen Sather, centre, with assistants Dave Dryden, left, and Bryan Watson. Dryden resigned soon after Watson was hired.

emies," wrote Dick Chubey in *The Edmonton Sun* the next morning.

Watson was one of Sather's best buddies.

But in moving himself back behind the bench, Sather said something else that indicated he certainly had the mental toughness for the job.

"It's like Sam Pollock used to say: 'The league comes first, your team comes second, your family comes third and your friends come last,'" quoted Sather of the famed Montreal Canadiens GM.

And so the dirty deed was done.

Watson, 4-9-4, was gonzo. And Sather was on his way to the Hockey Hall of Fame. Mind you, not before he heard the odd leather-lung shout "Bring Back Bugsy!" from the cheap seats because Sather's record, for the next few months, wasn't any better than Watson's.

Sather also heard, in early January, the singular voice of Harold Ballard.

When the Toronto Maple Leafs came to town, the bombastic Ballard offered to trade his entire team for Gretzky.

"I'd throw in our farm team in Moncton, too," said the Leafs owner.

"I'd trade my whole team for that kid. Might as well; if I got Gretzky I'd have nobody to play him with anyhow."

Actually, that was kind of Glen Sather's problem, too. So far, in the first 120 games of the Oilers' NHL hockey history, Gretzky's wingers had been Dave Semenko, Don Murdoch, Brett Callighen, Jari Kurri, Blair MacDonald, Mark Messier, Glenn Anderson and Don Ashby.

"Every day, my No. 1 priority is to find a goalscorer for Gretzky," said Slats. "We have to have somebody on that line who can score and score every night. If I could find somebody either in a trade or through the draft, who could score 50 or 60 goals ... The only thing I worry about,

An Edmonton fan gives owner Peter Pocklington an A-plus approval rating.

until I find him, is that I'm going to burn him out."

Meanwhile, Sather had decided to put Lowe and Coffey, the Oilers' No. 1 draft choices in their first two times to the annual NHL lottery, together as the youngest defensive pairing in the league.

"At first it was suicide," offered goalie Eddie Mio. "But now it's nice to watch, isn't it?"

Sather explained his thinking.

"They have to lean on each other. They see themselves growing up together. And the result is giving them both a lot of confidence."

Some nights they were woeful. And other nights they were wonderful. But there was no night more wonderful for Lowe, Coffey and everybody else in Oiler silks during that regular season than Jan. 28.

The Montreal Canadiens.

Again.

In hockey terms, this deserved a mention in Ripley's *"Believe It Or Not."*

Edmonton 9, Montreal 1.

To find a Montreal massacre which could compare you had to go back to 1974 when the New York Rangers beat the Habs 9-2 in Madison Square Garden, or that same season when the Canadiens were crushed 8-0 by the Boston Bruins. But 9-2 and 8-0 were not worse defeats than 9-1 by the just-out-of-the-WHA and, at this moment, out-of-the-playoffs Oilers.

"I don't think it's ever happened that we've been beaten worse," said Guy Lafleur. "I've never seen so many goals scored against us."

Actually, if you went back to the 1943-44 season, Montreal lost 10-0 that year to Detroit.

"It was a game we'll remember all of our lives," said goalie Mio, who was brilliant early when the Canadiens actually dominated the game.

"It was the thrill of a lifetime to beat Montreal 5-3 last year in our first

The Oilers visit the set of the television show M*A*S*H as guests of hockey fan Jamie (Corporal Klinger) Farr (front row, Oilers jersey).

NHL game against them. But this ... nobody beats the Montreal Canadiens like this."

What were they saying in the Montreal dressing room?

"I don't know," reported visitors room stick boy Lyle Kulchisky. "But there sure were a lot of 'Tabernacles.'"

That was definitely the Oilers' No. 1 "I was there" game to that point of their NHL history. Except for owner Peter Pocklington. He wasn't there.

"I was flying back from Toronto," said Peter Puck. "I ran from the plane to my car to hear Rod Phillips screaming and carrying on. I couldn't believe it. The greatest day in Oilers' history and I wasn't there."

Pocklington was able to laugh about it.

"When my wife returned from the game she told me I should stay away more often," the owner reported.

It was a night of significance for another reason.

Gretzky had five points. Kurri had three goals. And Sather was calling off his search for Gretzky's go-to guy.

A week later, against Winnipeg, No. 99 had a six point night to vault the 20-year-old past Marcel Dionne in the scoring race. They were Gretzky points Nos. 95, 96, 97, 98, 99 and 100.

In mid-February the Oilers ran it up again, 9-2 over the St. Louis Blues in front of legendary Hockey Hall of Fame goalie Glenn Henry Hall. This was a guy who had faced all the greats. Gordie Howe. Rocket Richard. Bobby Hull. Bobby Orr. And he said he'd never seen anything to compare with what he witnessed that night as Gretzky scored five goals.

"Wayne Gretzky is the greatest player I've ever seen," said Hall as the seconds ticked off the clock.

"Some year he's going to get 250 points in a season. He'll score 100 and get 150 assists."

It was a seven-point night for Gretzky.

Four goals in one period tied an NHL record owned by Busher Jackson.

"Busher Jackson?" said Gretzky.

Tough guy Dave Semenko hears from a young fan. Below, jockey with the '99' silks.

"Who's that? He must have broken in before Gordie Howe, eh? I've never heard of the Busher."

He had heard of Red Berenson. The Red Beren owned the record for six goals in a game. And Berenson was behind the Blues bench that night figuring he was going to lose his record, live and in person.

"I remember Berenson getting that record," said Gretzky. "I was eight."

While the Oilers struggled to make the playoffs again, it was almost as if the team was a sidebar to the Gretzky story.

At the all-star game Gretzky's dad, Walter, whispered his prediction: "He'll win the scoring race by 22 points."

Gretzky hadn't won the Art Ross Trophy the year before because the NHL rules stipulated that in the case of a tie, the title and the trophy would go to the player with the most goals. And that was Marcel Dionne. Not that Gretzky ended up empty-handed. He won the Hart Trophy as the league MVP. And they gave him the Lady Byng as something of a consolation prize for being deemed ineligible for the Calder Trophy as top rookie because of having played a year in the WHA. That was back on June 5, which went down in hockey history as the day Gordie Howe officially retired for good (again) and Gretzky officially ascended his throne.

Gretzky's stated goal in his second NHL season was "to score one more goal than Marcel Dionne." He also said he wanted to average two points a game.

In early March, in his 145th NHL game, he scored his 100th NHL goal. And the first real Great Gretzky Watch was under way.

In just his second NHL season, No. 99 was closing in on Phil Esposito's single-season record of 152 points. By the last week of March Gretzky was only five points back.

"I'm just sitting here trying to figure out where and when," said Esposito in New York.

Oilers vs. North Stars.

Stan Weir, right, celebrates a goal against the Washington Capitals.

Gretzky tied Espo's record in Detroit with a pass to Risto Siltanen in a 4-2 win over the Wings. And the following evening, in Pittsburgh, he assisted on goals by Messier, Kurri and Callighen.

One record was his. And now he went after the one he really wanted.

"If I'm ever going to break a record, Bobby Orr's assist record would be the one I want. I consider myself a playmaker more than a goalscorer," he had said before he tied Billy Taylor's 33-year-old record for most assists in one game (seven).

In the Oilers' 78th game, a 4-4 tie with Colorado, Gretzky registered the assist to beat Orr's record of 102. He'd racked up 22 assists in the last night games to do it by Game 78, the same number of games Orr played in setting the record.

Gretzky finished his 80-game season with 55 goals and an incredible 164 points. That was 12 more goals than Esposito and seven more assists than Orr. Dionne was 29 points back. The next closest Oiler was 90 points back. And his second straight Hart Trophy was a slam dunk.

Gretzky had looked after his dad's 22-point prediction. And he'd also taken care of a couple of his own predictions. One of those was that the Oilers would finish 13th overall. He

Fans get a chance to skate with their hockey idol, Wayne Gretzky.

was wrong about that. The Oilers finished 14th. They actually tied for 13th, but the New York Rangers got the nod because of more wins.

The Oilers had lost only one of their last dozen games to charge into the Stanley Cup playoffs. And, thanks to losing the tie-breaking proceedings with the Rangers, the Oilers were headed to the Taj Mahal of hockey.

And there it was. On the marquee. Of the cathedral. Of the Montreal Forum:

Stanley Cup Playoffs

Canadiens

vs.

Edmonton

The Oilers had only lost one of their last 12 games but the Canadiens could call that with the fact they'd lost only three of their last 26 – and could raise it with the fact they'd lost only one of their last 27 at home.

"I guess it's the old story of David vs. Goliath," said Sather. "It's a little guy going against a big one."

The Oilers had exactly 162 games of playoff experience. The Canadiens had more than 1,000. Gary Unger, Lee Fogolin and Stan Weir led the Oilers in Stanley Cup experience with 39, 33 and 30 games respectively. Serge Savard, Guy Lapointe and Guy Lafleur topped the Canadiens with 120, 111 and 100 games respectively.

"Montreal has years of playoff experience and tradition. We don't have any. Just youth and desire," said Sather.

The Oilers also had this teensy-weensy little problem in goal.

Ron Low, who had been great against Philadelphia in the playoffs the year before, was out with a broken thumb. And Eddie Mio was out with a broken finger.

That left journeyman Gary Edwards, acquired by Minnesota in February, and a kid whose only previous playoff experience was with the Billings Bighorns in junior hockey 12 months earlier. A kid by the name of Andy Moog.

When the sirens sounded to end Game 1, it was Moog who was surrounded by all the microphones, cameras and poised pens. And he couldn't wait for the members of the media to finish with him.

"I can't wait to phone home to Penticton," he said.

And what would his first words be?

"Hey, look what I did!"

Moog, who in his NHL debut allowed a goal on the first shot he faced, flipped and flopped and stopped 28 shots as the Oilers won Game 1, 6-3. In only his seventh NHL game, Moog had just won the Oilers' first playoff game.

It was a scene to savour in the cramped Forum visiting dressing room.

"What an honour," raved Paul Coffey. "To beat the Montreal Canadiens in the Forum in a Stanley Cup playoff game. I can't think of a better word. What an honour."

"Unbelievable!" exulted Kevin Lowe. "What an unbelievable thrill! I'm a hero. A Stanley Cup hero!"

Gretzky had five assists to tie a Stanley Cup record; three assists in the first period to tie another one. He set up linemates Kurri and Callighen for two each and Glenn Anderson for another. But when the media came looking for him in the dressing room, he pointed to the corner of the room and correctly identified Moog as The Story.

"Andy Moog is the most confident 20-year-old I've ever met," said Gretzky. "And it's not cockiness. He's just confident. I've never seen a 20-year-old that confident."

Gretzky leaned over and whispered a personal aside.

"I sat with him on the plane and he told me, 'I'm going to put my name on the Vezina Trophy some day.' "

Moog, informed at the morning skate that he'd start, said that one thought kept going through his head throughout the game.

"What am I doing here?" he said. "I thought that from start to finish. What am I doing here?"

Moog repeated the wish to get free of the interview scene so he could get to a phone and call his dad, Don Moog, a former goaltender for the Penticton Vees who, Andy explained, would be just finishing his shift as a bus driver.

Meanwhile, it was beginning to dawn on the boys on the bus back to the hotel just what had happened here.

"I think that was as close to a humiliation for the Montreal Canadiens that you are going to get," said Lowe, who grew up in Quebec and totally understood what they'd done in Game 1.

They couldn't do it again, could they?

They couldn't win *two* in the Montreal Forum, could they?

"If Dave Hunter, Dave Lumley and Stan Weir continue to contain Guy Lafleur like that, we can," said Gretzky.

And they did.

This time it was 3-1.

"This is Fantasy Island," said 19-year-old Coffey.

Messier had struggled during the season but he was again a presence in the playoffs, bumping Larry Robinson while Hunter hounded The Flower.

Oilers forward Glenn Anderson.

More memorable than any goal, any save or anything else was the looks on the faces of the fans in the Forum at the end of the game. And the look on the face of Claude Ruel.

"They play with no nerves," said the Canadiens coach.

"Maybe we're so young that we're naive," said Fogolin.

"We told ourselves that they have all the pressure," said Gretzky. "So why get uptight? We made up our minds to just give it everything we could give it."

The Oilers did exactly that. And Moog did the rest.

"I was so confident today after last night," said Moog of the back-to-back games in the best-of-five semifinal that took him from a nobody to a coast-to-coast household name in 48 hours.

"That kid in their net did everything. And it was not just luck. He was challenging my shooters and stopping them," said Ruel. "He was not being lucky. We outshot them 41-27. My club came and gave it a hell

of a game. We can't play better than we did tonight. What do you want me to do?"

The atmosphere in the other room was giddy.

"Do you think anybody in the NHL believes it?" enthused Gretzky.

And so the series switched to Edmonton and Game 3.

"That'll be World War III," said Sather. "It doesn't mean anything until we beat them one more time."

The Canadiens were trying to tell the Oilers that now that they were headed home with a 2-0 lead, the pressure was all on them.

"I don't think so," said Gretzky. "Edmonton has been waiting 80 years for this sort of thing. It's going to be great."

The Montreal players took one last look at their dressing room the next morning before they boarded the plane to Edmonton. One last look at the famous words on the wall: *To You From Failing Hands We Throw The Torch.*

"If we don't come back and win this series there may not be a torch to throw," said Larry Robinson on behalf of the team the town had stopped referring to as Les Glorieux the night before.

For three full minutes the Edmonton fans stood and thundered an ovation for the Oilers when they stepped on the Coliseum ice for Game 3.

Messier would, years later, call it one of the most motivating moments in his career.

"When the fans believe in a team like that, it's scary. It was like they were willing us to win."

And win they did, 6-2. And the historians had to go back to 1952 and the Detroit Red Wings with Terry Sawchuk, Red Kelly, Marcel Pronovost, Ted Lindsey, Sid Abel and Gordie Howe to find the last time the Canadiens had been swept in a series.

If Glenn Hall wasn't then Terry Sawchuk was the greatest goalie in the history of hockey. This was Andy Moog.

"An-dy! An-dy! An-dy!" the Coliseum crowd chanted.

The game had been over for an hour. The reporters had all left the dressing room. But there was Moog, still in uniform, sitting alone.

"It was the first chance I really had to sit down and realize what had happened to me," said Moog. "I just sat there. And then all of a sudden, I realized it. I was shaking.

"It had really started to sink in. For the first time I really realized that I had accomplished something – we'd all accomplished something. At that point I was really shaking. I was trembling."

Gretzky had his own thought.

"We just beat the best team in hockey. Who knows what we can do?"

Ah, hold that thought.

When the Oilers arrived in Uniondale, N.Y., for their next series against the New York Islanders, the first thing they noticed was that only one Stanley Cup pennant hung from the ceiling, not 22. But it was the

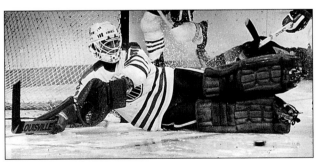

Netminder Andy Moog.

Wayne Gretzky embraces New York's Butch Goring after the Islanders eliminated the Oilers in the 1981 playoffs. Above, goalie Ron Low.

most recent pennant. And the Islanders, according to a headline in the *New York Post*, did not like No. 99's attitude coming off the Montreal series.

ISLES HOPE
TO MAKE GRETZKY
EAT HIS WORDS

So screamed the largest sports headline in the edition.

Gretzky had meant that they had beaten the greatest franchise in hockey history. But the Islanders chose to take it as an insult to the defending Stanley Cup champions.

"The Canadiens were the greatest team in hockey, but not now," said Stephan Persson. "I think Gretzky got it backwards."

And you'd have figured the Islanders pretty much delivered that message in person when they won the first two games, 6-3 and 8-2.

"I think we got a pretty good idea of why they're Stanley Cup champions," said captain Fogolin.

But Easter Sunday was another day of Oilers confirmation.

Gretzky again.

Gretzky scored three goals to put the Canadiens away in the first Stanley Cup playoff win in Edmonton. And he did it again to keep the Oilers alive as Coliseum fans watched their cardiac kids beat the Stanley Cup champions 5-2 in Game 3. But Ken Morrow scored at 5:41 of overtime in Game 4 and the series switched back to Long Island with midnight one loss away for Glen Sather's Cinderfellas.

If you didn't know it already, it was in Game 5 that you found out for sure that the Stanley Cup playoffs had never seen a team quite like this one.

Four minutes remained in the game and the Oilers were sitting on the bench. Singing!

"Here we go, Oilers, here we go!

"Here we go, Oilers, here we go!

"Here we go, Oilers, here we go!"

The team Claude Ruel said "had no nerves" was messing up the minds of every hockey man in the world now.

There's no singing on the bench in the Stanley Cup playoffs.

"This is getting to be fun," said Kevin Lowe.

"Every time we got into trouble we started singing," said Sather.

"Teenagers," assistant coach Harris shook his head.

The Edmonton Boys Choir was formed during the second period intermission.

"Here we go, Oilers, here we go!

"Here we go, Oilers, here we go!

"Here we go, Oilers, here we go!"

"I think it was Mark Messier who started it," said Coffey.

"It just felt right to start singing.

"We don't know how to be goodie-goodies yet. We're a young team. We don't know how to take it all in stride."

Just when you figured the story was over, it got better. Two wins in the Montreal Forum. Now one in the Nassau County Coliseum. And there were seven players in the lineup young enough to be playing in the Memorial Cup.

"It's proof of what everybody is saying back in Edmonton," said Gretzky in the dressing room that night after Matti Hagman scored the winner in the 4-3 thriller.

"We're the youngest team in the NHL. Just a bunch of kids. And all we're doing is saying to ourselves, 'Let's give it our best shot.' It's wrong to say we're going to beat them. And we're not going to say that. All we're saying is that we've got nothing to lose."

As Gretzky spoke, from out of the showers came the song again.

'It wasn't like playing Philadelphia or Montreal. It wasn't normal like that. It was all based on emotion and desire. It was so tough to play them. They made it so frustrating. It was weird playing them. It was like we were playing ourselves from five years ago.'

– Denis Potvin on playing the Oilers

A dejected Andy Moog after losing to the Islanders.

"Here we go, Oilers, here we go!

"Here we go, Oilers, here we go!

"Here we go, Oilers, here we go!"

But the Islanders had the last chorus.

The champions weren't interested in testing this team in a seventh game. They put an end to it with a 5-2 win in Game 6 and the Oilers formed a line to shake hands.

"Can I have your stick?" Messier asked Bob Nystrom as he shook hands. "I'd like a memento of this series. Something to remember."

Nystrom, stunned, gave him the stick.

And the Islanders, like the Philadelphia Flyers the year before, gave the Oilers nothing but praise when it was over.

"I've never been in a series like this one," said Denis Potvin. "It wasn't like playing Philadelphia or Montreal. It wasn't normal like that. It was all based on emotion and desire. It was so tough to play them. They made it so frustrating. It was weird playing them. It was like we were playing ourselves from five years ago."

Nystrom said of all his teammates, he'd be the last guy to praise another team.

"I'm not one to dole out compliments. But they were tremendous."

While reporters interviewed coach Al Arbour in the hall outside the New York room, the Islanders started to sing a slightly rewritten version of the song the Oilers had been singing on their bench in their rink.

"Here we go, Islanders, here we go!

"Here we go, Islanders, here we go!

"Here we go, Islanders, here we go!"

The Islanders went on to win their second straight Stanley Cup. But they left Edmonton that night knowing there would come a day ...

"That proves we're going to be *there!*" Lowe said to the walls in the Oilers room.

Chapter 5

Miracle On Manchester

he beautiful butterfly that emerged from the cocoon against the Montreal Canadiens and New York Islanders in the playoffs the previous spring had learned to fly in the NHL by the Edmonton Oilers' third year in the league. And not just fly. Fly high.

It was pedal to the metal from the start of the season. Instead of a mad scramble to make the playoffs in the final weeks of the schedule, this time making the post-season wasn't going to be a worry.

The Kiddie Corps led the league more days than not during the 1981-82 season. And had any team ever had as many plots going at the same time?

The season began with one scenario that could only happen with these talented toddlers.

This was an NHL club actually daring to go into a season with 19- and 21-year-old netminders?

The Oilers, at the June draft, had picked a goalie who was once cut by both the Sherwood Park Crusaders and St. Albert Saints of the Alberta Junior Hockey League. A kid named Grant Fuhr.

"He's the best prospect since Bernie Parent," said chief scout Barry Fraser. "I think he can play in the NHL this season."

The native of Spruce Grove, who celebrated his 19th birthday 15 days after the start of training camp, had been brilliant with the Victoria Cougars in the Western Hockey League the previous two seasons.

Fuhr had been rated as a "nine" on the Oilers' scouting sheets.

**The Battle of Alberta.
Opposite: Premier Peter
Lougheed shows
allegiance to both
Alberta NHL teams.**

Goalie Grant Fuhr in his Victoria Cougars junior hockey uniform.

Back then they had a 10-point rating system which looked like this:

1. **Reject.**
2. **Reject with one good quality.**
3. **Eastern Hockey League.**
4. **Minor pro.**
5. **Sure minor pro with NHL chance.**
6. **NHL prospect.**
7. **NHL prospect with good potential.**
8. **NHL.**
9. **Cinch NHL.**
10. **Gretzky.**

"When I drafted him, I believed he could step in and play," said Fraser. "He's extremely good at directing the puck into corners. He has the best blocker I have ever seen at any level. He has a good catching hand. And he always knows where the puck is behind him. The only thing he lacks is NHL experience."

You get the idea. Suddenly the Oilers' goaltending picture was getting kind of crowded. Andy Moog was the Oilers' playoff hero from the spring before. Ron Low was the playoff hero from the year before that. And then there was Eddie Mio, Gary Edwards and Edmonton native Gord Garbutt.

"We'll start three and go down to two by Christmas," said Glen Sather.

He kept the two kids, Fuhr and Moog. And he kept the old pro Low.

"I don't believe in the philosophy which has existed in hockey for 50 years that a young goaltender has to suffer for a year or two in the minors before starting in the NHL," said Sather.

If all Fuhr was lacking was NHL experience, Sather decided to cure that little problem by getting it for him quickly. And he was something special.

Fuhr lost his NHL debut 4-2 to the Winnipeg Jets. He was unbeaten in his next seven in which he gave up the grand total of four goals, two of them on breakaways.

And he just kept going. He eventually made it a 23-game unbeaten binge. He was supposed to be good, but nobody expected him to lose his first game and then go three months before he lost again. It was Jan. 16 in Toronto when he recorded his second loss. And he bounced back to be the first star the next night in a 4-4 tie against Detroit, then continued winning until Feb. 3 against Montreal.

"I couldn't help but look at him and the way he handled the first half of his first year and compare it to me and my first half of my rookie year the year before," Paul Coffey said. "I was in awe until mid-December. I didn't play my game at all. And he came in like it was nothing."

Fuhr lost that one game and went on another tear that lasted until March 6 before he lost back-to-back games to Colorado and Los Angeles. But that was it for the regular season. He never lost again. Grant Fuhr in his rookie season started 48 games and lost only five of them.

There were other compelling stories this most amazing of seasons. Such as Dave Lumley.

On Dec. 3, Dave Lumley, not Wayne Gretzky, not Jari Kurri, not Mark Messier, not Coffey, not Glenn Anderson – Dave Lumley – set the Oilers' team record for the longest consecutive games streak for goalscoring with seven.

Within a week the entire hockey world was following the saga of "Lumley In Wonderland."

Ten goals in 10 games. And counting.

"It's almost embarrassing," he said.

"It's like one of those quiz items. Which of the following names doesn't belong on this list? a. Bobby Hull, b. Andy Bathgate, c. Mike Bossy, d. Dave Lumley. Those are the three guys I'm tied with for 10 goals in 10 games. I can't help but wonder what all the other players in the NHL are thinking. They've watched me play. I know what they're all thinking: 'How in hell can *Dave Lumley* score goals in 10 straight games?' I'm not a goalscorer. I'm Dave Lumley. I'm the guy who went 16 games with-

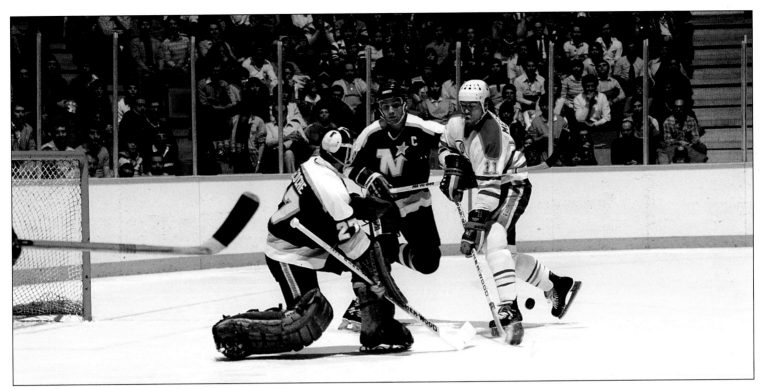

Mark Messier takes a shot against the Minnesota North Stars.

out scoring a goal for the Nova Scotia Voyageurs. I spent 13 games in the press box this year. Last year I didn't even want to get the puck. I didn't want to have anything to do with the puck. I knew that somehow I'd manage to screw it up."

On the other hand ...

"It's just grrrreat! I just feel so gooooood. I feel so loose and I'm just having the time of my life."

One day, when *Sun* hockey writer Dick Chubey came to him on a flight, carrying a copy of the NHL record book, Lumley told him to take a hike.

"Stay away from me. I've got nothing to say to you. I'm serious. Two years in a row you've done articles on me and I was booted upstairs to the press box. You're a jinx."

Chubey had the book turned to page 135:

Longest Consecutive Goalscoring Streak:

* 16 games – Harry (Punch) Broadbent, Ottawa Senators, 1921-22.
* 14 games – Joe Malone, Montreal Canadiens, 1917-18.
* 13 games – Newsy Lalonde, Montreal Canadiens, 1920-21.
* 13 games – Charlie Simmer, Los Angeles Kings, 1979-80.

On Dec. 16, in Denver, Lumley made it 12 games. And he scored two.

But all good things come to an end. In Calgary, Lumley failed to make it 13 games in a row. Simmer and the old-timers were safe.

"It was fun while it lasted," he said. "Now I can go back to being an unknown."

That wasn't going to happen to Messier.

He might have been a late bloomer compared to Gretzky. But boy, did he bloom that year.

On Feb. 17 the 21-year-old scored his 40th goal and his first home hat trick. And he was going for 50.

By Game 77 he had 48.

"I think I have a chance," said No. 11. "I know I don't want to finish with 49. Nobody remembers guys who come close."

Messier and Lumley combined in the next game, in Los Angeles, for a record.

Lumley scored on a breakaway at 0:24 of the first period, 10 seconds after Messier had notched No. 49. It set the record – by a full five seconds – for the fastest two goals at the start of a game.

The actual shot, and the puck denting the twine with less than a minute left in the Oilers' second-last game of the season for Messier's 50th, is probably a little fuzzy now to most of the fans who were there. But everybody must still remember Messier's celebration of the goal.

Messier set an NHL record for artistic impression as he turned the entire Coliseum ice surface into his own personal dance floor.

To describe his reaction is difficult. But imagine a human being as a balloon. Somebody lets out the air...

Messier went from one end of the ice to the other, his arms and legs out of control.

"I just lost it," he remembers.

"It was such a feeling of exhilaration. I just lost control of everything in my body and we just took a trip together. If the game had been played on a river, I'd have skated all the way like that to the next province."

Some of Messier's teammates couldn't help but laugh.

Like Lumley.

"Gretz should take celebration lessons from the Moose," he said.

"I don't think anybody realized how determined he was to get 50," said Gretzky. "It was more than a goal. It was a commitment."

Messier, Lumley, Fuhr ... there was no shortage of young Oilers blooming and having super seasons. Kurri had his first 50-goal season, too, making the modest jump from 43 goals to 54. Coffey went from nine goals to 29. Anderson jumped from 53 points to 105. Even Semenko scored 12 goals.

Dave Lumley put together a 12-game scoring streak early in the 1981-82 season.

But this was Gretzky's season to become hockey's icon.

And No. 99 called his shot again.

"I think it's time I started shooting more," he had said at training camp. "I think it's time to go for more goals. The teams are starting to get wise to me. They figure that nine times out of 10 I'm going to pass."

The previous year only Mike Bossy, Marcel Dionne and Charlie Simmer managed to score more than the 55 goals Gretzky scored, yet the young Oilers superstar was 17th when it came to shots on goal.

By the 14th game of the season Gretzky had 15 goals. Baseball season had just ended and football season was just beginning to peak, and people were asking Gretzky about the possibility of breaking some of the game's most treasured records.

The magic marker in hockey, for years and years, was 50 goals in 50 games.

"It's a little early to say I'm shooting for it," said No. 99 at that stage.

Gretzky, who took time out from his game plan of shooting to feed passes to Lumley during his run for a record, reverted to a goalscorer again at the end of the Lumley streak as Sather started to long-shift and double-shift him so that just about everybody on the team could claim to be his winger.

"I've got maybe six to eight minutes more ice time this year than last year," Gretzky observed at one point.

By Christmas Gretzky had scored 41 goals in 37 games. And he'd owned Christmas.

Oilers sweaters, most of them with No. 99 on the back, were the No. 1 Christmas gift in Canada.

"The Oilers outsold the Canadiens and Leafs *combined* at least two-to-one," Jerry Sabourin, an executive with the NHL rights-holding

Coach Glen (Slats) Sather.

Grant Emblems reported. "I've never seen a demand for any one team even remotely close to the demand for the Oilers. For every one Oilers crest that goes out, there's only one from all the other teams in the NHL combined that we sent out."

Gretzky's agent, Gus Badali, and his dad Walter had circled Game 47, in Toronto, as the day for Rocket Richard's famed record to fall. And that seemed about right. But it didn't work out that way.

The Los Angeles Kings were the first holiday-season visitors to Northlands Coliseum. And Gretzky scored four.

"It's like trying to throw a blanket over a ghost," said L.A. coach Parker MacDonald.

Now Gretzky had 45 goals and 102 points in just 38 games. That broke Phil Esposito's record from 11 years earlier for the fastest 100 points. And now there was no question. The Rocket was going to be shot down.

And how was Mr. Richard taking all of this?

"It's hard to believe," he said. "I started thinking about my record being equalled when the first expansion came. But I never thought it would be surpassed. And he's going to make it, maybe before his 42nd game! Every time he scores a goal, it looks easy. Everything he does looks easy. He plays everywhere. He's all over the ice. He's great. There's no doubt about it. There's no way anybody will stop him from being the greatest star in hockey."

The other 50-50 man was handling it well, too.

"Gretzky isn't just anybody," said Mike Bossy, the New York Islander who tied Richard's record the year before.

"This isn't the first record he'll break. He seems on course for a 100-goal season. And I think he can do it."

The next game was against the Philadelphia Flyers.

Dec. 30, 1981.

It was a fully accredited great moment in hockey history. It was the day the Rocket's red glare would look like a flick of a Bic.

Gretzky was lighting up the league, but writers went away from this game calling it the greatest game ever played by the greatest player in the history of the game to break the greatest record ever set in the game. And even Gretzky, he of the "I'll-play-'em-you-rate-'em" school, had to agree.

"It probably was," he said.

Five goals in one night. Nine in the last two nights. Fifty goals in 39 games!

"People are going to have to re-evaluate their stars of the century," said Sather in the post-game dressing room. "And I don't think we've seen the best of Wayne yet."

Pete Peeters was in goal that night for the Philadelphia Flyers.

"What he did was absolutely amazing," said Peeters, who was at least saved from going down in history as the goalie who gave up the 50th. Gretzky scored it into an empty net with three minutes left to play.

"This is absolutely crazy," said Flyers captain Bobby Clarke. "At least with Bobby Orr, you'd see him wind up in his own end and you could try to set up some kind of defence to stop him. Gretzky ... he just comes out of nowhere. It's scary."

Gretzky had scored on 15 of his last 32 shots.

Oiler Don Jackson stretches during training camp, 1981. Opposite: Wayne Gretzky takes a breather.

Wayne Gretzky shakes hands with his idol, Gordie Howe, at a celebrity softball tournament at Edmonton's John Ducey Park.

Gretzky's roommate, Kevin Lowe, said he knew it was coming when the two were sitting down to bacon and eggs (cooked by Gretzky) for breakfast that morning.

"He doesn't say much before his goals," reported Lowe. "But when I talked to him he said there was no reason he couldn't score five against the Flyers."

Gretzky, of course, was not in any position to compare his record to the Rocket's because he wasn't born by 1944-45, although he said he did remember seeing the Rocket on a between-periods interview once.

"I can't even remember seeing any Original Six NHL games on TV," he said.

One thing's for sure. By not just breaking the record, but absolutely smashing it to smithereens, Gretzky had taken away any ridicule of his record because of expansion, style of play or whatever other sacred excuses might have been out there at the time.

The numbers were already staggering.

Fifty goals in 39 games. One hundred and eight points in 39 games. One hundred and fifty-six goals and 409 points in a game shy of 2½ NHL seasons. And for the calendar year 1981, 95 goals with

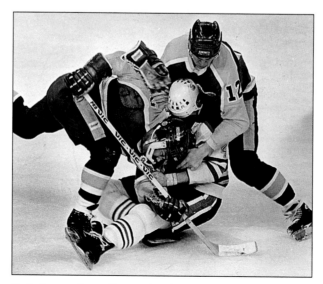

Kevin Lowe gets royally crunched by a pair of Kings.

142 assists for 237 points. And he had yet to reach his 21st birthday!

He still had half a season to go.

"I think I can double everything," said Gretzky as he left the dressing room that night.

The Oilers were about to hit the road to the eastern seaboard. And Gretzky and the Oilers were the hottest story in sport. A film crew was shooting *A Day in the Life of Wayne Gretzky.*

"Wayne is the most patient guy I have ever seen," observed Sather during that tour. "I know I don't have the patience. Wayne answers everyone. He is still willing to accept it as part of the game. I don't know how much longer he can remain the way he is. After a while, when so many people demand a piece of your life ..."

Gretzky did admit he couldn't wait to get back to Edmonton.

"Edmonton is a blessing. I can find time for myself when I'm home in Edmonton. I doubt if it would be like that in a place like New York."

But Gretzky was also enjoying the idea that all the interviews weren't just for him now. Everybody thought it was hilarious when *Ebony Magazine* showed up in Philadelphia to interview Fuhr. Ron Low suggested that was the first time Fuhr knew he was black.

When the team hit Toronto, it was nuts.

On the four-game tour which took the team from Washington to Philadelphia to Toronto to Detroit, there were 132 interview requests. In Toronto, the Oilers PR department decided the only way to handle the media was to hold a two-hour press conference.

Veteran Toronto sportswriters wondered if there had ever been such a reception for a Canadian athlete.

Peter Smith, who managed Toronto's Westin Hotel, compared it to a royal visit.

"The only time I've seen anything that came close was when I was the manager of the Edmonton Plaza Hotel (now the Westin) in 1978 and we had Queen Elizabeth and Prince Philip in the hotel for the Commonwealth Games."

Owner Pocklington took it all in.

"This scene is absolutely unbelievable. If you weren't convinced before, you have to be convinced now that Wayne has done more to put Edmonton on the map than all of the other 650,000 citizens of Edmonton combined."

Gretzky read it right.

"I guess what happened to me here this afternoon is just about the greatest compliment ever paid to me," he said.

After the game, Semenko and a couple of Oiler teammates had to act as plainclothes bodyguards to get Gretzky on the bus, which was surrounded by a bunch of teenaged girls screaming with delight just to get a glimpse of him or actually touch him.

"I feel like the Beatles," he said in an embarrassed sort of way as he worked his way down the aisle to the back of the bus.

Suddenly, both Gretzky and the Oilers had a new challenge.

The Oilers, who were wowing the hockey world with 25 wins, eight losses and six ties after the Gretzky game against the Flyers, had a terrible trip. They didn't win a game. And the losses were by scores of 8-2 in Philadelphia and 7-1 in Toronto.

"We should have realized how this would be sooner or later," said captain Lee Fogolin. "It wasn't long ago when we were the club in 18th place and we were treating those games when the Montreal Canadiens came into our rink like it was the moon. Obviously, we weren't prepared to handle it when it happened to us."

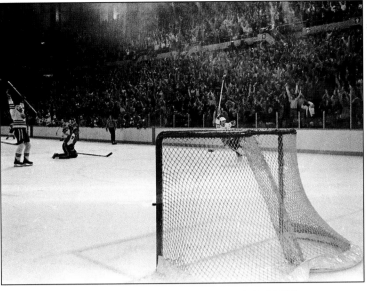

The empty-net goal that gave Wayne Gretzky 50 goals in 39 NHL games.

and NHL president John Ziegler, who informed them they'd be travelling with the team until Gretzky scored the historic goal.

"Our instructions to Wayne are to go out and get a bunch of assists and no goals. We figure it'd be nice if you could hang around with us at least as far as Pittsburgh," assistant coach Billy Harris joked with Esposito.

"Pittsburgh!" exclaimed Espo in horror. "I don't even want to go to Buffalo."

Gretzky tied the record in Detroit, taking a perfect relay from Anderson before beating goaltender Bob Sauve at 16:34 of the third period. He had scored 76 goals on 293 shots. When Esposito established the record he had taken 550 shots.

It was so obvious that Gretzky was going to break this record that he was taking everything in stride.

"The only thing I felt anxious about was that Phil was there and I wanted to do it so he could get back to work," No. 99 remembers.

When it happened, it was a bonus.

They came to see him score No. 77.

He scored No. 77, No. 78 and No. 79.

And Esposito had been saving an anecdote for the moment.

"Seven years ago I got a call from my dad in Sault Ste. Marie," said Esposito. "He said, 'There's a boy here who will break all your records one day. He's 14 years old and he's playing junior in the Soo. His name is Gretzky ... Wayne Gretzky.'"

In Game 76 against the Flames in Calgary, Gretzky notched his 200th, 201st, 202nd and 203rd regular-season points.

Gretzky had his own theory.

"I think we had been so successful that we got to the point where we started to believe that all we had to do was throw our sticks out on the ice. At the same time that happened, we became kind of a trophy for other teams."

The Oilers snapped out of it that time. But they would prove soon enough that they didn't learn the lesson.

With Gretzky's 50 goals in 39 games, nobody was holding out much hope for Esposito's NHL single-season record of 76 goals. And when the Oilers arrived in Detroit for Game 63, they were met by Esposito

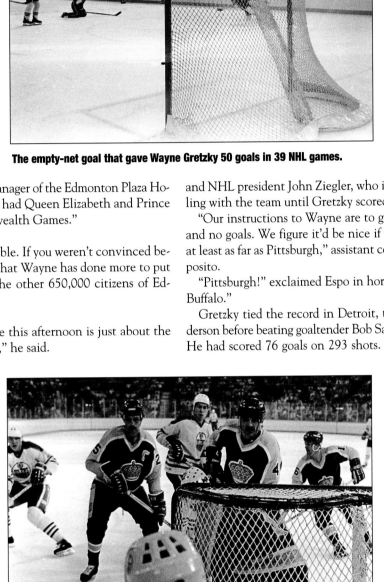

The Great One sets up in his office behind the net.

Glenn Anderson takes a shot against the Soviets.

And he was cheered! In Calgary!

"I've been booed before, but here they really mean it," said Gretzky.

When the moment came and Gretzky put up No. 200 at 9:16 of the first period, it *started* with a chorus of boos. But then, one by one, they started cheering him. And then, one by one, they came to their feet. Eventually everyone was standing, making it more than memorable for the young man who was well on his way to becoming hockey's No. 1 memory maker.

"I thought this was the last place in the world this would ever happen to me," said Gretzky. "Because of the ovation they gave me it meant a little bit more to me than what happened in Buffalo when I broke Phil Esposito's record. I think it showed when a Canadian does something special, they'll drop everything to stand behind him and show their appreciation as fellow Canadians."

Gretzky ended the regular season with 92 goals, 120 assists and 212 points – all NHL records.

Some of his amazing accomplishments in his third NHL season:

* A margin of 65 more points than scoring race runner-up Bossy.

* An average of 2.65 points per game, the first player in the history of the NHL to average more than two points a game during a season.

* A league-leading 12 winning goals.

* The fastest 500 points ever attained. At the end of three seasons his total was 513 points in 239 regular-season games, including 198 goals.

* An NHL record for 10 hat tricks.

* An NHL record with two short-handed goals in a span of 27 seconds.

* An NHL record with 50 goals in 39 games.

* An NHL record with 79 goals in 66 games to break Esposito's NHL record of 76 goals in 78 games.

Gretzky, of course, in addition to his second straight Art Ross Trophy, would win his third straight Hart Trophy. But it was the all-star voting that told the tale of this season. No. 99 wasn't flying solo any more. Messier joined him on the first team as the left-winger. Fuhr was the second-team goalie in his rookie season. And Coffey made the second team on defence. The whole team was on a magic carpet ride.

In mid-season a Calgary radio station hired a witch to try to stop them.

A California-based witch by the name of Zee Budapest was engaged by CFCN disc jockey Doug Veronelly to "hex the Oilers for the rest of the season and to brew up a real rivalry."

Budapest's voodoo worked for one night, when the Flames beat the Oilers 7-2 in Calgary, but Edmonton kept rolling along.

"We didn't want to slip back to being the kind of hockey club we were throughout most of the previous year," remembered Fogolin. "The play-offs allowed us to to discover how good we could really play if we put our minds to it. The year before we didn't expect as much as we should have expected from ourselves. We didn't prepare for a lot of those games. We were always ready for the big teams. We enjoyed great success in beating the good teams. But we were seldom ready to play the rest of the teams in the league."

By Jan. 28 the Oilers were one win away from equalling their 74-point total of the previous year. By Feb. 22, they had won 12 and lost only one in a 16-game span after that embarrassing loss to Toronto on The Trip. They were in first place overall, ahead of the back-to-back Stanley Cup-champion New York Islanders.

One of the great team nights of the season came in Denver when the Oilers went for the NHL team record for most goals in a single season. The Boston Bruins owned the record with 399 goals. And the Oilers were going for No. 400.

On the day of the game, the team was talking about who would be the best guy to get what they were calling the milestone marker.

"A couple of weeks ago we were all hoping it would be Bims," said Messier of Garry Lariviere. "We all felt he should have the honour. It would be his first goal of the season and it would be No. 400 to break the record. But he screwed it up and scored it a couple of weeks early."

"My choice would be Lee Fogolin," said Sather. "He was the first player we picked in the merger draft. He's our captain. That would be perfect for me.

Wayne Gretzky scores his 500th career point in Calgary in March 1982.

"Paul Coffey," said Harris.

"I'd like to see somebody like Cement," said Gretzky of Semenko.

It was Lumley. It was his year for being a hero.

"Does this mean I get inducted into the Hall of Fame?" he asked.

"Man, I wish we had the pool we were going to have. We were each going to throw $10 into the pool, but the defencemen figured they should only have to pay $5 and negotiations broke down before the game."

On March 13, the Oilers won their 100th all-time NHL game. They became the youngest NHL team ever to accomplish that feat. And in a matter of a few more days, they hit the 100-point plateau in the regular-season standings, becoming the youngest franchise to do that, too.

"It's big," said Low. "Bigger than most players on this team probably realize. There's something about 100 points. Just like there's something about winning 100 games in baseball. The biggest thing, because we're such a young club, is to prove we're really as good as everybody says we are. But when you get that 100 points, it's there as proof that we can do it. If we can do it once, we can do it again."

Fogolin said it's the number that separates the very top teams from the rest of the good teams in the league.

"The elite teams find a way to hit 100 points," he said. "Next year and in subsequent years we'll have that magic number to shoot for to stay in the elite."

A rare sight: Wayne Gretzky and Mark Messier together in the penalty box.

it bad enough we had to kill so many penalties in the first two periods without being stupid enough to take even more in the third period? We were stupid enough to think it couldn't catch up. It did. You don't win in the playoffs by playing stupid."

The No. 1 goat was Garry Unger, who took a five-minute high-sticking penalty with five minutes to go.

It became known as the Miracle On Manchester.

"In all my 30 years in hockey I've never seen anything like that," said the Kings new coach Don Perry. "Never!"

While it was only Game 3 of the best-of-five series, people would remember it as if it was a deciding game. The Oilers won

The Oilers ended up with 48 wins, 17 losses and 15 ties for 111 points. They finished second overall, seven points behind the Islanders. They scored 417 goals. And thus it was that the 1981-82 Edmonton Oilers would head into the Stanley Cup playoffs in a very strange space.

You could call it a "change of life." Their age of innocence was over. Their "*Fantasy Island*" days were done. Suddenly they went from being the hunters to the hunted.

They were a third-year NHL club and they went into the playoffs with the very clear understanding, probably too clear, that if they didn't make it to the Stanley Cup final people were going to be disappointed.

Assistant coach Harris put it perfectly.

"Last year we beat the Montreal Canadiens. In a way we've kind of *become* a Montreal Canadiens. Instead of getting better year by year, we did it all at once. Now strange thoughts cross your mind. Like, could the bubble burst?"

Coffey offered a thought or two, too.

"Last year if we had lost to Montreal, big deal. Now we have to worry about not being a Montreal and losing to the underdogs. We've just finished a season we'd like to be able to frame. But if we lose out in the first round ..."

The Oilers' first series in the playoffs was against the Los Angeles Kings. It would also be their only series. And Game 1 at the Coliseum pretty much telegraphed it.

The Oilers came out and grabbed a 4-1 lead and then gave the game away.

"Maybe it was nervousness," said Sather that night. "Panic seemed to set in. You could see it. All of a sudden the puck was a hot potato. Our entire game fell apart. We made dreadful mistakes. The only game I think we played worse all season was against Buffalo in the pre-season. We were horrible."

The final score was 10-8.

"That wasn't a Stanley Cup playoff game," said Lumley. "That was a joke."

Fuhr, who was as bad in goal in Game 1 as the score would suggest, stood on his head in Game 2 and the Oilers won 3-2.

And then came the loss which would be the Oilers' most famous defeat ever ... or at least until Steve Smith.

How do you blow, absolutely gas, a 5-0 lead in the third period of a Stanley Cup playoff game and then lose it in overtime?

"Stupid hockey," Gretzky correctly answered the question. "Wasn't

3-2, again, in Game 4. But back in Edmonton they went down 7-4 and headed into the off-season with their sensational season spoiled.

An Oilers doll hung from the ceiling in the Kings dressing room. It was quickly constructed by the Kings using an oil can. Attached to it were wobbly legs and weak knees and a pea-sized head.

And so it was that I was inspired to write The Paragraph.

"From today until they've won a playoff series again, they are weak-kneed wimps who thought they were God's gift to the National Hockey League but found out they were nothing but adolescent front-running good-time Charlies who couldn't handle adversity."

Eventually most of the members of that team would come around to the same conclusion. A couple of others needed only a few hours.

Like future Oilers coach Ron Low.

"If you are going to be as cocky as this team was, you have to stay cocky. You can't be cocky and then be overcome with self-doubts when it comes to the crunch."

From God's gift to the NHL to weak-kneed ...

Harris came clean about what really had happened.

"We have to get away from our cocky and antagonistic attitude," he began. "If you are going to be cocky, you have to be the best. Unquestionably the best. Our cockiness and our antagonistic attitude is the biggest reason we're not still playing.

"Remember how I told you after Game 3 in Los Angeles that for the first time all season I had nothing to say? Now I'll tell you why.

"We were leading 4-0 when it happened. Four to nothing! And Los Angeles had a power play. And at the time our bench, our entire bench, was *booing* the Los Angeles power play!"

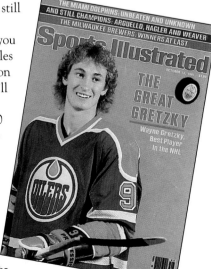

Gretzky's first appearance on the cover of *Sports Illustrated*, Oct. 12, 1981.

Chapter 6

Final Jeopardy

So, what was it like being weak-kneed wimps?

When the Oilers gathered for their fourth NHL training camp the storyline was their long, *hot* summer.

"It was incredible the way it went with the fans," said Kevin Lowe as he checked in. "It must have happened a thousand times. Somebody would come up to me and ... well, it never varied. Everybody would begin by asking exactly the same thing:

" *'I hate to ask you this but ...'*

"Then they'd pause. Then they'd spit it out.

" *'But ... what the hell happened?'*

"It was kind of tough all summer. I got tired of hearing that question over and over and over. I guess that's what we had to expect and I hope we'll remember it all year. It'll make us a better team."

Stunning the sport with a 417-goal, 111-point season and then losing spectacularly to a team that had finished 17th overall left Lowe and several Oilers in Europe as Team Canada pickups for the world championships.

"That's where it was most uncomfortable," said Lowe. "All the other players from all the other teams were the first to start asking it and I got the definite impression they were all delighted to see it happen to us. They didn't mind us losing out one bit. We did a lot to make other teams look bad.

"I think I know what it's going to be like for us this year. We ground a lot of people's noses into it last year and from talking to other players on other teams, there are a lot of teams who are going to come in here for revenge games."

Mark Messier lies on the ice. Opposite: Messier dazzles the crowd at a charity softball game.

Lowe, for one, didn't mind going public with the idea that the Oilers' largest lesson from the summer was that they had to grow up. He said booing the L.A. Kings' power play while on the bench and blowing a 5-0 lead emphasized it more than anything.

"Billy Harris pointed it out and he was right in saying what he did. When we did that, we gave Los Angeles a lift. We were trying to demoralize them but it worked in reverse. We looked stupid in the end. We've tried to pattern ourselves after the Islanders in a lot of ways. We have to become like the Islanders in that way, too. The Islanders don't rub other teams' noses in it. We've got to grow out of it and we've had all summer to drive that fact home."

And so it was the Oilers began the 1982-83 season.

There were changes. The year before the Oilers had added two coaches to the organization: Teddy Green, who joined the NHL staff, and John Muckler, who took on the job of coaching the farm team. Muckler was moved up to the big team to replace the fired Harris. And as the season started, only seven players who were there for the Oilers' first game in the NHL still remained with the club.

Randy Gregg, the former University of Alberta Golden Bear and the only medical doctor playing in the NHL, had returned from two years in Japan with the Kokudo Bunnies. Without having played a regular-season game, he'd dressed for four playoff games the year before "to settle Paul Coffey down," as Glen Sather put it. And Charlie Huddy, who hadn't even been drafted, had made it up from the minors for 41 games the year before and was now a full-timer. That allowed Sather to make a terrific trade, sending Risto Siltanen to Philadelphia for Ken (The Rat) Linseman.

"I feel like I'm sending my son to Siberia," said Flyers' owner Ed Snider.

So much for Alberta being a "rat-free" province.

Sather the GM was smart enough to know that Sather the coach needed a man like Muckler who possessed strengths to match his weaknesses. He also knew he had to do the same with the lineup. He spent the off-season working on finding someone who had all the qualities of The Rat.

Sather said he wanted Linseman to be an Oiler since a day in the WHA. A real chirper on the bench back then, Sather shouted at Linseman on the ice something like, "You're wet behind the ears!" Linseman promptly scored the winning

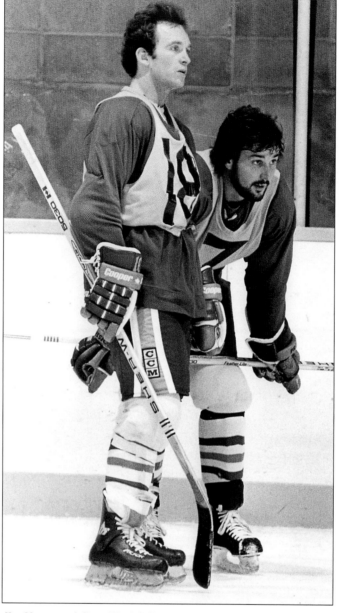

Ken Linseman, left, and Paul Coffey, 1982. Below: Wayne Gretzky.

goal, fished it out of the net, skated by the Oilers bench and flipped it at Sather, saying, "I may be wet behind the ears, but I'm a helluva player."

"We scored 400 goals but we didn't win when it counted," said Sather when he announced the deal. "We needed more speed and aggressiveness at centre. We needed a sparkplug. Gretzky leads with his talent. But we needed somebody to get things going. Somebody tenacious. Somebody teams love to hate. After what happened to us against L.A. ... when they got aggressive against us we didn't have many people to get aggressive back. We knew we had to make changes. We had to find players like Linseman. He's a winner. He's 24. He's young. He's healthy. And who, Ken Linseman included, wouldn't be happy coming to a team like this?"

Actually, Linseman wasn't all that thrilled to be coming to Siberia. But he'd change his tune soon enough. "I was lucky to come here," he said in a matter of months.

Another newcomer was Jaroslav Pouzar, a 30-year-old Czech national team member.

As the schedule began, the editorializing was to the effect that this time the regular season was essentially going to be an 80-game exhibition schedule and that the real season would start on April 5. And Sather wasn't discouraging it.

"I knew we were in trouble before the playoffs when blood tests on four players showed they were anemic," said Sather. "Wayne Gretzky, Mark Messier, Kevin Lowe and Dave Semenko were worn out."

Yet Sather said they really couldn't have played it much differently. "It was a once-in-a-lifetime thing. Everybody all over hockey got caught up in it."

There was a lot of talk about getting used to the system.

"This team never played under a system," said Linseman. "Grant just sort of kicked out the puck and they just took off from there. They just let it fly."

Lowe corrected him. Sort of.

"It wasn't that we didn't have a system, it's that everybody we played was afraid of getting blown out last year, and the wingers were already turned around and headed back up the ice and we were walking out at will. It was easy. But it's not going to be like that this year. Teams are going to be better prepared against us this year."

And they were. Especially early.

After 11 games the Oilers were 3-5-3.

Gretzky, however, didn't miss a beat. And he took

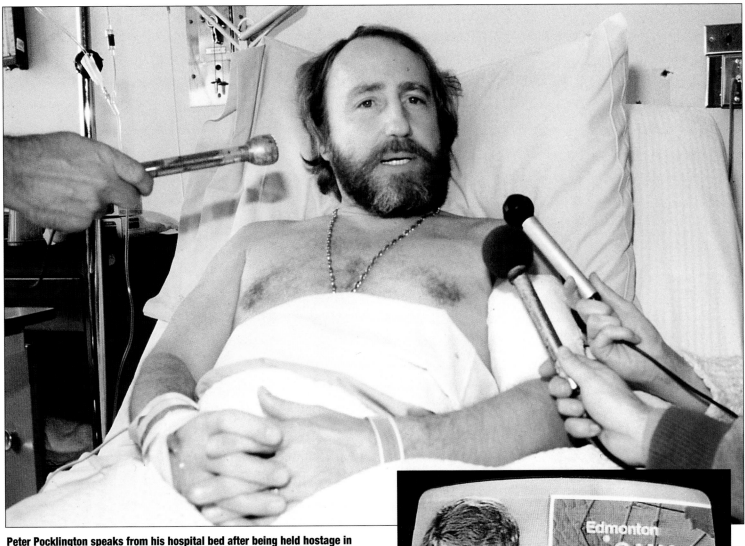

Peter Pocklington speaks from his hospital bed after being held hostage in April, 1982. The event even made Ted Koppel's ABC-TV news broadcast.

some of the focus off the early season struggles. Quietly. By Dec. 3 the 21-year-old had a different gig going this season. He was going after Guy Lafleur's NHL record for points in 28 consecutive games. *Sun* scribe Dick Chubey approached him to talk about closing in on the mark and came away with a more-or-less empty notebook which, in itself, qualified as news.

"The Silent One" was the *Sun* headline.

"I'm silent on this one," Gretzky told Ice Chubes. "I haven't talked about it until now and I'm not about to start at this time. I'll talk about the weather. I'll talk about the Eskimos' fifth straight Grey Cup. I'll talk about whatever you want. But ..."

On Dec. 5 Gretzky matched The Flower's record. And he ran it to 31 games.

At the time the Oilers were 10th overall with 32 points. That was 13 more than two years earlier and eight points fewer than the year before.

When the Montreal Canadiens came to town it was, as always, a special game. The Oilers won 5-2. But the emotion was entirely different. They played it differently, wanting to win it at both ends of the rink.

Gretzky gave the team a rare speech.

"He said we had everything here to win," reported Coffey. "He said everybody on this team now has a job to do and if everybody does their jobs we can be a complete hockey club. He said we have guys here to take the man, guys who are supposed to play defence, guys who are here to check and guys who are here to score goals. He said if we all start doing what Glen Sather put us here to do, we're going to win. I noticed one thing tonight which was different. We used to get incredibly high before a Canadiens game. It was all emotion. And it worked then. But

that's changed. I mean, we still get up for them because they are the Canadiens. But we've played them a few times. Now we believe we are as good a team as they are. Tonight we just wanted to go out and prove it. It was a credibility game."

Gretzky, however, had a bit of a brain cramp one night. Nowhere was it written in *his* job description that he was a fighter. That's right. He got into a fight.

"You coulda got a penalty for delay of game," said Semenko.

Neal Broten of the Minnesota North Stars and Gretzky were jostling behind the net when No. 99 threw a jab and dropped his gloves. Broten dropped Gretzky.

"I just got tired of people asking me when my last fight was," said No. 99, admitting he probably had just taken himself out of the Lady Byng voting.

The Oilers weren't the story they were the year before, but few players were failing on their mid-term report cards – except for Fuhr. The year before, in his rookie season, he was the second-team all-star goalie.

Coach Sather directs Kevin Lowe, Dave Semenko and Gary Lariviere at practice.

Wayne and Walter Gretzky share some ice time with Vladislav Tretiak in preparation for an Oilers vs. Russians exhibition game.

And Andy Moog, playoff hero from two years earlier, ended up playing 40 games in the minors. Moog was back and going great with a 14-3-5 record. And Fuhr was floundering.

On Jan. 9 he snapped.

To that point in his career, Fuhr hadn't opened his mouth. But that night he opened it wider than the hole between his pads where four super-soft goals had dribbled through to cost the Oilers a game against the Detroit Red Wings. Edmonton fans were on him good and for good reason. And Fuhr decided he'd become allergic to them.

"Edmonton fans are horse----," he began.

"I couldn't care less about Edmonton fans. They're all a bunch of jerks. They paid their money so they can chirp all the way, but I've given up on them. I mean, they're so quiet at the best of times. It's easier to play when it's noisy. But make a mistake and they start with the sarcastic cheers and boos and they call you a bum. All the usual stuff you get from fans on the road. I'd rather play on the road than here. These fans are jerks."

The next day under the watchful eye of Sather, Fuhr issued a public apology.

"I'd like to say I'm sorry," he said. "It wasn't a very bright thing to do. I did it more out of frustration than anything. This was the first time I've been booed by fans and for me, I guess, it was different.

"I knew it was a dumb thing to do when I woke up this morning. It's never right to say things like that about the fans. I've got enough problems trying to stop the puck. I don't need the fans getting on me."

On Jan. 24 Fuhr found out how Moog felt the year before. He was sent to Moncton, where the Oilers had moved their minor-league team.

"I'm not surprised," he said. "I knew a trip to Moncton was coming sooner or later."

By the end of February, Fuhr was back for good, and Sather traded Ron Low to New Jersey to let Moog and Fuhr get on with it as a dynamic duo. The Coliseum fans welcomed Fuhr back with open arms. When PA announcer Gord Ross announced Fuhr's name as the starting goaltender for the first time in the building since his "The Fans Are Jerks" tirade, the jerks applauded.

"I could hear it in the dressing room," said Fuhr.

"Grant was very nervous," said Slats. "He's gone through a lot of stress. It's been almost two months since he played here last and I was glad they gave him such a welcome back. These are still the best fans in the league. As far as Grant's concerned, I think his career is on an upward surge once again."

Gretzky's career continued on an upward surge even if the numbers were marginally down. He was playing great all year, but not with the same notice as the year before. Every morning, every hockey fan in existence would open the paper to find out how many points he produced the night before. He finished the season with 71 goals and 125 assists for 196 points.

The rave reviews kept coming. So did the records. And his career numbers were simply getting scary. At the end of his fourth season he'd accumulated statistics and records that already defied comparison with any other player, past or present. With 709 points in 319 regular-season games, he was four years ahead of Guy Lafleur, who had previously reached that number in the least number of games. And he was a full seven years ahead of the pace of Gordie Howe. In 26 seasons, Howe established 21 NHL records. After four seasons, Gretzky owned 37 records, including 18 he'd tied or broken during the season at hand, some of which were his own. He finally even managed to score on a penalty shot.

A third straight Art Ross and a fourth straight Hart Trophy were in the bag by the all-star break. And if there was one Gretzky game that would be remembered more than any other from this season, it was probably the all-star game.

Through his first 11 periods of play in the annual showcase, hockey's No. 1 star hadn't been much of an all-star. This time he scored four goals in one period.

"I got tired of everybody saying how poorly

Wayne Gretzky in his Ninety-nine jersey.

I always play in the all-star game," said Gretzky of stealing the MVP car, a $14,000 Camaro, from goalie John Garrett and earning a share of Ted Lindsay's 1950 record. "I received so much criticism that it started to bother me. I decided I could play well in this game, too."

Gretzky's greatest accomplishment all year, however, might have been his shutout. That's right. His shutout.

Before a late February game against the Winnipeg Jets he called it.

"Shutout!" he shouted out.

The 'O' in Oilers has seldom stood for zero. And it sure didn't back then.

"Shutout!" Gretzky shouted again.

And the team picked up the chant.

"Shutout! Shutout! Shutout!"

A called-shot shutout? By the Edmonton Oilers? Who woulda thunk it?

It had been 279 games between shutouts – 1,176 days since Eddie Mio managed the only previous shutout in Oilers' history. At the time of that last shutout Gretzky's career NHL stats were 11 goals and 27 assists for 37 points.

"Gretz had a feeling we'd get a shutout tonight and he was serious," said defenceman Don Jackson. "But I guess everybody could figure that out when he started showing up in our defensive corners and when he blocked a shot."

There was method to Gretzky's madness.

"I figured if everybody saw *me* talking shutout ... I figured if I started thinking that way, maybe everybody would. So I said, 'This is the game!' I mean, let's face it. We won a game 10-7 in Pittsburgh. That's ridiculous. The time has come for this team to get together in its own end. It's not funny any more."

Gretzky's shutout was officially registered under Moog's name.

When the season ended the Oilers led the league, as was becoming common, in a great many statistical areas. One included dollars. The Oilers topped the league in gate receipts with $9,749,260. The Rangers and Islanders were second and third.

The Oilers ended up with 47 wins and 106 points, only five fewer than the previous season. They scored 424 goals and gave up 315. By the numbers it wasn't much different, really, than the year before. And there was no need to push for first place overall because all the Oilers had to do was finish first in their division. The NHL that year had come up with a quirky new rule in which home-ice advantage for the playoffs was pre-

Top: Glenn Anderson, Gary Lariviere and goalie Grant Fuhr follow the puck along with Chicago's Rich Preston. Middle: Defenceman Kevin Lowe takes a flying leap. Bottom: Dave Hunter celebrates a goal with Lee Fogolin.

determined for conference and Stanley Cup finals and the Smythe Division and Campbell Conference were trump.

Messier didn't make it to 50 goals. He had 48. But he also had 106 points. Glenn Anderson also had 48 goals and Jari Kurri 45. But both had 104 points. The Oilers ended the season with *four* 100-point players. And Coffey had 29 goals and 96 points to lead all NHL defencemen. That left him with more points in his first three years in the league than Bobby Orr. And Charlie Huddy won the Emery Edge Trophy for the best plus-minus stats in the league. All in all, it was a heck of a season. And the *real* season hadn't started yet.

After the last league game I wrote: "This was Edmonton's best season yet because the Oilers became a team with some substance. Last year they were a bunch of cocky kids on a roll. This year they rocked more than they rolled. The big change this year is in the personality of the team. This is the year, I think history will record, that coach Glen Sather grew up. As a result, for the first time ever, I have the feeling Sather isn't going to screw up. And that reason, more than any other, is why the Oilers will make it all the way to the Stanley Cup final."

The Oilers didn't know it then, but the hockey gods had decided their road to the Stanley Cup final must always go through Winnipeg. To get to all six finals, including the five they won, Winnipeg was always a stop for a playoff series.

That year it was the first stop. And that year the Oilers made sure there was no stupidity in Game 1. They won it 6-3.

"This game was ooooh-so important," said Lee Fogolin when it was over. "It means so much in a best-of-five series to get started with some momentum."

The Oilers had a 6-1 lead after two periods but memories of blowing a 5-0 lead against L.A. rattled around under their helmets.

Stuff happens in hockey. And if all the stuff seemed to happen to the Oilers in the L.A. series the year before, stuff happened the other way in Game 2 against the Jets.

Officially, it was Messier's second goal of the game with 1:44 remaining that provided the Oilers with a 4-3 win. But it was Coffey's goal 15 minutes earlier that turned it. And it wasn't a goal. Replays proved it beyond a doubt. But Los Angeles goal judge Rick Lundgren turned on the red light and referee Kerry Fraser signalled his agreement and that was

that.

The Oilers made it bingo-bango-bongo in Winnipeg. But Linseman made it memorable. The Jets led the Oilers 2-1 going into the third period of Game 3 but Linseman scored unassisted at 18:46 to win it 4-3. And it was that game, more than the series, which suggested that the Oilers, indeed, were coming of age.

"I don't think we would have won that game last year because we didn't have the maturity," said Sather.

And with Linseman scoring, it was Sather who was the ultimate hero. His trade with the Jets of Laurie Boschman for Willie Lindstrom paid off when Lindstrom scored at 17:08. And his trade of Risto Siltanen for Linseman won it on the same night the Philadelphia Flyers were eliminated from the playoffs.

Sather wasn't taking any deep bows. But he did have a look of satisfaction on his face.

"Certainly the trades make me feel satisfied," he said. "But the most satisfaction about this series is the way Paul Coffey played. Look at what he did."

Gretzky called Coffey the poster boy for the before-after nature of what they were dealing with. "Paul was the biggest difference. He represented the difference in this team from last year to this year."

Coffey wasn't arguing.

"I have more satisfaction from this series than I did from the series against Montreal two years ago. In the series against L.A. last year, I didn't help at all. And last year we didn't have the character to do what we did tonight. I'd like to believe I was part of that transition."

The last line of the column I filed that night from the Winnipeg arena: "Strong-kneed macho men?"

The next dispatch ran under the headline: "Broadway Wayne?"

Under the headline were the following paragraphs:

"Wayne Gretzky to the New York Rangers for $18 million so Peter Pocklington can save Fidelity Trust? That's the rumour. Repeat. Rumour.

"Gus Badali, Gretzky's agent, was tipped on it from a source in Calgary who called his Toronto office. He reacted by putting in a call to Pocklington. Mike Barnett of the Sierra Sports Group, which manages Gretzky's endorsements, says he's heard it 'six or eight times' in the last 48 hours."

Pocklington, at the time, was trying to win the leadership of the

Islanders vs. Oilers: confrontation along the boards. Opposite: Wayne Gretzky and his bodyguard, Dave Semenko.

begin.

"If it had happened before this, it would have required an asterisk," said Flames GM Cliff Fletcher. "The thing that people don't understand is that we're just now becoming the *Calgary* Flames. It's only happened in the last 2½ months. Before then we were the Atlanta Flames relocated in Calgary, and not very damn happy about it. The biggest problem I had was that I had a group of players who all had their houses on golf courses and were used to playing golf 12 months of the year."

Fletcher wasn't promising anything immediate.

Conservative party so he could become prime minister of Canada.

"Nonsense," screamed Pocklington. "Wayne is more valuable to me than the family jewels. I'd never sell him. Never is a long time in my life, but I'd *never* sell him. It's absolutely false. I promised Edmonton on Day 1 that Wayne Gretzky would be here for 20 years and nothing has changed. Trade Gretzky to New York for $18 million, eh? If I traded Gretzky out of Canada nobody would vote for me."

The story went away for another day.

The Calgary Flames had won their opening-round playoff series against the Vancouver Canucks. The first Battle of Alberta of the Stanley Cup playoffs was about to

"This is the first Edmonton-Calgary playoff series. The Oilers proved over 80 games that they are one hell of a lot better than we are. But we've proved a few things in the last month and a half, too. Whatever happens, I guarantee you there are going to be many, many more."

The two towns built it up big time.

The Oilers won 6-3 for openers. And Messier equalled the Oilers' playoff record, established in Game 1 against Winnipeg by Gretzky, with four goals.

He was inspired. It was the first time all year that his dad, Doug Messier, the coach of the Oilers farm club in Moncton that season, and his mom Mary-Jean were able to occupy the family seats in Section V, Row 17, Seats 11 and 12.

"Mom and dad were my inspiration tonight," said Mark. "It was weird all year with my dad in Moncton, to look up at those seats and not see them watching me.

"I wanted to win this for dad. He's the one who got me here. And mom ... Mom always sits in Seat 11 because that's my uniform number. A gorilla couldn't take that ticket

Dave Lumley tries to annoy public enemy number 1, goalie Billy Smith.

out of her hands. That's her lucky seat."

"I'm pretty proud of him," said Doug. "But mostly I'm just happy for him that he's healthy this year and that he's able to do what he's doing. Last year he was one hurt buckaroo. He was hurt a lot worse than anybody knew.

"I've seen it so many times as a coach and way back when I was a player. But it's pretty pleasing watching as a parent when you see the maturing. It's always difficult for a young player like that when they discover the glamour and the bright lights. Like a lot of them, he stumbled. Now he's succeeding."

There were less likely heroes in Game 2.

Islanders' Billy Smith is flanked by Mark Messier, left, and Wayne Gretzky.

Don Jackson and Randy Gregg scored key goals in a 5-1 win. And journeyman Jackson was the first star.

"First time I got one of those," he said. "I had to ask what to do, where to go and who goes on the ice first?"

Subsequent Oiler-Flame playoff series would be magic but the first Alberta Civil War, after two games, was far too civil and was being called the Sominex Series.

"It's the pigeons vs. the statues," wrote one foreign correspondent.

"If this series were being played in my backyard, I'd draw the drapes," wrote another.

"We should be playing one hell of a lot better," said Calgary GM Fletcher as the series shifted to Calgary. "We're down 2-0 and Gretzky hasn't even got on track yet."

Famous last words.

Gretzky snapped a four-game playoff drought with a Stanley Cup playoff-record seven-point performance, including four goals, as the Oilers whupped the Flames 10-2 in Game 3.

Lanny McDonald, returning to the lineup hobbling on a tender ankle, scored a goal and two assists as the Flames won Game 4, 6-5. But back in Edmonton for Game 5 they were the Calgary Flameouts, losing 9-1 in an unmerciful killing.

It was the atom bomb vs. the bow and arrow. The Oilers set a playoff record for a series of any length with 35 goals.

There was a banner to hang from the rafters of the Coliseum. The Oilers were eight wins away from the Stanley Cup. And there were dreams dancing in the minds of everybody in Edmonton – especially in the Oilers dressing room where Lee Fogolin Jr. sat.

"My dad's name is on that Cup," he said in the emotion of the series ending that night. "We're playing the best hockey we've ever played at either end of the ice. Gawd, the way I feel right now I wish we could play eight nights in a row and get it over with."

They were getting giddy again.

"I think we all started feeling the goosebumps in the second period when we knew we had the game and the series won," said Coffey. "We're going to get pretty high in the next couple of days just thinking

Wayne Gretzky signs autographs in Churchill Square in May 1983.

about it. Thank goodness we had that vivid reminder from last year of what can happen when you get too high. We'll come back down in time."

Gretzky made a point.

"We're playing the best, most complete, hockey the Edmonton Oilers have ever played. But we can't ignore the facts. The teams we have beat to this point weren't in the top 10. The teams we play from here are in the top four."

Or as *Sun* scribe Chubey wrote: "On to the Campbell Conference final where men are men and scores are respectable."

Well, that was the theory.

The Oilers won the first two games in Edmonton against Chicago by scores of 8-4 and 8-2.

And Mount Orval erupted.

"I'm ashamed," said Blackhawks coach Orval Tessier. "I've been in hockey a long time. I've never been this embarrassed before. I'm highly embarrassed. This is the ultimate embarrassment. What do we do now? Put in a call to the Mayo Clinic for 18 heart transplants so we can get 'em done by Sunday? Probably can't."

Sixteen goals the Oilers scored at home in two Campbell Conference final playoff games – and it was plumbers Ray Cote, Dave Hunter and Pat Hughes who were getting the rave reviews.

"Forget the rest of us," said Gretzky, who along with Messier had 10 goals in the Calgary series. "Hughes, Hunter and Cote are the stars of this series so far. They're driving them crazy."

The Oilers, when they walked into Chicago Stadium, couldn't help but think back to Oct. 19, 1979 and their first game in the NHL in the place. And this was only the spring of 1983.

"We've come a long way, baby," said Fogolin. "That first year we were in 21st place at Christmas. Now we're a couple of wins away from the Stanley Cup final. Amazing, isn't it?"

Darryl Sutter's voice was breaking as he forced himself to stand in the Blackhawks dressing room as the unofficial player spokesman after Game 3.

"I don't know what to say," he said. "We forced them to play another style of game and they played it. They *played* it!"

With Moog the hero in goal, the Oilers won 3-2. It was over. A 6-3 win in Game 4 sent the Oilers to the final against the New York Islanders.

The first-time finalists had an 11-1 record in the playoffs and a 25-3-2 record dating back to the regular season. And the playoff goal count was at a staggering 74.

It wasn't a hard series to hype. The Islanders had won three straight and were now trying to match the Montreal Canadiens, who had won four in a row from 1976 to 1979 and five straight from 1956 to 1960. And they were playing the team everybody had labelled as their heir apparent.

"It's the Big Apple vs. the Little Country Boys," said Sather. "We're the new kids on the block trying to take their marbles. Heck, some of the kids on our team haven't played in the league as many years as the Islanders have been winning the Cup."

"It's like *Star Wars*," said Kevin Lowe of the Stanley Cup final matchup. "It's like Sugar Ray Leonard vs. Roberto Duran. We're Sugar Ray, of course. The smoothies, the glamour boys. And the Islanders, they're the hard-nosed solid vets."

And it was here we go, Oilers ... sans the song. The Oilers were learning decorum. At the same time, it seemed, the Islanders were losing theirs.

A couple of pre-series quotes:

"We want to beat them more than anything. You know why? Because they think they're the greatest thing since sliced bread," said Clarke Gillies.

"They think they're so hot. They're so cocky. The thing that really bugs me is that they don't give us any respect. The Flyers respect us. The Bruins respect us. The Rangers respect us. Edmonton doesn't respect anyone," said Bob Bourne.

Nobody asked Billy Smith. He was brilliant in scoring a 2-0 shutout in a game Gretzky suggested might have been the best the Oilers ever played when losing.

Smith, well known as a stick-swinger, chopped down Anderson in the game. And by the time they dropped the puck for Game 2, there were "Public Enemy No. 1" headlines and full-page "Evil Eyes" aimed at Battlin' Billy.

If Smith won Game 1, Moog knew he lost Game 2.

Gretzky and goaltending had been the key to the Oilers since they played their first NHL game. But the Islanders took Gretzky out of both

Mark Messier gets up close and personal with the Clarence Campbell Bowl after the Oilers won the conference championship in May 1983.

'That's the difference. They were wounded. We lost and we were fine.'

– Kevin Lowe after losing to the New York Islanders

0 because of Billy Smith."

The Oilers weren't the story any more. The Islanders were going for a four-game sweep to win a fourth straight Stanley Cup. The champs won Game 4 by a 4-2 score to become an official dynasty. And it was well after that game, as the Oilers trudged out of the Nassau County Coliseum, that they learned maybe their final and most important lesson about winning a Stanley Cup.

"Kevin Lowe and I were walking out of the rink after the final game and we walked by the Islanders dressing room," Gretzky would later recall. "As we got closer and closer, we noticed it was pretty quiet in there. As we looked in, the people who were doing the celebrating were management, family and wives. The players themselves were so exhausted, so tired, and had so many ice packs, we could really see the price they had paid. Guys like Denis Potvin, I remember, were really beat up. And we were fine. No problems at all. We got on the bus and Kevin said, 'That's the difference.' They were wounded. We lost and we were fine."

games in the Coliseum and they got to Moog to win 6-3 in Game 2.

In one dressing room the media mob surrounded Smith to talk about his flagrant stick-swinging against Gretzky. But in the other room, Moog knew he was the story, the whole story and nothing but the story.

"Goaltending is what it comes down to," said Moog. "I let them down. In the Stanley Cup final, your team depends on you to be there. And tonight, I let them down. The second and third goals were brutal. I haven't had the feeling of playing poorly for a long time. I don't like the feeling. I hope it won't come again."

It had been a wonderful scene as Edmonton experienced its first taste of playing host for the Stanley Cup final. But the Game 5 and Game 7 tickets would go unused. In Game 3 Gretzky kept shooting blanks. And Smith couldn't be rattled by Sather or Edmonton newspaper headlines, which Doug Gould of the *New York Post* summarized in four words: "Hitler. Stalin. And Billy."

The Isles took a 3-0 lead with a 5-1 win.

"What do we say?" said Lowe in the post-game Oilers morgue. "We're down 3-

Charlie Huddy accepts the Emery Edge award from Gordie Howe.

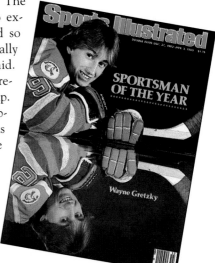

Wayne Gretzky: *Sports Illustrated*'s Sportsman of the Year, 1982.

Chapter 7

We Are The Champions

It was the usual scene in the dressing room after practice on the morning of Oct. 4, 1983. There was the regular game of ping-pong in progress in the middle of the room. Trainer Barrie Stafford was administering to a training camp casualty. Equipment man Lyle (Sparky) Kulchisky was giving a lecture to a rookie. And members of the media were scattered around the room sitting with individual players, working on their chosen angles for the day.

Once the last player had left the ice, Lee Fogolin stood up and made the unusual request that the media leave the room. When we returned, Wayne Gretzky was the new captain of the Edmonton Oilers.

"I've talked about it with Glen Sather for some time," he said. "Maybe a change like this will help us win a Stanley Cup. Not that I'm saying it would have made a heck of a lot of difference if we had won the Cup last spring. We probably would still have made the change."

It was time. Hockey has long had a history of the greats of the game wearing the "C." And while he was only entering his fifth season, Gretzky had already registered 269 goals, 440 assists and 709 points in the regular season plus 33 more goals, 26 more assists and 74 more points in the playoffs. Sather saw a practical advantage in Gretzky wearing the "C" as well. This was a team that loved to have fun. And most of the players who liked to party were the same age as their superstar. He needed one of them to convince the others when it was time to go home.

Oilers coaches Glen Sather, Ted Green and John Muckler. Opposite: Wayne Gretzky and Paul Coffey hoist the Stanley Cup.

"Fogie's a little older and we've got a young team. Wayne's their age and could have a big influence on off-the-ice situations."

The Oilers won their first seven games for Captain Gretzky.

Gretzky, until he was given the captain's "C," had never climbed on a soapbox and made a passionate speech about anything. But after the Oilers got off to a 10-2-1 start he did.

"Our record is 3-0," he said. "Out-of-division games are *designated* games."

It wouldn't be much longer before Gretzky threw the soapbox away.

On Nov. 19 the Oilers beat the New Jersey Devils 13-4. Gretzky had his first eight-point night in the NHL and Jari Kurri scored five. After the game, *The Sun's* Dick Chubey asked a question that pushed the wrong button. Gretzky called the Devils "Mickey Mouse."

Ron Low was in goal for the Devils for most of the long night. And it was no fun at all for Gretzky to be running up the score on his old teammate and friend.

"It got to the point where it wasn't even funny," said Gretzky. "How long has it been for them? Three years? Five? Seven? Probably closer to nine. Well, it's about time they got their act together. They're ruining the whole league. They better stop running a Mickey Mouse organization and put somebody on the ice. I feel damn sorry for Ron Low and Chico Resch."

Kurri, for his own part, enjoyed the evening. He scored five of the goals.

"I never thought I'd get five goals in an NHL game," Kurri said. "That was unbelievable."

Gretzky didn't take many wrong steps during his career, but the words "Mickey Mouse" were two he wished he could take back. He knew it the next day.

"The Devils Made Me Do It" was the headline in *The Sun.* And before the sun went down Gretzky had telexed an apology to the Devils. Billy MacMillan had been fired as coach after that game – the 18th loss in 20 games for the Devils – and replaced by Tommy McVie.

Lee Fogolin turns over the captain's 'C' to Wayne Gretzky.

"In the apology, basically what I said was that I regretted the statements I made," Gretzky said. "It's not my business to say anything like that."

McVie, from New Jersey, defended Gretzky.

"The reason Wayne took a shot at the Devils was that he has a close friend in Ron Low and when he saw his good friend having all those goals scored against him, he said something that he normally wouldn't say," said McVie. "He's a class young man."

The Oilers didn't need any hissing contests with the Devils. They already had one ongoing with the Islanders. And smack dab in the middle of their schedule were three games against the four-time Stanley Cup-champion Islanders, the ultimate of Gretzky's designated credibility games.

Credibility Game 1 was in Edmonton. And while it didn't have the same setup as the Stanley Cup final the year before, there was no lack of buzz before the game.

"There are a lot of feelings," said Gretzky.

"Last year, psychologically, they weren't intimidated by us, knowing they had beat us easily during the season," said Lowe.

And the Oilers lost again. It was now eight straight.

"At some point in time you have to get tired of saying it was a learning experience," said Sather.

They got themselves up for the next one, two weeks later on Long Island.

"Every time we play the Islanders it can do nothing but help our hockey club," said assistant coach John Muckler. "It's better to play them and lose than to beat the bleep out of some team 10-1. A 10-1 game is only good for your ego. And front-runners can find themselves getting too cocky. I'd like to play them 12 or 15 times a year. Each time you play them, you have to learn. The Russian hockey club didn't become great playing weak teams. Years ago they always wanted to play Canada."

Added to the lineup for a little of that Islander experience, it must be mentioned, was one Kevin McClelland. Sather, already making a name for himself as a deal-maker, traded Tom Roulson to Pittsburgh for McClelland, then languishing with their Baltimore farm club. The trade would later prove to be more than significant.

In Credibility Game 2 the Oilers were down 4-0 by the end of the first period. It soiled and spoiled the occasion of Gretzky scoring his 300th NHL goal and setting another record with a point in 31 consecutive games.

Back on the island for the third and final regular-season game, the Oilers struck out again. In fact, in the nine credibility games they'd circled, three each against the Islanders, the Bruins and the Flyers, the Oilers' record was a less-than-inspiring two wins, six losses and a tie. This time it was a 5-3 loss to the Islanders. It was a bump-and-grind game and Sather said the Oilers may have lost on the scoreboard, but he liked what he saw.

"That's the way we'll continue to play against them," said the coach and GM. "We hit them a lot. We played tough."

Still, counting the sweep in the Stanley Cup final, it meant if the Oilers returned for a rematch, the Islanders would have the confidence of knowing they'd won 10 straight games against Edmonton.

Not that they were adopting that kind of game on a nightly basis. There was the game against the Minnesota North Stars. For a minute there it looked as if the two teams would break the record for most goals in a game set 64 years earlier when the Montreal Canadiens beat the Toronto St. Patricks by a converted touchdown, 14-7. This one ended up 10-8 Oilers.

"You can't be proud of a 10-8 game no matter which dressing room you're in," said Gretzky, who backed off after scoring four goals and four assists in the first two periods and settled for the eight points.

Credibility games aside, Gretzky was becoming a big national story again.

It took a while. Next to nobody noticed when he scored 50 goals in 42 games. If his 50 in 39 was regarded as the most incredible accomplishment in the history of hockey, then you'd figure 50 in 42 would be the second most incredible accomplishment. But it went by with next to no notice.

"That's the second-fastest 50 of all time and there's no hoopla," said Muckler. "It's taken for granted. I guess that shows how great he is."

Gretzky said it's the way the world works.

"It's nice to get 50 in 42. But it's not 50 in 39."

Gretzky's points of reference now resided in other sports. He was already being referred to as the Babe Ruth of hockey. But as the calendar changed, the storyline switched to Pete Rose and Joe DiMaggio.

Rose had the National League record for most consecutive games with at least one hit, with 44. And DiMaggio had the major-league record with 56.

As he closed in on Rose, scoring points in 40 straight games, Gretzky thought about it.

"I really don't know how to compare it," he said. "I really can't explain why nobody has ever come close to a streak like the one I have when all those baseball players have long ones. Logic says it's tougher to do in baseball. I have more than four or five shifts a game to get my points. A baseball player is going to get four or five times at bat and he could get walked every time. Really, I have to think it's tougher in baseball."

Gretzky loved this one.

"I have no pressure at all. The greatest thing about this streak is that it doesn't bother me. When I set the record for the streak the first time, when it was 28, I thought about it a lot. There was a lot of pressure to get it. This year, it's been fun."

Before I headed off to cover the Super Bowl, I mentioned to members of *The Sun* sports staff that if Gretzky's streak was still intact when I got back, I'd try to track down Joe DiMaggio and see what he thought. DiMaggio, back then, had a reputation of being writer-unfriendly. The staffers said, "Yeah, right."

So there I was, sitting beside Joltin' Joe on Northwest Airlines Flight 735 from Chicago to Tampa Bay on Jan. 16. An hour earlier I'd been sitting at Gate 6 talking to a young man from Edmonton who had won a free trip to the Super Bowl when he looked up and said, "Mr. Coffee!"

To me, Joe DiMaggio was the Yankee Clipper, the man who married Marilyn Monroe. To the kid he was a guy who hustled coffee machines on TV.

As we boarded I explained Gretzky's streak and that the only remaining comparison was DiMaggio's 56-game run in baseball. I asked if I could have a minute when the plane landed. The stewardess came to the back of the plane and asked if I was the person who had been talking to Joe DiMaggio before the flight. I said yes. She said, "He's invited you to sit beside him in first class for a few minutes."

"I don't know if I'm going to be much help to you," he said, but added he'd read something about Gretzky's streak a week or so earlier and had started to follow it.

New Jersey fans get on Wayne Gretzky's case after he called their NHL franchise 'Mickey Mouse.'

"Nobody in hockey has ever had a streak like this? And my baseball streak is the only one to compare him to? Where's he at now?"

"One shy of your record if you count the ones from the end of last year," I said.

"You can't count the ones from last year," said DiMaggio. "They don't allow you to count the ones from last year in baseball.

"One thing he doesn't have to worry about that I had to worry about. He won't have to worry about a hockey game getting rained out in the middle of the second period. I was at 35 or 40 games when my streak was almost called on account of rain."

DiMaggio discussed it for more than half an hour. He asked as many questions as he answered.

"I think his streak is remarkable," he said. "And I think he's remarkable. And from what I can gather, he doesn't need any advice from me. He can carry on."

Gretzky, when he reached 46 (legitimate from the start of the season), wasn't thinking of DiMaggio's 56 hits in baseball. He was in New Jersey. And it was Mickey Mouse Night. Fans showed up wearing Mickey Mouse ears and sweaters and holding up hundreds of signs.

"I might get a standing boo," said Gretzky before the game in reference to his statements earlier in the season.

Phil Russell, an ex-Oil King, was a Devil in those days. He played in the 13-4 game in Edmonton and called it "the most embarrassing game in which I've ever been involved." He humourously offered fair warning as the Oilers arrived in New Jersey. "We've really improved. We've moved up. If we were playing like Mickey Mouse then, maybe we're like Donald Duck now."

It turned out to be a terrific game, the Oilers winning 5-4. Gretzky had a three-point night. But it was a long three-point night for him. He saw all the signs and even laughed at some of them. His favourite was one that read "Gretzky is Goofy."

Mark Messier and Kevin Lowe go through their paces in training camp.

"I kind of felt my way through that game," he said. "I learned something from all of this. I'm 22, going on 23, and I made a mistake."

Ron Low, the ex-Oiler and friend whose tough night in goal in Edmonton inspired the "Mickey Mouse" quote, said it for everybody. "He's got a pretty flawless record. If that's the only mistake of his lifetime, he'll be a pretty lucky guy."

Gretzky went from Mickey Mouse Night to the cover of *Sports Illustrated* with the heading "Greater And Greater." And people began to speculate not just whether he could match DiMaggio's number but if it was possible for him to get a point in every single game of the season.

"Five hundred to one," Sonny Reizer, the most flamboyant and well-known oddsmaker in Las Vegas, quoted the odds.

"Wayne Gretzky is capable of being the highest scorer in the NHL, the NFL and the NBA combined. I've never hung a number on anything like this before. But even as great as Gretzky is, somewhere along the line, it's inevitable; his streak has to be stopped."

Gretzky pushed it to the limit one night in Chicago. He scored an empty-net goal at 19:58 of the third period.

Finally, at 51, it came to an end. The L.A. Kings beat the Oilers 4-1. And Gretzky had the hole in the doughnut.

"I'm disappointed that it's over," said Gretzky. "But it's a relief, too. I guess I didn't win any money for anybody with those 500-to-1 odds."

It wouldn't have lasted much longer anyway. Gretzky injured a shoulder and missed six games, the first time in his pro career he was sidelined.

No problem. Gretzky's first night sitting out, journeyman Pat Hughes decided he'd be Gretzky for the night and scored five goals against Calgary.

"Every time I shot the puck it went into the net," said Hughes in disbelief. "I'm having trouble remembering five goals in a month."

But then the Oilers went East. And the team went in the toilet. In Hartford, with Gretzky and Kurri out of the lineup, the Oilers suffered their worst defeat of all time: 11-0. They hadn't been shut out in 228 games. And it was their fifth loss in five games on a road trip in which they were outscored 33-9.

"I don't think I'm going grocery shopping when we get home," said Charlie Huddy of having to face Edmonton fans. "My wife is on her own."

"I think I'll start going to church," said Dave Hunter.

It was a weird year. The Oilers won an unprecedented 57 games, scored 446 goals and finished first overall with 119 points to claim another banner for the roof of the Coliseum.

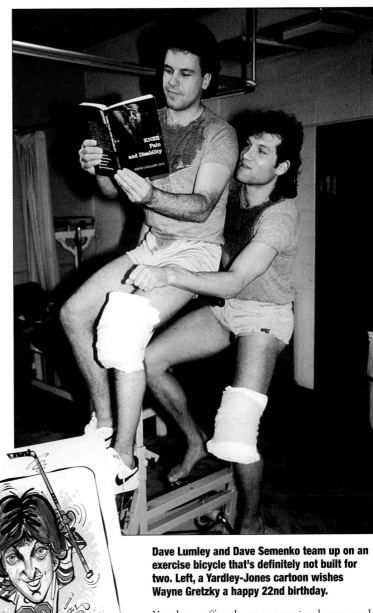

Dave Lumley and Dave Semenko team up on an exercise bicycle that's definitely not built for two. Left, a Yardley-Jones cartoon wishes Wayne Gretzky a happy 22nd birthday.

Yet they suffered some stunning losses, such as 9-2 to the Washington Capitals, 7-1 to the St. Louis Blues and 8-3 to the absolutely awful Toronto Maple Leafs. The loss to the Leafs inspired *Sun* hockey writer Dick Chubey to open his game story from the press box in Maple Leaf Gardens:

"TORONTO – The Stanley what?

"Steamer? Garage-door opener?"

The Oilers rewrote the record book again. But with the blowout and their uninspired record in credibility games, I suggested at one point the Oilers looked like a team that was built to break your heart and advocated maybe it was time to trade some goals for some guts, some calibre for some character. Fortunately, Sather ignored the free advice.

Six Oilers – Gretzky, Kurri, Messier, Coffey, Fuhr and Lowe – played in the all-star game.

Gretzky ended up with 87 goals and 118 assists for 205 points. That made it 393 goals, 558 assists and 914 points for his first five NHL seasons. Again he won the Art Ross and Hart trophies.

Kurri had 52 goals, 61 assists and 113 points, all personal bests. And long before the NHL awards were passed out, the Oilers were lamenting that he'd scored too much to win the trophy he deserved most, the Selke for defensive play.

"Going for 50?" Gretzky had asked Kurri.

"No way," said the Fabulous Finn.

"Why not?" said Gretzky.

Dave Semenko chats with Paul Coffey on the bench.

Dave Semenko, Dave Lumley and Charlie Huddy on the right track.

"I'm a two-way player," said Kurri.

Anderson had his first 50-goal season with 54. That made it three 50-goalscorers and that was an Oilers first.

Paul Coffey's 40 goals and 126-point season gave the Oilers four 100-point men. Messier had 113. Anderson would have made it five, but ended up one short with 99 points.

Other than Gretzky, it was Coffey who was the story of the Oilers' season. He'd arrived. He'd taken a lot of criticism for a thoroughbred. An early nickname had been Paul Cough-Up. He was once called "a regular pastry chef ... turnovers, turnovers, turnovers."

"People said things about me and they hurt," said Coffey. "But I deserved the criticism. I imagine I was pretty hard to live with in the dressing room. I'm sure I was just a jerk. The guys would joke, you know, and I'd take it the wrong way. It wasn't much fun. But I learned about character and mental toughness."

The question as the Oilers prepared for the playoffs was whether all of his equally young teammates had also learned enough about character and mental toughness to be able to make them Stanley Cup champions.

One thing for sure. The Oilers weren't lacking for coaching expertise. Not only had Sather assembled a first-rate staff with John Muckler and Ted Green, he added the temporarily unemployed Captain Video, Roger Neilson, to work the film room for the playoffs.

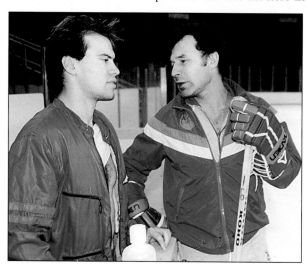

Ted Green has a word with an injured Mark Messier.

Again, the Oilers opened against Winnipeg in the playoffs. And after trying eight times in the regular season to beat Edmonton by conventional means, the Jets had been unable to win one.

Winnipeg GM John Ferguson tried to light their fire before it started.

"If you can't get fired up for the playoffs, you might as well go on vacation," he said. "We think we can win. We've got the youngest team in the league and we have a far better playoff team this year. We've got the team to do it. And what have the Oilers ever won? They have a lot of weaknesses, especially on defence. They're far from being a complete hockey club."

Fergy didn't sell anybody. He especially didn't sell the Jets. And he certainly didn't sell Edmonton that his hockey team was anything but the free space on the Stanley Cup bingo card. The Coliseum wasn't sold out for the first time in the Oilers' NHL history. After 242 consecutive sellouts, 301 empty seats and a 9-2 Oiler win in Game 1 said it all.

It's an old cliche to say the turning point of a lopsided game was the national anthem. But if that were ever true, it was on this night. Some might say it was actually 40 seconds after that, when the Oilers made it 1-0. But you could see it in the Jets' body language before the game. They skated in the warm-up the way a prisoner walks on the way to his execution. All that was missing was the cigarette and the blindfold. During the national anthem they stood like stiffs. And when the game started they played like stiffs. It was 4-0 by the 16th minute of the first period and 5-1 by the end of the period. And if the first period didn't tell the whole story, the scene in front of the Winnipeg bench in the third period, starring Kevin McClelland, said the rest.

"Could you believe that?" said *Hockey Night In Canada*'s Don Cherry after the game. "McClelland challenged the whole bench and nobody moved! I couldn't believe that would ever happen to a John Ferguson-coached team."

Ferguson conceded, "I'm (bleeping) embarrassed. If they are as embarrassed as I am, they'll do something tomorrow."

The Jets showed up for Game 2. The Oilers won it in 5-4 in overtime and if you were scoring it, Randy Gregg got the win and Grant Fuhr got the save. Fuhr was brilliant in goal and Gregg scored the winner 27 seconds into overtime.

"What do you mean was I thinking goal?" said Gregg in the post-game dressing room. "I can't remember the last time I thought goal. I was just hoping it wouldn't be blocked. I would have been happy if it went in off six legs."

He refused to say it was his greatest thrill.

"I beat Vladislav Tretiak in the Olympics. That's the one I'll remember forever. To the glove side," he added with pride.

In Winnipeg, Dave Semenko scored the winner as the Oilers put the Jets away 4-1 to sweep the best-of-five first-rounder. And there was no question who was the hero in that one.

"We had a wall in net," said Gretzky of the role Fuhr played in the win. "Grant played in the last two games like Billy Smith played against us in the first two games of last year's final. Grant's proving, like a lot of guys on this club are proving, that it takes a while to grow up. It takes time. And Grant's getting sharper and sharper."

As was the case the year before, the Calgary Flames were next. And they weren't expected to be much more than a speed bump either. In fact, Las Vegas quoted the Oilers 20-1 favourites to win the series. The Flames, you see, had this little problem winning in Edmonton (13 straight in the regular season and playoffs) and in Calgary (where the Oilers had won four straight in the brand new Saddledome).

Calgary figured out the problem. The Flames, game after game after game, would give up early goals and lose first periods badly.

"The key is the first 20 minutes," said Lanny McDonald. "If we can hang in there for the first 20 minutes, we can go from there."

Badger Bob Johnson wasn't making like John Ferguson.

"I know we're a better club than we were last year," said the Flames coach. "But we've never played well against Edmonton. We've played well against everybody else. But not Edmonton. I just hope that we do that for ourselves here."

In Game 1 the Flames did everything they wanted to do and still lost 5-2. They survived the first shift. They survived the first five minutes. And they scored first.

"We played them eight times this year and every time we were up 2-0 or 3-0 and I know they were telling themselves, like we tell ourselves going against the Islanders, that if we get up on them, it'll be different," said Kevin Lowe. "But our experience, and we have experience now with 10 of us on this team who are in our fifth Stanley Cup playoffs, showed tonight. There's nothing like experience. We didn't panic."

Game 2 was a different deal. While most people in the press box were expecting the second playoff "Airbus Series"

Wayne Gretzky pours out some Pro Stars cereal for a couple of hungry fans.

Kevin Lowe and Jari Kurri celebrate a goal against Calgary goalie Reggie Lemelin. Below, Dave Semenko views things from the other side of the camera.

to be a second "Airbust Series," the Calgary Flames flew home with the series tied 1-1. Canada's Sarajevo Olympics hero Carey Wilson – who scored three goals, including the winner, in Canada's 4-2 win over the U.S. – scored two, including the winner at 3:42 of overtime, for a 6-5 win.

"It was kind of like ... well, I don't want to compare it to that one in L.A.," said Lowe when it was over.

The Oilers blew a 4-1 lead.

"We just didn't have the killer instinct," said Messier.

"I knew something would go wrong," said Sather of waking up in the morning and realizing it was Friday the 13th. "I thought about it all day long."

OK. So Calgary finally had a win in Edmonton. Big deal. The Oilers went down to the Saddledome and won both games to take a commanding 3-1 series lead. But they were tough games, real tough, and the Oilers won them ugly.

"I don't know about ugly," said Gretzky. "But we won them *barely*."

In Game 3 the final score was 5-3 and in Game 4 it was 5-4. Gretzky said he hadn't been hit as often or as hard in his life. The same was true for Kurri and Anderson.

"They must have cranked me eight or nine times," said Gretzky of his rough ride in Game 4. Sather used the word

"maimed" in post-game interviews. Badger Bob hauled out the rule book. "Where does it say you can't hit Wayne Gretzky?"

Assistant coach John Muckler called the two wins "the greatest two Oiler games from a team point of view."

Lanny McDonald said, "She ain't over till it's over." And it wasn't over.

The Oilers didn't put the Flames away in Game 5. Grant Fuhr wasn't sharp. And again, the lack of a killer instinct was evident. "If we knew the reason, we'd all be champions," said Gretzky, packing his equipment bag for a return trip to Calgary.

One other Oilers problem to this point of their history was that they weren't much good at overtime playoff games. When Lanny McDonald scored 64 seconds into OT in Game 6 for a 5-4 victory to send the series to a seventh game, that made it six Oiler losses in eight overtime games in postseason play. McDonald blew a kiss to his wife Ardell in the stands and headed for the TV interview room, where he told the nation, "This goal ranks right up there with the one I scored for the Maple Leafs against the Islanders in the seventh game in '78."

Johnson kept it low-key.

"All we ever wanted was the opportunity for that one game to decide it all."

"When you play a seventh game it's a flip of the coin to see how it comes up," said Jim Peplinski.

The Oilers didn't flip out. Instead, they searched their souls. And nobody searched harder than No. 99.

"I spent the whole day thinking about it," said Gretzky. "All I thought about were the questions. Where was I? Why didn't I perform? I thought about other series like the Islanders last year and I told myself no way did I want all those questions again during the summer. This was the most critical game of my career. I was sweating yesterday and today. For whatever reasons, I wasn't doing my job. I had the flu and a few nagging injuries. But I wasn't doing my job. And I knew I had to make sure I went out there and had the game of my life. I knew this was going to be the biggest game of my career and the biggest game in the history of our organization."

The Oilers won it 7-4.

"We sat in this dressing room before the game and told ourselves that this was our 100th game and if we lost it, everything we'd done, the 440 goals and the 119 points in the standings wouldn't mean anything. We sat in here and said, 'We're a hell of a team. Let's prove it.'

"Maybe we found out a bit about what it takes now. To win the Stanley Cup you have to work your ass off as a team."

Lowe declared that what we'd just watched "may have been the best thing to ever happen to this team."

One thing everybody knew when it was over. The Battle of Alberta had finally been a battle. And that we hadn't seen the last of them. In the end both teams had won. "There's going to be a rivalry now for sure," said Gretzky.

Nobody mentioned it that night. But the Oilers' win wasn't just a matter of soul. It was heart, too. The dying words of a 12-year-old boy added to the inspiration. Todd, a friend of Sather's son Shannon, died of leukemia. Just before his death he told his mother, "Tell Mr. Sather for the Oilers to win because I'll be watching from heaven."

Sather told his team before the game.

"Our fans are criticized for being tough fans, but they live and die with this team. And when a little boy's last wish is for us to win ..." Dave Lumley couldn't finish the sentence.

"What hit home to all of us was that these were his last words. Whew!" said Randy Gregg, who like most players on the team had made a friend in Todd and had been pulling for him.

Such inspiration was not needed in the next round against the Minnesota North Stars.

Sather had a problem before the series started, however. In Game 7 of the Calgary series he started an ice-cold Andy Moog – as much as telling Fuhr he didn't trust him for the crucial game. Then, after Moog was left helpless in a 3-on-1 situation, Sather gave him the hook and threw in Fuhr. He won the game but now Sather had two unhappy goalies. He decided to go with Fuhr for Game 1 and was rewarded with several super saves early before the Oilers took control and eventually won in a breeze, 7-1.

You might have noticed a trend that playoff year: the Oilers specialized in Game 1, but Game 2 was not their strong suit.

"It's been deja vu, hasn't it?" said Gretzky as the Oilers counted themselves lucky to win 4-3 to take a 2-0 series lead back to the Twin Cities. Interesting thing about that game, though – Fuhr suffered a hyper-extended elbow and Moog finished up. And it was Moog who started in Game 3.

That game of the series would be remembered by the Oilers for a long time and, by Dave Lumley, probably forever. Lumley was given a five-minute spearing penalty and watched the North Stars score

Mark Hall of the Oilers, Edmonton mayor Laurence Decore and Sun publisher Patrick Harden unveil a new billboard.

Don Jackson and Paul Coffey wait to see who their Stanley Cup opponents will be.

three times while he was in the penalty box, to take a 5-2 lead in the Looney-Tune-iest game of the playoffs. It looked as if he was going to be a giant playoff goat. But his teammates bailed him out, scoring six straight goals to win it.

"I went from the lowest of lows to the highest of highs," said Lumley. "Boy, was I sweating in the penalty box while the goals were going in. The things that were going through my head ... I thought about going to Don Jackson's parents' place the next day with the entire team for lunch and how embarrassed and ashamed I'd be there."

The team thought about that, too.

"That game tells you something about this club," said Jackson. "That tells you how close we are. The biggest reason for that comeback was that we wanted to win that game for Dave Lumley. We didn't want one player to feel he personally lost a game. We had a guy on the hook and we wanted to take him off."

Everybody knew Lumley was guilty. But the team felt guilty, too.

"It was a bad penalty," said Gretzky. "But bad as it was, we killed it worse."

Everybody pitched in as the Oilers fought back. In order, the goals came from Coffey, Kurri, Anderson, Linseman, Messier and Gretzky, who scored his on a penalty shot. By then the game was well in hand and the Oilers were loose, knowing they were going back to the Stanley Cup final.

"Hey, Gretz," said Coffey in the dressing room after the 8-5 win. "You made me money."

"How's that?" asked Gretzky.

"When we were standing waiting for you to take the penalty shot, I bet Keith Acton of the North Stars $5 that you'd score. As you started off, I asked if that was Canadian or U.S. He said U.S."

Glen Sather, sounding remarkably like Wild Bill Hunter, called it "the greatest comeback in Oilers' history."

Fuhr was back in net as the Oilers won the fourth game 3-1 to sweep the series. But the story that night wasn't the game. It was the scene.

There was no emotion in the Oilers dressing room. There was no euphoria. It was reminiscent of another time and another place. It was like the Edmonton Eskimos dressing room in 1978 after they'd won the Western Final, a year after their 41-6 loss to the Montreal Alouettes in the Grey Cup. The Eskimos went on to win the Grey Cup – the first of five in a row.

"All of a sudden, after the game, the room went hush," said Gretzky. "All of a sudden our attitude was that we hadn't won anything yet. Last year we thought we'd won a whole lot. We discovered in a hurry that we'd won nothing."

Coffey put it best.

"Last year we couldn't believe it. This year we can believe it."

That year, the NHL had decided, the Stanley Cup final would adopt the baseball 2-3-2 format. And the series would open in Uniondale, New York.

It was the "Drive For Five" vs. "The Run For One." Or "Billy vs. The Kid."

Billy Smith adjusted his halo in the glow of the Islanders dressing room the night they beat the Montreal Canadiens to set up the rematch and said his wish was for peace on earth and goodwill towards the Edmonton Oilers this time.

"Both teams are great hockey teams. We don't need the cheap stickwork. We don't need all that yapping and everything we had last year. This time let's just have a great series."

Kevin Lowe greeted the media mob with a one-liner: "I hope you guys use more notebooks this year than last year."

We used more notebook pages on Game 1. If there's one Stanley Cup playoff game every Edmontonian will remember forever that *didn't* involve carrying the Stanley Cup around the ice, this is the one. Everybody remembers that Fuhr was great in getting the shutout and Mc-Clelland scored the only goal as Edmonton won a Stanley Cup playoff game 1-0.

Fuhr turned aside 34 shots, 14 in the first period as the Oilers came off a nine-day layoff for the win.

"Ah, it was a piece of cake," said Fuhr.

"It was the biggest win in our careers," said Coffey. "And this is the best feeling I've ever had in my life. We proved to everybody that we can be as disciplined as anybody if we put our minds to it."

"We're still a long way from winning it," said Coffey.

"But now we know we can play in it," said Kurri.

There wasn't much to say after Game 2.

"Tonight we didn't get it and we didn't deserve it," said Sather after the 6-1 loss. But it would be the last Oilers loss of the season. The next three games were in Edmonton. And Denis Potvin got his wish.

Before the series started, Potvin had pondered the idea that sooner or later the Islanders' Stanley Cup streak of four Cups and 19 consecutive playoff series wins would have to come to an end.

"When it happens, I'd like to feel like the team that beat us earned their victory like we've earned ours," he said.

Before the series started, Bryan Trottier said the thing about the Oilers is that "they're like a powder keg and you have to keep the lid on."

Kaboom!

Led by Messier with two goals, the Oilers won Game 3 by the staggering score, for a final series, of 7-2.

"I've never heard a crowd like this in Edmonton for a constant 60 minutes," said Messier, citing his inspiration.

It was 7-2 again in Game 4, with Moog back in goal the rest of the way due to a Fuhr shoulder injury. Gretzky finally scored (twice) to break a 10-game scoring slump against the Islanders. And Messier was huge once again.

One win away from the Stanley Cup.

"You gotta believe!" said Coffey.

"Belief. That's the biggest barrier we had to overcome. I mean, it's tough for a team to believe they can beat the four-time Stanley Cup champions. But now we believe. We *believe*!"

Fourteen years later the memory of what happened next moved Lowe to tears when, after a 19-year career, he announced his retirement as a player to embark on a career as an assistant coach with the Oilers.

Somebody asked what was his greatest thrill.

"May 19, 1984," was his instant response.

And then the tears came. In a flood. He looked at his wife Karen Percy-Lowe and his brother Ken, the Oilers trainer, brought him a bottle of water before he was able to go on.

"When Dave Lumley scored the empty-net goal," he said, his voice

'The Drive For Five is no longer alive because the Thirst For First shall be quenched tonight.'

– Sign in the Oilers dressing room

breaking. "It was pretty unbelievable. When the puck went in the net. That moment will forever be in my mind."

The Oilers had won the Stanley Cup!

It was a non-series. The Oilers won Game 5 by a score of 5-2. During the three games in Edmonton they outscored the Islanders 19-6. The defending champions had not merely been nudged off the throne, they'd been blown away. And the sign on the dressing room wall said it all: *The Drive For Five is no longer alive because the Thirst For First shall be quenched tonight.*

"Edmonton had tasted winning before but never like this," I observed in my column. "The Grey Cups were great. But, uh-uh. No way. Not even close. That was the greatest single sports experience this unbelievably fortunate city – Canada's City of Champions – has ever seen."

Soon there were signs on the outskirts of town declaring Edmonton the City of Champions.

To see Wayne Gretzky carry the Stanley Cup around the ice in front of a gone-mad Coliseum crowd after only five years in the league was one thing. But to do what the Oilers did to a dynasty, that was something else again. And inside the Oilers dressing room, everybody was drenched. Those who weren't were taken care of by Randy Gregg, who went around the room looking for candidates, shouting, "You're too dry!"

Peter Pocklington had an entire bottle of champagne with my name on it and insisted I wear it all. Then he said to this totally drenched scribe: "This is the most incredible high I've ever had in my life. When I said we'd win the Stanley Cup in five years the day we got into the league, I said it because I was a naive fool. But that's what I believed. And then that's what we all believed."

Messier was crying. Not only had he won the Stanley Cup, but he was such a force in the final they gave him the Conn Smythe Trophy, too.

"Messier's goal in Game 3 turned us into the team we had to be," said Coffey.

Wayne Gretzky celebrates a goal and Mark Messier sips from the Stanley Cup in this double-exposure photo.

"The Calgary series made all the difference," said Lowe. "Right there. That was the time and place. That's where we grew up. That's where we acquired the mental toughness to win the Stanley Cup."

Sather mentioned the World Hockey Association.

"I'm proud I had a chance to be in that league. People like Anders Hedberg and Ulf Nilsson showed us a lot about creative hockey. It started there."

Edmonton went crazy. The oil capital of Canada became the Oiler capital of Canada, the hockey capital of Canada. A crowd of between 100,000 and 200,000 people (police told Mayor Laurence Decore it was the latter) attended the biggest parade ever held in Edmonton.

And, thanks to the Oilers and a bet between mayors, 36 Long Island Ducks were moving into Edmonton's Storyland Valley Zoo.

Kevin Lowe and Ken Linseman enjoy the Stanley Cup victory parade.

Peter Pocklington and Glen Sather.

Jaroslav Pouzar, Mark Messier and Dave Hunter.

Mark Messier with the Conn Smythe trophy.

Willy Lindstrom and Randy Gregg.

Dave Semenko.

Dave Hunter and Lee Fogolin.

Wayne Gretzky with Stanley.

Kevin Lowe and Paul Coffey after the Oilers' first Stanley Cup victory.

Mark Messier hugs Lee Fogolin during the victory party.

Wayne Gretzky hoists the coveted Cup.

Messier, Lowe and Coffey sign a championship poster.

A jubilant Wayne Gretzky poses with his father, Walter, and brother Glen in the Oilers dressing room.

Chapter 8
The Cup Stays Here

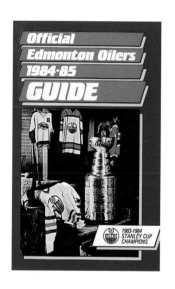

Picture the scene. It's the Bahamas. It's six weeks after the Oilers have won the Stanley Cup. And Wayne Gretzky and Kevin Lowe are sitting at a blackjack table in a casino.

"We look at each other. And we break into a big grin," says Lowe. "And at the same time we yell to the waiter: 'More champagne!'"

It's a Canada Cup year and Edmonton players, management and support staff dominate Team Canada. The Oilers are sitting around telling each other stories about their summer as they gather at training camp in Montreal.

"The only thing wrong with it is that it was too damned short," said Paul Coffey, who in a matter of weeks would become a hero again when he'd break up a two-on-one and take a shot that would be tipped by Mike Bossy to give Canada the win in the Canada Cup final against the Soviet Union.

"I admit it. I spent the summer *gloating*," said Gretzky. "And the best part of it was sharing it with everybody in Edmonton. We kept taking the Cup out to different restaurants and bars. We got a fantastic response. People in Edmonton had seen the Stanley Cup from a distance on television all those years when it was something the Montreal Canadiens used to win. To take it around sort of unannounced every night and to let thousands of people drink from it, that was probably the biggest kick of all. I can't wait until that first game in Edmonton when they raise the banner in the Coliseum and we're presented with the rings."

Wayne Gretzky became a magazine cover boy in no time. Opposite: Oilers Kevin Lowe, Jari Kurri and Dave Semenko savour their second Stanley Cup championship in May 1985.

Stanley is front and centre as coach Glen Sather, owner Peter Pocklington and the boys assemble for the annual team photo.

Gordie Howe presents Wayne Gretzky with the Emery Edge trophy.

Lowe seemed to be in the most awe of all.

"The reaction was more than I'd ever anticipated. The fan acceptance was wild. It was really nuts. Any fan who knew you were with the Oilers greeted you with open arms – especially, believe it or not, here in Montreal, which is my home town. It seemed people in this area were just as happy we'd won as the people in Edmonton. Montrealers like our team. They're happy we brought the Stanley Cup back to Canada. And they're especially happy that we didn't let the Islanders tie the Canadiens' record of five consecutive Cups."

Not everybody in the world was thrilled that the Stanley Cup was residing in Edmonton, Alberta, Canada, however. And hockey author, columnist and broadcaster Stan Fischler of New York topped the list. Fischler, writing in the *Village Voice*, called Northlands Coliseum "an oversized igloo," referred to Edmonton as "one of the bushest towns this side of Peoria" and referred to Wayne Gretzky as the "Pinocchio of the tundra."

Fischler wrote: "Edmonton should fervently embrace Lord Stanley's mug for the next 11 months for it will reside elsewhere in 1985."

And then, in the *Inside Sports* season preview, the prolific Fischler predicted a reverse result from the 1984 final.

Arbour's Empire Strikes Back

That was the main headline on the cover.

It's Only A One Year Dynasty For Gretzky And Team Arrogance.

That was the subhead.

In that article, Fischler called the Oilers "the reincarnation of the 1950 Detroit Red Wings who provided a brief respite from the Toronto Maple Leafs' three-consecutive-Cup reign, Toronto counterattacking and winning again in 1952."

He went on to explain the Oilers were a team that "won on a fluke last spring" who were "suffering from hallucinations – they suspect they have the makings of a dynasty, but if there is a one-year dynasty, the Oilers are it."

That was the scenario to start the season.

Glen Sather, who kept busy enough along with eight of his Oiler players leading Canada to victory in the Canada Cup, didn't stand pat with his own squad. He made several off-season trades that raised a lot of eyebrows. Ken Linseman was traded to

Billy Carroll vs. the Winnipeg Jets, 1985.

Boston for Mike Krushelnyski, and the Oilers lost Dave Lumley in the waiver draft, gaining Billy Carroll from the New York Islanders.

After a 2-2 tie in L.A. in the season opener, the Oilers came home to the Coliseum for the magic moment, the raising of their first Stanley Cup banner ... the sounds of *We Are The Champions*, the smoke, the spotlights ...

"That was something else," said St. Louis Blues coach Jacques Demers, who watched it all before sending his team out to play a game which, considering the scene, it had almost no chance to win. "I've never seen a night like this. I'm from Montreal. I've seen the Canadiens raise a lot of banners. But nothing like this."

While the fans were looking at the show, Sather was watching the fans.

"There were people behind the bench with tears in their eyes," he said.

There were some wet eyes on the ice, too.

"When I saw the banner going up, I knew that in 20 years, when I'm sitting in the stands, I'll be able to look up there and say I was part of the Edmonton Oilers when they won their first Stanley Cup," said Randy Gregg.

Even Carroll liked it, and he'd played for the other team in the final.

"This was much more glamourous than the ones I was there for," he said of being part of three of the four-in-a-row the Islanders had won. "Thing were always pretty low-key on the island."

A lot of teams can't make the transition from the hunters to the hunted. But this team knew what was coming and was totally prepared to go from winning the trophy to becoming the trophy.

"The first thing you notice is that the crowds are much louder when you are Stanley Cup champions," said Gretzky. "It's like when the Islanders came to Edmonton. It was almost like a playoff game. It's like that now for us when we go to other cities. And that's great. It gives us a push. It'll make us a better team."

He was speaking seven games into the season.

"Right now we have no losses. We already have the attitude, 'let's see how far we can go.' And when we lose one, we'll do the same thing with one loss."

They kept winning. And winning. And winning. Six straight wins. A tie. Four straight wins. A tie. Two more wins ...

"We're the champions," said Coffey. "We know we're the champions. But we have to prove it. If we'd got off to a bad start, it would have been back to the cocky thing again and that winning the Stanley Cup had given us all fat heads."

If the Oilers already looked like the greatest record-breakers in the history of record-breaking, the league hadn't seen anything yet.

The first one to fall was the NHL record for the longest undefeated streak at the start of a season as the Oilers went 15 games before losing, erasing the record set 41 years earlier by the

Oilers tough guy Kevin McClelland sinks his teeth into his work.

Wayne Gretzky and Glen Sather share a laugh during an Oilers workout.

1943-44 Montreal Canadiens. Toe Blake, the legendary Montreal Canadiens coach who played on that 1943-44 team, shrugged about losing that record. "I'm not worried about it. I'm more concerned about them beating our five Cups in a row."

Gretzky had a six-point outing to go with a hat trick by Jari Kurri in an 8-5 away win over the Washington Capitals to help make it happen.

When the team returned to the hotel there was a chilled bottle of expensive champagne in every room. Nobody knew where they had come from until Lowe found his bottle and read the attached note.

"Congratulations! Anything that's worth anything is hard to get. You guys did it!

"Congratulations ... from the Moose."

Mark Messier was at home, injured.

"What a guy! What a guy!" beamed Sather.

Messier had a strange season. He injured a knee in November and sat out 15 games while the Oilers established the record, then was suspended for 10 games for a violent act on Jamie Macoun of the Calgary Flames.

But Gretzky, Kurri and Coffey were all having spectacular seasons. With Mike Krushelnyski skating on their right side, making trader Sather look great again, Kurri and Gretzky were an entry. And as the season developed they set an interesting goal for each other.

Fifty in 50 times two!

One-two in scoring all season, the linemates figured if they were both to have 50-in-50 seasons they might be remembered as one of the greatest tag-teams of all time.

"It's starting to get interesting as we get closer and closer," said Kurri, who had 40, and Gretzky 42, going into the Oilers' 41st game. On his 24th birthday, Gretzky made it 50 in 49 for his part. But Kurri was injured before the 50th game. When he

Glenn Anderson and Mark Napier.

came back, he went after his own personal 50-in-50. Even though it would never show up in the record book, he wanted to be able to say he did it. And he did.

"It's my record now," said Kurri when he scored his 50th and 51st goals of the season. "I'm glad to get it in *my* 50th game. It feels much better now."

Kurri ended up setting a record for most goals by a right-winger, 73. Only Gretzky and Phil Esposito had previously beaten the 70-goal mark. With 52 assists and 135 points he finished second to Gretzky in the scoring race and bounced Mike Bossy as the first all-star team right-winger for the first time in five years. He also won the Lady Byng trophy.

Coffey was perking all season. Great in the Canada Cup, saving Canada's bacon at one end of the rink and then burning the Russians at the other, Coffey was rolling from the git-go and didn't cool off right through the playoffs. His best game was on Boxing Day in Calgary when he scored four goals, including the shorthanded winner with 3:14 remaining. Coffey was now good enough at both ends of the rink for the writers to vote him his first Norris Trophy. And even if a few of them still had doubts about his defensive ability, Coffey scored 37 goals, 84 assists and 121 points to finish fifth in regular-season scoring. The smooth-skating key to the Oilers' transition game was reinventing the position Bobby Orr had already once reinvented.

But, as always, Gretzky was the guy the world was watching.

In St. Louis, Gretzky had a five-goal night, the third of his career and his first since he broke Rocket Richard's record with five goals in Game 39 against Philadelphia. And nobody ever scored five goals in a game that were this gorgeous. Two were on breakaways and two were on absolutely brilliant spinarama moves.

His third goal was almost beyond description.

"I've never seen a goal like it," said Blues coach Demers. "That's the greatest goal I've ever seen. It must be pretty enjoyable for you guys to watch him every night. Just amazing."

Sather wasn't arguing in the other room.

"That goal's a first," he said of Gretzky's third, a creation which concluded with his spinning around to avoid defender Craig Levie and then hitting both posts. "He's the only player who could score that goal."

There was only one problem with Gretzky's big night. The five goals and an assist moved him to 998 career points. Edmonton was waiting to celebrate his 1,000th point at home. But the team still had a game to play in New Jersey.

No problem.

No. 99 set it up, making it 999.

"I guess Wayne's wish of wanting to get the record at home is going to come true after all," said Sather.

At home, against the L.A. Kings, The Great Gretzky became The "Grand" Gretzky. And he did in grand style. Not only did he get No. 1,000 – he added 1,001, 1,002, 1,003, 1,004 and 1,005 as well.

It was only Gretzky's 424th game in the league. He made it to 1,000 points a mind-boggling 296 games faster than Guy Lafleur, formerly the quickest to the milestone.

Sather, always trying to keep praise in balance with the rest of the best on his star-studded squad, took the opportunity to offer a testimonial.

"Bobby Orr and Gordie Howe were great players but what makes Wayne *the* best is that over his career so far, I don't think I've seen him take two or three games off. Every game there's guys trying to check him but he has more determination than anybody. That's what makes him great."

No sooner had Gretzky done it, however, than the story that wouldn't go away came back.

"I asked how much Gretzky would cost and I was told $18 million. They want $18 million," Toronto's Harold Ballard told me for publication in *The Edmonton Sun*. "I know they tried New York. Pocklington will deny it. But I know they tried New York. And he asked me once."

Pocklington denied it.

"Happy Harold has obviously lost all his marbles," the Oilers' owner said. "No, absolutely, no. He belongs to me and I expect he always will. It's absolute rubbish."

Once again the story went away for another day.

Gretzky played all 80 games and ended up with 73 goals, 87 assists and 205 points. That made it his fifth consecutive Art Ross Trophy and his sixth straight Hart Trophy. He ended up holding or sharing a total of 38 NHL regular-season, playoff and all-star records.

It was a most interesting season. And a lot of interesting incidents hap-

pened as the champs defended.

Like the night Ken Linseman *bit* Lee Fogolin. And confessed on the spot. "Yeah, I bit him. I should have done a lot worse to him." Obviously The Rat was having no trouble making the transition to not being an Oiler any more.

Then there was the day Dave Lumley was traded back to Edmonton.

"I'm a one-man Cinderella story," Lumley declared. "Can you believe it? They send me to Hartford and I get paid in American money all year, and then they bring me back for the Stanley Cup playoffs!"

Sather also added Mark Napier in a trade with Minnesota for Gord Sherven and a minor-leaguer. And, on a quiet day in February, Sather made a quiet deal with old Boston Bruins mentor Harry Sinden for Craig MacTavish – who had just served 276 days of a 365-day sentence for vehicular homicide – to give him a fresh start with the Oilers when he was released from jail.

Nobody was paying much attention to what was going on off the ice. The show on the ice had everybody mesmerized.

When the Oilers beat the Flames 6-4 at one point, coach Bob Johnson asked: "When was the last time that team lost?"

Moog and Fuhr were alternating, causing John Muckler to observe: "I've never seen them so happy. They're like pigs in mud."

Moog, at one point in the season: "I can't remember the last time we lost a game."

Canucks coach Bill LaForge, after losing to the Oilers Nov. 17: "Being Grey Cup week, I guess it's only right that they win by a converted touchdown."

Winnipeg coach Barry Long, after the Jets lost their 18th straight game against the Oilers: "Is there a law of averages? I'm really starting to doubt it."

Boston coach Gerry Cheevers: "You don't beat the Oilers when you pick up the paper and read 'Gretzky from Kurri, Kurri from Gretzky, Krushelnyski from Gretzky and Kurri, Coffey from Gretzky and Kurri, Gretzky from Coffey ...'"

NHL superstars Wayne Gretzky (99) and Pittsburgh's Mario Lemieux (66) faced off against each other for the first time on Nov. 6, 1984, at the Coliseum.

All year it had been like that. But as the playoffs drew near, the mighty Oilermobile started to cough and sputter some.

The only real knock on the Oilers during that sensational season was the way they played their last 18 games: L, L, L, W, T, L, W, T, L, W, T, W, L, L, W, W, T, L. Cooling off at the end of the schedule left Edmonton with 109 points in the final standings, four behind the Philadelphia Flyers.

If they'd lost their focus at the finish, it was no problem to find it again as they prepared for the playoffs.

The Miracle On Manchester wasn't that long ago. There had been a lot of changes since the spring of '82 for the Los Angeles Kings. The coach, the general manager, virtually the entire front office and all but eight players had long since shipped out. Dr. Jerry Buss was still the owner, but he had left his seat when it was 5-0 in that famed game that turned the 1982 series around.

Could it happen again?

"No," swore Sather. "It's completely different. They have different players. It can never happen again."

The Oilers just wanted closure.

"If we win this series maybe people will stop bringing it up," said Fuhr. "You kind of get tired of it after three years. For three years that series has been in mothballs and we'd like to put it back into mothballs for good."

That, of course, would never be possible. But the Oilers had no trouble putting the Kings into mothballs for the summer.

Lee Fogolin was the hero of Game 1. He scored the winner at 3:01 of overtime, then grabbed the puck. In his 11-year NHL career to that point, he had saved only one other puck.

"My first goal," he said. "To tell you how long ago it was, it was from the first game against the Oakland Seals. That says it all right there, doesn't it?"

Fogolin, who convinced a lot of rookies to phone their moms after their first goal, refused to phone anybody. "After 11 years in the league, I don't think my dad would appreciate being awakened at 2 a.m."

Winners by a 3-2 count in Game 1, it was 4-2 the next night with Krushelnyski scoring the winner in regulation. And Anderson put it away with a 4-3 overtime winner at the 46-minute mark in Game 3 in the Fabulous Forum.

With not a whole lot of fanfare, the Oilers had won of 12 of their last 13 playoff games and waited for the Winnipeg Jets – who would take years to win their first playoff game against Edmonton – to move on and be swept in four straight.

The Jets were becoming something of an Oilers coffee break on their Stanley Cup trails. But this year it was, if you'll excuse the expression, a Coffey break. Wow, did he have a series.

It started with the Oilers defenceman scoring to snap a 2-2 tie to send Edmonton to a 4-2 win in Game 1. But that was nothing compared to the two incredible

Wayne Gretzky helps Vic Mah cook up a storm at the Blue Willow Restaurant.

Team Canada vs. the U.S. in Canada Cup action.

Mark Messier skates away after elbowing Vladimir Kovin in September 1984.

goals and three assists he manufactured to lead the Oilers to a 5-2 win in Game 2.

"I guess both offensively and defensively, that was probably the strongest game I've ever played," said No. 7.

"I've never seen anyone play better, including Himself," said Teddy Green.

Himself, of course, was in reference to Bobby Orr, with whom Green played as a Boston Bruin.

"I guess that's the greatest compliment I've ever received," said Coffey when a scribe repeated the quote.

Coffey had not just been the hero at the Canada Cup but he already had 10 points for the playoffs and the Oilers had only played five games so far.

When the Oilers won 5-4 in Game 3 – with Gretzky scoring the winner and Messier and Anderson having big nights – the Jets knew they were done like dinner.

"We can't play any better than that," said coach Barry Long, an ex-Oiler from the WHA days. "It's like a kid with his finger in the holes in the dyke. You think you've got them stopped and they burst through in another place. Tonight Messier and Anderson burst through. Every night somebody bursts through. It kills you."

The Oilers were now 6-0 for the Stanley Cup season. As they waited for Game 4 they started adding it up. Two more wins and the Oilers, who had won their last three in the final series the year before against the Islanders, would tie the record set by four of the greatest teams ever for most consecutive playoff wins, with 11.

"That's not a bad record," said Coffey. "Any time you get in the same category as those great Montreal teams and that great Boston team ... I think it would be better to have a record like that than any individual records we might get."

Some of the Oilers were way ahead of that. Why not try to become the only team to go through an entire four-series Stanley Cup playoff year without losing a game?

"It would be great to go through the playoffs and not lose a game," volunteered Fogolin, adding that the Oilers were allowed to think that thought, having won, at this point, 15 of their last 16 playoff games. "It would be something to do that."

But possible?

"Yup," said Gretzky. "I think it's very possible."

Gretzky scored three times and added four assists to turn Winnipeg into "Waynerpeg," as the headline writers had it, to take care of the Jets for another season.

The fans in the Winnipeg arena had tried singing a soccer-style "Gretzky-Gretzky-Gretzky" to No. 99 to get him off his game. Not a good move. He *loved* it.

"My dad once told me not to get mad about the things fans chant. He said, 'Don't get mad, get even.' I think I got even."

The Oilers headed back to Edmonton and gathered in groups to watch other Stanley Cup series on TV. And they were together, almost the entire team, the night the Empire struck out.

"It's kind of sad. They carried the championship well and inspired us, I think, to want to be the same when we won the Cup," said Kevin Lowe of the New York Islanders' exit.

"The Islanders were our educators," said Andy Moog. "We learned so much from them. They taught everybody on our team so much about winning. It's strange to think they're out of it. It presents a whole new hockey season. It's something very unusual for our young hockey team. They've always been there."

Next up, Chicago. And the Revenge of Captain Video?

Roger Neilson, the man who had hired on as the Oilers' secret weapon behind the scenes for the playoff run the year before, was now in the employ of the Blackhawks. And Pocklington hadn't given him a Stanley Cup ring.

Pocklington's short arms and deep pockets, when it came to a ring for Roger, weren't a factor in Game 1.

Where was Mount Orval (Tessier) when you needed him? Bob Pulford was the coach now. And it was 11-2 Oilers for openers.

"It seemed like Glenn Anderson scored when they were playing the national anthem," said goalie

How sweet it is: A jubilant Mark Messier has a firm grip on the Stanley Cup.

Mark Messier escorts a Klondike Kitten through a welcoming line of Eskimo SUNshine girls in the spring of '85.

Murray Bannerman.

Larry (Bud) Melnyk proved to be the hero of the Oilers' much more respectable 7-3 win in Game 2. Who could be less likely? He'd never scored an NHL goal before. Not even one. The net had always been something of a mirage, an illusion, at the other end of the ice to Melnyk. And scoring the winner meant he got to go on *Hockey Night In Canada*. He'd never been there before, either.

"My heart really started pumping fast when they took me into the interview room," he said. "I was nervous. I'd always watched all the other guys on TV. Never me," said the veteran of 139 NHL games who had spent most of the year with the Oilers' farm team in Halifax.

The Oilers had the record. Twelve straight playoff wins. Six more and a second straight Cup would be theirs.

As the series shifted to Chicago, Blackhawks' Bob Murray came up with the quote of the series: "Edmonton plays hockey the way it's supposed to be played. We can't let them play it that way."

And then the 'Hawks played their best two games of the season.

"Hawkey Shock!" was *The Sun's* headline the next morning when the 'Hawks followed a 5-2 win in Game 3 with an 8-6 win in Game 4 to send the series back to Edmonton tied at two.

Fuhr was willing to take the blame for Game 4: "Don't ask. I've got nothing to say. Put bluntly, I had a bad night. I didn't make any @#$%&*# saves."

Other than that, it was a heck of an ambush by the Blackhawks. They played great.

"We're on a roll and they're thinking now," said Ed Olczyk as he packed his bag for the trip back to the Big E. "Six more wins and *we* win the Stanley Cup. And we're counting down. They're thinking and talking now. On the ice tonight they were talking. Not only to us but they were talking to themselves. They were a little bit tense."

And suddenly the Revenge of Captain Video was a story.

"Roger Neilson has had 60 to 70 per cent to do with it," said

Fun on the run: Paul Coffey, Wayne Gretzky and Kevin Lowe carry the Cup across the field during the victory party at Commonwealth Stadium on June 2, 1985.

Edmonton native Ken Yaremchuk. "He gave us the system to go by to beat these guys. He knows that hockey team. He worked with them last year. He knows how to stop them. Roger kept telling us we have to keep stepping into them and not let them get that European game going. He finally convinced us that when they can't freewheel they get frustrated," he said of the artful Roger.

The Oilers had heard enough. They decided Neilson wasn't going to get a Stanley Cup ring that year, either. In Game 5 the cream of the crop rose to the top. All the big guys had big games. The Oilers won 10-5. And they broke more records. Coffey broke three with a six-point night, Kurri broke another with his third hat trick of the playoff year and, with at least one game to play, the Oilers set the record for most goals in a series with 36. But it was Gretzky's two goals to break a 4-4 tie that were the key.

The Oilers made sure there was no ambush in Game 6 back in Chicago Stadium, winning 8-2. They were back in the Stanley Cup final for a third straight season!

Captain Video congratulated Sather after the game and made him laugh, too.

"Pully (head coach Pulford) said it's a good thing he and I are defensive coaches because we held you to 45 goals in the series," he quipped.

In the Oilers room Gretzky was telling whoever would listen, which was almost nobody, that the Oilers ought to be underdogs because the Flyers had finished higher in the final standings and had beaten the Oil-

> ## "All I know is that 15 years from now I'm going to say, 'Gawd, I played on a great hockey team.'"
>
> – Wayne Gretzky after winning back-to-back Stanley Cups

ers all three times they played them during the regular season.

As the media gathered in Philadelphia for the start of the series, the Oilers weren't the storyline. That honor belonged to Mike Keenan. In the Stanley Cup final in his rookie year as an NHL coach, he was getting a wide and varied assortment of questioning, little of which had anything to do with what we were about to watch.

Someone asked him if he'd ever seen the Stanley Cup. In person.

"Once," he said. "Bill Torrey brought Stanley to the same banquet once. It was the year I won the Calder Cup. When I saw Stanley, I decided to leave Calder in the car."

Bobby Clarke was in his first year as Flyers GM and he was a story, too.

"After all those years of playing the Edmonton Oil Kings in the final in junior in Flin Flon, it's quite the coincidence it's Edmonton in my first year as GM," he said. "Those series were battles. This one should be, too."

In the Flyers dressing room Mark Howe was getting the treatment from his teammates.

"Hey Mark, how many Cups did your dad win?" shouted somebody from the shower.

"Three or four," Howe answered.

"Don't count those @#$%&*@ Avco things. How many Stanley Cups did he win?"

"Three or four," answered Howe.

It looked like the son was going to have one after Game 1. The Oilers were supposed to be the high fire-power squad, not the Flyers. But Philadelphia won 4-1, outshot the Oilers 41-26, had 17 registered scoring chances to four by Edmonton and had five breakaways on Grant Fuhr. Not only that, but Viking's Ron Sutter smothered Gretzky. He didn't get a shot.

People seemed shocked. But the Flyers had lost only twice in the Spectrum since Dec. 6 and only five times in their past 50 home games.

"They did everything our coaches told us they would after watching their films," said Coffey. "There were no surprises. We were just horrible. They outworked us, outmanned us, outhit us, outskated us, outchecked us, beat us to every loose puck .. we were out-everythinged."

Sather knew he had to do something.

"We needed something to give our

This muscle-bound silver spaceman stepped out of a smoky haze holding the Cup high at the Oilers' home opener in October 1985.

team a lift. I've never seen our team so down like they were the next morning. I walked into our dressing room and it was like a morgue. They were totally depressed. They needed something."

Enter 20-year-old Esa Tikkanen, direct from Finland, making his NHL debut in the Stanley Cup final.

Tikkanen refused to back down in a first period incident with Rick Tocchet and was a one-man adrenalin hit for the entire team. Few on the team knew a whole heck of a lot about him, including Sather.

"I must have asked him 100 times before the game if he was nervous and he kept saying no," said Gretzky. "And he wasn't."

"I'd never seen him play outside of practice," said Sather, who took the word of coaches and scouts in the organization.

"I'd skated 20 minutes with him," Gretzky told the media. "You guys probably know more about him than I do."

If the team was down the day before, it had more than managed to get back up, as was evidenced by Gretzky's short exchange with *Sun* scribe Dick Chubey as he waited for the bus outside the hotel.

"See you in the winner's circle," he promised.

Gretzky opened the scoring and Willy Lindstrom and Dave Hunter fired the others as the Oilers won 3-1 in Game 2.

"I don't think they've had to play too many games like that," said Keenan. "But from time to time they've demonstrated it in their run to the Stanley Cup. They were on top of the puck carrier and played a real pressure-type defence."

After what happened next – again – the NHL returned to the 2-2-1-1 best-of-seven format in the final after taking a try at baseball's 2-3-2 format.

"All we needed was the last line change to get Gretzky away from Ron Sutter," said Mark Napier.

It didn't hurt, either, to get on the NHL's fastest sheet of ice. And well-

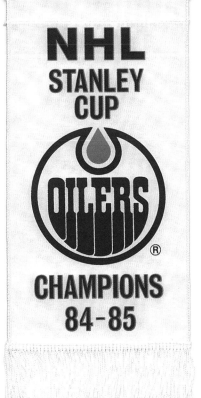

frozen pucks.

In Game 3, Gretzky scored two goals in the first 75 seconds and another in the 13th minute and that was enough for a 4-3 Oilers win.

"I don't know if it was a slow start or that the Oilers are such a great first-strike hockey club," said Keenan. "Maybe I should rephrase that. Mr. Gretzky didn't waste any time showing his abilities."

In Game 4 it was the other way around. Philadelphia led 3-1 after 11½ minutes.

"The slow start had me awfully concerned," said Sather. "I chewed my nails to the quick. We got ourselves in an enormous hole. It seemed like they'd brought the pucks from Philly."

It was a penalty-shot save by Fuhr on Ron Sutter, who had scored the winner in Game 1, that turned the tide.

Gretzky fed Kurri and Coffey with behind-the-back passes for goals, Messier scored on two breakaways and the Oilers had a 5-3 win and a chance to carry the Cup for a second straight year on Coliseum ice.

The crowd chanted, "The Cup Stays Here! The Cups Stays Here!" throughout the game as the Oilers ended up handling the Flyers like the Islanders the year before, winning Game 5 with ease, 8-3, to put the series away.

The Oilers had won all 10 playoff games in front of the Coliseum crowd and, with their last six from the year before, broke another Montreal Canadiens record: most consecutive home wins in the playoffs, dating back to the late '60s.

Sather and his stars had won two Stanley Cups and a Canada Cup in a span of 53 weeks.

"There's not much more to say after you've won two Stanley Cups and one Canada Cup in one year," is how Lowe put it.

Kurri and Coffey both set several playoff records and Fuhr was first-rate. But it was Gretzky who won the Conn Smythe.

"It was probably the toughest one ever picked," said the captain. "I wish I could have Paul Coffey's and Grant Fuhr's names on that trophy with me."

In a poll conducted by *Hockey Night In Canada* and *The Edmonton Sun* before the final game, the fans picked Coffey (3,667) and Fuhr (2,625) ahead of Gretzky (2,625).

"We all get our names on the Stanley Cup. That's all that matters. We've got to be rated as good as any team that ever won two in a row," bubbled Gretzky as he poured the bubbly. "All I know is that 15 years from now I'm going to say, 'Gawd, I played on a great hockey team.'

"In terms of emotion and excitement, the first one was bigger. But to do what we had to do to win the Cup twice ...

"We proved a lot of things by winning it twice. And I'll say the same thing now that I said last year. It's going to take a darn good team to take it away from us."

Chapter 9

Biggest Blunder Ever?

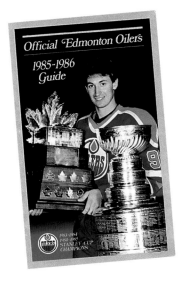

Carrying the Stanley Cup around the ice is nice. But the ring's the thing.

"This is what it's all about," said Wayne Gretzky as he slipped his second Stanley Cup ring on his finger on the first day of training camp.

"You can't carry the Stanley Cup around forever. You can only see the trophy once in a while. The most treasured thing is the ring. Carrying the Cup around the ice may be the greatest thrill of your life. But you wear the ring and every time you look at it, you see something different. You see the good times and the bad, the success and the sweat. To me, having the ring is more valuable than having your name on the Cup. If I had to make a choice, I'd take the ring."

As the Oilers gathered for their seventh NHL season, Gretzky and teammates were left to wonder how many rings this team might collect. They all knew the magic number was five – the record for consecutive Cups by the Montreal Canadiens. Matching that would obviously be the goal. But it would be a double-barrelled goal because of the local standard, also five: Hugh Campbell's Edmonton Eskimos won five straight Grey Cup rings.

"If we stick together and keep improving, there's no reason we can't win this year and next year and give ourselves a chance at a fifth," said Gretzky.

And No. 99 didn't think it was unrealistic for a team that had won two to be talking about a whole handful.

The Calgary Flames celebrate their playoff win over the Oilers. Opposite, rookie defenceman Steve Smith after the famous 'own goal' that ended the Oilers' post-season.

83

"As silly as it sounds, things are getting a little easier for me. Our guys are all getting better. Jari Kurri. Paul Coffey. Mark Messier. They've improved so much it makes it easier for me to play," said the 24-year-old who started the season in 14th place on the all-time points list at 1,123, with Gordie Howe's record of 1,850 already in his sights.

You'd figure the Oilers would all be happy campers with back-to-back Stanley Cups and people predicting they'd make it a fully accredited Edmonton Era with a third straight in the spring. But ... Pat Hughes, Jaroslav Pouzar, Willy Lindstrom and Billy Carroll had all been relocated. And Ted Green had retired as an assistant coach to pursue a private business project, replaced by Bob McCammon.

Captain Gretzky spoke to that as well before the season started.

"This is probably the closest team in professional sport," he said. "We're going to miss Pouzar, Pat and Willy. The players who are taking their jobs are great players and it's probably better for the team because they are younger. I'm not against trades and I don't do management's job. It's just when you play with guys, you live with guys. I'm the godfather of Willy's son. It's hard."

The newcomers were Esa Tikkanen, Craig MacTavish, Marty Mc-Sorley, Raimo Summanen ... and Steve Smith.

"Frank Selke Sr. once told me a team needs two or three changes every year," said Sather. "You need to bring in enthusiasm. You can't stay stagnant. Whether it's right or wrong, it's progress."

The Oilers came up with a space-age, laser-beamed way to celebrate the winning of their second Cup and to run up their second banner, after which they won their opener 4-3 over the Winnipeg Jets.

There was a thought that the Oilers' biggest obstacle this season might be boredom with the regular-season schedule as they hung around for the only months that mattered any more, April and May. But if that were true, it certainly didn't show early. The Oilers ripped off five wins in their first five games, lost, won, won three more, lost one, won two more, tied one, won one, lost two, tied one, won four, tied one, won three, tied one, won two, lost one, won three, lost one, won won, lost two, won five ... and it went that way all through the season.

And they still had games that made reading the summaries in the morning mandatory. Such as the night of Nov. 9.

Edmonton 13, Vancouver 0.

And Gretzky didn't get a goal. Dave Lumley had three.

"I've only had one other hat trick in my career," said Lumley. "I had three goals and three assists one night. I was second star. You-know-who was No. 1 star."

They set an Oiler record for

The usually mild-mannered Wayne Gretzky is restrained by Oilers trainer Lyle Kulchisky and linesman Ron Finn during 1986 playoff action.

the largest margin of victory, points (35) and most goals in a shutout. But they didn't get the NHL record. Forty-one years earlier Detroit had whupped New York 15-0.

The joy of hockey abounded with the most entertaining, exciting team in the history of the game ... until the Oilers hit Philadelphia in mid-month.

It should have been the first game of the season to draw hockey writers from far and wide – a rematch of the Stanley Cup final featuring the Flyers, off to a 12-2 start including 10 straight, and the Oilers, out of the gate at 11-3-1. And it was. But for all the wrong reasons.

Philadelphia goalie Pelle Lindbergh had just been killed in an accident when he drove his Turbo Porsche, valued at $117,300, into a cement wall. The Flyers held a Pelle Lindbergh Memorial prior to the game.

Sather offered to reschedule the game. For all the right reasons. But when the Flyers decided to stick with the schedule, Sather knew what the Oilers would face.

"If I was the opposing coach, if I was in Mike Keenan's boots, I'd be saying, 'Let's go out and play well for Pelle.' They'll be trying to tap the emotions of their players. If that's morbid, it's still a fact."

And that's the way it worked.

The highly emotional memorial lasted 50 minutes. And the Oilers, getting what they considered the most one-sided officiating they'd seen in seasons, lost it 5-3.

"We could have played all night and they wouldn't have let us win," said Gretzky.

It was the second game of a six-game road test the schedule maker had thrown at them to see how they handled things as back-to-back Stanley Cup champions.

"That's the toughest six-game road trip, in terms of the teams we had to play, I think we've ever had," said Lowe of the Washington-Philadelphia-Islander-Ranger-Quebec-Montreal run.

For the first time all year they lost two in a row and they needed two overtime wins to end up with a 3-2-1 record for the trip. It was at about that point that the Oilers began to see that they'd created something of a monster in themselves.

"When you lose two in a row, like we did at the start of the trip, you hear, 'What's wrong with the Oilers?' " said Gretzky.

Sather agreed. And was all in favour of it.

"It's gotten to the point in Edmonton where it's like it used to be in Montreal. When you lose, you leave the rink and the cab driver gives you hell."

Oilers Dave Semenko, Glenn Anderson, Don Jackson and Randy Gregg get into the Jazzercise spirit at a fund-raiser for Ronald McDonald House.

Oiler Glenn Anderson goes head first into the boards during Battle of Alberta action.

The Oilers were beginning to find out, the way the Eskimos had before them in their five-in-a-row Grey Cup run, that every year gets tougher. When you play 80 games before you get to the ones that matter, and you are so far ahead of your division six weeks into the season, there is a temptation to ask, "Do we really need these two points?"

It was different this year. And the Oilers were beginning to find that out.

"Before, because we were the new kids on the block and being from way far out west, and because we were all so young and everything, people kind of liked us," explained Lowe. "Now people are getting tired of us winning in the other cities. We're hearing a lot of snide remarks we never heard before."

But the Oilers were still putting in the pucks and putting up the Ws. And every second week they'd play one of those games that make memories.

A 5-3 win on Dec. 1 was one of them. It was the sort of night MacTavish had dreamed about when he lay awake behind prison bars. There he was. Back in the NHL. Before a capacity crowd. Scoring three straight goals. Almost single-handedly winning a game. And, as he came off the ice, a standing ovation.

He wasn't dreaming. It all happened.

After the game, when he emerged from the shower, he was surrounded by the Edmonton media, which as a group had interviewed him on the subject of vehicular manslaughter when he arrived for training camp and never mentioned the subject again. Not until MacTavish himself brought it up this night.

He said he thought a lot in jail about whether a crowd would ever support him again. And when he had the game he had this night, he said he wanted it more for the Edmonton fans than for himself.

He said his favourite moment in Edmonton so far wasn't this night but his first game, when he was embraced by the fans.

"It surprised me. It surprised me a lot."

At the time he wondered if they'd turn on him in a hurry when things weren't going good. They didn't. He had a terrible start. And, before this night, he had gone nine straight games without a point.

"It was wonderful," he said. "To get that standing ovation ... it felt real good. Considering the circumstances when I came here, it really meant a lot to me. I'm just going to savour this. It was my best night ever."

It wasn't quite in the ballpark with Bill Mosienko's three goals in 21 seconds or Jean Beliveau's three in 44 seconds. But three goals in six minutes and 38 seconds was magic to MacT.

A week later it was somebody else's turn.

Marty McSorley. Or Marty McScorely, as he was being called in *The Sun* the next morning. A guy who was hired to be a hockey hard hat, not a hockey hat trick, a guy who was not supposed to score five points but score on the five-point must system, stole the show from all the big boys as they were poised to reach milestones.

Kurri registered his 300th assist and scored his 250th goal. Gretzky

Oilers assistant equipment manager Joey Moss reacts after just missing a putt during the Wayne Gretzky Golf Classic in August, 1986.

played the 500th game of his career, tied Norm Ullman for 10th spot on the NHL's all-time assist list and left the rink with an 18-game point streak. And Coffey went home that night one point shy of the 500th of his career.

"I'm at a loss for words," said McSorley, the first star with two goals in a 4-3 win over Chicago. "But don't go away. I love being interviewed. And I don't think there are a lot of nights this is going to happen."

If the Oilers were getting tired of some of the kill-the-game strategies they were starting to see, they played a game in mid-December that featured nothing of the sort.

Edmonton 12, Chicago 9.

It tied an NHL record that had stood for nearly 65 years: most goals for two teams. Montreal Canadiens 14, Toronto St. Pats 7.

"How'd you like to say you scored the 10th goal and it was the winner?" said Lee Fogolin of Glenn Anderson's snipe.

Gretzky matched his own assist record of seven, which had broken Billy Taylor's record set in 1947.

"I lost count myself," said Gretzky. "At one point I thought I had eight. There'll never be another game like this one. We were up 7-1, then it was 8-6, then 10-6, 10-7, 11-8, 12-8, 12-9."

"That was the wildest game I've ever been in," said Grant Fuhr, who replaced Andy Moog when the 'Hawks cut the count to 7-5. "The only thing you can do is laugh. I was looking for a life preserver somebody was supposed to throw to save me."

Always the comedian, Lumley cracked: "If the goalies had been on, we would have won 12-0."

At the midway mark of the season the Oilers admitted it. Their biggest battle *was* to beat boredom.

"We're at the stage as individuals and as a team where the key is to maintain consistency and maintain our level of play," said Gretzky, who had 208 points the year before and had 103 at the halfway point this time. Paul Coffey had 121 the year before; at the half he had 60.

"Jari Kurri had 71 goals in 72 games last year," Gretzky continued. "It's going to be tough for him to improve on that. He has to score 80 in 80. Bobby Orr averaged 120 to 130 points a year. Paul Coffey is at that point of his career now where he's going to average 120 to 130 points a year as well."

As for Gretzky ...

His level had been out of this world since Day 1. But he, too, had reached his peak and accepted the new challenge of maintaining that level for as many years as he could. And this was a year he had distractions that went beyond the ones brought on by fame.

In February I broke the story:

Defenceman Paul Coffey with the puck from his 47th goal.

Gretzky had launched legal action against his money managers for the loss of more than $500,000 in an investment megabuck mess.

"It's been an education in business which was costly and very, very unnecessary," said Gretzky. "It's an expensive lesson I hope no other athlete has to go through."

He promised it wouldn't affect his hockey.

"I'm able to separate hockey from business and I think my statistics prove that."

What happened resulted in Gretzky's financial, legal and personal affairs all being handled from Edmonton instead of Toronto.

The Oilers, with 62 points at the half, were ahead of their pace of the year before, but were no longer consumed by any attempt to record the greatest regular season in NHL history.

John Muckler, now listed as co-coach, said in a way some things that were happening to the team were an aid.

"I think running into injuries and suspensions has been a blessing in disguise," he said of the loss of Fuhr, Messier and Krushelnyski as well as an eight-game suspension for Glenn Anderson.

There were a couple of other things. Serious things. *Sports Illustrated* magazine published an article alleging cocaine use on the team. Mark Messier was charged with dangerous driving when his sports car was allegedly rammed into three parked cars. And Dave Hunter was found guilty of his third impaired-driving charge and sentenced to time in jail. Half the headlines were not about hockey. And it was as if, for a significant part of the season at least, half the team was under journalistic investigation.

It certainly was not smooth sailing. Going to the games became a form of escapism, even for the sportswriters.

But now people were starting to wonder if they should read something into some of the stranger scores.

Two years before, the Oilers had suffered a loss that turned more heads than any of their wins, 11-0 to the Hartford Whalers.

This year, in Toronto, while not quite that stunning, they had another one. Toronto 11, Edmonton 9.

"Hard To Be-Leaf" was *The Sun*'s headline the next day.

"We embarrassed ourselves," said Sather.

But the quote of the night, one which would be worth noting in the spring, came from Muckler.

"It's like raising a family. Any time the kids get into trouble, they go back to the family. But any time they have success, they don't listen to the parents at all."

In late January all eyes were on Gretzky and Coffey. Both were

Mark Messier jokingly begs Glenn Anderson for an autograph during a 'meet the players' session at the Coliseum in 1986.

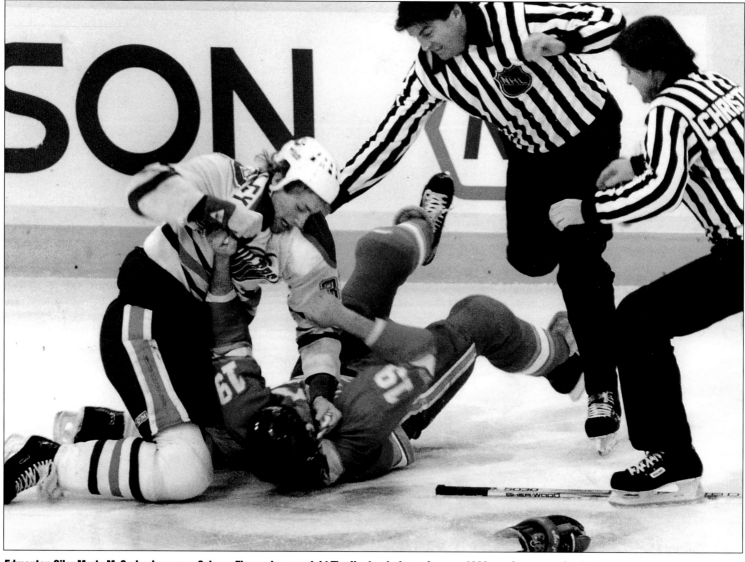

Edmonton Oiler Marty McSorley hammers Calgary Flames heavyweight Tim Hunter during a January 1986 regular-season bout.

streaking. Gretzky, who had already set the record with 51, had run up 39 straight games with at least a point . And Coffey, at 28, equalled Guy Lafleur's old record, as *Sun* hockey writer Dick Chubey phrased it, "for mere mortals."

Coffey admitted playing next to Gretzky's greatness did have that effect.

"Only one other guy has got 28 but it hasn't sunk in because of Gretz's 51," he said.

Both streaks ended the next night in Chicago.

Gretzky, who came right back with yet another seven-assist game against Quebec, and Coffey continued to be the focus individually.

On March 14, Coffey went into the record books in a big way. He had an eight-point night against the Red Wings to tie Tom Bladon's record for most points in a game by a defenceman.

And I didn't even stay in the rink to watch it. At the end of the second period, I left history in the making to see history in the quaking. Tom Bladon happened to be a couple thousand feet away at Northlands' Silver Slipper Saloon, where he'd organized an Edmonton Oil Kings reunion.

"I hope he gets it," said Bladon. "A record like that should be owned by a Bobby Orr or a Paul Coffey, not a Tom Bladon. I broke Orr's record and I never thought that was right. I kind of regarded it as a bit of a fluke. Every dog has his day and that was my day to be the dog. I was embarrassed to break it. Records like that are meant for players like Coffey. A player like him should have that record."

By the end of March, Coffey was taking dead aim at Orr. Coffey was one goal shy of Orr's record of goals for a defenceman, 46, and six points back of Orr's record of 139 for a defenceman. And Gretzky was three shy of his record NHL season of 212 points.

And it was, almost, ho-hum.

"Not only in Edmonton," said Sather. "But all around the league. I've been shocked at the lack of attention given to Coffey. These records are very difficult to break. He should be the showcase of the NHL."

Orr was paying attention. And he'd already kissed his record goodbye.

"It's his," he said during the countdown. "He'll get it. He'll probably break it easy. Want to bet your mortgage money against him?"

Coffey said he wanted to get at least one of Orr's records at home. And he did.

On the night of April 2, he not only became the NHL's all-time top-scoring defenceman, with his 46th and 47th markers, but was the star of an 8-4 win over the Vancouver Canucks.

The record breaker was a sight to behold, a vintage Coffey end-to-end work of art.

"I threw my arms up in the air, looked up at the scoreboard and saw a big 47," said Coffey. "Right then I felt like 1,000 pounds had been lifted off my back."

Coffey wasn't done yet. Neither was Gretzky.

With two games to go Coffey needed two points to equal yet another Orr record – most points in a season for a defenceman, 139. And Gretzky needed two points to break his record of 212 set in '81-82.

The next game was in Calgary.

"I don't expect to be cheered," said No. 99.

Gretzky had three assists. And the bad blood between the Calgary and Edmonton franchises boiled over in a game the Oilers lost 9-3, which featured 61 penalties and 242 minutes of sin-bin sitting.

It wasn't so much the fans. They were having a hoot yelling "Yahoo" every six minutes or so when the Flames scored. It was only the second time all season that their team had managed to beat the Oilers. What made it an incident was the Flames organization's refusal to acknowledge, in any way, shape or form, the fact that Gretzky had equalled and then broken the NHL's all-time single-season scoring record.

Sather was livid.

"Wayne set an all-time NHL record and the Flames didn't even have the class to announce it over the PA system. If Lanny McDonald had set a record in our building, you can be damned sure we'd announce it. Even if Calgary had beat us 25 times in a row. I think the game is bigger than the two teams and it's bigger than the people who come to watch the two teams. It's unfortunate people don't have minds big enough to understand some of that stuff."

Gretzky ended up with 52 goals and 163 assists, demolishing his old record of 135 and establishing the new points record at 215. He won the Art Ross Trophy for the sixth straight year and the Hart for the seventh straight season. He scored his 37th hat trick to tie Mike Bossy. In the entire season he was held scoreless only three times and recorded 61 multiple-point games. His NHL records count was now up to 41.

Coffey won the Norris Trophy for the second consecutive season. He ended up with 48 goals but, with 138 assists, fell one short of Orr's points record for a defenceman.

Kurri (68-63–131) and Anderson (54-48–102) also had big years. And Sather even got a trophy. He won the Jack Adams Trophy as NHL coach of the year.

Despite the tougher going at times because of the way teams were starting to play them, the Oilers matched their best year ever with 119 points in the final standings. Fifty-six wins. One hundred and nineteen points. And 426 goals. First overall by a dozen points. And 60 points ahead of their first-round playoff opponents, the Vancouver Canucks.

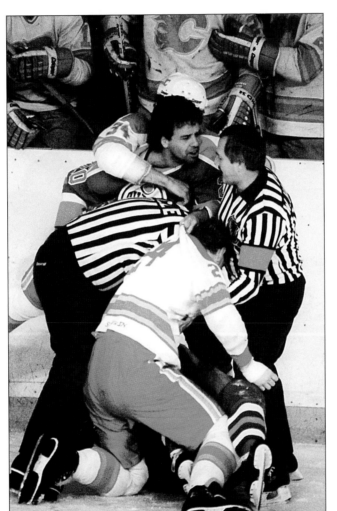

Provincial rivalry rears its ugly head again.

If ever there was a playoff series that was tough to get up for, this was it. First place overall vs. 18th overall. In eight regular-season games the Oilers went 7-0-1 against the Canucks and outscored the left-coast club 51-23.

The Oilers won Game 1 by a 7-3 count and it had regular-season game written all over it. Even the Oilers didn't like it.

"We weren't forechecking," said Mike Krushelnyski, who scored the winning goal in the game. "We had no enthusiasm."

And it wasn't much different the next night as the Oilers extended their record to 18 straight home playoff victories with a 5-1 win in Game 2. Moog played the game in goal, replacing Fuhr whose father died the night before.

In Vancouver the story was in the stands. Only 5,000 tickets had been sold for the game in the Pacific Coliseum.

"I couldn't believe it," said Mark Napier. "I skated out and looked up and nobody was there. It felt like an exhibition game."

Fuhr was back in goal for the final game of the best-of-five first-round series and said he'd had tougher practices. "It wasn't exactly a tough game. There weren't any tough shots."

Edmonton won it 5-1.

The real Stanley Cup playoffs would start soon enough. Calgary was next. And there was a heaping helping of hype to fan the fires of hockey's civil war where the Mason-Dixon line was drawn on the floor in the middle of a bar in Red Deer.

"This is where men are men and the boys don't win," declared Lowe.

"This is like one of those old westerns," said Calgary coach Bob Johnson. "One guy in the middle of the street, against the top gun in the whole town, thinking he's going to be gunned down. We want to be John Wayne. We want to be one against 50 and ride in there and win."

The Flames' Perry Berezan said he didn't know about the old West but this was always the way it was since he was born in Edmonton.

"Ever since the day I was born I was brought up to understand that Edmontonians hate Calgarians and Calgarians hate Edmontonians. It's always been that way. It'll always be that way."

Calgary Sun columnist Larry Tucker got it going by reminding the province of Sather's quotes during the regular season.

"The GM/coach of the Edmonton Oilers called the Flames 'cowards' and 'homers' and 'a no-class organization,'" wrote Tucker, who had moved to Calgary after working as an *Edmonton Sun* sportswriter.

This quote from Sather ran in italics at the top of his column, dated April 18, 1985:

"I think Badger should go back to his school books. He's got a theory for a theory and a meeting for a meeting. The Calgary team is so paranoid about trying to beat us, they intimidate us and forget about their own game."

Sather, who always believed gamesmanship was part of the playoff package, said he couldn't believe it when he found out the Flames were dressing their practice goalie in an Oilers jersey.

"That must be something you do in college in the States," he said. "Of course, he's an American. He thinks differently than I do. I'm a Canadian, born in Alberta. I probably think a little more logically than he does."

John Tonelli was a Flame now and he had no problem getting with the program, declaring that the Oilers made him sick. Figuratively. And, once, literally.

"They made me sick," said the former New York Islander, talking about the Oilers taking a fifth Stanley Cup ring off his finger. "I felt awful. I

A devastated Oilers bench, including a tearful Steve Smith, tries to come to grips with the fact that the playoff run is over after a Game 7 loss to Calgary.

felt like they took something away from me that belonged to me. I was physically ill after that series. I was in bed for three weeks after that series and the Oilers put me there."

And so it went.

"Enough already," said Lowe after the five-day wait before the first faceoff. "Deal the cards. Let's get going."

After Game 1 he wanted to call a misdeal.

"We didn't play worth a damn," said Sather after the 4-1 loss. "Absolutely zippo. Calgary seemed to want it a lot more than we did. We didn't get untracked. A lot of our players were awfully tentative. I don't know whether it was nerves or not. There wasn't the skating or the composure there should have been."

The Oilers came close to losing Game 2, too. But Anderson, on a brilliant play by Lumley, was sent in alone on Reggie Lemelin 64 seconds into OT to win it 6-5.

The game was to hockey what *Raiders of the Lost Ark* was to the movies that year. It had it all. Comedy. Action. Drama. Thrills. Chills. Spills. And if you didn't like that particular movie analogy, one crazed Calgarian carried a *Ghostbusters* sign around the Coliseum, declaring, "We ain't afraid of our hosts."

"It was an adventure," said Fuhr who allowed possibly the longest tip-in in Stanley Cup history on a 110-foot shot. "I couldn't believe that one. It was from the tee box. Just once I'd like to make one from that far away on the golf course. My daughter could have stopped that. That's how hard it was going. That's going to go down as the worst goal I ever

let in. I expect to see that one someday on *Bloops And Blunders*."

The Oilers, understandably, headed for Calgary more than a little bit rattled.

"I'll tell you one thing," said Coffey. "I'm scared right now! I'm afraid of losing the Stanley Cup!"

That made Game 3 a fright night. The Flames won it 3-2 to take a 2-1 series lead.

"It's obvious after three games that Calgary is the hungrier hockey club," said assistant coach Bob McCammon. "Our guys want it but there are degrees of wanting."

One other thing was obvious. This was already one hell of a Stanley Cup playoff series.

"It's scary," said Tonelli. "I wish it was the Stanley Cup final so everybody could watch it. The whole country should be seeing this series. You watch our games, with this incredible pace every night, and then you watch the other games. They look like slow motion."

The Oilers were talking about a need to go back to the blackboard.

"We have to change our game plan a little bit," said Kurri, still trying to get a handle on the English language. "This is going to be a long *serious*."

The major change in Game 4 was that Gretzky broke loose. Three goals. Two assists. Seven-four. The Oilers had finally won back home-ice advantage.

"Wayne had one of those games you can dream about," said Sather. "Wayne took it upon himself to win this game for us and he did," said

MacTavish.

Indeed. On this night a pair of nines beat everything. The rest didn't count.

Gretzky had heard the boo-birds before. Four years earlier in L.A., the fans chanted "Gretzky Sucks" all night, every night. But he couldn't even go to the racetrack between games without getting it in Calgary. There he was, sitting at a table in the clubhouse, when people at the tables on either side of him started to chant "Whiner. Whiner. Whiner."

Signs were everywhere.

"I brought the cheese, who has the whine?" read one.

"Keep the Cup shiny, whiny," read another.

And then there was the most popular local joke making the rounds.

"Q: What do you call a basement full of Wayne Gretzkys?

"A: A whine cellar."

The Whiner was The Winner this night. But all was still not right. Word was leaking out of the Oilers dressing room after they were spanked 4-1 in Game 5 that the coaches felt they were giving the players the game plan to win but the players were refusing to listen.

Roger Neilson was scouting the series for Chicago and made a couple of interesting observations himself.

"What has happened so far is not a matter of luck," he said. "The difference is, Calgary is doing what you have to do in the playoffs. They won on the boards. They finished every check. They were shooting at every opportunity. And they were going with short shifts. I don't think Edmonton is doing those things. If I were to offer any advice, I'd tell them to get the go-go going. It's tough to get the go-go going with those long shifts. If you want to get the go-go going, you have to go with the short shifts."

Suddenly, in Game 6 back in Calgary, it was win or else for the Oilers.

"I guess what happens next will show whether or not we're a great team," said Charlie Huddy.

In Game 6 the Oilers were a great team.

"We gutted it out," said Gretzky of the 5-2 win that forced a seventh and deciding game back in Edmonton. "Messier scored the biggest goal of his life. Fuhr ... what do you say? He's the best goaltender in the game and he showed it tonight. Everybody showed up."

They claimed to have been scared straight.

"It had to be the game of our lives and we went out and did it," said Huddy. "We were on the brink of elimination. It's the biggest game I ever played."

And so it went to Game 7. And everybody remembers what happened next.

The next morning I wrote the following in *The Sun* under the headline:

"BIGGEST BLUNDER EVER?"

"On the back of a raw rookie, a dynasty died.

"Steve Smith, on his 23rd birthday, ended one of the greatest series in the history of hockey with one of the biggest bonehead plays in the history of all sport.

"As the Coliseum crowd sat in stunned disbelief, watching the Calgary Flames celebrate, sportswriters from all over North America tried to remember a bigger blunder.

"Roy Reigel running the wrong way for a touchdown in the Rose Bowl. The famous Gene Tunney long count when he stood over Jack Dempsey, allowing Dempsey time to recover, get up and come back to win the fight. Bonehead Merkle of the New York Giants who failed to touch second base on a hit that would have won the World Series. Mickey Owen dropping a third strike that would have ended a World Series game. Chuck Hunsinger's fumble which Jackie Parker ran back to win the 1954 Grey Cup game.

"But has such a super-duper blooper ever cost a club, which had won two straight championships, a chance to be an all-time team and win three straight?

"This one, obviously, ranks right up with any bonehead play in a championship situation, anywhere, any time, any place, ever!

"It stopped a Stanley Cup streak in its tracks.

"When Steve Smith passed the puck from behind his own net and hit goaltender Grant Fuhr on the back of his left leg, the puck bounced into the net, breaking a 2-2 tie and breaking the backs of the back-to-back Stanley Cup champions.

"Smith had tears in his eyes as he bravely walked across the Oilers dressing room, where few other players chose to make an appearance, and sat in his stall, instantly surrounded by every media man in the room.

" 'Sooner or later I have to face it,' said the rookie, who was not allowed to return to the ice after his incredible error at 5:14 of the third period.

" 'I've got to keep on living. I don't know if I'll ever live this down, but I have to keep on living. The sun will come up tomorrow.

" 'The players have stuck by me. But this is just a time I have to spend by myself right now. It was a human error. I'll have to live by it.' "

"And live with it forever. No matter what Steve Smith does in his career, he'll go down in history as the player who cost the Edmonton Oilers their third straight Stanley Cup."

The Edmonton native on the Calgary roster, Perry Berezan, received official credit for the goal. The Flames headed home to be met by an airport full of fans. And Edmonton headed into the off-season.

The next morning *The Sun* received hundreds of phone calls, a record that stands to this day. Almost all were sympathetic to Smith and steamed at me. Smith hadn't even looked at the papers when I called him the next day.

"I haven't left the apartment," he said. "I tried to sleep but I couldn't."

On the way home from an Oilers wake, in which he sat much of the night by himself at the other end of the bar, he noticed the newspapers were in the boxes.

"On the way home I passed a *Sun* box and saw the picture of me on the front page," he said. "When I saw the photographers taking pictures of me on the ice and in the dressing room, it's what I expected."

He said he had no chance to monitor the public outpouring of compassion that dominated the day after the Oilers died. He was told of the record number of calls to *The Sun* switchboard.

"That makes me feel good," he said. "I'm happy to hear it. I really don't know what to expect from the fans."

A local psychiatrist said the city woke up the next morning and "couldn't find it in their hearts to blame the rookie on his birthday and decided to get mad at Terry Jones instead."

Whatever, Edmonton was wonderful.

The best analogy came from a caller who said Smith was Mrs. O'Leary's cow. Smith kicked over the lantern. But it wasn't his fault that the Oilers left it on the floor.

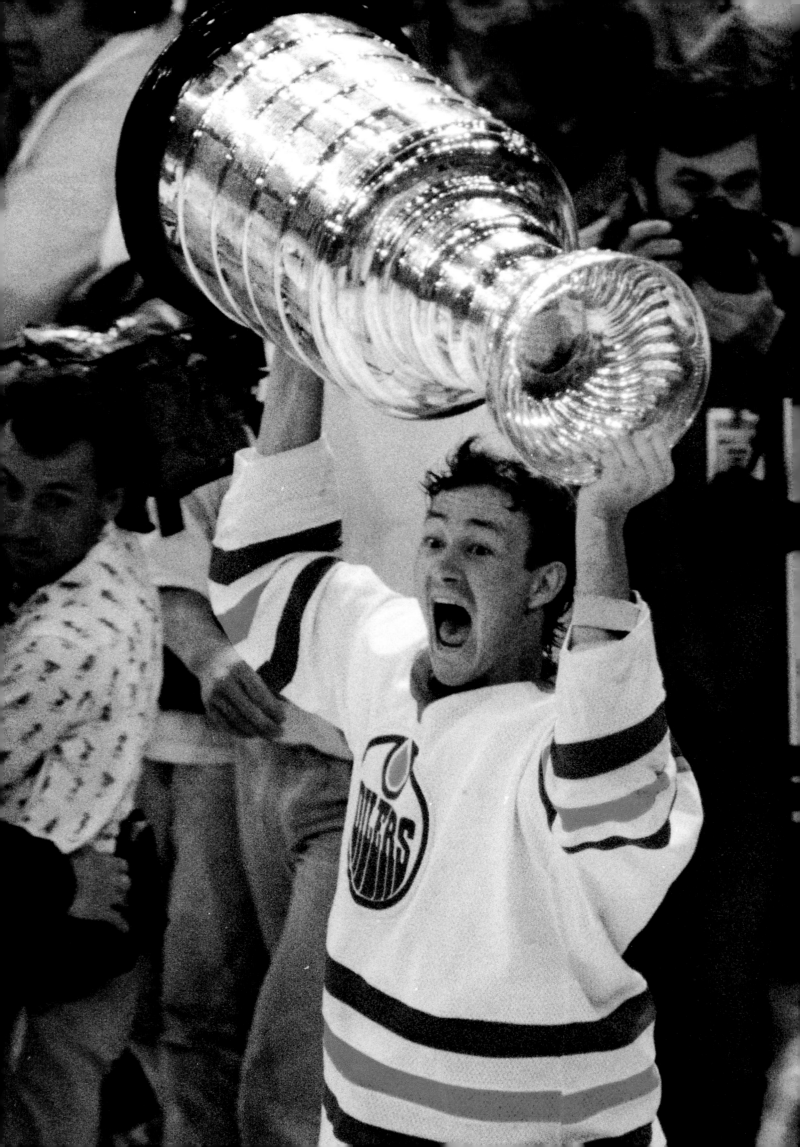

Chapter 10

Still The One

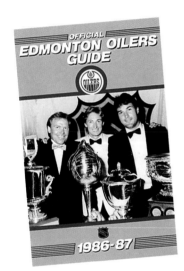

Following an afternoon on the golf course in Phoenix, three members of the dethroned Edmonton Oilers were playing 8-ball in a sports bar.

"Coming up next on ESPN, exciting Stanley Cup semifinal action with the St. Louis Blues and the Calg ....."

Paul Coffey calmly walked over and pulled the plug on the TV set. Wayne Gretzky and Kevin Lowe kept their eyes on the stripes and solids and the game continued. Nobody said a word.

"Any time the games came on, wherever we were, even a mention of the word hockey for those first few weeks and you got a sick feeling in your stomach," said Lowe.

If they weren't thinking it to themselves, they were saying it out loud.

"Damn, I can't believe we lost."

The Calgary Flames made it to the Stanley Cup final against Montreal in the Oilers' place, making it four straight seasons the final was played on Alberta soil. It had been one of those years. The Oilers weren't the only top team to end up upset after being upset in the playoffs. The final featured the fifth- and sixth-place teams overall. But the Oilers were the back-to-back defending Stanley Cup champions and the backbone of the Canada Cup-winning team in between. And when they arrived at training camp they still couldn't believe it.

John Muckler, Glen Sather, Dr. Gordon Cameron, Peter Pocklington and Ted Green in the winning dressing room. Opposite: All is forgiven, Steve Smith.

"We'd won two Stanley Cups in a row," said Paul Coffey. "We had seven great months. And now nothing but that Calgary series will be remembered."

In the off-season Glen Sather had come to some sobering conclusions.

"You could see we were winning when we weren't playing the way we should," he said. "But to tell them that … they didn't want to hear it."

Like the players, the coaching staff had spent the off-season trying to make sure they knew what went wrong so they could supply the cure and get the Stanley Cup back in their grasp again.

"I think we were too predictable," said co-coach John Muckler. "I think we continued to do things that we do awfully well for too long. I think a lot of study has gone into how to beat the Oilers and I think we have to become unpredictable."

Sather said there was still room to grow.

"We still have some growing up to do. This is a great hockey team. But there still are people who don't believe in what their coaches tell them. They were doing things that work during the regular season. In the playoffs you have to devise strategies and overcome them."

And one other thing.

"We have to respect our end of the ice a lot more," said co-coach Muckler.

Could they turn the Happy Hooker into Doris Day? Maybe yes. Maybe no. One way or the other, as the Oilers prepared to open their eighth NHL campaign, most everybody involved suspected it was going to be their longest season.

The Oilers opened in Philadelphia in what the schedule makers figured would have been a lid-lifter featuring the Stanley Cup finalists. The Oilers played defence. They lost 2-1 as they ran into a hot goalie, a kid by the name of Ron Hextall playing his first NHL game. But the coaches claimed to be pleased.

"I'd have to say we're happy," said defensive coach Ted Green, back with the team after a year away in private business. "We did things well in our own zone. We lost the game, but playing that way will benefit us as the season goes on and we get into the playoffs."

The Oilers claimed to want to change their game and change some people, too. Craig Muni was signed as a free agent. Jeff Beukeboom, who had played 44 games the year before, was now a regular. And Don Jackson had been traded away for the rights to Reijo Ruotsalainen once his contract obligations were fulfilled with the Bern Bears in Switzerland at the end of the season. Dave Lumley, as expected, retired.

The Oilers played the Flames three times early in the season and lost all three, leaving them with a not-too-spectacular 8-6-1 record getting out of the gate.

Calgary wasn't the entire problem. Edmonton was the problem.

"We don't seem to have the emotion of the past – that burning desire," Sather observed of the Oilers' slow start.

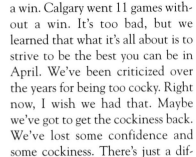
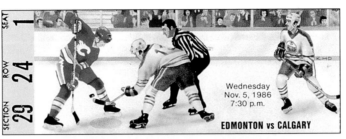

Wednesday
Nov. 5, 1986
7:30 p.m.

EDMONTON vs CALGARY

Gretzky tried to put his finger on it.

"It's a hard thing to explain. There's a whole different attitude. A whole different atmosphere. Last year we had such a great year. It was an outstanding year. All through the regular season we strove to be the best. And what good did it do us? Montreal went seven games without a win. Calgary went 11 games without a win. It's too bad, but we learned that what it's all about is to strive to be the best you can be in April. We've been criticized over the years for being too cocky. Right now, I wish we had that. Maybe we've got to get the cockiness back. We've lost some confidence and some cockiness. There's just a different feeling this season."

The Oilers, during Grey Cup week, lost to the Flames for a fourth time and four nights later lost to Chicago at the Coliseum. And now even the visiting teams were trying to figure out what was wrong with the Oilers.

"They looked flat. They're not playing with much fire," suggested Darryl Sutter.

If the Oilers had found out in the spring that their loss to the Flames was popular outside of Edmonton and area, Gretzky was finding the same thing personally.

"People are looking for a new hockey hero," he told me in early December. "They want somebody else to take over. I've won the Art Ross and Hart trophies too many times. Let's say I end up with 160 points in the scoring race. Would I get the Hart Trophy? Definitely not. Nobody has ever managed to get more than 160. But that's the way it would be."

Gretzky was off to a slow start by his standards, too. Why, if he kept the same pace all year he'd end up with *only* 189 points, his *worst* season since he set a record with 164 points in '80-81.

Two weeks before Christmas Sather made a move. He traded Dave Semenko to Hartford for a draft pick.

Gretzky was choked up.

"Words don't have to be said what a good guy he is," said Gretzky.

Semenko took it better.

"I don't think it'll be as bad as the riots in Montreal when Rocket Richard was suspended," he said.

Gretzky scored his 500th NHL goal early in the season without much notice. And when he had his first big game of the season with four goals and an assist in a 5-3 win over Quebec, he was upstaged by Semenko ... on the out-of-town scoreboard. Sammy scored twice in his Whalers debut.

Craig MacTavish leaned over on the Oilers bench and whispered to Wayne, "Gretz, the big guy doesn't miss you."

But Gretzky got it going. He scored 17 goals in 14 games. And slowly but surely the Oilers began to become, in equal parts, the team they had been and the team they wanted to be.

With a six-game winning streak, followed by a three-gamer and a five-gamer, the Oilers were rolling in January. And they beat the Flames! And

Glenn Anderson and Wayne Gretzky: Daily workouts are a joy when you're winning.

Grant Fuhr, Ray Bourque, Rod Langway and Wayne Gretzky pose for the all-star team photo.

there was discipline!

The dressing-room talk after the 5-3 win was fascinating. Ever since the Oilers had been eliminated by the Flames in the playoffs, the most popular theory about what happened was that the players refused to listen to the coaches. The coaches said they were telling their team to dump it in, dump it in, dump it in until they were blue in the face. On this night the team finally dumped it in, and dump-it-in equalled win.

"It was obvious," said Muckler in the Oilers dressing room. "We shot the puck in. We made their team turn and work. We finally proved to everybody tonight that we could be a disciplined team. We have to be a disciplined team because the Flames are a disciplined team. By dumping it in and forechecking, we got to use our speed to an advantage. It worked. We got the puck in. We penetrated. And we made their defence twist and turn. We played the majority of the game in their zone. We used speed to create the flow. Our plays were not being broken up at the blueline. And by not having our plays broken up at the blueline, we weren't creating three-on-twos and two-on-ones the other way."

So the coaches finally got it through the players' thick skulls, huh?

Not so fast, suggested a couple of prime-time players. It wasn't that the players finally listened, but that finally they had a game plan worth listening to.

"Last year in the playoffs they wanted us to play outside to inside," said Gretzky. "This time we played inside to outside. When you go in from the outside, it's tougher to get through to the net. Tonight, we sent people through the middle. The point is where we were dumping the puck in *from*. We had a different game plan tonight than we did last year. Our coaches studied how other clubs succeeded against Calgary. We put that in our game plan tonight."

Coffey made the same point.

"Instead of dumping it in, we had a *purpose*," he said.

Neither the players nor the coaches were interested in continuing the controversy. Finally, they were on the same page.

But as soon as they got there, the league called time out and the Oilers stars headed for Quebec City for Rendez-Vous, a short series against the Soviets replacing the annual NHL All-Star game. Gretzky was named the NHL's MVP in the event. But the series took plenty out of the participants and when they resumed the NHL schedule with a tough road trip, Gretzky was held without a point in back-to-back games for the first time since October of 1980.

They hit Scottsdale, Arizona, for a little rest and relaxation and a golf game with ex-president Gerald Ford at the Troon Golf Club.

"I've never seen Gretz play a worse game," said Sather of a 5-2 loss in Washington that capped the first three-game losing streak of the season for the team. "But what do you expect? Those were two emotional games against the Soviets. He's only human."

The Oilers won their next seven straight. But they couldn't prevent change. Sather made two more moves.

The first, during the stop in Scottsdale, was to announce that Jaroslav Pouzar was returning to the team.

"I don't come back for money," said the Czech who had been playing in Germany. "I want to help win the Stanley Cup.

"When I left everybody was happy and smiling," said the popular Pouzar of the celebrations after the Oilers won their second straight Stanley Cup. "I came back to visit this summer and saw people on the streets not smiling. Everybody was sad. I came back for a visit and found this team very different. I'd like to help win the Stanley Cup back."

Sather's next move was a real eyebrow-raiser. He obtained Kent Nilsson from Minnesota for a draft choice that hinged on how Edmonton did in the playoffs. And Calgary, where he'd previously played, partially as the Magic Man and partially as one Calgary columnist referred to him as "a cancer," would be paying part of his salary, as Calgary had when he went to the North Stars.

Gretzky was excited.

"He's a great asset. He's the purest, most talented player in the league. Great player. Great shot."

In Minnesota, GM Lou Nanne explained the trade.

"What do I have to lose? My coach won't play him."

When Nilsson left Calgary, GM Cliff Fletcher said there was no debate.

"It was unanimous. Everybody agreed we'd be better off without him.

It became so frustrating because of his inconsistent play. He's an enigma. He's one of the most skilled players I've ever watched. I'm sure Glen Sather took him for the short term. Who knows? Put him on the same team with Gretzky and on the same line as Mark Messier and Glenn Anderson. Who knows? No one has ever questioned his talent. He might be a major contributor to the Oilers the rest of the way."

Reijo Ruotsalainen.

The best line came from assistant coach Ted Green.

"He's like the little girl with the curl. When he's good, he's very, very good. When he's bad ... you have to send out a missing person's report."

Nilsson was delighted with the deal.

"It's nice to be traded to the best team. If I win a Stanley Cup that will be the highlight of my career."

Gretzky invited him to live with him. And when he checked into the Oilers dressing room, he found he'd been placed in the stall beside Messier. Good cop, bad cop.

No sooner had Nilsson checked in than Reijo Ruotsalainen arrived to tell Edmonton fans to please call him Rexi.

"People can pronounce Rexi," he said.

Ruotsalainen arrived in Edmonton after 18 hours flying time from Bern and said his last month had been a long month in the Swiss league and said that was mostly thanks to the columnist.

The quotes got back. A month earlier I had visited him in Bern and he'd said a few things. Like: "I felt like I wasted a year of my career."

And: "This is not professional. You have to bring your own tape for your stick and that's just a little thing. You can't pass the puck to your defensive partner without worrying it will end up in your own net."

And: "Come over here when you are 30. Don't come earlier."

Ruotsalainen was happy to escape.

"There was a little trouble with the newspapers," he said.

Ruotsalainen's arrival coincided with the departure of Lee Fogolin and Mark Napier to Buffalo in exchange for Normand Lacombe, Wayne Van Dorp and a draft pick.

Watching Fogolin pack his bags and leave was tough enough for everybody, but particularly tough for Lowe. Fogolin was his original defence partner and roommate.

"I roomed with him after our very first game in Chicago. After the game we went back to the hotel and ordered room service. He asked me if I was going to phone my mom. I asked why. He said, 'Well, you scored your first goal.' I phoned her. It was just little things like that. He weaned me. When I heard he was traded, eight years passed before my eyes in a couple of minutes. Of all the guys who have ever gone it was the toughest to see

him go. From the first day of training camp in '79 he took me aside and kind of kept a special eye on me – on and off the ice."

When the big moves had all been made, Sather had achieved the desired effect.

"I don't think I've ever felt this team as excited as we've been the last few days," said Gretzky. "There was a real excitement when Kent and Rexi showed up. It's such a positive feeling here. I don't think I've ever felt it this excited."

The Oilers would have skated merrily, merrily into the playoffs except for ... well, Calgary. Three of their final 10 games were against the Flames. Loss. Loss. Tie.

And in one of the losses in the Saddledome, was that who we thought it was who scored the winning goal?

"Yes, it was," confirmed Harry Neale when he emerged from watching the replays in the TV booth.

Steve Smith. Own goal again.

"He's getting better, though. He's gone from his stick to his foot," laughed Neale.

The Calgary fans wanted playoff deja vu and got it. The Calgary crowd was already dressed in their "sea of red" playoff get-ups. And some of the fans were wearing $15 T-shirts with headlines from the previous spring, "What A Flaming Night" and "Edmonton Dies By Own Hand" and "Calgary Reigns On Oilers Parade."

When the Oilers' longest season ended it was, however, another unqualified success. The Oilers again finished first overall with 106 points, six more than Philadelphia. The Oilers won 50 and lost 24.

Gretzky, while he didn't finish strong (one goal in his last eight games), won his seventh Art Ross and eighth straight Hart trophy as he became the fourth NHLer ever to hit 1,500 points, ending up with 62 goals and 121 assists for 183 points. Kurri enjoyed a 54-goal season and finished second with 108 points, one more than Messier and Mario Lemieux. Coffey missed a quarter of the season due to injury.

But none of the numbers meant much to the team this time around.

Finally it was over.

"This season really dragged on," said Messier. "This year, more than any other, seemed to go on forever. We didn't care as much about finishing first and accomplishing a lot of things that used to be important to us. The playoffs are where it's at. We never knew it as much as we knew it this year."

Sather agreed.

"It's been a long, tough season," said the boss, adding the Oilers deserved a lot more credit for finishing first overall than they were accorded. "For a lot of reasons it was very difficult. A lot of it came back to last year and the defeat. We made some changes and traded away some veterans who had meant a lot to the club in the past and that wasn't easy on anybody. And Rendez-Vous '87 kicked the hell out of us. We just started recovering. I'm far more anxious to get going in these playoffs than ever. I think the team is like that, too."

All eyes were on the prize. But

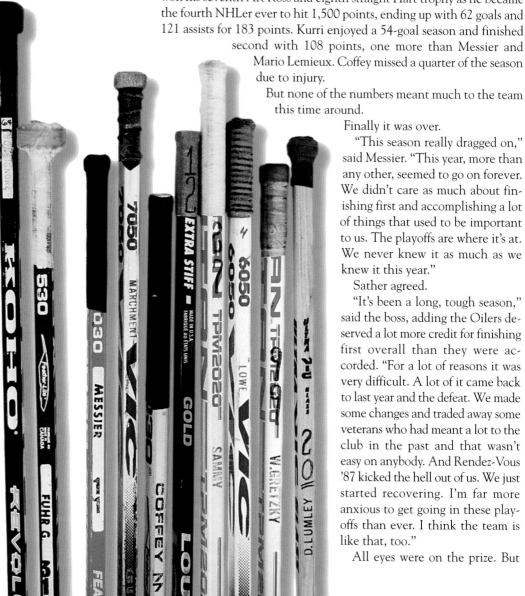

Coach and GM Glen Sather works with goaltenders Andy Moog, left, and Grant Fuhr in April, during a 1987 practice.

there were other eyes on the same prize now. Suddenly the Smythe Division had become the toughest division in hockey. The first question wasn't whether the Oilers would win another Stanley Cup but if they could put another banner up on the ceiling of the Coliseum where there were three Smythe Division, three Campbell Conference and two Stanley Cup championship banners.

"We've got something to prove and just about everything we have to prove is wrapped up in that next banner," said Grant Fuhr.

Unlike previous playoffs, the Oilers weren't being picked to win by everybody this time around. In fact ...

I took a pre-playoff poll.

"I've covered seven of the eight games they played against Calgary for TV and I can't see any reason why Calgary will lose to them," said Harry Neale. "Edmonton has now lost its aura of invincibility. I don't think Edmonton will win the Stanley Cup."

John Davidson and Dave Hodge agreed.

But Don Cherry went the other way.

"I can't see them losing. Not again. They're the best team. I can't believe it. Every open-line radio show I dial into all I hear is Calgary, Philadelphia, Montreal . . . like everybody is ignoring Edmonton this year and that's ridiculous. If you pick a team and I pick a team and I get to pick first, I'm gonna pick Edmonton!"

Grapes might have changed his mind after Game 1 of the Oilers' opening-round series against the L.A. Kings. After the longest season waiting to get to the real season – they no-showed. The were woeful. Lost 5-2. The Oilers, who had swept four straight best-of-five series since their Miracle On Manchester opening series, had no memorable explanations. But this was the year the NHL made all playoff series best-of-seven, so the panic level was minimal.

They did their talking in Game 2 as they went

from awful to awesome. They went from playing one of their most pathetic home playoff games to one in which 20 NHL and club records were set. In fact, the Oilers had six more records this night than Los Angeles had shots on goal as they folded, spindled and mutilated the Kings to the count of 13-3.

"Still The One."

Thirteen times they played the Oilers' playoff theme song that night. After every Oilers goal.

"Still the one. Still the one. We're still having fun. And we're still the one."

How could they play as terrible as they did in Game 1 and as terrific as they did in Game 2?

"I wish I could tell you," said Randy Gregg. "I'm sure the coaches wish they could tell you, too."

One of the records, surprise, surprise, belonged to Gretzky. When he set up Kurri for the Oilers' first goal it was his 177th playoff point and broke Jean Beliveau's all-time playoff points record. The 13 goals broke the 1944 Montreal Canadiens' mark of 11 which the Oilers tied in '85. Kurri had four goals and an assist. Gretzky's count was one goal and six assists. Messier had two goals and two assists, including his eighth shorthanded goal to tie a playoff record. But the most interesting stat was that Moog, replacing Game 1 starter Fuhr, could have made just two saves and the Oilers still would have won.

Moog didn't have much work but he hoped the start would get him back in goal for Game 3. And he hoped that maybe this would be his year to be the Oilers' Stanley Cup stopper. He did get the start in the next one but he was shaky, making a 6-5 Oilers win a lot closer than the play as Edmonton outshot L.A. 35-23.

"We won the hockey game, that's all that counts," said Sather, who made it clear he was switching back to Fuhr for Game 4.

It was the last game Andy Moog played as an Edmonton Oiler.

The Oilers mob forward Jari Kurri after his overtime goal beat the Philadelphia Flyers in Game 2 of the 1987 Stanley Cup final.

Between games Gregg and Coffey arrived at the rink early to ride the exercise bike. To get to the equipment they had to go through the Kings dressing room. When they did, they saw it with their own four eyes: Los Angeles had a hit list on their dressing-room wall.

"It's a damned hit list, all right," said Sather. "Right up on their wall. They can call it anything they want to call it. But it's a hit list. Can you believe that? Mike Murphy ... one of the biggest pansies ever to play the game. And he has a hit list? Jari Kurri's name is there. So is Wayne Gretzky's. And Rexi Ruotsalainen. And Paul Coffey."

No. 1 on their hit parade, according to the hit list, was Kurri.

"What they are doing is by design," said Muckler. "No question about it. They're running Wayne. But more so Jari. They don't want to start

World War III so they are going more at Jari than at Wayne."

Kurri had six goals in the first three games. Other than Steve Smith, it was Coffey and Kurri who took the most heat for what had happened against Calgary the year before. And Kurri said he was determined to prove he was made of the right stuff, no matter if he was at the top of a hit list or one of the points on Badger Bob Johnson's seven-point plan for beating the Oilers.

"Last year I wasn't playing my own game. I was worried about those guys and what they were doing to me," said Kurri. "This year I'm trying to play so that the more whacks I get, the more it gets me going. I'm more hungry now. I know I have to pay the price. I don't know that I'm trying to show that I have more guts. I'm just trying to show I learned a lot last year."

Game 4 belonged to Gretzky with a goal and four assists in a 6-3 win in an afternoon game to take a 3-1 lead in the series. When it was over, the team quickly showered and headed for the Melody Bar and Grill so they could watch the Flames and Jets on a big-screen TV. And they weren't cheering for the Flames, who they'd only managed to beat once in eight games during the season.

"With our track record against Calgary, we'd rather play Winnipeg," admitted Gretzky.

Back home, the Oilers put the Kings away as Anderson scored the series-winning goal in a 5-4 game.

The Oilers got their wish. The Jets upset the Flames.

"Edmonton just won the Stanley Cup," declared Calgary GM Cliff Fletcher.

There was no reason to believe the Oilers wouldn't beat the Jets in the series. If the Oilers couldn't beat Calgary, they were having no trouble at all with Winnipeg. And the Jets went into the series 0-10 against the Oilers in the playoffs.

For openers the Jets gave them trouble, taking Game 1 into overtime where Sudden Death Glenn did it again. Then Anderson, for the third time in the last four consecutive Oilers' OT playoff wins, fired the winner. And he didn't waste any time. Thirty-six seconds.

"He's a money man," said Gretzky after the 3-2 win. "He's something else under pressure."

In Game 2, Dave Hunter and trade-deadline acquisition Moe Lemay scored the big goals in a 5-3 win but it was Messier, winning an incredible 21 of 25 faceoffs, who was the story.

The series shifted to Winnipeg and when Grant Fuhr skated onto the ice he thought he was in the middle of a Ku Klux Klan convention. It was his first look at a Winnipeg Whiteout.

"They should have worn black," observed the Oilers goalie. "I couldn't believe how easy the puck was to see in here with everybody dressed in white. Seriously! It really brightened the place up. Normally it's a pretty dark building. But all those white shirts, all the light reflected off all the white. It was easier to pick the puck out of it. I'm not kidding. I *like* white."

The Whiteout was a 5-2 wipeout and Fuhr was the first star as the Jets outshot the Oilers 37-25.

"Grant was back to his old self – bulletproof," said owner Pocklington, a man quite qualified to speak on the subject, having stopped a bullet himself when a gunman tried to hold him hostage in his Edmonton home.

"They say Fuhr was playing bad," said Winnipeg assistant coach Billy Sutherland. "I'd hate to see him when he was playing good."

It was Fuhr again to leave the Jets 0-14 vs. the Oilers in NHL postseason play.

"We knew Grant would get better. We knew sooner or later Grant

would be Grant," said Gretzky after their 4-2 win in Game 4.

The Oilers had achieved their short-term goal. The bells could ring out and another Smythe Division banner would fly.

"We mentioned that banner before the game," said Lowe. "It was tough getting another one up there."

Looking up, in Edmonton, meant eyeballing those banners. In Detroit, you looked up for flying octopuses.

Playing Detroit in a Stanley Cup playoff series was a new deal for the Oilers and, considering his idol was Gordie Howe, Gretzky's education was sadly lacking when it came to the Red Wings.

"We're gonna ogle octopus. We're going to see squid," he was informed.

One fan's explanation for the real reason behind the Flyers' defeat.

"You're kidding," he said. "I never heard of that. *Real* octopuses?"

"Octopi, Wayne. Flying octopi!"

No. 99 looked almost frightened.

"How many?"

"One night they threw 55 of 'em," said Detroit sportswriting legend Joe Falls, who explained that back in the Original Six days of the NHL you needed eight wins to capture a Stanley Cup, and an octopus has eight legs, and somebody threw one on the ice to deliver the message that the Wings would win eight straight. Or something like that.

"To tell you the truth, these octopi aren't like the ones in the old days," Falls told Gretzky. "They look undernourished. When the old octopi hit the ice there was a jelly-like effect. Let's be honest. These are *expansion* octopi."

"When do they throw them?" asked No. 99. "During the play?"

"No, after Detroit goals."

"Aren't they full of ink?" asked Fuhr.

"Yup, just like a sportswriter," he was told.

The Oilers wouldn't see any octopi until Game 3 in Detroit but the Red Wings decided to play the Oilers like octopi in Edmonton, wrapping their arms around them at every opportunity. And Game 1 was "the Night of the Living Dead Things," Detroit snapping an Oilers' 13-game winning streak in games involving the two teams with a 3-1 victory.

"Detroit outplayed us and beat us," said Sather. "You sit around and do nothing for eight days but practice, this is what happens."

The Oilers adjusted to the clutch-and-grab game and won Game 2 by a 4-1 count.

"We had to prove to the Red Wings that if we have to, we can be as patient and as disciplined as they are," said Lowe.

Marty McSorley and Craig MacTavish were the heroes of Game 3 in Detroit as the Oilers scored two and held the Wings to one octopus opportunity. And it was Krushelnyski with the winner in a 3-2 Edmonton win in Game 3. You get the picture. In Detroit it was Grant and the Grinders. The octopi were not a factor.

Philadelphia netminder Ron Hextall was the centre of controversy after this chop against Edmonton's Kent Nilsson in the final series.

It was over when the Oilers won 6-3 back in Edmonton to run up another banner and make it to the Stanley Cup for the fourth time in five years. It really hadn't been much of a series. The Red Wings had managed to take Gretzky away – he didn't get a goal in the series and only had three so far in the playoffs. And Detroit forced Kurri, Coffey, Nilsson and Anderson to have quiet series. But when it was over and Wings coach Jacques Demers added everything up, he knew which Oiler, with the possible exception of Fuhr, meant the most to Edmonton in the series.

"Just too much Mark Messier," he said.

Messier wasn't much interested in any gee-whiz interviews after the game.

"I just want to win. Last year was a big disappointment and I don't think we should be going overboard about what we've done yet just because we're back in the Stanley Cup final. We haven't accomplished anything yet. We haven't done what we've come to do."

Nilsson, who scored the fifth and sixth goals after Messier had scored the tying and winning goals, had been introduced to Messier's playoff pre-game glare a few times now.

"He just looks at you," he marvelled. "I'll tell you, he has a helluva look. One of those looks at you and you know you better get going. He's

the guy who gets everybody going."

As the hundreds of sports reporters headed for Edmonton and a final that would match the Oilers and Mike Keenan's Philadelphia Flyers again, Ron Hextall was the story.

"We would not be here without Ron Hextall," said Flyers GM Bobby Clarke. "We wouldn't even be close without him."

Hextall wasn't just building up frequent Flyer first-star awards in the playoffs, he was building up frequent-flyer airline points. Even if the Flyers were swept in this series, they'd set a record for most playoff games played, single season, with 24. And if the series went seven, they'd shatter it with one less than the maximum.

Hextall said he was going to be calm, cool and collected in goal for Game 1 of the final against the Oilers – at least compared to the way he was in Game 1 of the season opener against the same squad.

"That was tougher, no doubt about it," said the rookie. "Unless there's a seventh game in this series. That might be worse."

If Keenan had guts to throw rookie Hextall in the nets against the NHL's all-time scoring machine, what about Sather starting Kelly Buchberger for his first-ever Oiler game in Game 1 of the Stanley Cup final?

Buchberger had been to a training camp two years earlier – and he

Edmonton fans never tired of the sight of Oilers captain Wayne Gretzky carrying the Stanley Cup.

was still having nightmares about that.

His roomie was MacTavish.

"Where did you play last year?" asked MacTavish when the two checked in to their room.

"Moose Jaw," said Buchberger.

Wanting to appear just as friendly as MacTavish, Buchberger returned the question.

"Where did you spend last year?"

Ouch. It was not, first of all, a question you asked a five-year NHL veteran. And it was definitely not one you asked a guy who had just spent the previous year in jail for vehicular homicide.

"I didn't know Craig. I've never been so embarrassed in my life," Buchberger told the story on himself after he played a great game and helped the Oilers win the opener 4-2.

The 21-year-old native of Langenberg, Sask., was one of those warm, fuzzy, Stanley Cup dream-come-true stories.

Nervous?

"Let's put it this way," said Muckler. "If he were a horse, we would have had to scratch him."

Ron Low, who would one day become coach and name Buchberger his captain, will never forget the day.

"Bucky was so nervous that when guys started drifting into the dressing room at 4 p.m., the first thing they saw was Kelly sitting at his stall already dressed for the game."

He didn't even phone home.

"I figured they'd watch the game," said Buchberger. "I didn't think they'd be going out to a movie."

He was right. Bill and Linda Buchberger didn't go to a movie.

"We were over at my cousin's house. We had a big barbecue. About 40 people. We turned on the TV and lots of guys were watching the introductions, when suddenly everybody started hooting and hollering. I tell you, we had one big, happy Buchberger family," said his dad.

OK. Buchberger didn't win the game by himself.

"The guy for us was Gretzky," said Sather in the interview room. "Wayne showed us why he is the greatest player in the world. There was pressure mounting on him. He heard so much conversation about only scoring three goals in the playoffs."

Gretzky, held to two shots on goal during the Detroit series, conceded the fact.

"I thought I had forgotten where the net was," he said.

The Oilers put another Stanley Cup sticker on the dressing-room door in Game 2 and this time it was Kurri who was the hero with the win-

Streamers fill the air at Northlands Coliseum as the Edmonton Oilers close in on another Stanley Cup championship for the City of Champions.

ner at 6:50 of overtime.

"Until tonight my biggest goal was in the final of the world junior against the Soviet Union," said Kurri. "It was overtime. The fifth period of the game. It was Finland's first-ever medal. Until now that was my biggest goal. But now this is the biggest goal of my life."

The Flyers were 9-0 going into the third period with a lead in the playoffs and 45-1-4 with that scenario during the season, but Anderson scored the only goal of the third period to give Kurri the chance to be a hero and move the Oilers to within two wins of three Stanley Cups in four years.

But, as I reported the next morning, it ain't over until the dead lady sings.

In a macabre move, the Flyers exhumed Kate Smith for Game 3.

Alive, the old gal was 55-9-2 singing *God Bless America* before key Flyer games. Near death, she was 1-0 on Bobby Clarke's retirement night. And this would make her 2-0 after death (on video) as the inspired Flyers came back from the dead with a 5-3 win.

Class act: Captain Wayne Gretzky presents hockey's most coveted Cup to Oilers defenceman Steve Smith.

"They're sick here," said Oilers exec Bob McCammon, a former Flyers coach and GM. "It's like New York."

The Oilers were up 2-0 in the series and 3-0 in the game. It was over. But two dumb penalties, two fluke goals and ...

"I wouldn't say we were dead. But we were pretty close to the grave, weren't we?" said Rick Tocchet.

No problem. The Oilers beat Kate Smith and the Flyers in Game 4 by a 4-1 score.

"Finally all growed up?" I asked Muckler after the Game 4 win.

"I think so," said the co-coach. "I couldn't say that last year. Gawd, no."

The team may or may not have been "all growed up." But the town wasn't.

In a move you'd expect from a town that had never won anything before, Edmonton's mayor announced the parade route prior to Game 5!

"You shouldn't plan a parade for the next day when the series isn't over yet," said Tocchet. "Of course, that gave us extra motivation. It gets your dander up. It gives you some extra drive. We wanted to rain on their parade."

The only question was exactly when the Flyers got the parade news. The Oilers led the game 3-0. And then blew it!

"We got caught up in the environment," said Muckler. "We were going to blow them out and that's all there was to it."

"That Stanley Cup was hanging in the middle of the building and everybody saw it and everybody was too anxious," explained Sather.

Back to Philly. Up 2-0 again. And they lost again, 3-2. Who wrote this script?

"If you would have told me we'd come back three times from at least two-goal deficits, I'd have said you were crazy," said Hextall, who was simply brilliant as he had been all series.

There was no sense looking back. What was ahead was 60 minutes for all the marbles. And not just for a series and a season, but for being an all-time team.

When you're a kid playing on the pond, it's always Game 7 of the Stanley Cup final. But when you're a kid there are no historians perched around the pond ready to write against your name after one game. Not necessarily fair, but it's the way the world works.

Lose, especially after gassing games with 2-0, 3-0 and 2-0 leads after a 2-0 and 3-1 series lead, and the Oilers knew their mental makeup would be questioned. They'd go down in history as a talented team that couldn't make talent trump to become an all-time team.

Win, and so what if they blew a chance to become a five-in-a-row team like the Montreal Canadiens or a four-in-a-row team like the New York Islanders? They would be like the '45-oops-1947-'48-'49-oops-1951-Toronto Maple Leafs or the 1950-oops-'52-oops-1954-'55 Detroit Red Wings or the 1965-'66-oops-1968-'69-oops-'71-oops-'73 Montreal Canadiens, dynasties all.

Game 7 was Oilers playoff game No. 101. They'd won 69 and lost 31. They were going for their 17th series win against five series losses.

They won!

Messier, Kurri and Anderson scored as the Oilers won it 3-1, outshooting the Flyers 43-20 to take the Stanley Cup but not the Conn Smythe, which Hextall lugged off the ice to the objection of nobody.

The Oilers Stanley Cup dressing room was a scene to behold.

A year and a month after his 23rd birthday, Steve Smith was crying again.

"I was in tears last year and I'm in tears again this year. This time they're tears of joy," he said.

"This is the greatest," said Kurri, who scored the Cup-winning goal. "We won the Stanley Cup in the seventh game. You can't compare the other two to this one. We'll remember this one the most."

Huddy made a point as he poured champagne.

"This one feels better because we had to work harder to get it and because it says so much more about us. We can control our emotions. We can play with patience. We can play defensive. We can play with discipline."

Sather said winning it was one thing.

"It was a classic," he said. "I'd always said the Team Canada win over the Russians was the best game in which I'd ever been involved, but right now I think this is the best. I saw Kent Nilsson with tears in his eyes on the bench."

Randy Gregg said it was seventh heaven.

"The first one was so exciting because everybody was so young and we'd never done it before. The second one was so satisfying because we did it two years in a row. But this one ... in the seventh game ... after what happened last year ..."

The freeze-frame moment came when the Oilers were still on the ice and Gretzky had the Cup over his head. As the captain began to lower it, he carried it over and handed it to Steve Smith to carry first.

It would go down as one of the classiest acts in the history of sport.

Chapter 11
Stanley Had Fun In Edmonton

Stanley had a rough night after the Oilers won him for the third time. They poured champagne out of him in the dressing room. Then beer. The first-time players posed with him for picture after picture. From there Stanley went to the Silver Slipper for a private team party. Then to Barry T's nightclub. Then to several other spots. Rough night. But not as rough as some of the players. The Oilers had planned a team picture with Stanley for 4 p.m. the next day. Only half the players showed. It had to be rescheduled for the next day, following the parade.

'You think it's easy running a hockey team?'
— GM/coach Glen Sather

"You think it's easy running a hockey team?" asked GM/coach Glen Sather, shaking his head at Mark Messier who walked in wearing sunglasses – still at the peak of the party which for some of the others had died about daybreak.

There was a tradition with the Oilers that each player won the right to have Stanley for a day. Messier, told that the team picture was off, decided to claim Day 1. He took Stanley across the street to the Forum Inn and Stanley went straight on stage with a stripper.

Stanley definitely had more fun in Edmonton.

Grant Fuhr asked, when Messier was done having fun, if he could take Stanley for a round of golf.

Kent Nilsson had a better idea.

"I'd like to take it for a day and go down to Calgary and have my own parade down there," he said.

Craig Muni said he wanted to take a bath with it.

And Kelly Buchberger wondered if it would be OK if he took it out of province, all the way to Langenberg, Sask.

Thanks to the Oilers, Stanley visited places he'd never been before ... including the strippers' stage at the Forum Inn. Opposite: Oilers trainer Ken Lowe catches a few winks on a plane with the Cup by his side.

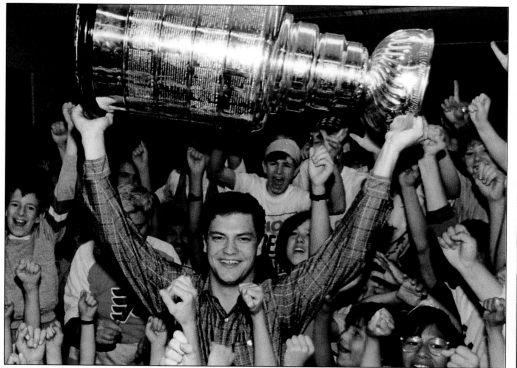

"If I could have it for a day, everybody in Langenberg (population 700) would drink from it."

They voted Buchberger his day in Saskatchewan. And Bucky made damned sure just about everybody in Langenberg *did* drink from it.

"There never was a city where Stanley met so many people and spent so much time with the players," said Kevin Lowe. "No question, Stanley had more fun in Edmonton."

Lowe and Messier began the tradition when they took Stanley into the Bruin Inn in St. Albert, the Edmonton suburb where Messier had grown up. The young Oilers stars wanted to share the Cup with their fans. They wanted everybody to be able to see the Cup, touch it, and, yes, even sip champagne (although most often it would be beer) from the oldest trophy in North American pro sport. A lot of it had to do with the reality that for most of the people who would come in contact with the team, Lord Stanley's famous silverware was something they never expected to see, live and in person, much less in Edmonton.

And to drink from it ...

It was a dream sequence played over and over again all over town. The older fans would take a respectful sip out of it, sometimes even

Top left, Esa Tikkanen took the Cup to a local school; top right, Stanley helped Charlie Huddy celebrate his birthday in style; above, Mark Messier toured with the trophy in his home town of St. Albert.

of the fun Stanley had wasn't of the restricted adult variety.

The Stanley Cup served as a centrepiece at Randy Gregg's wedding after the Oilers won it the first year.

"I also took a walk with it one day," remembers Gregg. "That was great. I'd walk down the street and somebody would drive past and look at the Cup like they didn't believe what they were seeing. Then they'd get about two blocks away and all of a sudden they'd slam on the brakes and drive back, climb out of the car and ask if they could touch it."

But wherever Stanley was by day, you could usually find him at a watering hole at night. One year team photographer Bob Mummery was assigned to follow it around. "It ended up in damned near every bar in Edmonton and a few outside Edmonton. Everybody took it into their favourite bar. Every Joe in town got a chance to have a drink out of it. The party went on for two weeks. Those two weeks of my life are lost forever. I can barely remember them."

"We left the Cup in a couple of places," remembered Pat Hughes. "It was Sparky's job to make sure the Cup got back to where it needed to be. I know he had to put it back together once."

with a tear in their eye or a lump in their throat. And to look in the eyes of the kids who had a chance to hoist Stanley over their heads, just like their heroes had done after they'd won the Cup, was unforgettable. There must be more pictures of more regular people with the Stanley Cup in Edmonton rumpus rooms than anywhere else on earth.

"Sharing it with the people was half the fun of winning it," said Kevin McClelland.

The Oilers took the Cup to local pubs, to schools and, at Glenn Anderson's insistence, to Northlands Park racetrack. And, of course, there was Stanley's appearance on stage at the strip joint, where an enterprising *Sun* photographer found himself shooting the treasured trophy. But most

Sparky is Lyle Kulchisky, the Oilers longtime equipment man.

"One morning the boys brought Stanley in after a really hard run the night before and Stanley was in two pieces," remembers Sparky. "I had to get Stanley to a noon-hour function downtown and I didn't know what to do. So I took it to the Freedom Ford body shop. They fixed Stanley as good as new, just in time to make it for the function."

The team called Kulchisky, an Oiler NHL Day Oner, "the Keeper of the Cup."

"Being the Keeper of the Cup is about as good as it gets," he said. "And I got to do it five times so far. Each time was greater than the time before. It never got old watching the look on people's faces. Whether it was young kids at a school or old-timers at a function, you could see in their faces how the Stanley Cup was something almost sacred."

The Oilers and the CFL Eskimos organized a joint picture-taking session at 60,000-seat Commonwealth Stadium where regular fans lined up for hours to have their pictures taken with the Stanley Cup and the Grey Cup, won in the same season.

The Oilers were big Eskimo fans. The day the Eskimos beat the Toronto Argos in the 1987 Grey Cup game – which arguably was the greatest Grey Cup game ever played – Messier and Gretzky came up to *Sun* scribe Dick Chubey before the Oilers game in Buffalo and asked if he would do the team a favour. Chubes, in those days, wore a fedora everywhere but to bed. The players knew there was a TV in the Buffalo press box that would get CBC from the other side of the border. They worked out a communications system involving Chubes' chapeau. If the players looked up at the press box and his hat was on, the Eskimos were winning. If they looked up and his hat was off, they were losing. Chubes' hat was on and off so many times that day, people in the press box were looking at him like he was some sort of weirdo. But the hockey players followed the game that way from start to finish.

Several Oilers and Eskimos have keeper pictures of each other with both the Grey Cup and Stanley Cup from that season.

"The Oilers always had the attitude that the Stanley Cup belonged to the fans," said Glen Sather. "The league developed the idea that the Cup should be worshipped."

The NHL came to decide that Stanley shouldn't be having such a good time. By law, now, Stanley is much more stuffy. What the league never understood was that nowhere was he worshipped more than in Edmonton. Despite his, er, affair with the stripper. Despite the isolated incidents. Edmonton is the heartland of Canadian hockey and the Oilers, when they found out how hard you had to work for the Cup, decided they'd play just as hard with Stanley after they'd won the pleasure of his company.

This wasn't just a team that could play hockey. This team could *play*.

The fun-loving Oilers led the league in good times.

Oh, it backfired a few times in the beginning. For example, the Oilers' last trip of the regular season the year of the Miracle On Manchester – when they blew a 5-0 lead in Los Angeles and lost the playoff series – was to Los Angeles. And the good times were really rolling on that trip.

"I wouldn't trade this for anything," said Dave Lumley at the time. "We're the cockiest, most arrogant, fun-loving bunch of bananas in the league. We're

Edmonton police officer Bryan Bolanger had his moment with the Cup.

having the time of our lives."

The team had just scored a big win over the Kings the night after several players had attended a Hollywood party in the company of such beautiful people as Morgan Fairchild, the hot Hollywood sex symbol of the moment, Priscilla Barnes of the popular TV show *Three's Company* and TV hosts Mike Douglas and Alan Thicke.

"I'm sitting in the penalty box tonight," said Lumley, who had made several trips to that location, "and I couldn't keep my eyes off Morgan Fairchild. I'm sitting there staring at her, paying no attention at all to the game. Half the guys on the bench are staring at her all night. And I'm sitting there thinking, 'This is unreal.' She's here because guys on this team got her tickets."

A player from any other team wouldn't sit down in the dressing room and tell a sports columnist the likes of myself, like Lumley eventually did, that maybe, just maybe, he might have taken a couple of penalties just so he could sit in the penalty box and look at Ms. Fairchild.

Of course I quoted him.

"This is unreal," said Messier in that same dressing room. "I had the puck on one shift tonight and we were having so much fun that I couldn't help myself when I skated past the bench. I was laughing.

"I don't know how to explain it. But what other club in pro sport would come back from a 20-day road trip, after seeing each other's faces every day, and make plans for as soon as we landed back in Edmonton to go out and have a few beers together?"

Also in the stands that night were M*A*S*H stars Mike Farrell and Jamie Farr. They'd become regular Oiler fans.

The Oilers were regular visitors to the set of the No. 1 TV sitcom in those days. Farr, in particular, was a big fan who loved to go on radio between periods with Rod Phillips on the Oilers broadcasts and loved inviting the team over to the set.

On one of those visits, Messier got off the bus at the gates of 20th Century-Fox and stood on the street. "I want to get discovered," he explained.

Gretzky got discovered.

The Young And The Restless.

He became a soap opera star. Well, OK, to say he starred is a stretch. *Edmonton Sun* TV writer Lucinda Chodan's review of his appearance on the show was not particularly positive.

"He shoots! He misses!" was her first paragraph.

Gretzky's cameo featured him

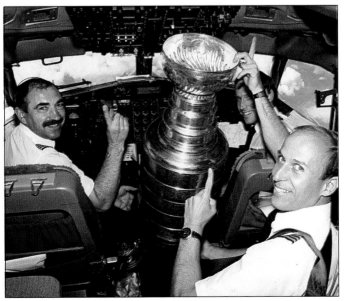
Even the airline pilots got to spend some quality time with Stanley.

being introduced as "the man from our Edmonton operation."

Gretzky leered unconvincingly at his leading lady, Nikki, and winked.

"Call me Wayne, everybody does."

It was his one and only line.

A few other Oilers managed a little more airtime than that. CBC-TV aired a special half-hour show titled *Dr. Gregg and Mr. Semenko*. And Lowe accepted an offer from CBC Radio to be a radio actor. He even spent part of a summer working at *The Edmonton Sun*. Lowe spent two weeks in the promotions department, a week in production and a few days in advertising. He also contributed a weekly column in the sports section for a couple of seasons.

And the entire team starred in an 85-minute video titled *Boys On The Bus*, which turned into a two-year project after Steve Smith scored on his own net and director Bob McKeown decided to shoot for another year. Lowe, who narrated the excellent video (which is even more fun to watch all these years later), gave it a rave review in his *Sun* column after the premiere at Edmonton's Citadel Theatre.

"The detour," he wrote of the extra year of filming, "made it even better."

"Uniquely realistic," he said in his review.

• • •

A wise man once said that he who collects the most experiences in life wins.

The Oilers were real winners.

In their third season, the NHL all-star game was in Washington, D.C.

The players were invited to the White House to meet president Ronald Reagan and his old Hollywood pal, Bob Hope.

"I was in a fog all day," said Gretzky. "I couldn't believe it was me sitting there at the White House with them. Even just being in the White House was a big thrill."

Fuhr, Messier and Coffey played in the all-star game that year, too, and Fuhr managed to come up with his best (and only) one-liner of the season when he remarked about meeting president Reagan: "I was even more stuck for words than I usually am."

Fuhr was more nervous than for a game.

"The worst thing was to figure out something to say to him. I just said 'hi.' That's all I could think of to say to him."

Messier offered his impressions.

"Nice lunch," he said. "The plates had so much gold in them, I could barely lift one."

Gretzky, who by that point was getting used to rubbing shoulders with the rich and famous, wasn't at ease in that situation. He

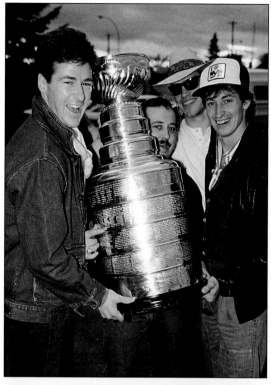

Top: Kevin Lowe, Mark Messier and Wayne Gretzky made sure Stanley got around during his visits to Edmonton. Bottom: On the links, Wayne Gretzky seems in awe of a shot by Sun sports writer Dick Chubey.

was glad that Reagan, once a play-by-play sports announcer, had invited Gordie Howe along, too.

Howe said he was invited so Reagan would have somebody his own age there to relate to. It was the youngest average age of any NHL all-star game in history, with 25 first-time players.

"He told me his dad took him to watch me play when he was a kid," Howe laughed.

"I kept looking at Gordie and doing exactly what he was doing," said Gretzky.

"I told Wayne, 'Just pretend he's not there. Finish your meal. And don't look up,' " said Howe.

The Oilers became regulars, playing a yearly golf game at various famous courses – like Pebble Beach – with ex-president Gerald Ford.

Gretzky remembers the first time. He was paired with the president.

"Was I nervous?" gasped Gretzky after shooting a 93 at the luxurious Thunderbird Golf and Country Club in Palm Springs. "I knew I was in trouble when I went triple, triple, triple on the first three holes."

Golf was always big with the bunch. And then there was Grant Fuhr, who would play 36 holes on the day off between games in the playoffs.

"We feel fortunate we had Grant in goal tonight," said Sather after one stand-on-his-head Stanley Cup performance. "Grant had a chance to golf 36 holes and was well-refreshed. He seems to play better after he plays a game of golf."

Fuhr agreed.

"But I play a worse game of golf after a game of goal," he laughed.

One year in Winnipeg, Fuhr played 18 holes at the St. Charles course before practice and 18 holes at Niakawa after practice.

"I don't think any goalie has ever played 36 holes of golf between games in the Stanley Cup playoffs," said Gretzky at the time. "I don't think anybody other than Grant ever will."

Fuhr didn't much mind who he was playing golf with as long as he was playing. But it was a regular Who's Who of celebrities when Gretzky, Lowe, Huddy, Fuhr and others held their own golf tournaments.

The Oilers were a team celebrities wanted to be around because celebrities are attracted to other celebrities. There always seemed to be a rock band visiting the Oilers dressing room.

It was amazing the number of invitations some of the players received.

One particular stop certainly qualified as a magic memory maker. Messier, Gretzky and Lowe ate dinner with Hugh Hefner at the Playboy Mansion.

Another time the whole team visited the

Alan Thicke, Wayne Gretzky and Ed Marinaro have their hands full with an Eskimo SUNshine girl.

home of Muhammad Ali. Everybody but Gretzky, who was unable to attend because of a commitment to sit at Kenny Rogers' table at the American Music Awards. But Gretzky had met the champ before – in New York, when he was travelling with Gordie Howe the summer he signed with the WHA.

"Best day of my life," said Gretzky back then. "I got to meet Ali, Bobby Hull and Debbie Boone all on the same day."

The Ali connection was Messier. His uncle, Larry Messier of Edmonton, was a key member of Ali's entourage in those days.

"I feel like I'm on a field trip," said Don Jackson as a cavalcade with the Oilers' entourage snaked

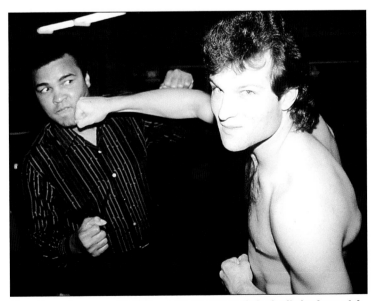

Dave Semenko spars with Muhammad Ali prior to their charity boxing match.

off Wilshire Boulevard, through the guarded gates into Ali's secluded neighbourhood in Beverly Hills where Mick Jagger and Jane Fonda were his neighbours.

The Oilers brought a special chocolate cake decorated with boxing gloves for the champ and also presented him with a stick autographed by members of the National Hockey League club.

"I love your company, I admire your style, but to give a gift so cheap, don't come back for a while," Ali the poet teased the team.

He asked if there were any "brothers" on the team. When Grant Fuhr stepped forward, he did the Ali shuffle for him.

"I've never had so many white people in my house at one time," cracked Ali.

One of them was Dave Semenko, who would become the answer to another trivia question (besides *who scored the last goal in the history of the WHA?*). He ended up being the last opponent to face former world heavyweight boxing champion Muhammad Ali.

"Ali is doing this, first of all, for charity," trumpeted Messier's uncle Larry, on the phone from Beverly Hills announcing the exhibition match. "And because he thinks, 'Who does this Dave Semenko think he is, beating everyone up?'"

The early reviews of the concept were not positive. It was viewed as a farce fight featuring Ali floating like the Titanic and stinging like a marshmallow. But it was news. And I ended up in Ali's house, alone with the champ, for a two-hour interview. When Ali hit town and made an appearance at West Edmonton Mall, it was a love-in. He did his disappearing Kleenex magic trick and introduced Joe Frazier in the crowd ("Oh, I'm sorry, lady, you look just like Joe Frazier.")

And he recited a poem he wrote for the Semenko fight:

Ali comes to meet Semenko
But Semenko starts to retreat
If Semenko goes back an inch further
He'll end up in a ringside seat

Ali swings with a left
Ali swings with a right
The punch knocks Semenko
Clean out of sight

Semenko is still rising
But the referee wears a frown
For he can't start counting
Until Semenko comes down

Semenko disappears from view
The crowd gets in a frantic
Radar has located him.
He's somewhere off the Atlantic!

Who would have thought
When they came to the fight
That they would have watched the launching
Of a Canadian satellite.

It was trash sport. But 5,500 people bought tickets. And they loved it.

When Gordon Ross introduced Semenko as "the uncrowned, yet undisputed heavyweight champion of the National Hockey League" and Butch Goring of the New York Islanders and Ron Low of the New Jersey Devils showed up as his cornermen, there was a tremendous roar of approval.

Ali and Semenko wore 20-ounce gloves and it wasn't even a good pillow fight. But it was fun. And Slammin' Sammy survived.

That was Semenko's nickname – Sammy. The Oilers didn't hand out great nicknames. Coff. Gretz. Mess. That was the best they could do. But they came up with a good one for Coffey's beard one day. They called it "the Western." Huddy explained that was "because of all the wide open spaces."

Coffey was a source of humour in his first years with the team.

Once he was fined by Sather for being late for practice. Sather couldn't believe Coffey was late. He couldn't possibly have written the practice time any bigger on the blackboard after the game.

"What's the last thing you do when you leave the dressing room?" asked Slats.

"I say goodbye to the guys," said Coffey, wondering why his coach would ask such a stupid question.

Coffey once showed up with five minutes left in a team function. The time of the event was listed on the invitation as "5 to 7." Coffey showed up at five minutes to seven.

Even the Stanley Cup needs a tuneup once in a while. Sparky Kulchisky took the trophy to Freedom Ford's autobody shop for refurbishing.

Coffey created a lot of humour intentionally, too.

There was the time in the Oilers' third season when Gretzky showed up and discovered he had a girl for a winger.

Mary Campbell, a 25-year-old Ottawa recreation department worker, was Gretzky's winger for 15 minutes in a workout. It was a special shoot for a CTV show titled *Thrill Of A Lifetime.*

"I've never skated with a girl before," said Gretzky.

"You've never done anything with a girl before," quipped Coffey.

In the Oilers' first NHL season Gretzky lived in a modest four-storey walk-up apartment on Edmonton's south side with the lovely Kevin Lowe.

It was Felix Lowe and Oscar Gretzky.

One day Gretzky came to the rink raving about something Lowe had cooked up the night before.

"He's amazing. Kevin cooks roasts, makes fondues, bakes lasagna. Last night he even cooked a huge cherry cheesecake for dessert."

Lowe looked at him.

"I can't be that good," he deadpanned. "I can't get him fattened up."

Practical jokes were big with this team.

On one trip, I was asleep on a plane and woke up with most of a can of shaving cream on my head. Or maybe that wasn't a practical joke. Maybe it was something I'd written.

One of the best adventures was the Great Snipe Hunt. It became a tradition with the team.

Noted hunter Dick Chubey (he's always in the woods hunting for golf balls) reported on the original Snipe Hunt in 1981:

"With an abundance of naive young men to choose from at Glen Sather's Day-care Centre, hunting the elusive snipe was on the itinerary for Sunday's day of R & R.

"Let us, shall we, venture to the wooded area outside of St. Albert.

"'Have we got everything we need?' inquired captain Lee Fogolin, who was checking to make sure that the nets were securely fastened to the blades of four hockey sticks. He also made sure there were whistles, duck calls, and even a flashlight as dusk does come early at this time of year.

"Those assigned to the nets were veteran Garry Unger, Kevin Lowe, Risto Siltanen and Andy Moog.

"Kurri, who was flamboyantly decked out in an orange fluorescent hunting suit, was obviously the chaps' choice as the Great Snipe Hunter. But just as the safari was about to begin, other potential candidates surfaced.

"'What's a snipe?' innocently asked centre Tom Roulston, a city boy who once worked as an all-night deejay in Winnipeg and therefore could be excused for his unfamiliarity towards rural wildlife.

" 'It's a small game bird about six inches high,' replied Unger, attempting to hold back his laughter.

" 'Is it like a pheasant?' asked Finnish defenceman Risto Siltanen. 'We have those in Finland, you know ...'

" 'Enough small talk,' interjected Fogolin. 'Let's go out and get us some snipes. After all, we're going to need them for the barbecue afterwards.'

"Quickly the scouts were dispatched ahead of the gallant hunters, who set out to snare their elusive game bird, licking their chops in anticipation of the feast afterwards.

" 'I thought I saw one!' said the vulnerable Roulston, spotting some underbrush movement.

"No one had any luck, however, as time passed and darkness began to set in.

"Then out of nowhere they came – the law enforcement officers. The gendarmes. The fuzz. The jig was up!

"As the police put the arm on Moog and Kurri, Lowe threw his net down and fled. Unger, the cagey veteran, handed his to Roulston, who cussed, 'I don't want the @#$&%$# thing.' Then he found a large tree to hide behind.

"The charges laid against Kurri and Moog were for trespassing, poaching and for hunting snipes on the Sabbath.

" 'Why?' inquired Roulston as his two teammates were being herded into a squad car. 'Do wildlife get Sundays off here or what?'

"Moog, the 21-year-old goaltender who looks 14 going on 16, was later dismissed, presumably due to the fact police had him pegged as a minor. Kurri was detained for more than an hour while his mates posted a bond and the word was that he would be lucky to escape with a $1,500 fine."

The next day at practice they finally let the snipe out of the bag. It, of course, was all a gag.

Kurri would go down in hockey history as one of the great snipers of all time. And Gretzky would set him up for a good number of his snipes.

They manufactured memories like those on purpose. And they made memories by accident.

There was the night in the Oilers' first year in the NHL when Peter Driscoll thought Oilers play-by-play man Rod (This Is No Place For A Nervous Person) Phillips had stolen his shoes on a plane and stuffed them into his suit bag. Driscoll decided to get them back and get even at the same time and, along with an Oiler accomplice, snuck into what he thought was Phillips' hotel room. Rummaging through luggage, he pulled out a .457 Magnum. Only then did it occur to Driscoll that he might be in the wrong room.

The team liked to play hard. And stay out late.

One of the great stories involved tennis star Martina Navratilova, who once made headlines – after coming out as a lesbian – by saying she'd like to have Wayne Gretzky's baby. Navratilova enjoyed hanging around the Oilers, who enjoyed hanging around the bar.

One day the team was in Chicago, where she was playing in a tennis tournament. It was getting late, but last call was still a couple of hours away. She said she had to leave because she had an early game in the morning.

That's when Dave Semenko, who'd had a couple, put his arm around her and is said to have slurred, "Martina, baby, in all my 'sperience as a professssshional athlete, I know one thing. You play better guilty. Have another drink."

Kevin Lowe remembers the first year and his first players-only team meeting.

"It was in Vancouver. The team had checked in to the Hotel Vancouver and a meeting had been called, but I didn't catch the location," he recalled years later in his *Edmonton Sun* column. "The only guy I could find in the hotel lobby was Cowboy Flett. He took the little lost sheep under his wing and brought me to my first team meeting. At first I thought he was putting one over on me when we walked into the beverage room at the Ritz Hotel. Little did I know, there was a lot to learn about pro life."

Then there was the time Dave Hunter was serving a jail sentence for drunk driving. It was a serious situation, of course, and one which ought not to have inspired any humour. But it did.

Paul Coffey went to visit him.

Jail officials told him Hunter would be unable to see him because he was in a floor hockey game going into overtime.

"What do you mean?" said Coffey. "Hunter never gets to play in overtime."

Then there was the time Messier came home from an around-the-world vacation after winning a Stanley Cup.

He served up a quote to Chubey about his stop in Bangkok, which the hockey scribe dutifully printed the next day:

"I think I'll leave it to the people's imagination ... Put it this way. You could see the most beautiful temples in the world to the poorest slum areas to the most outrageous sexual fantasies imaginable. That pretty much sums up the whole infield right there."

It was the off-season and Messier found himself on the commissioner's carpet. And he couldn't bring the stripper with the Stanley Cup as a character witness.

They were the glory of their times. And they gloried in having a good time.

Craig Simpson and Edmonton singer Lin Elder watch as Mark Messier tickles the ivories to hype the Red Cross Society's New Year's Eve Red and White Gala.

Chapter 12
The Double Double

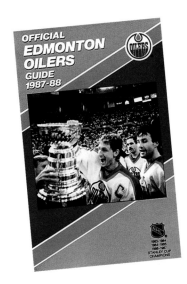

E ventually the party was over. And when it was over, the Edmonton Oilers suddenly turned into the Edmonton Turmoilers.

Suddenly, taking another bite out of the carrot was not everything for everybody.

The carrot?

On every Oilers' Stanley Cup ring there is a carrot. The first one has one bite out of the carrot. The second one has two. The third one has three ... You get the idea. In there somewhere was the concept that if this team could stick together, they could keep taking bites out of the carrot.

For years the cry around the NHL had been "Break Up The Oilers." And this was the season – 1987-88– that it would start to happen.

It was another Canada Cup year and, again, the Oilers were well-represented. And if Paul Coffey's superb play to win the previous Canada Cup was a freeze-frame for the ages, Wayne Gretzky's setup of Mario Lemieux at 10:07 of second overtime to beat the Soviets – and the two greats of the game leaping into each other's arms with Larry Murphy – could only be trumped by Paul Henderson's famous goal that beat the Russians in '72.

When the Canada Cup was over – even before it started – it was obvious the lineup changes this year would go beyond, way beyond, Glen Sather's belief that every team needs three or four changes a year to prevent it from becoming stagnant.

1988: We are the champions ... again.

Three Amigos: Mark Messier, Wayne Gretzky and Kevin Lowe celebrate the 1988 Stanley Cup victory. It was Gretzky's last game as an Oiler.

Several changes they saw coming. A couple were telegraphed to reporters as the players drank champagne in the Oilers dressing room while celebrating their third Stanley Cup, and headed out to party together for weeks on end. But now the Oilers were beginning to wonder if what was happening was the beginning of the end.

Randy Gregg had made it known throughout the previous year that his dream was to return and play for the Canadian Olympic team in the Calgary 1988 Winter Olympics.

"We respect that," said Sather. "I'd say it's 95 per cent he will be back with us before the end of the season."

Rexi Ruotsalainen was back on the other side of the ocean.

Kent Nilsson, knowing he was a short-term project with the Oilers, decided to play in Bolsano, Italy, and hoped he'd get a springtime call from Sather, too.

No problem with any of that.

But Andy Moog had sat and watched Grant Fuhr start in too many Stanley Cup playoff games while he sat on the bench. He was outta here. But he didn't know where. Free agency then wasn't what it is now. The Oilers had a right to match any offer and trade him. And, knowing that, nobody was making any offers. Moog's solution was the Olympics, too.

The Oilers had signed Gretzky to a $1-million-a-year contract prior to the Canada Cup. But he was no longer tied to the team until 1999. In fact, the reality of the deal Peter Pocklington had done would hit him soon enough. In effect, Gretzky's new contract had managed to make No. 99 a depreciating asset.

And with Gretzky getting the big raise, everybody else formed a line to the right to ask for something close to what the going rates had become around the league.

Kevin Lowe signed a new deal. But when the Canada Cup was over, Mark Messier and Paul Coffey both informed me they were going to hold out and not report for training camp. Then Glenn Anderson didn't show up as scheduled for an Oilers pre-season game in Toronto.

"Coff has settled into his usual spot in the doghouse. Glenn is hovering around the door," was how Sather put it.

Anderson ended his brief holdout after a half-hour meeting with Pocklington. But when Peter Puck emerged from the meeting, the hole was dug deeper with Coffey. "As far as I'm concerned, Paul can cool his heels forever," said the owner.

For 10 days Coffey stayed silent. But when I discovered him at a Toronto Blue Jays pennant race game, he decided to speak his mind.

"I just want to be treated fairly," he said. "I don't want to be traded. I want to stay in Edmonton. I've had seven good years in Edmonton. I love playing in that city. I want to play there for the rest of my career. But I believe if I don't take this stand, I'm going to end up in exactly the same boat as Andy Moog two years down the road. I don't want to end up like Mooger."

Mike Krushelnyski was a holdout, too, but with all the Canada Cuppers out with their tin cups, he wasn't getting any notice.

On Oct. 2 the big headline in *The Sun* was one word: "SUSPENDED!"

The subhead: "Messier the latest Oiler to bolt."

Doug Messier, acting as his son's agent, informed the Oilers that Mark wasn't going to report. In fact he was in Mannheim, West Germany, visiting his brother Paul and working out with his team.

"I didn't want to suspend him because we had been negotiating," said Sather.

On the day Sather finally signed Krushelnyski to a new deal, Messier flew to town under the cover of darkness, intentionally avoiding Sather's media advisers.

"We didn't want him besieged by reporters," said Slats. "We wanted him left alone until we have a chance to talk to each other."

On Oct. 9, his deal was done.

"Mark's an Edmonton Oiler," announced his dad. "Things are resolved. Mark still wanted to play here and the Oilers still wanted to have him."

That left Coffey.

"TRADE HIM"

That was the next headline over my copy.

"I don't think there's any going back now," said Coffey. "It would be tough to go back and play for the guy you've been negotiating with when he's your coach. It would be almost impossible after all of this. The longer it goes, the worse it gets. I'm sure Slats feels the same way. Obviously they don't want me back. And obviously it would now be tough to go back."

Agent Gus Badali had come to the same conclusion. "Yes, basically that's the way it is now. I don't think there is any alternative but to trade him. I don't think Paul can go back there."

"BLOCKBUSTER"

That was the headline in *The Sun* the next day.

Sather gave Coffey his wish. And Oiler fans were delighted with his deal.

Coffey, the aging Dave Hunter and borderline NHLer Wayne VanDorp to the Pittsburgh Penguins for Craig Simpson, Moe Mantha, Dave Hannan and Chris Joseph.

The deal, during Grey Cup week, knocked football off the sports pages from coast to coast. And the trade was reviewed by just about everybody, except Sather himself, as a steal of a deal considering the circumstances.

"You always wonder when you trade a guy like Paul whether or not you've made the right trade," said Sather. "It doesn't matter who you get back, you can't replace Coffey. Paul is just coming into the best years of his career, but his attitude changed to the point where we couldn't reconcile the situation here."

Two weeks earlier, Muckler had gone on record as saying the Oilers weren't good enough to repeat as Stanley Cup champions.

"I think we are now," he said.

"I believe Edmonton is a better team for the future than they were yesterday," declared Calgary GM Cliff Fletcher 20 minutes after the deal was done. "Craig Simpson is already a great young forward. At 20 he has a great career ahead of him."

Finally, in the middle of December, it was hockey season.

On Dec. 15 the Oilers and Calgary Flames were tied for first in the Smythe Division. And Wayne Gretzky was in his first battle for the scoring title since his first season in the league. The guy he'd set up for that

Craig Simpson celebrates a goal against former Oiler Paul Coffey and the Pittsburgh Penguins.

unforgettable Canada Cup-winning goal, Mario Lemieux, had benefited from the experience and was now going after Gretzky.

The Race.

The Chase.

If the Oilers and Gretzky had been playing regular seasons for their own amazement and amusement before, now there was more to play for.

This was the season in which Gretzky registered his 1,000th NHL assist. The night he did it he knew he was moving into a new dimension.

"It's different now," he said. "Things change for me now. It used to be games and seasons. From now on it's milestones and longevity."

It seemed like just yesterday he was setting up Lowe for the first one.

"I can remember that first assist like it *was* yesterday," he said that night. "You don't forget your first game in the NHL. And you don't forget your first assist. I was pretty excited. Nine hundred and ninety-nine assists later and I'm still pretty excited.

"What makes this special is only one other guy has ever been there before and he's the greatest," said Gretzky of his idol, Gordie Howe, who ended his 26-year career with 1,049 and knew his record wasn't likely to survive the season.

"No. 1,050 is going to be very, very special."

No. 1,000 was special, too, because Gretzky beat Marcel Dionne to the plateau by one. And Dionne, a New York Ranger now, was on the same ice, playing in his 1,258th game in his 16th season.

Dionne managed a single assist and left the ice at 999.

"I had a tough time getting one point tonight and he had five," said Dionne. "He's a scoring machine. He makes plays that are incredible. He's going to get all of Gordie's records. Wayne Gretzky and Gordie Howe are going to go down in history in a special category together."

Gretzky had the fourth five-goal night of his career against St. Louis. Then, for the first time in his career, he suffered an injury, a sprained right knee that kept him out of the lineup for almost a month.

And so the buildup began.

The Chase.

"I'll probably be 25 points behind him when I get back," said Gretzky on Jan. 7 as he waited and watched Lemieux pull away. "It's tough to score in Hartford from my couch in Edmonton. I'll have a lot of ground to make up when I get back. But if I get back in time, it should be something that will be good for hockey. If I get back in time it looks like we'll have a *real* scoring race. It's supposed to be a scoring *race*. It's supposed to be something for the fans to talk about. This could be fun."

Gretzky finally managed to get back on Jan. 29. He was 19 points back of Lemieux's 105.

There was a feel to the fans when he came back, an electricity in the air that Gretzky said he hadn't really felt since his 50-in-39 season.

"It's very noticeable," he said after a three-point night to up his total to 10 in three games since his return. "I can really feel it. Just from the way they react to everything. I can feel everybody reacting around it. I can feel it with the fans and I can feel it with my teammates. Everybody is really into it."

Gretzky and Lemieux went head to head at the Coliseum on Feb. 20. But there was no show. Gretzky went down at 4:45 with an eye injury. And not long after Lemieux left the game with a broken nose.

Gretzky's injury, obviously, was more frightening.

"The thing is, that's the exact same spot on the ice where Brett Callighen got hit – right at the blueline," said Gretzky of his former linemate who never played another game after taking a stick in the eye.

Gretzky missed another 10 days.

But when he got back, he did it. The 27-year-old broke Howe's assist record of 1,049 in his 681st game – 1,086 fewer games than Howe required to establish it. And what pleased him most was he fed Jari Kurri to pull the trigger. Pleased Kurri a tad, too.

"I felt good, especially the way it happened," said Kurri. "We've scored a lot of goals like that. And it reminded me of the first one I got here

Wayne Gretzky holds the Canada Cup trophy with pride.

eight years ago. This will be a great memory."

There was no false modesty for Gretzky with this one. This was the one he wanted. This was the one which best defined who he was – the greatest playmaker in this history of hockey.

"It's No. 1," said No. 99. "It's No. 1 because it's one of those records people say will never be broken. This is the one which tells kids it doesn't matter who scores the goal, that an assist is just as important as a goal."

And Gretzky said his injuries made him appreciate it more, too.

"When I was injured and missed a month, I guess somebody up there was saying I needed a break and needed a rest. When I injured the eye, on the very edge of breaking the record, that's when I started to tell myself how thankful I am that I haven't been hurt."

Gretzky lost the chase. Lemieux, playing 77 games, ended up with 168 points. Gretzky, playing 64, ended up with 149.

Lemieux won the Art Ross. And for the first time in his nine seasons with the Oilers in the NHL, Gretzky didn't win the Hart Trophy. Lemieux got that, too.

Gretzky was the second all-star team centre; the only Oiler skater to win a spot on the all-star team that season.

Meanwhile, back at the ranch ...

The Race.

Being tied with the Flames in mid-December was something most Oilers fans hadn't expected. They were prepared for an upset in the playoffs; that had happened before. They were prepared for the Flames to win the season series with Edmonton. That had happened the year before when Calgary lost only once in eight games against the Oilers.

But *this* ...

"The Oilers started slowly," said Calgary GM Cliff Fletcher. "And we've been very fortunate the way our new players, Joe Nieuwendyk and Brett Hull, have turned out. But look at our record for the last 240 games. We've been averaging about 95 points a season. And that's the pace we're on again."

During Gretzky's injury time the Oilers went 4-4-4 through a tough period in the schedule. But the Flames were on fire. And by the time the two teams met each other on Boxing Day in Calgary, the Oilers were seven points back.

The Oilers won that night, 5-4.

"I think we said, 'Hey, we're a championship team,' " said Kevin Lowe. "There was a commitment to this game. And that's tough to get the day after Christmas. But you could feel it in the dressing room."

"We want to know if we're good enough," said Mark Messier. "We're in a bit of a transition period right now and we need to know we're still good enough."

Calgary assistant coach Pierre Page attended a game in the Coliseum in mid-January and said it was obvious the Oilers were playing a new game.

"I've never seen the Oilers with three men back as often as I saw them

Kevin Lowe jostles with assistant coach Ted Green during an Oilers workout.

with three men back tonight," he said. "You know what? I think they're a better team now than they were with Coffey. Before, there seemed to be rules for Coffey and rules for everybody else. And now, with Wayne out, they are able to play a completely different game. They seem to be able to accept the fact that they have to play *that* game in this situation and they're a better team for it. I think they are going to be a better playoff team without Coffey."

By early March the Oilers were still trailing in The Race.

"We're like Avis," said co-coach John Muckler. "If we try harder, maybe we can become Hertz again."

They finished the regular season as Avis.

The Flames finished first overall with 105 points, the Montreal Canadiens second with 103 and the Oilers finished up with a 44-25-11 record and 99 points.

But Randy Gregg was back from the Olympics. And Sather, after the

Olympics were over, pulled off the long-awaited deal: Andy Moog for Bill Ranford and Russ Courtnall.

The Coffey trade had worked out well. Craig Simpson, for the first time in his three-year NHL career, scored 50 goals to lead the team in that department with 56 – 19 more than Messier, who had a 111-point season, and 13 more than Kurri who had a 96-point year.

"The guys here made me feel comfortable immediately," said Simpson. "I didn't have to worry about fitting in. I came here full of fire, to try to establish myself. There are so many stars here, I didn't want to get lost in the shuffle."

The No. 1 star of the season wasn't Gretzky, Messier, Kurri, Anderson, Simpson or any of the other skaters, however. It was Grant Fuhr.

With Moog gone, Fuhr was playing twice as many games. And while no skater except Gretzky made the all-star team, Fuhr was the first-team goalie and won the Vezina Trophy as top netminder for the first time in his NHL career.

He established an NHL record for most games played by a goaltender in a single season, appearing in 75 of the Oilers' 80 games – breaking the record of 73 set by Bernie Parent. And Fuhr started 73 of the 75 games in which he played. Not to be forgotten was the fact he started the season as Canada's national netminder in the Canada Cup win over the Soviets.

Not unlike most of the big boys on the team, Fuhr went through contract stuff that same season. Except he seemed mostly oblivious to his dealings, which were being handled by Edmonton-based agent Rich Winter who later played a leading role in bringing down players association boss Alan Eagleson.

"I'm tired of the BS but I'm not tired of playing," said Fuhr. "I love it."

He was able to play the second half of the season sans the BS.

It was a sleazy scene on New Year's Eve when a few Edmonton sports reporters and I were called away from our families and festivities to the boardroom of a local law office by Winter's promise of a blockbuster story. We were there because he had threatened the withdrawal of Fuhr's services if his salary situation wasn't settled by the end of the calendar year – and it was the end of the calendar year.

While we sat in the boardroom, Winter was on the phone to Glen Sather. Eventually the agent, whose style was similar to Dave Semenko's, came into the room and said there would be no blockbuster news.

"I think we have an agreement. Grant will be an Edmonton Oiler for a long time."

At that point I asked Winter the question. Was he telling us he had brought us all to his boardroom on New Year's Eve for the express purpose of using us as pawns in negotiations with Sather?

"I'll leave you to speculate," he said.

Kevin Lowe and Mark Messier present Wayne Gretzky with a silver stick to commemorate his 1,000th point.

Lovely.

Fuhr, meanwhile, was certainly earning his money.

"I don't know how he does it," said defenceman Steve Smith. "The more he plays the better he gets."

Gerry Cheevers, in with the Bruins one night and as good an authority on goaltending as you're going to find, said this season was proving it.

"Fuhr's the best. He's playing with so much confidence and relaxation that he's toying with every situation."

But while he was the Oilers' tower of strength in the regular season, the worry was that he'd be a weakness in the playoffs, because after the Canada Cup and 75 regular-season games he couldn't help but collapse from fatigue in the post-season.

Reasons why the Oilers wouldn't win the Stanley Cup again this season were a dime a dozen:

• They'd grown weary.

• They were satisfied with three. When you have three, what do you need with four?

• They were terrible all season against the best, losing all three to Montreal and losing their last three to Calgary.

• They had a losing record on the road.

• The Oilers defence and third and fourth forward lines couldn't compare to Calgary and Montreal.

• Edmonton's stars were fading. Coffey and Moog were gone and Kurri, Anderson and even Gretzky didn't have the seasons they'd had in the past.

• The list of players without Stanley Cup experience was long – Bill Ranford, Dave Hannan, Craig Simpson, Normand Lacombe, and Keith Acton who had come to the team in a trade for Moe Mantha in the second half of the season.

I wrote a column in *The Sun* offering my own list of reasons why I felt the Edmonton Era was not about to come to a crashing conclusion:

• A 99-point season without Gretzky for 16 games and without the compensation for Coffey and Moog for far longer, wasn't so shabby.

• The Oilers veterans knew better than anybody else how meaningless the regular season is in the NHL.

• Gretzky didn't win the scoring race and would fail to win the Hart Trophy for the first time. That would make him the most motivated man in the playoffs.

• Fuhr thrived on playing goal in the playoffs.

• Anderson was never a regular-season great but always showed up in the playoffs.

• Messier's leadership and will to win were proving to be greater than that of any player in the league.

• Winners win.

• They were opening against Winnipeg – and every time they played Winnipeg in the playoffs ...

And there was another factor that ought to have been mentioned. New blood. The first-time Oilers knew this was as good a chance as they were going to get to win a Stanley Cup.

Hannan and Simpson had never played a single, solitary, playoff game. Suddenly they had visions of the Stanley Cup dancing in their heads.

"I wish I could describe the feeling," said Hannan. "I'm used to an empty feeling at this time of year. These guys wear their Stanley Cup rings and they wear them well. I want one. And I'm sure Craig wants one."

Glenn Anderson was the story of Game 1, coming and going.

On game-day morning he awoke to the following front-page headline in *The Edmonton Sun*:

"MAN DIES AFTER POOL
MISHAP AT OILER HOME"
"Cops Conduct Routine Probe Into Incident
At Glenn Anderson's House"

After the game, it wasn't the police who wanted to talk to Anderson, it was the hockey writers. Anderson had shaken off the story and the death of a close personal friend to score three goals and add two assists, singlehandedly leading the Oilers to a 7-4 victory.

Anderson left the dressing room before the door was opened to the media and was unavailable for comment.

Sather said he felt sick when he picked up *The Sun* and saw the scoop about the death of George Varvis, who had been pulled from the indoor pool at Anderson's home.

"I didn't stop worrying for the rest of the day after I saw that headline," said Sather.

About Anderson. About his team. Several of Anderson's teammates had been at Anderson's home the night the incident occurred.

"He lost a dear friend. That's a real tough thing for anybody to go through," said Sather.

What happened at Anderson's pool may have been the story of the day but what happened at the Coliseum was definitely the story of the night.

"For Glenn to overcome it ... the story of the game was what he did," said Sather. "I wish it was under different circumstances."

Simpson wasted no time in contributing to the cause. He scored the winner in Game 1 and again in Game 2 as the Oilers made it 16 playoff wins in a row against the Jets with a 3-2 win.

The Oilers embark on a Smythe Division showdown with the Calgary Flames.

scored two and Fuhr kicked out 32 shots as the Oilers came back from a 3-1 deficit.

Edmonton Eskimos GM Hugh Campbell – who knew something about winning, having coached his team to five straight Grey Cup wins – was now predicting the Oilers would do it. And he came up with the theme for their dream: Winning two straight Stanley Cups twice, he referred to as "The Double Double."

The Oilers came home and took care of the Jets 6-2. And this year there was no getting around them. The Calgary Flames were next. And Calgary was going crazy.

The sloppy hand-painted "Honk If You Love The Flames" signs were on lawns all over Calgary. Grade-schoolers had made cutout Flaming Cs which hung in front windows from Medicine Hat to Banff. A sign on one downtown building declared "Home Of The 1988 Stanley Cup Champion Flames." On a flight from Toronto a stewardess, upon landing, welcomed everybody to Calgary, "Home Of The 1988 Stanley Cup Champions." And when the Oilers arrived, there was no question Cowtown had already been painted red.

For the first time ever, an Oilers-Flames series opened in the Olympic Saddledome. But what was home-ice advantage with these two teams? The Flames had won three of four in Edmonton and the Oilers two of three in Calgary in the Steve Smith year. And in the regular season just completed, the Oilers lost three of four in the Coliseum while winning two and gaining a tie in the Saddledome.

"I don't know what it is," said Fuhr. "We play better there and they play better here."

Gretzky figured it might work out to be an Oiler advantage for another reason.

"There's a pressure on them they've never experienced before. This will be the first time they've played with the expectations for them to win. They'll be expected to win that first game."

They didn't.

Edmonton 3, Calgary 1.

"I kind of enjoyed that," said Sather when it was over. "I went to rent a car from Hertz to-

Finally, in Winnipeg, the Jets beat the streak in Game 3. The longest post-season losing streak in the history of all of pro sports in North America was over.

"I thought it would never end," said Jets GM John Ferguson. "How long ago was the WHA? That's the last time we beat those guys in the playoffs.'

It was 6-4 and the Jets were worthy winners.

The Oilers were worthy winners right back at 'em in Game 4.

"Anybody who watched that game has to realize that we're serious about winning another Stanley Cup," said Slats after a 5-3 victory in which Kurri

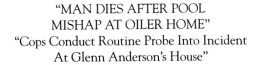

Keith Acton enjoys a well-deserved sip of champagne from the coveted Stanley Cup in May 1988.

day and when I got the car it had a 'Go Flames Go' sticker on the front of the licence plate."

How big a win was it?

It was so big that Gretzky sounded a lot like Wild Bill Hunter from another movie.

He called it the biggest win in Oilers history.

"I don't think we've ever had a bigger one," he said.

"This game will end up meaning a great deal," predicted Muckler. "The pressure was on Calgary tonight. It was really on Calgary. And it's double pressure on them now."

Gretzky, fuelled by the Calgary fans, sank the Flames in overtime of Game 2.

"They do get me going," said No. 99 after he scored his fourth goal of the playoffs at 7:54 of OT for the 5-4 win. "They're more worried about me than about their own team."

Gretzky's shot was never compared to that of Al MacInnis. But the one he ripped for the winner was a rocket.

"If Wayne has ever shot the puck harder, I don't think I've ever seen it," said Muckler of the man of the hour who brought the Oilers back from a 3-0 deficit to send them home with a 2-0 series lead.

Wild Wayne called it "the biggest goal I've ever scored."

After a 4-2 win in Game 3 and a 6-4 win in Game 4 the *Edmonton Sun* headline proclaimed: "How Sweep It Is!"

Calgarians could analyse the series until the cows came home and they'd have to come up with the same conclusion: The Flames lost in four because of the Oilers' big four.

"Too much Messier. Too much Gretzky. Too much Kurri. Too much Fuhr," Flames coach Terry Crisp said it for the record.

But the picture was worth a thousand words.

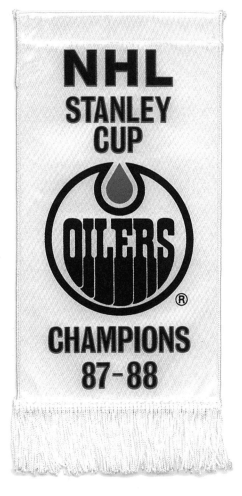

Calgary Mayor Ralph Klein, standing on the top of Edmonton's highest building wearing an Oilers sweater with the number 4-0 on the back and the name "Sweep" stitched across the back. He'd lost the mayors' bet with Edmonton's Laurence Decore.

"I don't like heights," said Klein as he waved the Oilers flag. "I particularly don't like heights in Edmonton."

Jacques Demers no doubt enjoyed the Klein coverage in the papers. But he still wasn't impressed by the reviews his Detroit Red Wings were getting when they hit town for the Campbell Conference final.

"I guess we're a little more *politely* received this year," Demers said as he scanned the papers prior to Game 1. "But we're *still* not given much respect."

Nor, after Game 1, did they deserve any.

It was the Oilers against air. The Red Wings weren't there. It was the irresistible force versus token resistance. Go-go vs. oh-no. Fast forward vs. slow mo. Or, as one press box wag put it, after the Calgary-Edmonton heavyweight championship fight this looked like a walkout bout.

The Oilers outshot the Wings 15-3 in the first period and 12-5 in the second, then called the dogs off in a 4-1 win, after which Demers admitted the score flattered Detroit.

"They played a perfect game," said the Wings coach. "That's the only time I've seen a 100 per cent perfect game. I had never seen a perfect game in hockey until tonight. And we stood there and watched it all night. They dominated every zone. They put a blanket on the whole ice. Every time a Wing thought about touching the puck an Oiler was there."

Maybe Demers was trying to make Edmonton feel overconfident.

Operating in neutral for 40 minutes, the Oilers waited until the third period to kick

Wayne Gretzky and Jeff Beukeboom accompany Stanley on one of his many parade trips down Edmonton's Jasper Avenue.

Game 2 into gear, scoring three goals in the first five minutes to win 5-3 and take a 2-0 series lead to Detroit.

The storyline coming out of Game 2 was a hit on Red Wings goalie Greg Stefan delivered by Oiler Craig Simpson. And in Game 3 the Red Wings looked like so many Detroit hit men. There appeared to be a price on the heads of both Simpson and Fuhr.

"Lee Norwood broke two sticks on Simpson's back!" said Sather.

But while the Red Wings seemed to be putting revenge ahead of winning, they did win, and by a 5-2 score at that.

Demers had guaranteed "No sweep" before the series and, if nothing else, the Norris Division reps avoided that fate.

The Red Wings came close to making it a series in Game 4. They took the Oilers into overtime. But Esa Tikkanen intercepted a Norwood pass and fed Kurri, who blasted a 25-foot shot past Glen Hanlon for his second goal of the night – and second career overtime playoff winner – at 11:02 of sudden-death OT to mercifully end hockey on a hot tin roof.

Game 4 was *Hockey Night In Hell*. Beating the heat was as much the game plan as beating the Red Wings.

"I read in the paper that Mike Illitch is worth $785 million," said Sather of the Detroit owner. "You'd think he'd be able to afford air-conditioning."

"It had to be 100 degrees on the ice," admitted Detroit's Demers.

"Unbelievable," said Simpson. "I have never been in a game when I was hotter than that. It was ridiculous. I've never sweated that much."

After that game, several Red Wings were obviously thirsty.

The story after the Oilers wrapped up the series wasn't Messier's big night to lead the Oilers to an 8-4 series-clinching win and send Edmonton to a fourth Stanley Cup final. The story was six Red Wings,

Calgary Mayor Ralph Klein sports an Oilers jersey with 'SWEEP' and '4-0' on the back after losing a bet with Edmonton Mayor Laurence Decore, right.

including Bob Probert and Petr Klima, who had been caught by assistant coach Colin Campbell drinking in an Edmonton nightclub past curfew the night before the game.

All six were fined "for showing no respect to the team," said Demers. "What those guys did had a tremendous effect on the team. What those guys did was tell everyone on the team that they couldn't win this game. They took the heart out of everything. I feel betrayed. It was unforgiv-

able."

And so the Edmonton Oilers stood on dynasty's doorstep, almost emotionless and expressionless.

"Every year it's a bigger challenge," said Messier. "I don't think anybody is satisfied with what we've accomplished."

Muckler put it best:

"We stopped celebrating getting to the Stanley Cup a long time ago," said the co-coach. "That was one of the first lessons this team learned. We celebrated the first year we got here and lost four straight."

That lesson was lost on the fans in Boston. The puck hadn't even been dropped for Game 7 of the Bruins' conference final against the New Jersey Devils when they were selling shirts outside the Boston Garden.

"Stanley's Back and He's Wearing Black," was the message emblazoned on the shirts, which also featured Bruins and Oilers logos and the likeness of the Stanley Cup.

When it was over the Gallery Gods and the rest of the inhabitants of the old building poured onto Causeway Street and began the chant.

"Edmonton! Edmonton! Edmonton!"

"They're sick out there," beer-soaked Bruins assistant trainer Bob Cocker broke into the dressing room to report. "They're picking up cars and stuff."

In a corner of the Bruins room Andy Moog said he couldn't wait for the final series to begin, although Reggie Lemelin had been handed the start in Game 7 and Moog had been No. 2 with the Canadian Olympic team and the Bruins since leaving the Oilers, because he'd had enough of being No. 2 behind Grant Fuhr.

In another corner of the Bruins room sat Ken Linseman, who had won two Cups with the Oilers.

"I've been experiencing all sorts of weird emotions," said The Rat. "You know the way I play. I'm *real* aggressive. And those guys are *real* good friends. It's going to be *real* interesting. It's going to be *real* weird."

When the Bruins arrived in Edmonton, Moog got the word.

"I'm going to play," he said.

"Terry O'Reilly wants to take advantage of all the cards he has in his

Wayne Gretzky poses with the Stanley Cup while his father, Walter, takes another historic snapshot for the family album.

hand. I'm one of those cards."

O'Reilly couldn't tell himself he had chosen wrong after Game 1. Andy was dandy. But Grant Fuhr won the goaltenders duel and the Oilers won the game 2-1, with Keith Acton firing the winner 75 seconds into the third period.

Before Game 2, Glen Gretzky walked up to his brother and couldn't believe his eyes.

"I saw that haircut and I did a double take," said Glen.

He said he thought Wayne looked like k.d. lang.

"Who cares?" said jubilant owner Peter Pocklington after Gretzky set up Anderson and Messier for goals, then fired the winner with 8½ minutes left as the Oilers sent the series back to Boston with a 4-2 win.

Historically, the Boston Garden had always been the Oilers' least favourite place to play. Two wins. Ten losses. Two ties. Their all-time record in the Boston barn said it all.

But Sather had something to say on the subject when the Oilers arrived in Beantown, where beating the building was more of a storyline than beating the Bruins.

"If the Oilers ever had the team to beat the building, this is it," he said. "This is the one."

They beat the building 6-3 in Game 3 and Gretzky had his best-ever game in the place with four assists, but Esa Tikkanen hogged the headlines with a three-goal night.

"I don't think there's ever been an Oiler team that's played better as a team," said Muckler.

O'Reilly wasn't arguing.

"That's a great team playing great hockey," said the Bruins coach.

The Oilers couldn't beat the building in Game 4. It was the night of May 24 and it was, as *The Sun* headline read the next morning, "The Game That Never Was."

It was the night the lights were supposed to go out on the Boston Bruins but, instead, went down in history as the night the lights went out on the Stanley Cup.

'It was done for everybody, the players and the people who have been behind this team for so long. They were all part of the picture. Nobody has ever done something like this before. It was a great idea. It was Wayne's idea.'

– Glen Sather on the on-ice team picture, below

Left in the dark with the teams tied 3-3, the league reached into the Dark Ages to find a rule to apply to the situation and declared the series would shift to Edmonton for Game 5 with a non-result in Game 4.

"We'll get a couple hundred grand out of it, enough to pay for the Stanley Cup rings," said Peter Pocklington.

The Oilers would get a chance to sweep the Bruins with the unfair advantage of playing three of the four games at home.

Game 4 had five fog delays before the lights went out with 23 minutes and 23 seconds remaining.

"Edmonton goal by ..." were the final words out of the mouth of PA announcer Joe Pearmutter as he tried to announce the Craig Simpson goal that had tied the game.

"IT'S AN OUT(R)AGE," screamed the front page headline in the *Boston Herald*.

"GARDEN FANS POWERLESS!" was another in Boston

"LEFT IN THE DARK," a Toronto paper declared.

The Oilers won 6-3 back home.

"In an unprecedented 4.67-game sweep ..." *Edmonton Sun* hockey writer Dick Chubey began in his game story.

The Oilers had won 16 and lost two in the playoffs. And thanks to the Boston Garden scenario, Edmonton had managed to go 11-0 at home.

The Oilers had found a new way to win a Stanley Cup. And after they carried it, they found a new way to celebrate it.

The theme was the team, not the talent. And the highlight of the night was an on-ice picture with the entire team and the Stanley Cup. The scene has been repeated by every Stanley Cup winner since, but had never been seen before.

"The picture made it perfect," said Sather. "It was done for everybody, the players and the people who have been behind this team for so long. They were all part of the picture. Nobody has ever done something like this before. It was a great idea. It was Wayne's idea."

Did he know? Did he have a premonition?

Chapter 13

99 Tears

The headline will be remembered almost as long as the day will be remembered.

"99 TEARS!"

There was a picture of Wayne Gretzky dabbing at his tears. There was no subhead. Just two lines of type over the microphones:

"Pages 2, 3, 4, 5, 6, 10, 11, 18, 19, 23, 30, 36, 37, 38, 39, 40, 41, 42, 43, 46 and 47."

It was the front page of *The Edmonton Sun* on Aug. 10, 1988.

Peter Pocklington did the dirty deed and sold Wayne Gretzky to Los Angeles Kings owner Bruce McNall for $15 million U.S. dollars – $18 million Cdn.

Fourteen months earlier Gretzky had signed a new contract.

"Today," said his new Edmonton-based financial adviser Ian Barrigan, "Wayne Gretzky is the highest-paid player in hockey."

For the first time in his career, No. 99 would be making more than a million dollars a year on the ice. And the new contract wiped out the one he had signed on the ice on his 18th birthday. The one that expired in 1999, remember?

Gretzky had managed to keep it quiet for a long time. But that day at centre ice, on his 18th birthday, he'd come oh-so-close to signing the name "Bob Smith" on that contract.

He even started signing the 'B.'

"The 'W' wasn't straight on that contract, it was kind of on a slant," Gretzky later revealed. "That's because it started out to be a 'B.' But I thought, 'I can't.' "

"Don't sign," one of the veterans had told him.

"But I've got to. They're having a ceremony at centre ice," said Gretzky.

"Well, sign 'Bob Smith,' " said the veteran. That way it's no good and you can wait until you're really sure."

Said Barrigan: "It's 20-20 hindsight to say the deal he signed at centre ice wasn't a good one. It was a bird-in-the-hand-is-better-than-two-in-the-bush deal. It wasn't that bad if Wayne had played to a level where most star players play at. But he has played at a level way beyond that."

Everybody was happy. Gretzky was the highest-paid player in the game.

Wayne Gretzky arrives in Los Angeles as the newest member of Bruce McNall's Kings. Opposite: Gretzky's tearful farewell to the Edmonton media.

The phrase "depreciating asset" wouldn't be mentioned for more than a year.

And Gretzky was happy. He headed for Canada Cup training camp, and one day at a Team Canada function in Glen Sather's backyard in Banff, he introduced a girl by the name of Janet Jones to everybody.

Some had seen her before. In *A Chorus Line*. In *American Anthem*. In *The Flamingo Kid*. And in the March issue of *Playboy*.

"She's a nice girl," said his mom, Phyllis Gretzky, who said she had no problem with the *Playboy* pictorial. "It doesn't bother Wayne so it doesn't bother me."

Gretzky said he'd met Janet about five years earlier but hadn't started dating her until a month or so before the 1987 Canada Cup.

Then came the day in January where I got scooped on the story. By myself.

At the time I was working for local radio station 630 CHED with Rob Christie, Audie Lynds and Janet From Another Planet as the sports guy on the Morning Crew. The radio station had a cash-for-news-tips thing going. And sometime overnight somebody had phoned to try to earn $1,000 by tipping that Gretzky and a gang of Oilers had been at Earl's Tin Palace after the game the night before and Gretzky had broken the news to the boys. He was getting married!

As CHED's sports guy until 9 a.m., I had this teensy-weensy, itsy-bitsy conflict of interest I'd never dreamed would be possible with the gig.

I checked out the tip.

It was fact.

And, rationalizing to myself that there was no way the story would survive the day anyway and if anybody was going to break it then it might as well be me ...

I broke it. On the air. Not in *The Sun*.

I followed it, however, with comprehensive coverage the next day, having had a real jump on the story.

"She said yes," said Wayne. "It's definite. We're getting married. We were meant to spend our lives together. She's a tremendous lady, a great person."

Wayne said he had proposed to her over the telephone to South Carolina where she was on location shooting a movie. He then phoned his mom and dad and went out and played against the Washington Capitals. At the Tin Palace after the game, he broke the news to the boys, buying a few bottles of Dom Perignon to celebrate.

"My last words to everybody were, 'Let's keep this quiet for a little while.' I guess it kept quiet for about four hours."

Gretzky's marketing man Mike Barnett said Wayne laughed when he heard it on the radio in the morning.

"He said, 'I should have phoned the radio station myself and made the $1,000,' " said Bar-

Edmonton's version of the royal wedding: St. Joseph's Basilica, July 16, 1988.

nett.

Janet was on the set in South Carolina. She wouldn't reveal the exact nature of Wayne's proposal.

"That's between Wayne and myself. We can't tell you everything. All I can say is that he proposed in a very special way. I'll never forget it for the rest of my life. It was very special," said the future Mrs. Gretzky, adding that it was "wonderfully romantic."

"Then, after the game, he kept calling me all night, getting friends and players on the phone. It sure sounded like they were really celebrating up there. But the nicest part was that he called my mother first. My family was thrilled."

While Janet was from St. Louis and Gretzky from Brantford, Ont., they both said there was no discussion on where the wedding would be. It would be in Edmonton.

There was no question. It would be the social event of the season. In fact, by the end of the day it was being called Canada's Royal Wedding.

Mark Messier and Kevin Lowe claimed to be the most thrilled.

"We win the bet!" said Messier.

"Gretz will have a new bride. Walter and Phyllis Gretzky will have a new daughter and Kevin and I get $1,000 each."

Messier explained the three had made the bet – which of the Three Amigos would end up at the altar first – when they were all 18 years old in their first season in the NHL.

The wedding coverage in *The Sun* was so extensive it was hard to envision any Gretzky event in the future that could possibly occupy more pages of the paper. There was a report on the bachelor bash at which best man Eddie Mio declared Wayne "the happiest I've seen him in 10 years." There was a story on the $250,000 worth of jewelry, most of it on one finger, that Janet would wear on her wedding day. There were stories on her wedding dress and about anybody who was anybody who had anything to do with the wedding or who had received an invitation to the event.

The guest list included virtually the entire Oilers family, Hollywood's Alan Thicke, David Foster and Tim Feehan; hockey's hierarchy including John Zeigler, Alan Eagleson, Mike Keenan, Vladislav Tretiak and Gordie Howe. Jackie Parker and several members of the Eskimos family were invited. And, yes, even a small number of media, including a hockey writer by the name of Chubey and a columnist by the name of Jones.

The hype had become so huge that the day before the wedding Gretzky was worried Edmonton had built it up to be so big that there'd be a letdown.

"I hope they aren't disappointed," he said. "There are not going to be 50 or 60 Hollywood or sports celebrities here. Obviously, because of the careers both Janet and I happen to have, there are going to be a few celebrities. But by far the majority of people are our friends – plain ordinary people from Brantford, St. Louis and Edmonton. I'm thrilled that Edmonton is so excited about the wedding but I don't want anybody to think it's going to be something it isn't."

I wrote the story at Gretzky's request. But it didn't make anybody less excited about the event.

As I explained to Gretzky, how do you downplay something when the prime minister is invited?

"I guess that's the problem," he laughed. "We know the prime minister."

The Sun produced a special section full of wedding-day coverage.

The lead story of that section, by *Edmonton Sun* staff writers:

"Edmonton's favourite son Wayne Douglas Gretzky took Janet Marie Jones for his wife in a colourful ceremony full of style and elegance.

"The bride, dressed in a magnificent white satin gown rumoured to have cost $40,000, and Wayne, looking slightly nervous throughout in his traditional black tuxedo, exchanged vows before more than 650 selected guests at St. Joseph's Basilica.

"While 3,000 well-wishers waited outside, the hushed audience inside listened as Wayne and Janet repeated their vows in unison.

"Each confidently answered 'I do' when asked during the 40-minute ecumenical service, conducted by retired minister Canon John Munro from an Anglican church in Gretzky's home town of Brantford and assisted by Rev. Mike McCaffery, rector of St. Joseph's.

"When they were pronounced man and wife by Canon Munro, they kissed and hugged, then smiled at each other and kissed and hugged again.

"Janet had earlier caused a stir by arriving two hours before the ceremony to dress in the church, disappointing crowds outside who had hoped to catch a glimpse of the radiant bride in her wedding gown.

"Wayne arrived 30 minutes before the service was to begin, accompanied by his best man, Eddie Mio.

"Groomsmen were Mark Messier, Kevin Lowe, Paul Coffey, brothers Glen, Brent and Keith Gretzky ...

"When he walked down the aisle it was at the side of his parents, Walter and Phyllis Gretzky, while members of the Edmonton Symphony Orchestra played *Trumpet Voluntary*.

"As he walked past his grandmother, 84-year-old Mary Gretzky, Wayne gave her a wink and the thumbs-up sign.

"Local rock star Tim Feehan sang Beethoven's *Ode to Joy*.

"While Feehan sang, Janet stood with her arm behind Wayne's back and gave him a playful tickle.

"When the pair left the church following the ceremony they were welcomed warmly by the crowd.

Groom Wayne Gretzky walks down the aisle accompanied by his father, Walter, and mother, Phyllis.

"Wayne looked relieved while his bride appeared overjoyed as they posed and kissed on the steps of St. Joseph's, much to the delight of cheering onlookers."

Nobody was disappointed.

Anne Alexander filled a page with a story on Janet's wedding dress and an interview with wedding co-ordinator Connie Duguid. Alexander and Kerry Diotte filled another page with reaction ("It was everything I hoped and more. No one could be happier than I am today") from the bride. David Quigley and Richard Watts covered the reception ("The only person not too happy with the wedding reception was the chef. He had to keep the food warm as the meal was delayed more than an hour while each of the guests personally congratulated the newlyweds."). Diotte interviewed the relatives ("Wayne told me he's happier than when he won any of the Stanley Cups," said 16-year-old brother Brett.). Gord Bannerman covered the crowd outside ("I love Wayne Gretzky and I wanted to see Janet's dress."). Chubey and Jones took the day off.

It looked for all the world that day as if Wayne and Janet and Edmonton would live happily ever after.

Then the story appeared under my byline on Aug. 4.

"The rumour has been running rampant for days: Wayne Gretzky to the Los Angeles Kings for $18 million.

" 'There is nothing to it,' said Oilers president, general manager and coach Glen Sather. 'Every summer it's a different rumour. This one goes in the same bin as all the other ones. Put it with the ones about him going to the New York Rangers, the Detroit Red Wings, the Vancouver Canucks and the Calgary Flames. I don't even know where Wayne and Janet are. If there was anything like that I assume Peter would let me know. There is nothing to it.'"

Where were you when John F. Kennedy was assassinated? Everybody remembers. And everybody in Edmonton will likely remember where they were when they heard the news that Wayne Gretzky had been traded to the Los Angeles Kings.

I will. I wasn't there. I'd taken Sather at face value and was on holiday with my son Shane in the Ozark Mountains, en route to Kansas City to take him to watch his favourite team, the Royals, in a three-game series, a combination birthday and high school graduation present. Maybe I had a premonition. I don't know. But for no real reason I phoned the office from Aurora, Missouri, that day. They informed me they'd tried to find me in hotels in six states. Gretzky had been sold.

And I wrote the following from a hotel room in Joplin, Missouri, while my son listened to the baseball game on the radio in the car:

"Shock. Outrage. Anger. None of those emotions quite cover it, do they?

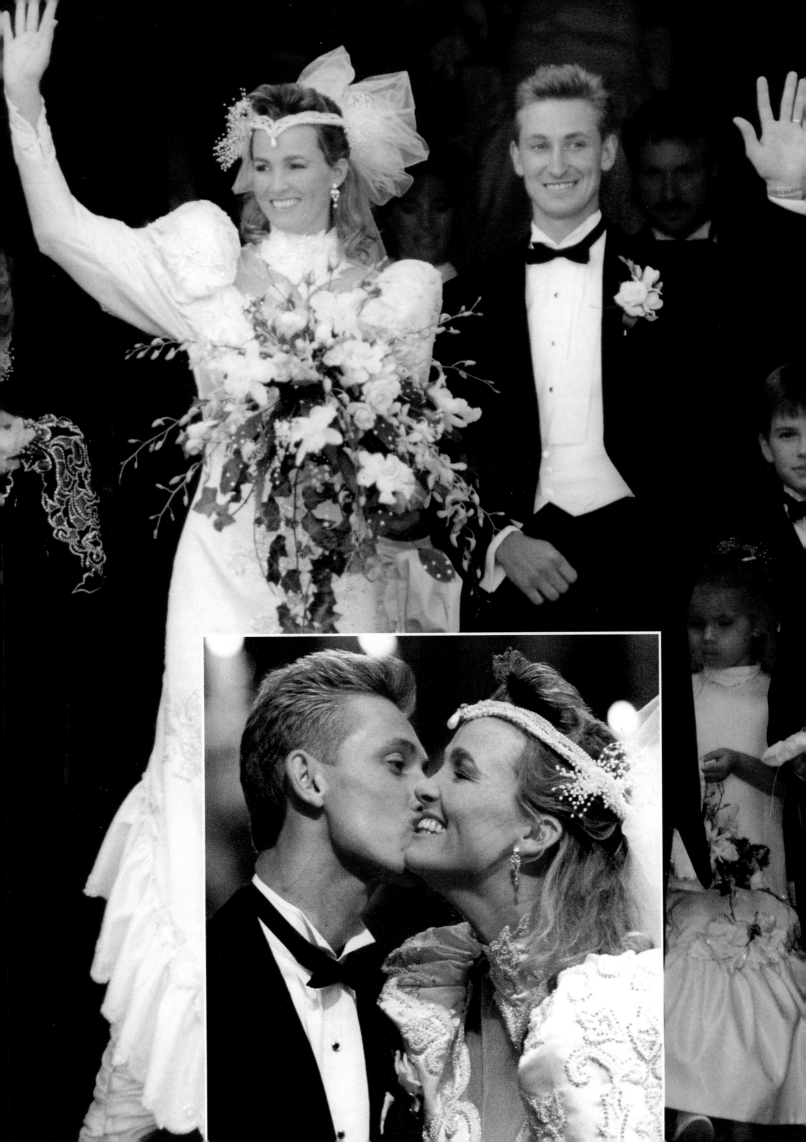

"The emotions we're dealing with here are not unlike those of a death in the family. A death not by natural causes.

"Wayne Gretzky is more than the greatest player in the history of hockey. He is more than the most dominant team sport athlete in history. He's that to the world. But to Edmonton ... Wayne Gretzky was our mark on the map. This morning our city can only be in a state of mourning.

"Babe Ruth was once traded from the Boston Braves to the New York Yankees. I can't think of anything else that can compare. And, really, even that doesn't do it. Babe Ruth wasn't Babe Ruth then. He hadn't put up the numbers which, to this day, separate him from everybody else who has ever played the game. He hadn't won the World Series four times yet. He wasn't in his prime, at the very peak of his career.

"This, unquestionably, is the biggest deal in hockey history. This, arguably, is the biggest deal in the history of professional sport.

"Was it for love? Or money?

"How did it happen?

"You can believe what you want. I know what I believe. With every bone in my body, I know what I believe.

"I know the instant reaction is to first finger the blushing bride. She stole our Wayne away. You can believe, if you wish, all the white-knight stuff about doing what Wayne wanted. I don't buy it ... I believe the suggestion that the whole thing was Wayne's idea is quite likely a crock."

I fingered Peter Pocklington.

Chubey and several *Sun* staffers covered the press conference at Molson House and Dan Barnes flew to Los Angeles to cover the second stage of the press conference down there. Reaction was gathered by the entire *Sun* sports staff. Coverage on pages 2, 3, 4, 5, 6, 10, 11, 18, 19, 23, 30, 36, 37, 38, 39, 40, 41, 42, 43, 46 and 47 indeed.

Assistant sports editor (now sports editor) Phil Rivers wrote the famous "99 Tears" front-page headline.

Chubey found co-coach John Muckler: "Thank God I believe in life after death. Are the police on call out there?"

Laurie MacFayden found Don Cherry: "I'd like to say I knew it was coming, but I must admit I thought Wayne Gretzky would never leave Edmonton. It's very hard for me to believe."

While it was the sale of century, players were also involved. Marty McSorley and Mike Krushelnyski went to the Kings and Jimmy Carson and Martin Gelinas came to Edmonton. There were stories on all.

The headline on Graham Hicks' column was "Jezebel Janet!"

There was even a story on Joey Moss, the mentally handicapped brother of Gretzky's old girlfriend Vikki Moss who Wayne found work for in the Oilers dressing room.

Peter Stockland from *The Sun's* Ottawa bureau filed a story on NDP House leader Nelson Riis "demanding the Mulroney government immediately block the Gretzky trade."

The next day Pocklington went on record as saying he didn't think Gretzky's tears at the press conference were real.

"Wayne has an ego the size of Manhattan. He's a great actor."

The social event of the year: the marriage of hockey superstar Wayne Gretzky to actress Janet Jones.

Best man Mio went on the record as saying there was no way Gretzky asked for the trade: "Gretzky never initiated any deal. Wayne loves Edmonton. He never wanted to leave. It's really important people know this wasn't Wayne and Janet's idea."

Coffey checked in with a similar quote: "I talked with Wayne after the Stanley Cup and he said, 'I'm happy. I'll play here forever.'"

Sather had very little to say. And Gretzky was refusing to say anything.

But Janet Jones-Gretzky phoned me in Kansas City and said she was not going to let her husband sit silent and go down in hockey history as an egomaniac and a Canadian treasure-turned-traitor.

"Peter Pocklington is the reason Wayne Gretzky is no longer an Edmonton Oiler," she began.

"The key to everything that happened was an event five days after our wedding. Pocklington gave Bruce McNall permission to take Wayne if he could do it. And that did it!

"I never intended to talk. But let's talk. The story of the trade as presented by Peter Pocklington is false. Pocklington is the reason Wayne is gone. I know the real story. I know the whole story. I know Wayne didn't deserve any of this. He wouldn't let Edmonton fans, Canada and, most important, his teammates down without good reason.

"Wayne speaks from the heart. People who aren't good at lying aren't good at lying. The tears that came out were not all an act. To see Wayne hurt like this hurts me. That's why I'm making the call to you.

"This is what happened. The day after the Stanley Cup, Pocklington told Wayne about an offer from Vancouver. Wayne said to Pocklington: 'I can't believe you coming to me with this the day after we win the Stanley Cup.' It was obvious Peter did not have Wayne's backing and he backed out of the Vancouver deal.

"Before the wedding, Wayne had heard so many rumours about being traded and sold he asked Pocklington about them. Pocklington suggested Wayne come to his office to talk about it. He told Wayne there was nothing to them. Wayne told me, 'Janet, all the rumours are false.' This was the day before our wedding. I brought my car to Edmonton. We had every intention of living the rest of our lives in Edmonton.

"Five days after the wedding, Wayne got a call from Bruce McNall. He told Wayne that he had talked to Pocklington and Peter had told him, 'If you can swing him over, you've got him.'

"Five days after the wedding, Wayne had no intention of leaving the Edmonton Oilers."

Ten years later, on the anniversary, Gretzky looked back.

"It's the hardest thing I've ever been through. I think about it a lot still. I don't think there's an Aug. 9 that's gone by when I haven't thought about it.

"It still seems like yesterday, not like 10 years. And it was something I thought would never end. At the time we were the cream of the crop. We'd just won our fourth Stanley Cup. And I played as well as I ever played in that final. Then all of a sudden, things happen. And, unfortunately, it all ended a little too quick.

"I've said it many times in private but never in public until now. But because of that day, playing in Edmonton has never been a good feeling for me. I hate it. I look in the crowd and I still see the faces. The

Proud parents Janet and Wayne cuddle with their daughter Paulina.

No longer an Oiler, Wayne Gretzky musters a smile with his new boss, L.A. Kings owner Bruce McNall.

fans felt like my friends. I skate on the ice in Edmonton and still see those faces and it's difficult to this day for me to play in Edmonton.

"I think we could have won seven or eight Stanley Cups.

"I'll tell you one thing I'll go to my grave believing. There may have been better teams that have won the Stanley Cup, but those Edmonton teams were the most exciting teams ever to win it. That team had so much emotion, energy and excitement."

Ten years later and he was still having trouble talking about it.

But that day, despite how he publicly appeared to stand in support of his owner, Glen Sather was working the other way behind the scenes.

"Glen really wanted me to stay," said Gretzky. "It became an even bigger decision."

Gretzky says he's friends with Pocklington again. And he never stopped having a special relationship with Sather.

"In fact, somehow, some way, I can see myself being connected with the Oilers when it's done," he says.

"I'll always be an Oiler when it's done."

How would history have changed if Sather had talked Gretzky out of it? How many more Stanley Cups would the Edmonton Oilers have won?

A Cup of happiness: Wayne and Janet pose with their bundle of joy, daughter Paulina.

How much longer would it have taken for the NHL's salary structure to go crazy?

What would the NHL look like today?

"I guess I think about that all the time. I think about it every time I see him," said Sather on the anniversary. "I think about it every time I see something about him in the paper. I wonder what we could have accomplished. That team was settling in pretty good that summer. It had become so strong internally. There wouldn't have been much that could have torn it apart. But that was the one thing that definitely would have done it."

Aug. 9, 1988.

Ten years later, with Pocklington out of the picture, Sather was willing to tell the whole story.

"I took Wayne into a room with just the two of us at Molson House where we held the press conference. I talked to him for a few minutes. I told him I'd stop the deal. I told him I'd tell Peter I'd resign if he didn't stop the deal. But Wayne decided not to because he felt it was all beyond repair at that point.

"I was the last to know. We went to the Arctic fishing. I think everybody on the Arctic trip knew about the deal except for me. When that was over Peter invited me to president Ford's golf tournament in Beaver Creek, Colorado. That's when he told me. I got on the phone to Bruce

Wayne Gretzky returned to the Coliseum in October 1988 to face his former Oiler teammates for the first time as a Los Angeles King.

McNall from there. That's when I began to understand that the deal was already done.

"Peter was afraid to tell me.

"And I don't blame him.

"Krushelnyski and McSorley were already part of the deal. Gretzky had got them in. By the time I got involved, I got Gelinas and Carson and the draft picks out of McNall by convincing him I would queer the deal. But to me it didn't matter. It didn't make any difference. It wouldn't be the same."

Sather says it didn't have to happen in 1988. Or 1989. Or 1990. Or maybe even 1991.

"If the team had been a separate entity, if Peter was not involved in the other businesses, I think we could have kept that team together for quite a while longer.

"It was so close-knit. And they could all see the things they could accomplish together historically.

"I know we would have won more than one more Stanley Cup. Probably two or three. We were too good at that point. I think, financially, we would have been able to keep that team together another three or four years. It was just starting to hit it. They were just going into the prime of their careers."

Sather isn't sure what the dollars would be like in the game today. Gretzky going to L.A. was the one deal that started the spiral.

"McNall was giving money away as if it didn't mean anything," said Sather. "Because it didn't mean anything."

After scoring 583 goals and 1,086 assists for 1,669 points in 696 regular-season games and adding 81 goals and 171 assists for 252 points in 120 playoff games, setting 43 NHL records, winning eight Hart Trophies, seven Art Ross Trophies, four Stanley Cups and two Conn Smythes in nine NHL seasons in Edmonton, Wayne Gretzky was gone.

The memories stay, but do not grow greater with time because this was one case where that wasn't possible.

In a year there'd be a statue outside the Coliseum of Gretzky holding the Stanley Cup over his head – a reminder to Edmontonians every time they attended an Oiler game that they had watched the greatest player in the history of hockey when he was at his best.

Lightning dramatically lights up the night sky above the statue of Wayne Gretzky.

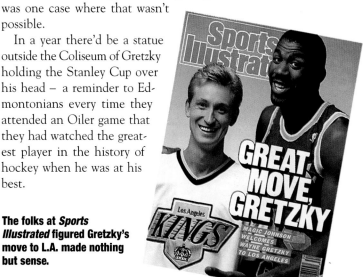

The folks at *Sports Illustrated* figured Gretzky's move to L.A. made nothing but sense.

Chapter 14

The Title Wave

Wayne Gretzky is gone. Life goes on. If only it could have been that easy.

There was nothing easy about the 1988-89 season. Gretzky was never out of mind, seldom even out of sight.

The NHL schedule maker saw to it that Gretzky and the Oilers hooked up for a home-and-home media event, early.

The first reunion was in Edmonton on Oct. 19. And it was a game like no other. Oiler players were actually encouraging Edmonton fans to welcome Gretzky with cheers. In fact, "Cheers Wayne!" was *The Sun*'s headline on the day of the big game.

"I hope they do cheer," said Craig MacTavish. "This is a night for memories and he's been a part of them all."

Kevin Lowe said if it feels good, do it.

"If the fans cheer for him and not us, I don't think the players will take it personally. This isn't like any other game for any of us – the players or the fans."

Mark Messier said if he was sitting in the stands he'd be cheering for Gretzky.

"He's Wayne Gretzky. He's the greatest player who ever played the game. And he's a friend."

O where have you gone? Missing letter aside, there's no doubt who these fans were honouring. Opposite: The Oilers won the 1990 Stanley Cup without the Great One.

It might have been the first time in hockey history that 234 sports reporters came to cover a crowd. Everybody involved, including the fans, knew they had to get this game by the boards before they could even contemplate moving forward toward closure. And that, of course, included Gretzky.

"The things you think about now are all the memories and all the fun. We had something that very few teams ever had. We were the Green Bay Packers of our time," he said. "We were in a small city, grew up together and had a great relationship with each other and the city."

Messier took charge and held Gretzky without a goal, and won the game for the Oilers with the

Mark (Moose) Messier thumps Washington's Bob Gould in January 1988.

two goals that made the difference in an 8-6 win. But the scene was the story. After 99 Tears, the storyline this night was 99 Cheers. And *The Sun*'s picture said it all. Gretzky, his stick across his knees, stood on the Los Angeles Kings' side of centre ice while Oilers Charlie Huddy and MacTavish stood staring at the back of the man who, as the sign in the Coliseum said, was "Back In Black."

The city, which never had a chance to say goodbye, tried to pay Gretzky back for a million memories as it rode an emotional roller coaster to nowhere. When he stepped on the ice for the pre-game warm-up, several hundred fans crowded behind the L.A. bench. They applauded him when he appeared. They applauded him again when he left. And he kept peeking back to see if they were peeking back at him.

"I didn't talk to anybody and nobody talked to me," said No. 99.

The minute the Kings started to file back onto the ice the ovation began. Then they chanted "Gretzky! Gretzky! Gretzky!" The ovation lasted four minutes before Tim Feehan, who had sung at Gretzky's wedding, could sing the national anthem.

"To come out to that ovation ... it was a great feeling. Words cannot describe it," said Gretzky.

The crowd cheered Gretzky when he had the puck and cheered the Oilers when he didn't. But in the end, when the game was 6-5 and the Kings had a five-minute power play, it was Edmonton vs. Los Angeles. Us vs. Them. And he was Them.

Breaking up is hard to do, and Gretzky didn't make it any easier when the two teams travelled to Los Angeles a few days later to do it all over again. He invited the en-

Young fans watch as the Oilers are shuttled back to the Coliseum after a practice at the nearby AgriCom.

tire team to his new $2.7-million house three doors down from Michael Jackson before the second game of the Homecoming-And-Home series.

Wife Janet said her husband didn't leave his last tear in Edmonton.

"He was teary-eyed when we drove up to our house and all the other guys were standing there. He loves those guys so much, you can just see it pulling his heartstrings when they're around."

One tour group from Edmonton bought 500 tickets for the game. Again the Oilers won, 5-4 this time, and it was Jimmy Carson who scored the prettiest goal of the game.

The Oilers could get on with it now. But not for long. This was the year the NHL All-Star Game was held in Edmonton.

"There are a lot of people who have watched hockey for a long time in this city," said Messier. "And if you'd told them 10, 15, 20 or 30 years ago that they'd be watching the NHL All-Star Game in Edmonton one day ...

"And with Wayne coming back ...

"One year we had eight Oilers in the all-star game. This year we have seven. Of course, that's counting Gretzky and Paul Coffey."

Gretzky had always treated the all-star game as if it was public skating. But he insisted he wouldn't for this one.

"This is the last game when I'll be on the team Edmonton fans are cheering for," he said. "It would be nice to have a great game. It would be nice to win."

It was one last time for old times' sake. And he made it magic.

"I had a great time," he said when it was over and his Campbell Conference team had beat Mario Lemieux's Wales Conference reps 9-5. "I couldn't stop smiling all night. I was tickled by everything. The ovation was something I'll remember forever. What happened to me here earlier in the year was special. This was extra-special."

Gretzky made it extra-special when he won another car as the all-star game MVP.

"I think I'm going to give this one to a guy who didn't get a lot of recognition for what he did for me in my career. I'm going to give this car to Dave Semenko."

Co-coach John Muckler made it extra-special, too. He put Gretzky on a line with Jari Kurri. In the middle of the second period

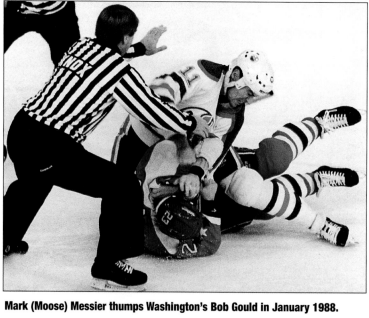

Kelly Buchberger, left, cheers as Jari Kurri stays loose with a game of table tennis during the Oilers' 1990 playoff drive for five.

End of an era: Glen Sather officially turned the head coaching reins over to John Muckler in June 1989.

he looked down the bench at them and said, "Gosh, it's nice to see you two together again."

Gretzky and Kurri each had a goal and two assists in the game. "We were giving and going, weren't we? It was fun to play with Jari again."

Now the Oilers could get on with their season. Well, at least until the playoffs.

Kurri was the story of the season. And some of us ended up eating our words on that subject. Like Don Cherry. He said it loudest. He said without Wayne around Kurri wouldn't score 25 goals. But I wrote it. I said it, too. I said Jari Kurri without Gretzky around wouldn't be Jari Kurri any more. But after the first 35 games, Kurri had four more goals and 14 more points than the year before.

Kurri ended up becoming the first player whose name wasn't Wayne Gretzky to lead the Oilers in scoring. His 102 points on 44 goals and 58 assists ranked eighth in the league. It was his seventh 40-goal year. He scored his 400th career goal, his 500th career assist and his 950th career point. And he made the second all-star team.

Carson was two points behind him with 100 for the year and Mark Messier had 94. Three Oilers in the top dozen was nothing to sneeze at. But the Oilers struggled as a team all year, falling back to the middle of the pack with teams that weren't sure if they were contenders or pretenders.

Grant Fuhr had the most frustrating year of anybody.

"I'm playing like a dog. I'm fighting the puck. I've had more bad games this year than in my first seven years as a pro," he said at one point.

It was the year Death Valley died.

For more than six seasons teams had been singing the Highway 2 Blues. You had to go back to 1982 to find the last team that found four points in back-to-back games in Edmonton and Calgary. It was Oct. 7-8, 1982 – the first two games of the season – when the defending Stanley Cup-champion New York Islanders did it.

Alberta, the province where the dinosaurs died, had became known far and wide in hockey as Death Valley. But you could see the end of that coming on New Year's Eve. The Montreal Canadiens had won in Calgary and headed to Edmonton red-hot, with the Oilers not.

Over the years, 136 teams had tried to do the Alberta double play and failed. But the Canadiens turned the trick. And Sather left the rink fuming at the Coliseum crowd which seemed to have more people cheering for Montreal than the Oilers.

"Somebody was waving the flag of France behind our bench. That's a joke. In our building!" said Sather, who had made a deal in early Feb-

ruary to acquire an attraction for the fans who had loved Dave Semenko: Dave Brown from Philadelphia for Keith Acton.

Finally, on April 2 in Calgary, the regular season was over. The Oilers barely managed to end up over .500 and finished third in their division behind Calgary and L.A. That meant they'd have to open the playoffs on the road for the first time since their second year in the league.

"Now it's over and who cares?" said MacTavish. "Now it doesn't matter any more. Who cares? It's forgotten. All of the things that were said, all of the nattering back and forth, it's forgotten if you do well in the playoffs. Obviously, the year didn't go well. Hopefully we'll go into the playoffs with the idea that we can salvage a poor season."

But it was Gretzky again.

Edmonton vs. Los Angeles.

The series was compelling in Canada. But, in the beginning, L.A. took no notice. For the first time in 21 years of the franchise, the Kings were opening the playoffs at home and the *L.A. Times* didn't have one word on the series the day the Oilers arrived in the middle of a heat wave. It was 104 F on the day of the series opener. And whatever you may have made of the regular season, Game 1 for the Oilers provided hope that the Oilers would get hot when it mattered most.

Esa Tikkanen and Craig Simpson scored 67 seconds apart to rally for a 4-3 win.

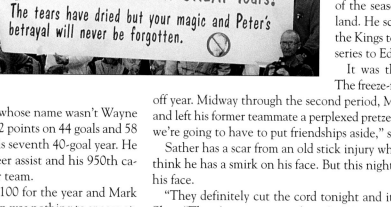

In Game 2, the Oilers were beaten by somebody by the name of Chris Kontos. Nobody had him in any playoff pool. He'd played most of the season in Kloeten, Switzerland. He scored three goals to lead the Kings to a 5-2 win and send the series to Edmonton tied 1-1.

It was there that it happened. The freeze-frame of the Oilers' playoff year. Midway through the second period, Messier ran over Gretzky and left his former teammate a perplexed pretzel on the ice. "Obviously, we're going to have to put friendships aside," said Messier.

Sather has a scar from an old stick injury which often makes people think he has a smirk on his face. But this night he *did* have a smirk on his face.

"They definitely cut the cord tonight and it was great to see," said Slats. "There's no reason to cheer for Wayne any more. The crowd was 100 per cent behind the team and I could tell the team was happy with

Kevin Lowe and Mark Lamb had plenty to smile about after the Oilers eliminated the Winnipeg Jets in the 1990 playoffs.

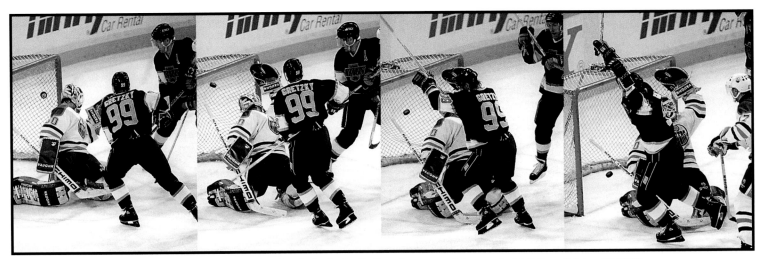

Wayne Gretzky made history on Edmonton ice yet again when he broke Gordie Howe's career points record of 1,850 on October 15, 1989.

that, too."

For the first time in five years Fuhr produced a playoff shutout. The Oilers won 4-0.

In Game 4, the much-maligned Steve Smith got to be a Stanley Cup playoff hero. He scored with 26 seconds remaining for a 4-3 win and a commanding 3-1 series lead.

Back in L.A., at poolside, Messier and I talked at length. In what should have been an upbeat, positive time, I didn't have to possess special powers to see that it wasn't. Not for Messier. He'd hit Gretzky hard in Game 3. But it was Messier who ended up hurting on the inside. And sitting there, waiting for Game 5 and a chance to put Gretzky out of play, he poured his heart out.

"This is no damn fun," he said.

"It just doesn't seem right.

"Obviously, I have responsibilities to the guys on my team now and to the Oilers organization. But I can honestly say it hasn't been real enjoyable.

"I just want to win this series and get it over with. I've played with this guy so long. We've been so close. I'm godfather to his daughter Paulina. To go out there and slam his head through the boards isn't easy. It's the most difficult thing I've ever had to do."

The Kings used a letter from then U.S. president Ronald Reagan for motivational purposes prior to the game. They also had a message from Sylvester Stallone. Rocky on hockey didn't hurt, either. ("This is perfect. This is just like Rocky. You're the underdog. Come back and win the series.")

Suddenly Hollywood had discovered the Kings. Tom Hanks was at the game. Dudley Moore. Mary Fran. Larry Mann. John Candy. And the Kings won, 4-2.

Los Angeles became the sixth team in Stanley Cup playoff history to come from behind three games to one and win a series. A 4-1 win in Edmonton and a 6-3 win back home in Game 7. Edmonton native Kelly Hrudey was wonderful in the L.A. nets and Kontos scored his eighth goal of the series to end it for the Oilers.

"I feel deeply sorry for the Edmonton players, especially Mark and Kevin," said Gretzky. "I wanted to talk to them, but I couldn't. No one takes losing as hard as those two guys. We just beat the best play-

off team in the league. Now we play the best team in the league."

The Calgary Flames got rid of Gretzky and his new gang in four straight, going on to bring the Stanley Cup final to Alberta soil for the seventh straight season and then win it.

Sather waited only a few days after the Flames' triumph to make the first major news of the next hockey season. He called a press conference to announce he was stepping down as coach.

"It's an easy transition. I've been with John Muckler for a long time and it seems I've been with Teddy Green all my life. It's not like I'm passing this job to somebody I don't know or trust."

Head coach Muckler hired Ron Low as a new assistant and Muck's men came to camp in a much different frame of mind.

"Last year, every day somebody was upset about something," said Lowe. "Sooner or later you have to get the chip off your shoulder before it's too late. Last year was enough of that for an entire career as far as I'm concerned. I want to work in a happier environment."

But Gretzky had one more play before he would begin to go away.

There is something about Gretzky's sense of stage which is amazing. You just knew it would work out this way. Gretzky was on the verge of breaking Gordie Howe's record of 1,850 career points. And one look at the schedule and you knew exactly where and when it was going to happen.

Edmonton. Oct. 15, 1989.

I returned from the World Series for one day to cover the event. And it *was* an event. The crowd had come to cheer for Gretzky yet again. They were hoping that one last time they'd sit in on Gretzky making history at the Coliseum. And it wasn't enough for The Great One to break Howe's record on the ice he used to own. He waited until 5.3 seconds remained in the game to get a goal to send it into overtime. Then he scored the winner in overtime!

"I don't know who writes his scripts," said Howe. "There is no end to his brilliance."

The ovation lasted 10 minutes.

Howe was part of a presentation on the ice. The Kings presented a crystal hologram engraved with the image of

Legends: Gretz and Gordie chat outside the Coliseum.

Gretzky. And the Oilers presented him with a diamond bracelet with the inscription: "A great man is made up of qualities that meet or make great occasions. Presented in friendship by the Edmonton Oilers Hockey Club, 1989-90."

Could they get on with it now?

For anybody still focused on the Gretzky "trade," Sather gave them a new trade, a real trade, to chew on. And it turned out to be one of the greatest trades of his career. The highly unpopular Jimmy Carson and the aging Kevin McClelland were dealt to Detroit for Joe Murphy, Adam Graves and Petr Klima.

"We're committed to getting this team back on track again," said Slats. "All these guys are world-class skaters. Murphy and Graves are young guys with great potential. We have some great experienced players to teach them. And I'm convinced speed is the way hockey is going to go in the '90s."

Two weeks later Messier made the pronouncement: "We're going to win the Stanley Cup this year."

It wasn't *that* he said it. Talk is cheap. It was *when* he said it. The Oilers had a worse record in the middle of November that year than they had the previous year.

"The standings don't show it. But we're light years ahead of where we were last year," said Messier. "Last year there was no light at the end of the tunnel. This year we can see the light. And it's a bright light.

"We're definitely going to start talking Stanley Cup around here. I think it's important that the veterans start talking about what it was like to win a Stanley Cup around all of the new players and making them feel like we can win it. You can see the veterans getting excited. You can see Kevin, Doc Gregg, Charlie Huddy and Steve Smith starting to get pumped. I'm starting to think about what it was like to win that first one. It was great. To come back and win another one now ... that would be incredible."

Four days before Christmas, Grant Fuhr suffered a shoulder injury that would keep him out until just prior to the playoffs. No matter who had come and gone, there was always Fuhr to play goal in the playoffs. But all of sudden the odds were long that he'd be there this time. And there was still a half-schedule of regular-season hockey to play. Could the Oilers be the Oilers without Fuhr in goal?

"Let's find out," said Muckler.

It was Bill Ranford's team now.

"I want to prove I can win," said Ranford. "I don't care about stats. I want to win as many games as possible and play as well as I can play. All I care about are wins."

And the wins were starting to come. The Oilers had a record of 6-9-4 on Nov. 12. By Dec. 29, when they beat the Montreal Canadiens 6-2, they were 21-11-7. And while Gretzky wasn't around to manufacture milestones any more, Kurri substituted quite nicely. On Jan. 3 he scored his 1,000th NHL point, scoring his 461st goal and adding two

In June 1990, Geoff Smith, Mark Lamb and Kelly Buchberger were three of the Oilers' most eligible bachelors.

Oilers heavyweight big, bad Dave Brown.

assists as the Oilers beat the Blues 6-4 in St. Louis.

Among the highlights of the season were the highly hyped home-and-home heavyweight fight nights featuring Big Bad Dave Brown, Meanest Man In The Whole Damn Town vs. Stu (The Grim Reaper) Grimson.

The second fight, in Calgary, was one of the most incredible beatings in the history of the heavyweight division in hockey.

Grimson, who had claimed he had never lost a fight, lost his claim to fame. Brown hit Grimson with 15 overhand lefts and rights, with Grimson not managing one punch in return. The hero of a 3-2 overtime win was Martin Gelinas.

"That's a major win," said Muckler. "I think this hockey team grew up a bit tonight."

Sather managed to get Rexi Ruotsalainen back for another spring with a deadline deal for Jeff Sharples, a throw-in with Graves, Murphy and Klima in the Jimmy Carson trade. And the mood around the team was entirely different than it had been the year before.

Calgary won the division again with 90 points, nine more than the 38-38-14 Oilers. But the Winnipeg Jets had finished third and that meant Edmonton got its lucky matchup that translated to the Stanley Cup final every time.

And Edmonton was celebrating players wearing the Oiler uniform again, none with more gusto than Edmonton native Messier who stepped up and took his place as a great of the game this season, if he hadn't before.

Gretzky beat him in the scoring race, 142 points to 129. But Messier won the trophy that Gretzky had owned for his first eight years in the league. Edging Boston defenceman Ray Bourque by two votes in the closest voting in the history of the league's MVP award, Messier won the Hart Trophy. It was his career year. And now it was the part of the year he liked best. The playoffs.

That's also the part of the year Glen Sather likes best. But, for the first time, he wasn't coaching the club and his first problem in adjusting to the situation was location.

"I don't know where I'm going to sit. I could sit with my wife, but that would be too tough on her. Sitting with the fans in the stands might be too tough on me. There are a lot of places I might prefer to the press box. I'd like some place down at ice level to watch it, but I don't know if there is such a place," said Slats, who had a 21-6 playoff series record and a .706 winning percentage in Stanley Cup play.

The playoffs, Sather could tell you, are no place for a n-n-n-nervous person. But Ranford had to play anyway. And it was shake, rattle and roll as Ranford's knees knocked and the Jets won Game 1.

The Jets had a 3-0 lead before they had what might be called their first real scoring chance. It was that kind of a night as the Jets, 1-18

A shoulder injury to No. 1 netminder Grant Fuhr meant the Oilers had to sink or swim with Billy Ranford down the stretch. He didn't let them down.

against the Oilers in post-season play, scored a 7-5 win, their first ever playoff win in the Coliseum.

"He's not the first goalie to have his troubles in a game and he's not going to be the last," said Muckler. "It's up to Billy to fight back."

Fuhr wasn't healthy enough to be an option. It was sink or swim with Ranford.

"Billy doesn't have to be Grant Fuhr," said Messier. "He just has to be Bill Ranford. He got us to where we were this year. Now we're here and he has to relax and enjoy it. There's no use getting uptight and nervous and missing out on all the fun."

Every playoff year the least likely of players gets to be a Stanley Cup hero. And Mark Lamb was the man in Game 2, scoring the winner at 4:21 of overtime to leave the Jets with a 0-5 OT record against the Oilers in the playoffs.

"They sent me on for the faceoff and I was supposed to come right off," said Lamb. "I'm sure glad I didn't."

As rancid as Ranford was in Game 1, he was great in Game 3. But the result was the same. He'd gone from the ridiculous to the sublime – and superb – in three games of the series, but the hockey gods weren't warming up to him.

"That's probably the best game I've played in ..." He didn't end the sentence.

A Craig Simpson turnover resulted in a Dale Hawerchuk goal with 4:30 left in regulation to win it 2-1 for the Jets and give Winnipeg a 2-1 series lead.

And that's when the Oilers received a major motivation.

Winnipeg columnist Jack Matheson called the Oilers "bewildered clowns."

"The Oilers aren't a hockey machine any more and they are having trouble hacking mediocrity," wrote the father of *Journal* hockey writer Jim Matheson. "The glamour is gone. The Oilers never did learn how to lose. And why would they? They've never had much practice."

But it was Jets assistant coach Alpo Suhonen who checked in with the best stuff. He dished up juicy quotes, saying the Oilers were "confused" and "arrogant" and "completely lost." He also observed that "every empire goes over the hill" and theorized that "they've been winning these series for 10 years but once you go over the hill it's very hard to come back."

Game 4 was one for the memory bank. The old Winnipeg Arena was turned into a duplicate din of Chicago Stadium and the Oilers and Jets gave hockey one of those games you couldn't help but appreciate regardless of how it ended. It ended 65 seconds into the second overtime period with the two teams skating in sand and the crowd too tense to put its tonsils to a further test, until it all escaped in one euphoric release when Dave Ellett scored to win it 4-3 for the Jets, ending an eight-game Oilers playoff overtime winning streak.

"I'm glad they have a roof on this place," said Ellett. "I don't think I've ever jumped that high. The best thing about winning is that we don't have to know how it feels to lose that game."

Muckler knew what he had watched.

"It was a great, great hockey game. It was a gallant effort. Our team can't work any harder. We gave so much."

The scene back home between games was hardly what you would've expected.

"A little more positive around here than you might have thought?" inquired Simpson.

They'd just been kicked in the stomach for the third time in the series, but they flew home, slept, woke up, noticed that the sun had come up, and decided to take the attitude that they were still alive so there was no sense being bummed out by anything. There would be plenty of time for that in the summer if that's the way it worked out. Besides, the Oilers had given up a 3-1 series lead the year before. They decided they kind of liked the idea of trying to turn the trick themselves and become the seventh team in the history of the Stanley Cup playoffs to come back from a dreaded 3-1 deficit.

"It's been great hockey. It's been great TV. Now we've got to win, that's all. And the players are dead confident they are going to come out of this thing," said Muckler.

How confident they were when Hawerchuk broke in alone and ripped a 30-footer with four minutes remaining and the Oilers leading 4-3, you had to wonder.

Adam Graves.

Ranford was certainly candid about how he felt.

"My heart was pounding so hard," he said.

He made an amazing save.

"I guess it was one of the most critical saves I've ever made. The best playoff save, anyway," he said.

Simpson scored at the other end and the series returned to Winnipeg for Game 6 with the Oilers making the point that for the first time there'd be pressure, real Stanley Cup playoff pressure, on the Jets.

"We've got guys who have been to five finals and have won four Stanley Cups," said Muckler. "If we have an advantage, that's it."

If the Jets were playoff patsies for the Oilers in the past, they weren't this year.

"They're like a cockroach," said assistant GM Bruce MacGregor. "Kill one and there are two. Kill two and there are four."

The Oilers took a 3-0 lead in Game 6, but still needed a world-class goal from Kurri with just over six minutes to play to win it 4-3. Another great game.

"I think this series should go on forever," said Muckler.

Sather wasn't quite so pumped.

"I'm in jail," he said of watching the series from the press box instead of coaching.

"Did you see that shot?" Esa Tikkanen shouted in the dressing room after Kurri beat Bob Essensa to win it. "Nobody saw that shot. Not even me."

Muckler marvelled.

"Terry Sawchuk wouldn't have stopped that. Johnny Bower wouldn't have stopped that. No goalie in the history of hockey would have stopped that shot. It was labelled. It was like a bullet."

Mark Messier celebrates Esa Tikkanen's goal against former teammate Andy Moog during Game 3 of the playoff series against the Bruins.

Back to Edmonton and a Game 7 ... and when it was over, the question was "Grant who?"

Ranford, the great goat of Game 1, went on to become the series hero and the first star of Game 7 as the Oilers scored a 4-1 win to put the Jets away.

"I think I proved I can win in pressure playoff games," he said.

It was Gretzky and the Kings again. But this time with a difference.

"I don't think we've forgotten how they eliminated us last year," said Muckler. "And I know I'll never forget the enjoyment Wayne got. All of those things stick in your mind."

There had been enough passage of time. Now the Oilers wanted to prove that there was more to them than Gretzky, that they could win a Stanley Cup without Gretzky.

While the hockey world had been expecting an Oilers-Flames series, there was nothing wrong with the way this series set up. If the Oilers were going to be great again, they'd have to beat the guy who made them great. The Great Gretzky.

The Kings, who had scored a stunning upset over the Flames in the first round, winning games by scores of 5-3, 2-1, 12-4 and 4-3, were beaten 7-0 in the lid-lifter of the Smythe Division final.

Said L.A. coach Tom Webster: "Humiliated. Embarrassed. We didn't show up. We've got to get our pride back. That's all I have to say."

The Oilers had easier opening games in their Stanley Cup playoff history. But only three could compare. In '85 there was the 11-2 win over Chicago. A year earlier Edmonton ran it up 9-2 over Winnipeg. And the same year the Oilers massaged Minnesota 7-1.

"This game was a breather," reported Ranford, who refused to make much of his first Stanley Cup shutout. Gretzky looked injured. And Tikkanen had refined the art of Grate vs. Great, checking against his old linemate.

Game 2 was Game 1 all over again. Except this time it was 6-1. Kurri scored his 87th career playoff goal to move one behind Gretzky, and a Ranford breakaway save against Gretzky only 85 seconds into the game was considered the turning point.

All of a sudden, things were too good to be true. Overcoming negatives, you may have noticed by now, has been a constant in Oilers history. And between games, a sign on Kurri's lawn had the potential to rip this team apart again: "For Sale."

But the Oilers were getting used to handling the speed bumps now.

"Yeah, I heard about this," said Tikkanen of the "For Sale" sign. "The big thing if he's going away is not to worry about that right now. We have to think about now, not next year. But it's not easy. He's a big player in the last 10 years."

After the long series against Winnipeg, the Oilers knew they needed a short series if there was any chance they were going to win Lord Stanley's modern-day marathon.

Again, Ranford was great in goal as the Oilers won 5-4. Messier had two assists to tie Larry Robinson on the Stanley Cup list with 111. Only Gretzky with 188 had more. And

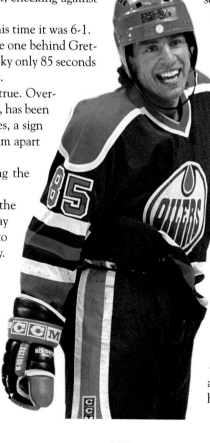

What's up, Doc? Stay-at-home defenceman Randy Gregg dances in celebration of a rare goal against Chicago in May 1990. Below: Petr Klima.

Gretzky wouldn't get any more this season. He was too injured to play in Game 4.

And so it was that the Ghost of Gretzky was exorcised. The ghost was gone and the Oilers moved on as Joe Murphy fired the winner four minutes and 42 seconds into overtime.

"We knew we were going to put Wayne behind us at the start of the year," said captain Messier.

"I think we became a team after that first game, that loss to Winnipeg," said Sather. "The team is a team now. Last year we were a collection of people."

In the L.A. room Gretzky was predicting a fifth Stanley Cup for his old teammates.

"They could be pretty much unstoppable," he said. "Messier keeps getting stronger and stronger and if Ranford continues to be as tough as he was in this series ... A lot of people forget they won the Cup two years ago. I think it's one thing that they got over my trade, but I think it was the trade with Detroit that made them a better team. One of those guys, Joe Murphy, scored the winning goal in overtime tonight. I think it was more that trade than getting over me that made the Oilers what they are right now. Glen made a great trade. Those guys fit right into the Oilers' style."

It was shades of Mount Orval as the Oilers opened their Campbell Conference series final. Chicago Blackhawks deja vu.

In the spring of '83, the 'Hawks had lost a playoff game 8-2 to the Oilers. When it was over coach Orval Tessier said he was "ashamed" and said his players "should be sent to the Mayo Clinic for heart transplants."

Game 1 was 5-2 Edmonton. And Mike Keenan was declaring "we embarrassed ourselves."

Keenan and his star Denis Savard engaged in a shouting session in the hall outside the visitors dressing room after the first period. Savard had two 30-second shifts in the first period. In the second period he played a grand total of 276 seconds.

Four-letter words filled the air.

"A fly on the dressing-room wall would have had a really good time," said Doug Wilson of the goings-on that night.

Keenan made sure his team was motivated for Game 2 and it was Wilson who sailed a 55-footer past Lowe's hand and by Ranford, with 119 seconds to play, to win it 4-3, ending an eight-game Oilers win streak that went back to Game 5 against Winnipeg. And back in Chicago, Greg Millen stopped 31 shots as the 'Hawks stunned the Oilers 5-1.

Suddenly the Oilers were a team in trouble again.

Much has been written over the years about the famous Mark Messier stare and glare. Prior to Game 4 in Chicago was where his teammates saw it emerge full force for the first time.

This was his hockey team now. And he came to the rink with that refuse-to-lose look in his eyes.

"He wasn't saying anything," said MacTavish. "He didn't say a word. He had his skates on more than half an hour before he would normally put them on. You just had to take one look at him and know how up he was,

Stanley comin' through: Mark Messier makes his way through the Edmonton crowd after the Oilers brought the Cup back from Boston in May 1990.

how ready he was. One look at him and you knew he was going to take charge."

The Oilers won 4-2 to even the series. Messier took the entire load on his shoulders, scoring two goals and adding two assists.

"He did the job for us. The rest of us were the supporting cast," said MacTavish. "We took one look at him and knew he was going to win that game no matter how the rest of us played."

Sather wasn't complaining about where he was sitting to watch this one.

"Mark was awesome," he said. "Whenever you need it, he's the guy who comes through for you. He's been doing this since the Islanders in '84. But tonight he was the dominant force. That was his best game of the playoffs. Maybe the best game ever."

Back home Messier set up Kurri for the winner in a 4-3 game and the Oilers packed their bags for an eight-day road trip. To Chicago ... and Boston.

Messier had won the series in Game 4 and everybody knew it. It was 8-4 in Game 6 as the Oilers advanced to their sixth Stanley Cup final in eight years.

"Title Wave" seemed like such a silly slogan during the season. But it fit as the Oilers headed to Boston for games 1 and 2 of the final series to win a ring for their thumb, the same thumb they were sucking the year before without Gretzky.

Back in the Stanley Cup final 21 months after Pocklington sold Gretzky. Astonishing.

In business in the NHL for 11 years and making the final this year meant they had played in the finals more years than not. Mind-boggling.

If every team's fair playoff share was an appearance in the final every 10½ years, then Edmonton had now enjoyed its share up to the year 2043. And if the

The 6,000-kg statue of Wayne Gretzky found a permanent home in front of the Coliseum in August 1989.

Oilers beat the Bruins in the final, the City of Champions would be up to the year 2085 for Cups copped.

Spoiled? Rotten!

Funny the way it worked. Going for their fifth Stanley Cup felt more like going for the first one than any other.

"This year it's extra-special," declared Messier upon arrival in Boston. "It's so unbelievable. These kids came so far, so fast," he said, making special reference to the Kid Line of Martin Gelinas, Adam Graves and Joe Murphy, who had only played three games together prior to the playoffs. "They're seasoned veterans now. That's what is so great. That's what going through three series can do for a player. You learn in a hurry. And Billy ... Billy Ranford found out that all he has to be is Billy Ranford. If he doesn't get all caught up about being in Boston where he used to play, he'll be fine."

We thought we were there to cover the Stanley Cup final, not the Boston Marathon. But Game 1 will always be remembered in Stanley Cup history as the Boston Marathon. And if Petr Klima's name lives on in hockey history, it'll be for the game in which he didn't play, yet managed to score the winning goal.

It was the longest game in the history of the Stanley Cup finals. At 1:23 a.m., with 4:47 left on the clock in the third overtime period – after 115 minutes and 13 seconds of hockey – Klima won it 3-2 for the Oilers.

Klima didn't get on the ice until well into the third overtime. When it was over, I asked the happy hero when he'd taken his last shift before that.

"About 10 o'clock," he said. "Maybe 9 o'clock or

something.

"When I got the shot, I didn't just shoot, I shot for the five-hole between Andy Moog's legs. At 1:30 in the morning you have to make a good shot."

Before Klima lit the lamp, the lights went out in the Boston Garden *again*. Two years earlier, a game had to be postponed when the lights went out with 23 minutes and 23 seconds to play in regulation. But this time they came back on and everybody in the building was praying they wouldn't go off again because everybody knew they were sitting in on Stanley Cup playoff history – a game that would never be forgotten. And everybody knew that somebody's name would be attached to this game forever.

"I don't care about having my name on a game, I just care about having my name on the Stanley Cup," said Klima.

The Oilers didn't practise the next day. They wouldn't have been able to even if they had wanted to.

"It's going to take two days for our equipment to dry out," said Steve Smith. "We all wore a couple of different sweaters. We all changed underwear and socks at least three times during the game. Everybody's gloves were just sopping wet. It was tough to hang on to your stick."

Kurri may have had a "For Sale" sign out on his lawn but he put the down payment on the Oilers' fifth Stanley Cup when he scored playoff goals Nos. 90, 91 and 92, in addition to a pair of assists, in leading Edmonton to a 7-2 win in the Garden party which was Game 2 and on his 30th birthday.

"What can you say? It was one of those nights when everything was going my way," said Kurri, who also passed Gretzky as the all-time Stanley Cup goalscorer and became the only player in playoff history not named Gretzky to hit the 200-point plateau.

"Turning 30, getting three goals, breaking Gretzky's record. That's a pretty good day," he said.

When the Oilers returned from Boston they were met by the largest number of fans ever to greet them at an airport. There was only one thing wrong with the scene. They hadn't won the Cup yet. The Bruins took advantage of the cocky mood and attitude in town as Andy Moog was the hero of a 2-1 win in Game 3.

With Messier seizing the moment again, after much speculation that he was playing hurt, the Oilers won 5-1 in Game 4. And the Oilers headed back to Beantown to try to do something they'd never done before: win a Cup on the road.

"We want to win it here because it's something we've never done in our history," said Craig Muni. "We got a taste of what it would be like at the airport when we came home up two games to nothing."

The fans in Edmonton had seen them carry four Cups. That never gets old hat. But ...

"Don't get us wrong," said Lowe. "We don't want to sound picky and choosy. But we'd like to experience bringing it home together on the plane and winning it like that."

And that they would.

With one minute and three seconds to go, Messier and Anderson said

Three men and a Stanley: Kevin Lowe, Mark Messier and Jari Kurri take the Cup for a victory spin around the track at Commonwealth Stadium.

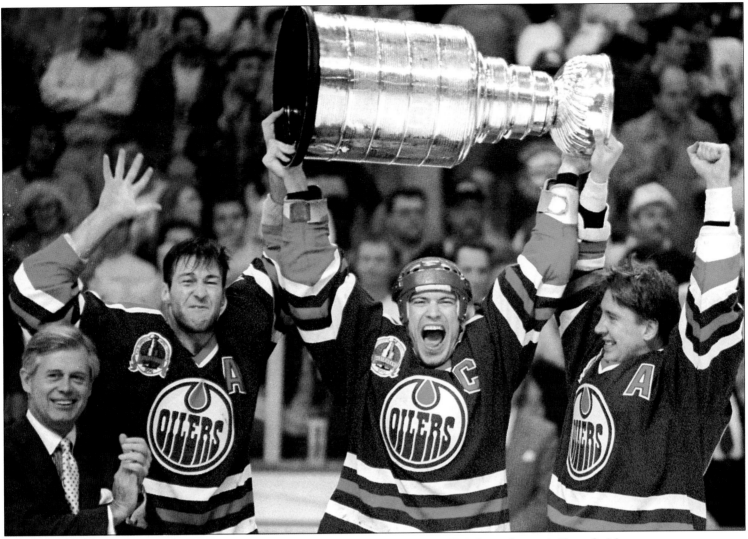

Five alive! Kevin Lowe, Mark Messier and Jari Kurri dedicated their fifth Stanley Cup championship to former teammate Wayne Gretzky.

to hell with it and threw their arms around each other on the bench. A split second later, Gelinas, Graves and Murphy melted into each other's arms. Messier then went to their end of the bench and started hugging them. Lowe, Huddy and Randy Gregg looked at each other and laughed.

"Somebody said we've got 15 Cups between the three of us," said Huddy. "I couldn't help but sit there thinking I turned a mediocre career into a pretty good one."

In the final minute, garbage bags emerged from behind the bench. In went the gloves and helmets. You could tell this team had been there and done this before.

Finally, when it was over, they got to mob Conn Smythe Trophy winner Ranford.

Craig Simpson's 16th goal of the playoffs turned out to be the Stanley Cup winner as the Oilers put the Bruins away 4-1.

Five Stanley Cups in seven seasons!

After 11 seasons in the league the Oilers could boast that only three franchises had won more Cups than they had.

There was now no denying they were a dynasty.

We were all dreaming, weren't we? Soon we were all going to wake up and Clarence Campbell would still be president of the NHL and Foster Hewitt would still be in the gondola a million miles away. Soon we'd wake up and it would still be a six-team league, and any suggestion Edmonton would win five Stanley Cups might be good for a lifetime pass to the mental institution of your choice.

"We just stepped into another era," said Lowe. "Five Cups! How many did Henri Richard win? Eleven? That's my goal now."

Messier paraded the Cup. And then the ritual of passing it from player to player began. To Graves. To Murphy. To Ranford and Anderson who carried it together. Ranford again. After they were done, they remembered the on-ice picture Gretzky had choreographed two years earlier.

"This one is for the G-man," said Lowe in the dressing room. "This afternoon Mark and I were in our room and saying, 'Let's win this one for Wayne.' He was a big part of our lives. He was a big part of this whole thing. We followed on his coattails and developed our pride, our abilities and our winning attitude."

On the plane ride home Anderson sang the theme song *Simply The Best – Better Than All The Rest.*

And when the Oilers returned home, they were given the high-five. There can only be one first time with hundreds of thousands of people in the streets for a parade. But this was the best of the rest.

Muckler took the stage in the middle of Commonwealth Stadium and told the fans about the great dessert his wife made him when he returned home.

"Boston creamed pie," he said.

But this wasn't a day to hear speeches. It was a day to see faces. And, as always, the face of all faces belonged to Messier and his goalmouth-sized smile.

"This was a lot like the first year," he said. "It was like winning it for the first time all over again."

Chapter 15

Two More 'Banner' Years

The theme for the dream changed after the Edmonton Oilers won their fifth Stanley Cup. It went from "Win One Without Wayne" to "Win One More For the Final Five With Five."

The list was getting shorter now. Mark Messier. Kevin Lowe. Glenn Anderson. Grant Fuhr. And Charlie Huddy. Five with five. Alive.

The old gang was breaking up. It was only a matter of time before they'd all be gone.

The "For Sale" sign was no joke. Jari Kurri was gone. He went off to play for a year with the Milan Devils of the Italian league and became the highest-paid player in European hockey history.

Everyone saw that coming. But not what happened next. In late August, Grant Fuhr confessed to drug abuse.

The team, scheduled to spend 16 days of the pre-season on a European tour, left without him, not expecting to see him for many months and not likely wearing an Oiler uniform then.

It was a nice trip for the defending Stanley Cup champions. But they couldn't convince themselves the Epson Cup was the Stanley Cup. They lost 10-1 to the St. Louis Blues. They did, however, beat West Germany 2-0 for the silver medal as the fans chanted "Oilers, Oilers, ha, ha, ha."

Another day, another victory over the Flames. Opposite: Mark Messier cracks up while posing for the annual team picture in May 1991.

"Something to cherish for life," said Craig MacTavish of the silver medal.

The Oilers travelled by boat down the Rhine River, took a 6½-hour train ride past quaint villages, hillside vineyards and castles. It was a terrific tour. But eventually ...

"I'm all cultured out," said Adam Graves.

When they returned NHL president John Ziegler had come down with his suspension for Fuhr.

One year.

"I have considered that his conduct went on for a period of six to seven years in spite of a clear league policy that if you use illegal drugs you will be suspended. Mr. Fuhr's actions were in defiance of this policy. He must suffer the consequences," said Ziegler after a 72-hour hearing in Toronto.

Glen Sather had left Randy Gregg unprotected and Vancouver Canucks coach Bob McCammon picked him off. Rexi Ruotsalainen chose to return to Europe again. No fewer than eight Oilers were playing out their options ...

None of that, however, took anything away from the scene on Oct. 6 when lightning, thunder, strobes and fireworks filled the air and there was proof through the night in Northlands Coliseum that another flag was up there. The Stanley Cup champions came onto the ice through a mist and were ushered to centre ice by strobe lights. The capacity crowd watched Mark Messier emerge through runway landing lights with the Stanley Cup held high over his head and the five-time champions replayed the scene from the Boston Garden the year before as they passed the Cup from player to player. Finally, as indoor fireworks flared, the banner was hoisted to the rafters where, now, 20 hung from the girders – 10 orange Smythe Division and Campbell Conference banners, three blue President's Trophy flags and five white Stanley Cup standards.

"It was excellent. It was a nice touch that we had a victory parade with the Cup," said coach John Muckler. "All the others were won at home. The fans were able to see the players parade with the Cup. They got that tonight."

Craig Muni said all the previous ceremonies were more for the fans than the players, but not this one.

"The players were more involved in this one. It was great to carry the Cup around one more time."

The season had barely begun when Messier went down with a medial ligament strain which, doctors said, would keep him out until mid-December.

That season became a "what have you done for us lately" scenario in a hurry. In a 12-game span the Oilers lost 11, including nine in a row. With a 2-11-2 record, they were off to their worst start in franchise history. And on the night of Nov. 12, the champs of the NHL were suddenly the chumps of the NHL, falling to 21st place in a 21-team league.

All this and Billy Ranford was playing *well*!

He lost two straight 1-0 games, including one to the Winnipeg Jets in overtime.

Ranford had a 2.78 goals-against average. And he had *two* wins.

The morning after the second straight 1-0 loss Ranford showed up for practice at West Edmonton Mall, saying he was thinking about taking a vow of silence and not talking until he won.

"I couldn't sleep last night. I just sat there thinking about the way things are going. Things may be going well for me, but when you lose 1-0, especially 1-0 in overtime ..."

Craig Simpson said he thought he recognized the problem.

"Bums like me are not scoring," he said.

Sather knew the problem was beyond that.

"There are so many things that are screwing it all up. Injuries. Sus-

Team captain Mark Messier made a dramatic entrance with the Stanley Cup prior to the Oilers' home opener on Oct. 6, 1990.

Oilers captain Glenn Anderson tangles with Mike Modano of the Minnesota North Stars. Below: Jari Kurri.

The Kid Line of Adam Graves, Joe Murphy and Martin Gelinas played like seasoned veterans throughout much of the 1989-90 campaign.

pensions. Walkouts. They all throw the timing off."

That and the sophomore jinx.

Martin Gelinas, Adam Graves and Joe Murphy were all struggling. On Nov. 14 they finally snapped out of it and at least ended the nine-game losing streak. And they found a wild and wacky way to do it.

"It was Looney-Toon," said Vancouver Canucks goalie Troy Gamble. "That will be on every hockey highlight film they ever make."

Five minutes were left in the second period, the Oilers losing 2-1. Stan Smyl and Messier started shoving in front of the benches. Garth Butcher stepped in and took a run at Messier. Esa Tikkanen and Steve Smith entered the picture while Jyrke Lumme, Brian Bradley and Steve Bozek plunged in for the Canucks. Three Oilers. Five Canucks. The puck was behind the Oilers' net. Chris Joseph passed it to Simpson. The two skated the length of the ice. Suddenly the crowd reacted. The battle in front of the benches stopped. The players stared in total disbelief. Referee Andy van Hellemond hadn't blown his whistle! Simpson, across the redline. Across the blueline. Simpson shoots! Scores!!!

It was one of those *Believe It Or Not* moments in sports people talk about years later. It transcended winning and losing. The Oilers took the goal and the win but ... "If that had happened to me when I was coaching, I'd have gone on the ice and chased van Hellemond around until I caught him, and been suspended for life," said Sather.

There was one other contributing factor to the win that night. Messier was back.

"He's the best leader in sports," said Graves. "Mess was definitely the best player on the ice by far. But it goes further than that. Just him being here makes the other guys play harder."

On Dec. 12, Graves scored his first goal of the season. In fact, all three members of the Kid Line scored in the same game.

"I wore my playoff suit to the game," said Graves. "This time it was clean. By the end of the playoffs last year it was all wrinkled and had spots on it."

On Feb. 4 Ziegler granted Fuhr reinstatement effective Feb. 12. It wasn't until Feb. 18, however, that he played his first game. It was one he'd remember.

On his first night back he registered a shutout against the New Jersey Devils. There was something odd about him, though. His

mask. It was white. Blank.

"I figured why waste the paint?" said Fuhr, who expected to be traded. "I figure why waste all the time and trouble of designing and decorating my mask until I know for sure what colours to use."

It was the week of the trading deadline.

"The trade deadline is Tuesday. We play Wednesday. If I'm still here, I'll get it painted Thursday."

He was still there. He got it painted Thursday.

All the deadline deals fell through, including a big one involving eight players which died two minutes before deadline. And the Oilers went into the playoffs with the team that struggled to finish 37-37-6, in third place in the Smythe Division. Esa Tikkanen led the team in points with 69, one more than Petr Klima and five more than Messier. Ranford had a 27-27 record in goal.

The defending Stanley Cup champions viewed the playoffs as a chance to change their batteries and forget the frustration of their regular season.

"I don't care how you slice it, it hasn't been easy playing this year," said Messier. "No matter what the problems are, no matter what you're going through, the No. 1 thing is that the only person you can hurt in the long run is yourself. We all know that. Most of us have had a lot of experience. We've always been able to put our problems aside because we have a group of guys here who have so much respect for each other. We don't need any extra motivation. We don't need to be kick-started. The only motivation we need is the Cup."

Any extra motivation came from the first-round matchup. Another Battle of Alberta Stanley Cup playoff series. And this one, when it was over, would be viewed by many as the best single playoff series ever played. I've never seen a better one.

Fuhr had 94 games of playoff experience when he entered the nets in the Saddledome for Game 1, something less than his old calm, cool and collected self.

"I'll tell you what," said assistant coach Ron Low. "He was *nervous.*"

"It was weird," said Fuhr. "I wasn't real comfortable. It's been a long time since I played a playoff game."

Fuhr fell on his face early. But he stood on his head the rest of the way and was the story as the Oilers scored a 3-1 win in Game 1.

The series hit the boiling point in Game 2.

Don Cherry was at the game.

"You could make *Rock 'Em, Sock 'Em III* out of that one," said the *Hockey Night In Canada* commentator. "They don't come more physical than that one."

There were 120 hits in the game, most registering on the Richter scale. The most memorable was when Flames' Ric Nattress took a world-class elbow from Messier and, eyes rolling and knees wobbling, staggered back to the bench.

"Thank God I went to the right bench," said Nattress.

Muckler said they should have given the almost-out-on-his-feet Nattress "the standing eight count."

Jeff Beukeboom put Gary Roberts in la-la land. Graves scored a TKO over Frank Musil. And two Oilers gave Mike Vernon what he described as "whiplash – I had to take a couple of minutes to get my bearings back."

Calgary's Jamie Macoun stands by as the Oilers celebrate a goal.

The Oilers beat the Flames in the back alley but the Flames won the game 3-1, thanks mostly to Vernon's 35-save night.

The Flames weren't crying about the rockin' and sockin'.

"Whadya think this is, a dance?" said Vernon. "These are the playoffs. It's them or us. What it boils down to is who is willing to go to the mat and do what has to be done."

Calgary coach Doug Risebrough, who once used his skates to slash Marty McSorley's Oilers sweater in the playoffs, wasn't moaning and groaning either.

"It's playoff hockey, I guess. I'll tell you one thing. Kerry Fraser had his selection out there, didn't he?"

Up in the press box where CBC's Chris Cuthbert declared this "the mother of all series" before it began, Rod Phillips stepped out of his broadcast booth after the first period of Game 3 and called the breakneck battle "the most unbelievable period of hockey I've broadcast in 18 years."

Enforcer Luke Richardson dukes it out with Calgary's Ron Stern.

Down in the dressing room when it was over, losing coach Risebrough's first words were "great game!"

In the other dressing room, Muckler described it as "as good a game as I've ever seen."

Murphy scored with 14 seconds left after Anderson had brought the Oilers back to tie it. Simpson set up both goals.

"I don't know what it was like to watch, but it was fun to play," said Huddy. "It's more fun that we won. But it had to be fun for Calgary to play, too."

Murphy scored on his first shot of the game.

"That's as big a goal as I've ever scored," he said. "I had the winner in the fourth game against Los Angeles last year. But this was such a great game. And it was like overtime. What a game. It had great

hits, great goaltending, great plays and I can't believe the speed. As hard as everybody is skating, everybody is hitting just as hard, too. It's so intense. It's just incredible out there. I've never played a more exciting game. And you know what's the most incredible thing about this series? There's more to come!"

The Oilers didn't win Game 4. It was more that they refused to lose it.

"If you're going to win a championship," said Muckler, "that's what you have to do."

Calgary was ahead 2-0 when the Oilers were forced to kill a five-minute penalty.

"It didn't look good for us," said penalty killer MacTavish. "But that's where experience really comes into play."

Fuhr said what he watched inspired him to keep his net empty as he backstopped the Oilers to a 5-2 win and a 3-1 series lead.

"That was the finest example of penalty killing I've ever seen," said Fuhr, who didn't have to make a save or even move a muscle.

"We must have made 20 line changes in that five minutes," said Messier.

There was more raving about the series being so good it ought to be bottled as the scene shifted back to Calgary for Game 5. That's where Carey Wilson was the hero with two goals in a 5-3 Flames win. But compared to the first four games, this one almost looked like a dud.

"I think the first four games took their toll on both teams," said Huddy. "Neither team played with the pace of the first four games. It was like we just both decided to take a break from it."

They dialled it back up again in Edmonton for Game 6 where Messier, the most valuable man on the five-time Stanley Cup championship team, passed away the puck and gave away the game.

Theo Fleury, the heart and soul of the Flames, saw it coming, read it like a book and skated in to score the winning goal. His celebration of that goal will be remembered by Calgary fans for ages.

"Let's go back to Calgary!" he screamed.

"The sea of red is going to be redder than red can be for Game 7. That's definitely the biggest goal of my career."

Messier, head down in the Oilers room, didn't dodge it.

"I'm the guy who is supposed to score the goal, not give it away," he said.

The series had it all, including a

The Battle of Alberta: Bench strength, Oilers' style.

Game seventh heaven: An overtime goal by Esa Tikkanen, left, moved the Oilers past the Flames in the Smythe Division final.

Game 7 to savour for the ages. Arguably the greatest playoff series ever played, it ended with one of the wildest and craziest seventh games you'll ever see in any sport. And it ended with an absolutely anything-goes overtime. Only two things were missing when it was over; champagne. And the Stanley Cup.

"Seventh game. Overtime. Last shot. What a great way to end it," said Muckler. "As long as you're the ones who won it."

Shouts and screams came from the showers where the Oilers frolicked after Tikkanen scored his third goal of the game to win it 5-4 at 6:58 of OT. And when they weren't shouting and screaming, the Oilers were looking at each other, shaking their heads, rolling their eyes and grinning the greatest grins. Yet when asked how it felt to come back from 3-0 to win a Game 7 in overtime, their first words were for the Flames.

"I know how I feel," said Muckler. "I turned 55 the other day and now I feel like I'm 35. But I know how I'd feel in that other room. I'd feel like crying. I'd be sick. If I'd been in that other room, I'd have been proud of those guys. Doug Risebrough did a great job. If we'd lost it I'd have been proud of these guys. I really feel like we should be getting the Stanley Cup but we've only won one round."

What was it like?

"Wanna know something?" asked Graves. "That's the most fun I ever had playing hockey other than the last few minutes of the Stanley Cup final in Boston when we knew we were going to win."

The hat trick for Tikkanen was his second in Stanley Cup play. It was his first playoff overtime goal.

"When Esa scored that first one, we all saw something," said Mac-

Tavish. "Their team really tightened up. Not only that, but their crowd really tightened up. It was like, 'Here we go!' "

Strangely, the most subdued player in the Oilers dressing room was Tikkanen.

"Everybody in this room knows how to win a Stanley Cup," he said. "We know we can win the big games. We can do it. We've done it before. I just got the puck at the blueline. I went to pass the puck to Petr Klima but he was covered. So I shot and scored."

"Winners win" was the bottom line, according to Muckler.

"I don't think we should ever be doubted again. No matter what things look like at the time, we should never be doubted. I said it two months ago. This team should not be judged until we've played our final game."

So, it was on to the next round. And guess who, again? Wayne Gretzky and the Los Angeles Kings. And when Game 1 was over, the Oilers were having trouble remembering what it felt like to play a regulation-time game.

Luc Robitaille scored the tying goal to send it to overtime and then fired the winner past Ranford 2:13 into the sudden-death session for a 4-3 win.

Muckler made the decision to go with Ranford simply to give Fuhr a break.

"Grant had played seven games in 14 nights. None of them were easy. The last two were in overtime. We figured we'd go with Billy and Grant would be a heck of a lot sharper from here on out."

Game 2. Overtime again. Double overtime.

Mark Messier hugs Mark Lamb after another playoff triumph.

A dejected Wayne Gretzky shakes hands with former teammates after his Kings were eliminated by the Oilers.

"Petr has a habit. Any time after the first overtime, he's going to score," said Muckler of Klima, the hero of the triple-overtime game in Boston the year before who was the hero at 4:48 of the second overtime as the Oilers won Game 2, 4-3.

"I was waiting for the third overtime," Klima laughed. "But I got a chance in the second overtime, so I said, 'What the heck.'

"This team is in great shape. If it takes seven overtime games to win this series, we'll play seven overtime games."

Game 3. Overtime again. And this one went into the books beside the Montreal Canadiens and Toronto Maple Leafs, who went five straight games of overtime together in the 1951 Stanley Cup final.

Not only was it the fifth straight time, it was the second straight game that went to double overtime. And for the second time, Game 7 Battle of Alberta hero Tikkanen was the hero.

For the third straight time in the series the final score was 4-3.

The Kings were forced to play most of the game without Gretzky, who left late in the first period when he was hit on the ear by a shot from teammate Steve Duchesne and was cut for 25 stitches.

"It's too bad Wayne got hurt, but without him out there, I got to play my own game," said Tikkanen.

Game 4 was a refreshing change. No overtime. And a different score.

It was 4-2 instead of 4-3 as the Oilers moved within one victory of winning their 27th Stanley Cup playoff series in 33 attempts.

"I don't know what to do with the extra time," said Muckler. "I feel lost."

A new pattern emerged as the series returned to Los Angeles. First team to four goals wins. And it was Robitaille with a hat trick who put the Kings to the four-goal plateau en route to a 5-2 win, sending the se-ries back to Edmonton. There the Oilers ended it, for the fourth time in the series and sixth time in an eight-game stretch, in overtime. Craig MacTavish had the honour this time at the 16:57 mark for the, you guessed it, 4-3 win. Ranford relieved an injured Fuhr in mid-game and Tikkanen completed his masterful job of shadowing Gretzky, leaving him without a goal in the series.

For the seventh time in the last nine years, the Oilers had made it to the final four.

They had won 26 of their last 29 playoff series.

Edmonton went into the next series, against the Minnesota North Stars, a mentally and physically tired team. It showed in the opener,

'You want to do nothing but look forward. But it's impossible. When it comes to Edmonton, I was pretty bunkered in there. To tell Glen Sather to trade me is the toughest thing I may ever have to do.'
– Mark Messier

which they lost 3-1.

"If we had played like that against Calgary or Los Angeles, we wouldn't be here now," said Muckler.

Klima scored a natural hat trick in a span of five minutes and 13 seconds to give the Oilers Game 2, running up a 7-2 count. But in Minnesota, where the Stars had lost but two of their last 21 games, the Oilers lost 7-3 and 3-1, then returned home to lose 3-2. Series over.

"We were out of gas," said Lowe. "Calgary and Los Angeles took too much out of us."

Messier and half the team were walking wounded.

"By the time we got to this series, we were too beat up," said Messier.

Strange the way it worked out. The Oilers beat Calgary in a series they weren't supposed to win, beat Los Angeles in a series they weren't supposed to win, then lost to Minnesota in a series that they *were* supposed to win.

The Edmonton Sun's headline above a shot of the traditional end-of-season team picture taken the next day:

"Absence Of Chalice."

Absence of Muckler was the storyline as the 1991-92 season began. It was one thing for the players to be leaving, but now it was the coach...

The record book would forever say Glen Sather was one of the most successful coaches of all time. But Muckler was the man who made him. Muckler was the game-plan guy Sather the GM was smart enough to hire so that Sather the coach would be able to use his assets as a motivator and a bench boss to become the coaching success he became.

Now Muckler had shuffled off to Buffalo.

It was the old dial-out factor.

"You get tired of presenting the same story and the players get tired of listening to it," said Sather. "They need a fresh perspective after a while."

Enter Ted Green.

With the veterans leaving, one by one, to be replaced by as many young prospects as Sather could con out of their new teams, the GM suggested Green's mental makeup might make him better suited to their development than anybody else. Whatever, there wasn't an exhaustive search to find Muckler's replacement.

Hockey's ultimate leader returned as the enemy in a Rangers uniform.

"In my mind, there was nobody else to consider," Sather said.

It was a Canada Cup year and, as always, the Oilers supplied a significant number of players to the team, including Messier. Except, by the time the Canada Cup got going, it was obvious he'd soon be ex-Oiler Messier.

"Mark has informed me he'd like to be traded," said Sather with Team Canada in Toronto. "I told him I'd try to accommodate him."

The day before, Adam Graves had joined the New York Rangers.

"He signed a five-year deal for $2.4 million US. The guy had seven goals," said Slats.

But Graves wasn't Messier. Messier was an Edmonton icon.

"I'd say I've probably played my last game as an Oiler," Messier said as we sat on the bench at Maple Leaf Gardens after a Team Canada practice.

"I always wanted to stay and play out my career in Edmonton. But the way things have gone, I can honestly say I no longer want to stay. I think it's best for everybody if I move on now and not leave a bitter taste in anybody's mouth. It's been a great 12 years. If they want to get rid of the old guys, it's their team. They can do what they want. It's stopped being about money. If I did sign, it just wouldn't be fun any more. It's about winning. I see it starting to fall apart now. At this stage of my career, the only thing that matters is winning."

Lowe read the story back home in Edmonton.

"The old Oiler flag better be lowered to half-mast," he said. "They're taking away the blood and guts of the organization. It's a very sad day in Oilers history."

Messier sat in limbo after another Canada Cup win, this one led by Billy Ranford as the national netminder.

As Oiler players were returning to training camp from the Canada Cup, the face of the team was changing dramatically day by day.

Fuhr and Anderson were traded to Toronto, along with Craig Berube, for Vincent Damphousse, Luke Richardson, Scott Thornton and Peter Ing.

"It's the end of an era," said Fuhr.

"It's tough because Grant and I have gone through so much together, more than any other player," Sather said of Fuhr's money and drug problems. "I hope this one works out for everyone."

Charlie Huddy went to join Edmonton West in Los Angeles. And Oiler fans waited for Sather to make the Messier deal to create the beginning of Edmonton East with the New York Rangers.

I asked a kid in my neighbourhood what he thought about Messier leaving the Oilers.

Bernie Nicholls, right, and Kelly Buchburger at Millwoods Golf Course in April 1992, when the NHL strike signalled an early start to golf season.

'The old Oiler flag better be lowered to half-mast, they're taking away the blood and guts of the organization. It's a very sad day in Oilers history.'

– Kevin Lowe on the trading of Mark Messier

"It's like Christmas," the kid said. "I know what I'm giving. I can hardly wait to find out what I'm going to get."

When the deal was finally done, I asked the kid if he enjoyed his Christmas. "It was like getting clothes," he said.

Exactly.

Messier for Bernie Nicholls, Louie DeBrusk and Steven Rice.

Rumours leaked from around the league that Peter Pocklington was putting $5 million US into his pocket from the deal as well. When, a couple of weeks later, the Oilers swapped Jeff Beukeboom for David Shaw "to complete the deal," as Rangers GM Neil Smith put it, Beukeboom said, "Obviously the Oilers wanted the money."

Messier was shocked at how it felt when the day finally came and the deal was done.

"I felt like I just fell in a hole," he said. "I felt like the bottom just fell out of everything. I'm glad I didn't have to have a press conference in Edmonton like Wayne. I would have lost it. I would have bawled like a baby. You want to do nothing but look forward. But it's impossible. When it comes to Edmonton, I was pretty bunkered in there. To tell Glen Sather to trade me is the toughest thing I may ever have to do."

So, Teddy, how do you like your hockey team? All these years you waited to become a head coach and by the time you get the job and actually start the job, players possessing a total of 34 Stanley Cup rings depart.

"A lot of people were smiling on Sept. 4," said Green of picking up his paper and reading the daily dispatches of the destruction of his dynasty. "A lot of people thought they were looking at the end of the Oilers. When we started camp, all the wheels were falling off. It wasn't easy to walk into that. It was all doom and gloom."

Green said he liked the challenge.

"Forge steel," he said of what he had to do as a head coach. "We had a lot of guys who were like forged steel. They'd been in the fire. They'd survived it. We have to forge some more steel. When we do that, we've got a team. And don't forget, the coach has a plate of forged steel in his head," he added of his souvenir of the famed Wayne Maki incident from way back when he was a Boston Bruin player.

"The young guys have to learn how to win. The most important thing I have to do is develop the will to win."

Sather offered hope.

"I think we'll do better in the regular season. We have a great attitude. The attitude of this year's team is 100 per cent better than last year's team."

Oh yeah? The Oilers got out of the gate with a 1-5-1 record. After their first 23 games they had 13 losses and a run of two wins in their last 11 games.

"I think we have some under-achievers on this hockey club, no doubt about that," said Green.

And that was before Bernie Nicholls finally showed up on Dec. 7.

By Jan. 12, the Oilers were 16-22-7 and had four sellouts. And Nicholls and Petr Klima had become the focus of the fans' frustrations.

"You guys are calling Nicholls and Klima horsebleep. I *know* they're playing horsebleep," said Sather, who went on to say they were playing so horsebleep that he couldn't trade either one of them.

Of Nicholls in particular, he said, "He's gone in the tank."

Nicholls fired back in *The Sun*.

"The Oilers could have won eight or nine Stanley Cups. Everybody knows that. Glen Sather traded away a dynasty for money. Don't blame Petr and I. Management never stands up and takes the blame. It's always the players, but management makes the deals and Glen dealt away a dynasty. He's starting to blame the players and that's not right. Treat people like human beings, like every other GM, and he'd still have a dynasty here."

Then there was Green's quote on the subject of Klima:

"Petr's been a coach killer wherever he's been. I don't give a damn about Petr Klima. I've run out of patience. Here's a guy who only cares about himself."

Happy campers.

It was Kevin Lowe's first year as Oilers captain and there'd never be a tougher year to be an Oilers captain.

"It's a daily challenge to maintain Oilers' pride," he said in mid-January.

This was the year the old "Ex-Oiler Great Returns to Face Former Mates in Front of Former Fans and Familiar Faces" angle got a real workout.

First it was Messier on Jan. 23. He scored the winner on a third-period power play with a Gretzky-like sense of stage.

Fuhr had the same kind of game when he showed up on March 5.

"Fuhrzie played great. Fuhrzie came in here and played the same way he played here for 12 years," said assistant coach Ron Low after the 5-2 Toronto Maple Leafs victory at the Coliseum. "And then Glenn Anderson scored their fourth goal on a breakaway ... that did as much to take us down as Fuhr did."

Defenceman Kevin Lowe fends off Mario Lemieux in December 1991.

York. But of all the relocated ex-Oilers, only Messier and Gretzky had more points than the 89 Vincent Damphousse manufactured. And when the Oilers came back from the strike, they actually were happy campers.

"There's a lot of electricity in this room. We were short-circuited. Somebody pulled the plug. But I think we can get it all back. When the strike started we were peaking for the playoffs. We had a barrel of confidence. I don't think we'll lose that," said Ranford.

The hockey gods may or may not be Oiler fans. But they certainly made sure just about every single season that the Oilers would find themselves in a scenario that would demand coverage by the national media.

If the Oilers vs. Wayne Gretzky and the L.A. Kings in the playoffs was starting to get stale, try it with Paul Coffey, Jari Kurri, Charlie Huddy and Marty McSorley wearing L.A. uniforms and most of Edmonton's other famous faces now departed.

It had been a strange hockey season in Los Angeles as well. Gretzky's back was injured during the Canada Cup and people were wondering if it was the end of his career. There was also the health problems of Wayne's father, Walter. Kurri bombed big in the regular season. Coffey was injured upon arrival. And coach Tom Webster was suspended for 12 games for a javelin toss of a hockey stick at referee Kerry

The NHL's 75th season was cut short by a players' strike. And it hit just as the Oilers seemed to have overcome all the obstacles.

"We've come a long way in a year," said Low. "Just about as far as you could come in a year."

Green was frustrated with the idea that everything he'd gone through might go for naught if the season were to be wiped out.

"It's been shift-by-shift, day-by-day. We've had all kinds of goals this year. The first was just to be competitive and exciting. Then we elevated that to staying close to the pack and not getting too far behind the teams in front of us. Then we set .500 as a goal. When we fell short about 10 times, we stopped talking about it. Then, in the middle of January, we sat down and looked at an 18-game stretch and our goal was to get 26 points from that. We did it. And we got the 26th point the same night we hit .500 ... "

The Oilers were 35-33-10 when the 12-day strike hit. They won one and lost one when the teams came back to complete the schedule. Green did manage to get the team in over .500. Messier won the Hart Trophy in New

Craig MacTavish scores the overtime winner in Game 6 against Los Angeles.

Fraser.

But everybody was back and healthy for the lid lifter. And Webster couldn't resist when he pencilled in his starting lineup.

Gretzky. Kurri. McSorley. Coffey. Huddy. And Edmonton-native Kelly Hrudey in goal.

The series, from an Edmonton point of view, was billed as Yesterday vs Tomorrow. And Game 1 was Tomorrowland and the Oilers offered fabulous forechecking, wonderful penalty killing and won almost all the little races to the puck which make all the difference in winning playoff hockey games.

"It was a perfect playoff game, really," said Ranford.

Brian Glynn got to be a playoff hero with two goals for the Oilers in the 3-1 win.

"The Fab Five," as Webster called Gretzky, Kurri, Coffey, Huddy and McSorley, were flying in Game 2.

The "Oil Kings" won it 8-5.

"Paul got those first two power-play goals. Gretzky fought through that checking all night. Kurri scored a very big goal. I believe they brought a great deal of pride to the rink tonight," said Webster.

Gretzky had four assists to bring his playoff total to 303. Kurri's goal was his 94th Stanley Cup snipe, moving him back into a tie with Gretzky. Huddy had a goal and an assist. Even McSorley scored. And it was Bruce McNall's birthday.

Bernie Nicholls got the hint. And it was the ex-King who won Game 3 for the Oilers. He scored two power-play goals, including the winner, in a 4-3 victory.

It took all year, but finally Broadway Bernie became Northlands Nicholls.

The running mate of Petr Klima in the balloting for Most Unpopular Oiler all season, Nicholls changed the storyline from Oilers vs. ex-Oilers to Kings vs. ex-King as Nicholls became the first Oiler ever to score three power-play goals in a single series, a fact he found totally shocking.

"I did?"

"Wayne didn't do that? I'm honoured."

Nicholls had two previous claims to fame in Oilers playoff hockey history. He was the King who scored the series-winning goals on both occasions in which Los Angeles beat Edmonton in a playoff series.

"I get real emotional in the playoffs," he said. "If there's any team I'd like to put out, it's L.A."

The storyline bounced back to ex-Oilers in Game 4 as Coffey perked up in a game *The Sun*'s headline writers captured with "Billy Goat, Kelly Hero." Ranford struggled and Hrudey played great and the Kings evened the series with a 4-3 win.

Coffey had two goals and an assist.

Minnesota's Dave Gagnon celebrates a playoff goal in front of Esa Tikkanen and Kevin Lowe.

Back in L.A., it looked as if the headline writers were going to call this one "Wayne's World" but in the end, well, "Hat Tikk!" was *The Sun*'s headline the next day.

For no logical reason other than coach's intuition, Green decided to put the Grate One against the Great One again. Kelly Buchberger had been doing an excellent job on Gretzky in the first four games of the series, but ...

Gretzky scored twice. Tikkanen scored thrice. The Oilers won 5-2. And Tikkanen shared the hero's halo with Ranford, who bounced back from his so-so Game 4 with a 42-save performance to send the series back to Edmonton with the Oilers leading 3-2.

"Tikk has had a rough road," said Green. "He has not been playing up to par."

He was invisible through the first four games, had one point and was a minus-three.

"I believe I score more when I'm checking Wayne," he said. "When I'm checking Wayne I have a lot more open ice. I'm not just going up and down my wing. I'm following him all over the place, not just staying on the left side. When the play goes the other way, I can do whatever I want."

The Oilers booted the boys in black out of the playoffs for the third straight season with a how-sweet-it-is win over Edmonton West in the sixth game back in the Coliseum.

Considering where they were at the start of the season, just to win a playoff series, much less *this* playoff series, was remarkable.

The Oilers era was over in the minds of everybody in hockey, but the Edmonton legend kept going. It was the Oilers' 28th playoff series win in 35 tries.

"We have a history to draw on," said Green. "Players can see it and sense it. They realize it's not just a lot of talking."

Nicholls, changing his tune dramatically, said it all for the new Oilers.

"You can't come to Edmonton and not respect the staff and management. How can you come to Edmonton and question anything? Edmonton knows how to win."

Could they win one more banner? Could they win one more series?

The Calgary Flames hadn't – and wouldn't, for at least the next 10 years – won another playoff series after their one and only Stanley Cup in 1989. But the Oilers, if nothing else, planned on being the last Canadian team still skating again.

That meant they had to beat the Vancouver Canucks in a series that opened on the left coast.

Vincent Damphousse.

For some reason, Vancouver was always Ranford's favourite place to play. And the guy they called Billy Goat a week earlier was Billy Great in Game 1 as the Oilers won 4-3.

"Simply fantastic," said Green of his goalie after the Grand Theft win.

"Billy was bulletproof. We won that game on the back of Billy Ranford. He hasn't let up a goal which has been anywhere near suspect since he gave up those three quickies in Game 4 against Los Angeles. He found his groove in Game 5 and now he's groovin'," said the coach of the Canada Cup MVP and the Conn Smythe Trophy winner for Edmonton's fifth Stanley Cup.

Ranford was dinged in the next one and sent to the dressing room with a shoulder injury.

"I thought they were going to get 73 shots on Billy tonight," said replacement Ron Tugnutt, a guy who knows how it felt, having once faced that many.

Vancouver won 4-0.

If there was one Oiler making a name for himself this playoff season, it was Joe Murphy. And he left his signature on the Oilers' Game 3 win.

"He's carrying this team right now," said Damphousse. "Tonight he stepped up to another level. He's doing it all right now, maybe more than anyone expected."

Murphy fired three goals, including the winner, in the 5-2 victory. He had a three-point night and scored the winner in overtime in Game 1. And with seven goals and 18 assists in nine playoff games, he was only one back of leading playoff scorer Mario Lemieux.

Lowe had no such numbers. But the Oilers captain, who Green called "the player with the highest pain threshold in the entire history of hockey," was leading by example, playing with a damaged shoulder, an ugly groin injury and several other hurts.

"The pain and pride that Kevin is showing ... I can't think of anyone else, ever, to be playing like he is," said Sather. "He's truly an inspiration."

Scott Mellanby scored the winner as the Oilers took a 3-1 series lead but the Oilers – despite know-

Top: Jari Kurri signs a Stanley Cup poster; middle: Jeff Beukeboom, left, and Esa Tikkanen passed around cigars when they became dads in March 1991; bottom: Kevin Lowe's golf stag was a wet and wild affair.

ing from years before what a long series could do to them – messed up Game 5 in Vancouver, losing 4-3.

Back home for Game 6, Ranford was brilliant in a 3-0 shutout. And a 22nd banner, representing their eighth Smythe Division championship in 10 years, soon hung from the rafters. It's the easiest one to spot up there today. It's the one on the end.

The Oilers, like the year before against Minnesota, expired in a four-game sweep against the Chicago Blackhawks – 8-2, 4-2, 4-3 and 5-1 – but in most Oiler fans' minds that series was quickly forgotten. They spent the summer marvelling at how in the world the Oilers, considering where they started the season, could have possibly made it back to the final four to once again be the last Canadian club skating.

Sather suggested maybe that banner ought to have some fringe on it or something else to set it apart.

"I don't like to compare them. But from a point of view of the team starting training camp as big an underdog as we were, and for this team to work as hard as they worked, yes, this one is as rewarding as it gets," he said.

"We had a lot of turmoil and a lot of adjustments had to be made. The patience of Ted Green ... he deserves most of the credit."

Green wasn't taking any bows he couldn't share.

"I'm really proud of what happened. We came into a situation where nobody expected us to make the playoffs. This was *total* reorganization. A lot of fans, the media and even the coach, at times, gave Glen Sather and Peter Pocklington a lot of heat. But they pointed the ship in the right direction."

The Oilers had still not missed the playoffs and still hadn't finished under .500 since their second season in the league. Could the beat continue? Could they simply reload instead of rebuild?

Despite the even stormier seas ahead, there were plenty of people willing to believe it just might be possible after the way Green's Oilers had salvaged the season and the way the Oilers had, despite being torn apart, made it to the final four again and again.

Chapter 16

Hall Of Fame Game

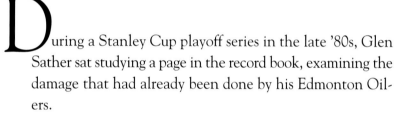

uring a Stanley Cup playoff series in the late '80s, Glen Sather sat studying a page in the record book, examining the damage that had already been done by his Edmonton Oilers.

"What's involved here is immortality," he said, with a rare faraway look in his eye.

One by one, he knew then, they'd be going into the Hockey Hall of Fame. Their immortality had already been assured.

Nine Hart Trophies had been won by players wearing Edmonton Oiler uniforms. Eight Art Ross. Six Lester B. Pearson. Four Conn Smythe. Four Emery Edge. Two Norris. Two Lady Byng. One Vezina. One Adams. One King Clancy. Fifteen Oilers were selected as NHL first team all-stars and 10 more as second team all-stars. And the Oilers had a remarkable 69 all-star game selections in 19 seasons. No other team in the last two decades came close to matching that collection, even if you didn't include the five Stanley Cups.

The Oilers, sometime soon, must decide what they want to do with all their about-to-be Hall of Famers.

Hang their numbers from the rafters as they do in so many other cities?

Create a special place for monuments to the greats such as they have in Yankee Stadium in New York?

**Glen (Slats) Sather:
Coach, general manager,
master tradesman.**

Give them all their own statues like the one Gretzky has outside the building in which they played their greatest games, won all or all but one of their Stanley Cups, and rang up their numbers like the scoreboard was a pinball machine?

It should be something special because, in this era of free-agency and athletes changing uniforms four and five times in a career, it may never happen again. The Edmonton Oilers may go down in hockey history as the Last Dynasty.

Gretzky, it was telegraphed when the three-year waiting period prior to Hall of Fame eligibility was waived for Mario Lemieux, will go directly into the Hall of Fame the moment he calls it a career.

But when will that be? After he registers his 3,000th point? After he scores his 1,000th goal?

Gretzky, with 885 goals and 1,910 assists in 1,417 NHL games to start the 1998-99 season, hit the 2,800-point plateau in his fourth game of his 20th NHL season. He scored 583 of those goals, 1,086 of the assists and 1,669 of the points in his 696 games in Edmonton.

Gretzky has 122 goals and 260 assists for 382 playoff points. His Oilers post-season totals include 81 goals with 171 assists for 252 points.

Owning or sharing 61 different NHL records, the vast majority of which he established as an Oiler, Gretzky's glory is going to be greater as the years pass.

Forget those never-to-be-broken big career numbers. Already some of the NHL records he set as an Oiler have the never-to-be-broken look about them:

Jari Kurri and Wayne Gretzky: poetry in motion.

- 92 goals in a season.
- 100 goals in a season including playoffs.
- 61 (twice) in his first 50 games of a season.
- 50 goals in 39 games.
- 163 assists in one season.
- 7 assists (three times) in one game.
- 215 points in one season.
- 255 points in a season including playoffs.
- 23-game goal-scoring streak.
- 51-game point-scoring streak.
- 31 assists, one playoff year.
- 49 points, one playoff year.

Gretzky received one of the greatest honours of his incredible career when *The Hockey News* celebrated its 50th anniversary by naming No. 99 No. 1 in their blue-ribbon panel vote for the top 50 players of all time.

The announcement almost rated as a great moment in hockey history itself. Gretzky's agent, Mike Barnett, provided a special presentation he'd been waiting to find the right time and place to make to the star he'd signed when he ran an endorsement outfit in Edmonton. He'd had Gretzky's old skates bronzed, the set he'd worn for his first game as an Edmonton Oiler in the NHL in 1979.

"Those are pretty cool," said Gretzky at the unveiling, which ranked as just as cool as about any other treasure in the Hall of Fame.

"I'm a little embarrassed to be standing up here," he told the select crowd. "If I was voting, I'd vote for Gordie Howe and Bobby Orr and be happy to be third."

Orr was second. Howe was third.

Howe helped make that moment.

"I'm in the money. Win. Place. I'm show.

"I'm almost as proud of Wayne as Phyllis and Wally," Howe said of Gretzky's parents. "I'm proud of the fact that many years ago I shook the hand of this young man in Brantford and had that opportunity to play with him in that WHA all-star game in Edmonton. I'm proud of the fact I was there when this young man started. If anyone thinks I'm jealous, don't. This is how I would have voted."

Gretzky said he was also thrilled for his Edmonton teammates.

"To have four guys from that Edmonton team end up in the top 50, that's pretty special."

Messier was selected No. 12.

Coffey was picked No. 28.

And Kurri was ranked No. 50.

You don't make *The Hockey News'* top 50 players of all time and not make it into the Hall of Fame.

The first Edmonton Oiler to make it into the Hall of Fame, however, was Sather.

Slats got the call to the Hall from Scotty Morrison, the former referees boss who now heads hockey's shrine in Toronto.

With all the dignity and the tone in which such a call should be made, Morrison informed Sather he'd been selected to join the 85 others in the Hall.

"The players category?" asked Sather.

Sather played 660 NHL games over 10 seasons with the Boston Bruins, Pittsburgh Penguins, New York Rangers, St. Louis Blues, Montreal Canadiens and Minnesota North Stars before joining the Oilers in the WHA. He had 293 NHL points. Eighty of them were goals.

Sather is never far from his sense of humour. Long viewed as an overgrown Dennis the Menace, the man with the permanent smirk, provided by a puck that sliced his lip, once climbed a 300-foot high microwave tower to hang a dummy of the Wainwright school principal as a Halloween prank.

And then there was the deal he once made with Red Fisher, the legendary Montreal hockey columnist. Sather had promised Fisher an Indian painting.

When Sather finally delivered, Fisher was looking at a photograph of "The Chief," former Oiler Jim Nielson, wearing full Indian headdress, painting the side of a house.

It wasn't that Sather wasn't impressed with the honour.

"It's very humbling," said Sather.

"I've been blessed to have been surrounded by good players. I don't think I'd be here if I hadn't been involved with Wayne Gretzky and Mark Messier."

It goes both ways.

"He played a huge, huge part in my career," says Messier. "We all showed up as boys and he turned us into men. He was our mentor. He showed us how to dress. He taught us how to act. He took us to a lot of different places. He gave us some culture. He was a father, a disciplinarian and a coach. He was unbelievable. He taught us how to compete and play. He taught us how to win."

Looking back, Sather said it was a seat-of-your-pants thing.

"I guess it was a combination, coaching and babysitting. But even when they were young, it was fun to be around them, making their silly little mistakes. The kidding around ... there was always an attitude there. They knew they were going to be good players."

Maybe it was because as a player he didn't have the talent. But as a coach and GM, Sather loves letting the thoroughbreds run.

"I like a fast-skating team that moves the puck," he said. "It's easier to play defensive hockey. But I don't particularly like that style.

"We started the free-flow game in the NHL. But I'm not going to take the credit for that. The ideas I got came from going to Finland in the WHA and watching a bunch of peewees practise in Turku. I said, boy, these kids have the right idea. And that year Winnipeg had all those great Swedes: Anders Hedberg, Ulf Nilsson and those guys. We just took it from there. It made it easier because we had Wayne. We had to create open ice for Wayne."

While all his stars eventually left, Sather stayed and still remains and that endears him to Edmonton as much as his success.

"It's home," he said. "It's not complicated. This is where my friends are. I never wanted to be a carpetbagger and leave for the wrong reasons. Preaching one thing to the players and doing something different myself wouldn't be the right thing to do. I've been in Edmonton most of my life. I plan on staying here most of my life. Edmonton is stuck with me."

In 842 regular-season games, Sather's coaching record is 464-268-110. That's a .616 winning percentage. The 464 wins ranks seventh in NHL history. Sather, as a coach, won four Stanley Cups. The other came after he appointed John Muckler as coach. Sather coached the Oilers to 21 playoff series victories in 27 attempts. His 89 victories in Stanley Cup playoff play ranks fourth. His .706 winning percentage ranks first.

As GM and coach of Team Canada in the World Cup of Hockey, Sather coached Canada's 1984 Canada Cup winner and was GM of the 1994 World Hockey Championship team. He was on the Team Canada management committee for the 1987 Canada Cup championship team.

Sather coached two Stanley Cup champions and a Canada Cup winner within a 53-week period.

Someone once wrote that the doors to the Hall of Fame open wide but that some go in the front and some go in the side. Sather was front-door material all the way. And so are more than a handful of his hockey greats who will follow.

"I'm sure there'll be a raft of guys joining me," said Slats.

"He'll have company in a few years. Gretzky, Messier, Coffey, Kurri and Fuhr for sure," said Boston Bruins boss Harry Sinden. "Glenn Anderson has a shot. So does Kevin Lowe."

Messier, like Gretzky, made it to his 20th season in the NHL and scored his 600th NHL goal early in the year in his second season with the Vancouver Canucks, having started the 1998-99 season with 597 to go with his 1,015 assists for a total of 1,612 points in 1,354 games. He is third all-time in Oilers scoring with 474 goals, 569 assists and 1,043 points in 851 games.

In the playoffs, Messier was in for all five Oiler Stanley Cups and won another with the New York Rangers. He set a record for most playoff games played with 236 and has 109 goals, 186 assists and 295 playoff points. He's second all-time in the Oilers books with 80 goals, 135 assists and 215 points.

Fourth all-time in points with only Gordie Howe (1,850) and Marcel Dionne (1,771) left ahead of him, Messier is second only to Gretzky in playoff goalscoring (109) where the top four are ex-Oilers, second only to Gretzky in playoff assists (186) where the top five are ex-Oilers and second only to Gretzky in playoff points (295) where the top five are ex-Oilers.

Messier owns the playoff record for most shorthanded goals in a career with 14.

Messier and Gretzky: The Hall of Fame beckons.

Messier. He came into the league wanting to be Mick Jagger. From St. Albert, he played for his dad Doug with the St. Albert Saints, where he made $7 for a win, $4 for a tie and $2 for a loss. Eight days older than Gretzky, it was Messier who went from St. Albert to Indianapolis to replace Gretzky when No. 99 became an Oiler.

Messier beat Raymond Bourque of Boston by two points to win his first Hart Trophy, the closest vote in the history of the award.

It was a Hart-tugging and Hart-breaking night.

"Whooooooo," was the first sound out of Messier's mouth.

"Oh, this is wild, man."

He tried to thank coaches John Muckler and Ted Green and then general manager Sather.

"To Wayne Gretzky," he said, his voice vibrating. "He's been a big part of my life ..."

His voice broke.

"And to my family ..."

That was it. It was all the mighty Messier could manage.

"You could see by his eyes that he wasn't going to make it," said his brother Paul. "Mark was really nervous about the whole thing. After 11 years it means so much for him to win. There were a lot of things he wanted to say, to dad and to Wayne."

Doug Messier said, that's his boy.

"He's an emotional player. He's an emotional guy."

Messier went from a kid who went to the wrong airport and ended up with a ticket to the minor leagues in his first year as an Oiler to a player who showed up five hours early for a playoff game and met his teammates with the famous stare that let them know they were going to win that night.

In New York he guaranteed a playoff win over the New Jersey Devils.

When he scored his 1,000th NHL point, Messier gave the puck to Anderson because it was his sidekick's 400th goal.

While Gordie Howe was Gretzky's idol, it was Messier who played like him.

One night a Messier elbow tore Soviet winger Vladimir Kovin's face for 28 stitches. Another time a fist broke Jamie Macoun's jaw in Calgary. Once he removed four of Rich Sutter's teeth with his stick.

His original nickname with the Oilers was Mad Dog. For most of his career in Edmonton he was known as Moose. In New York, where they hadn't won a Stanley Cup in 54 years until he arrived, they called him Messiah.

He's been called the greatest leader in the history of team sports by some of the greatest leaders in the history of team sports.

"Messier is the greatest leader in the game," said Mike Keenan after Messier made a special trip, with the Stanley Cup held over his head, to the bench and handed it to his coach when they won it in New York. "For him to come and give me the Cup at the bench was an unbelievable feeling. I have so much respect for Mark. He's such a strong character man."

His Oiler coach put it best.

"He has that unbeatable spirit, like a thoroughbred galloping in the wind," Sather once said. "He gets that look in his eye. I've only seen it once before, from Rocket Richard, but Mark has it even more. He gives everyone in the room that look and away they go."

Gretzky, when he got his first look at Jari Kurri, knew they were going to go a long way together.

"You could sort of see Gretz's eyes light up when Jari was at his first training camp," said Lowe. "To see a guy so young who could shoot so well ..."

Kurri would score 32, 32, 45, 52, 71, 68, 54, 43, 44 and 33 goals a season in his time as an Edmonton Oiler.

He learned to speak English watching *Happy Days* on TV.

There aren't many Jari Kurri stories, other than the Great Snipe Hunt, but teammates do remember the time he came to the bench one night on Long Island and fellow Finn Esa Tikkanen was telling Kurri about some mistake Kurri had made on the ice. The normally mild-mannered Kurri up and punched Tikkanen on the nose.

Eventually, like the rest of them, Kurri went on his way to the bigger payday.

"I spent 10 years of my life in Edmonton," he would look back. "That's a long time. I came when I was only 20 years old. I remember very well thinking that I would stay one year and go back to Finland."

Kurri, after stops in Los Angeles, New York, Anaheim and Colorado, called it a career after 14 seasons, in ninth place in all-time NHL goal-scoring with 601 snipes, 14th place in all-time NHL point production with 1,398 and 20th in the record book with 813 assists.

As an Oiler he ranks second all-time in points with 1,043, in goals with 474 and third in assists with 569.

Kurri completed his career second only to Gordie Howe in points by a right-winger and with the best statistics of any European ever to play in the NHL.

He won the Lady Byng Trophy in 1985.

"A lot of people make a big deal about regular-season statistics," says Kurri. "But I believe playoff stats mean the most. They say you were a winner. Playoff stats are much tougher to get. And winning the Cups, that is the best. That is so-o-o-o-o much fun."

Kurri's playoff totals include 225 games played, with 106 goals, third highest of all time; 127 assists, fourth highest of all time; and 233 points, third highest of all time.

Kurri owns the Oilers record for playoff goals with 92 and is third in assists (110) and points (202), having played 146 of his 200 Stanley Cup playoff games as an Oiler (and his last one, ironically, against the Oilers).

Kurri owns Stanley Cup records for most goals in a series (12), most three-or-more-goal games (4) and most three-or-more-goal games in one playoff series (3).

"I felt that 600 goals in the NHL and playing in the Olympics in Nagano would make a fine exit," Kurri said of his decision to call it a career.

He scored a goal in the bronze-medal game to help Finland beat Canada at the Olympics.

It would have been more fitting if Kurri had waited just one more night to score that 600th goal.

He became only the eighth NHLer to reach the magic milestone but it took him 36 games to get it. His Colorado Avalanche came to Edmonton to play the Oilers the next night.

There used to be an old hockey joke:

Q: Why are Finns like bananas?

A: Because they're green when you get them. Then they turn yellow. And after you've had them a while, they're rotten.

Jari Kurri forced hockey people to stop telling that joke.

"I could always count on him," said Gretzky. "Jari always got back. He was never out of position."

Sather said Kurri had a lot to do with the records Gretzky set as an Oiler.

"Wayne couldn't play like Wayne and the Oilers remain successful if Jari didn't do for him what he did," said Slats.

"Wayne spent so much time at the other end, Jari had to do what Wayne didn't do defensively.

"The thing that's always bugged me is that Jari didn't win the Selke Award. He should have won it three or four times but because he was so explosive offensively, so dominating, they wouldn't give it to him. Nobody could take a player out of the play without taking a penalty like Jari. He just angled players off the puck. He's one of the smartest players I ever saw."

In the beginning, nobody was raving about Paul Coffey's defensive game like that. And he's a defenceman.

Coffey, after playing for the same Junior B team as Gretzky, gave fans plenty of reason with his speed and style to believe he was going to be

Speedy blueliner Paul Coffey – the Bobby Orr of the '80s.

great. But in the beginning he was known as Paul Coff-up and fans used to jeer that the foulest smell in the Coliseum was burnt Coffey. But soon enough his reign of error was over.

And then he made the play to set up Mike Bossy to win the Canada Cup, a play that would likely rank third in most Canadians' international hockey memory banks, behind Paul Henderson's goal in 1972 and Wayne Gretzky's setup of Mario Lemieux to win the Canada Cup, which followed Coffey's 1984 memory maker.

"That's the best I ever felt in my life," said Coffey the night he made the play in a game that many would compare to the famed New Year's Eve game between the Montreal Canadiens and Red Army, thought of as the greatest hockey game ever played.

Oilers goaltending coach Pete Peeters, playing in goal for Canada that night, said it for everybody.

"I hope all those people who have knocked him saw his defensive ability tonight," Peeters said of the winning goal, which Coffey began by making the big play defensively before he gave Mike Bossy a live look at the famed Oilers transition game.

He became the Bobby Orr of the '80s.

"I never saw him live," said Coffey of the Bruins great. "And I'd never even met him until I went to Wayne's tennis tournament. I'd have loved to have played against Bobby Orr, to get to know how our styles were the same or different. I know he revolutionized the game of hockey for defencemen. He could kill a penalty all by himself. He was so much ahead of everybody then."

In 16 seasons in the NHL, after performing as a Pittsburgh Penguin, Los Angeles King, Detroit Red Wing and Philadelphia Flyer, Coffey became a Chicago Blackhawk.

A member of three Oiler Stanley Cup teams, who won one more as a Penguin, Coffey ranks first all-time among NHL defencemen in goals (383), assists (1,090) and points (1,473) and second all-time in assists behind only Gretzky, and seventh overall in all-time NHL point production.

Coffey also ranks third all-time with 131 Stanley Cup assists and fifth all-time with 195 playoff points.

As an Oiler he played 532 games, scored 209 goals, had 460 assists and 669 points. He played 94 of his playoff games in Edmonton, with 36 goals, 67 assists and 103 points.

A three-time winner of the Norris Trophy, with three Canada Cup trophies and a World Cup of Hockey silver medal to go with the numbers, he's a Hall of Fame automatic, too.

Coffey owns the record for most goals by a defenceman, career, most assists by a defenceman, career, and most points by a defenceman, career. He broke Orr's single-season record for goals when he scored 48 in '85-86 with the Oilers. He shares records for assists by a defenceman in a game (six) and points by a defenceman in a game (eight) and owns outright the longest point-scoring streak by a defenceman at 28 games.

In the Stanley Cup record book he owns others. Coffey's 12 goals by a defenceman in a playoff year, 25 assists by a defenceman in a playoff year, five assists by a defenceman in a playoff game, 37 points by a defenceman in a playoff year and six points by a defenceman in a playoff game are all records.

He was the first Oiler star to leave. And his spats with Slats were legendary.

"Glen Sather's last words to me were that I'd never win a Cup again," said No. 7, who won one with Mario Lemieux in Pittsburgh.

Coffey was thrilled to be able to play for Sather again in the World Cup of Hockey and, looking back, had mostly positive things to say about his old coach who used to ride him so hard.

"In those seven years he was so influential, so important to my career. The Oilers are a good organization. I had good teaching early. Sometimes I look at some players in the playoffs and shake my head at the way they play. But then I look at the organizations where they came from and I understand.

"I used to take a wide turn at the net all the time and Slats would be all over me. 'Cut sharp past the post,' he'd scream at me. I can still hear that."

Sather remembers the feuds with Coffey.

"The funny thing is that of all the guys who played in Edmonton, my kids Justin and Shannon liked Paul the best," said Sather. "He had a way with my kids. He was respectful. He talked to them. He was sincere. He was always their favourite."

Being a fan favourite was never Grant Fuhr's lot in life as an Oiler, especially after he called the Edmonton fans jerks and after he was suspended for admitting to cocaine use.

Adopted and raised by white parents in Spruce Grove, as many stories are told about Fuhr's life and times as an Oiler as about his greatness in goal.

"Fuhr saves" was said a lot when he was on the ice. But seldom when he was off it.

By the late 1980s Grant Fuhr was being called the world's greatest goalie.

There was always the temptation to call Fuhr a money goalie for his playoff play. Except you could never actually type that with a straight face. He was usually out of money, the garnisheed goalie.

"I had a tougher time learning to save money than learning to stop pucks," Fuhr once told me. "I was a pretty good example of too much, too soon."

Sather spoke of Fuhr in the *Sports Illustrated* article which painted the Oilers as a cocaine club.

"He threw money around like it was playing paper. He bought whatever he saw, videos, stereos, clothes ...

"Grant's not exactly a wizard when it comes to finances. He can't take care of money. The problem Grant's got comes from a kid who is dumb."

Fuhr didn't call Sather a jerk for those quotes.

"I was dumb," he said. "For the first couple years I was real dumb. I know that. I bought everything, including a couple of cars which weren't exactly practical. If I saw something I liked, I bought it."

More reasons to celebrate: Kevin Lowe congratulates teammates Mark Messier, who was presented with a silver stick in honour of his 1,000th NHL point, and Glenn Anderson, who was given a silver puck to mark his 400th goal, in January 1991.

Playing goal behind a team designed to go forward more than back left Fuhr underrated until the 1987 Canada Cup when, all of a sudden, people started speaking of the national netminder as the heir to Vladislav Tretiak's title of world's greatest goalie.

"Finally, people are beginning to believe it," said Gretzky at that Canada Cup. "I think he's been the best goaltender in the world for the last two or three years."

A year later the general managers finally gave Fuhr his due by voting him winner of the Vezina Trophy, and the Professional Hockey Writers Association voted him to the first all-star team for the first time.

"He has been the best in this league and the world for quite some time," said Sather. "He got overlooked because of the team. He deserves this."

Fuhr, who made stops in Toronto, Buffalo and Los Angeles before he became a St. Louis Blues goalie, ranked fifth on the all-time win list, going into his 18th NHL season with 382 victories. The Spruce Grove product was only 26 behind Stony Plain's Glenn Hall. Terry Sawchuk owns the record at 447. The record could be Fuhr's. And despite the big black mark on his career left by the drug suspension, that record is his key to the Hall of Fame regardless of what politics might be played.

On the Stanley Cup trail, Fuhr has appeared in the second-highest number of playoff games (137) and has the third-highest number of wins with 86, only two back of second-place Billy Smith.

Fuhr set one NHL regular-season record as an Oiler for longest undefeated streak by a goalie in his first NHL season (23).

And if he couldn't possibly set any records for goals-against average and the like playing for this team, Fuhr figured he might as well get in on the act.

He holds the record for most assists by a goaltender with 46 and most assists by a goaltender in a single season with 14 from the 1983-84 Oilers season.

If Fuhr doesn't have some of the numbers, how about Kevin Lowe?

There was the day in '86 when the team locked the dressing-room doors after practice and presented Lowe with a cake. The occasion was the first anniversary of his last goal.

"Happy Anniversary. Keep Up The Good Work" read the inscription in icing on the cake.

His teammates, on the other hand, didn't present him with a cake when he played his 700th game. But Lowe gave himself that extra tap on his own shin pads before he took the ice that night.

"You hit a number like 700 and it makes you think a bit," said the player who was the Oilers' first draft choice and scorer of their first goal. "You think about the heroes you had as a kid. Bobby Orr played less than 700. I looked up to Doug Barkley. He only played a couple hundred before he lost his eye. You get to this point and really realize you've been a lucky lad."

Lowe always had a sense of the big picture. That's why he was the last of the glory gang to leave, and that's why he came back with his eye on a coaching career here.

On a hot July day in 1987, Lowe invited the media to drop around to his house. There was a bucket of beer on ice for the media men, who, one by one, drifted through his home to the back patio where Lowe was taking turns doing one-on-one interviews to announce the signing of a five-year contract.

You could see it all with Kevin Lowe right there.

He understood the media. He understood the way the world works. He understood the value of being a citizen. He understood his city. He understood himself. He understood history. He understood tradition.

"All that stuff," said Sather. "He understands *all* that stuff."

Sather knew, all along, who Kevin Lowe wanted to be in Edmonton.

"Jean Beliveau," he once said.

Lowe talked about it that day.

"Somebody asked me if I'd like to finish my career playing for the Montreal Canadiens because I grew up there," said Lowe. "To me the Edmonton Oilers *are* the Montreal Canadiens. I have blue and orange blood in my veins.

"I look at a guy like Jackie Parker. I see his name up there at Commonwealth Stadium. I'd like to think that someday somebody may think of me that way. I'm conscious of the team's place in history. It's important to me that new players are proud of the traditions we're building here. I know Edmonton is a small city way up in the north of Canada. I also know the Edmonton Oilers are pretty big on the totem pole of sport."

While Gretzky had Edmonton's royal wedding, Kevin Lowe and Karen Percy had Banff's.

It was almost as big a story. And like the Gretzky-Jones engagement, I scooped myself on Lowe-Percy, too. Same deal. A tipster in search of the big news tip of the year prize at 630-CHED. Again I had to break the story on the Morning Crew, where I was moonlighting at daybreak.

This one nobody saw coming.

"We both moved pretty quick," said Lowe.

They met at Gretzky's softball tournament in Brantford.

"We looked at each other all night," said Karen.

Lowe eventually left to join Messier and Edmonton East with the Rangers. Then, although we're getting ahead of the storyline here, he came back.

"It didn't dawn on me when I left here," he said. "I was ready to go. Looking back on it later, I'd say, 'Geez, I'd played 966 games through all those years here and to not play 1,000 would be a shame.'"

Lowe ended up with 19 seasons and 1,254 games, 26th in NHL history. His 1,037 games in Oiler silks is a team record. Only 27 players have managed to hit the 1,000-game milestone with the same team.

His 214 playoff games ranks fifth in Stanley Cup history and his 18 seasons in the playoffs are only two short of the record of 20 shared by Gordie Howe and Larry Robinson. His 172-game playoff total is tops in Oilers history.

With six Stanley Cups, including one with the Rangers in New York, Lowe was a member of the 1984 Canada Cup team and played in seven NHL all-star games. Lowe also became the only player ever to win the King Clancy Memorial Trophy and the Budweiser Man of the Year Award in the same season.

Strictly a stay-at-home defenceman, Lowe did manage to score 84 goals and add 347 assists for 431 points. He ranks sixth on the Oilers'

all-time playoff assists list with 309 and seventh in playoff points with 383. In the playoffs Lowe ended up with 10 goals and 48 assists for 58 points, all but one of the goals and five of the assists registered with the Oilers.

Lowe's No. 4, Messier's No. 11 and Gretzky's No. 99 are the only three uniform numbers, other than Al Hamilton's retired No. 3, which haven't been made available to other Oilers.

Glenn Anderson wore No. 9. Jim Harrison and Kari Makkonen wore it before him. Then Bernie Nicholls and Shayne Corson wore it after him. Then Anderson wore it again, returning to the team to complete his career. Three others have worn it since.

At least Anderson wore it twice. That made it 99 for the space cadet who grew up with movie and TV star Michael J. Fox and once listed his boyhood idol as Wayne Gretzky. Anderson is three months older than No. 99.

Drafted by the Oilers, he opted instead to play for the Canadian Olympic team.

That's where they hung him with his nickname, Mork.

John Muckler probably described him best.

"Andy will do anything to win. He's a gifted skater and a daredevil. He goes to the net as well as anybody in the NHL. You have to be leery of him. You never know what will happen. He loses control."

His playing style was eventually described as kamikaze.

Anderson is going to be the toughest call for the Hall of Fame selection committee. He was a regular-season underachiever and a Stanley Cup playoff overachiever. That's if anybody who played 1,129 regular-season games and produced 1,099 points can be called an underachiever. Maybe you had to be there.

The radio voice of the Oilers, Rod Phillips, receives a silver stick from general manager Glen Sather in November 1997.

Given the chance to come back and complete his career in Edmonton and get his 500th goal, Anderson came up two goals short. In 16 NHL seasons Lanny McDonald hit the magic figure of 500 and in the same number of seasons Anderson came up two shy. They rank 26th and 27th on the all-time goal-scoring list. Anderson's 601 assists ranks 49th and his 1,099 points 37th. His Oiler totals from finishing his career with the club ended up at 845 games, 417 goals, 489 assists and 906 points.

If those end up as borderline Hall of Fame numbers, his playoff production is an entirely different story.

Ranked fourth all-time with 93 playoff goals, Anderson retired fifth in all-time post-season assists with 121, and fourth all-time in Stanley Cup points with 214.

His main claim to fame was coming through in the clutch. He scored 17 overtime goals in the playoffs.

Winning six Stanley Cups, including the one in New York with the Rangers, and being a regular with Team Canada in the Canada Cups with the other Oiler greats ought to be enough to send him in the front door of the Hockey Hall of Fame, the one marked "push," not the one marked "pull."

Chapter 17

Stay Oilers Stay

"**W**ait till next year" is the normal way of sport. But starting the 1992-93 season the Edmonton version was somewhat shorter and came with a question mark.

"Next year?"

Would there be one?

One by one there wouldn't be a next year in Quebec City, Winnipeg and Hartford. And there was no question the other WHA merger franchise was on the endangered species list.

Peter Pocklington called his first press conference to hold the town hostage. Edmonton Northlands and the Oilers' owner began their fight over the Coliseum, with as many of their press conferences televised locally as Oiler games.

Would the Oilers end up in Hamilton? Minnesota? Houston?

The gut-churning "Stay Oilers Stay" scenario would take the focus away from the games – which some nights maybe wasn't such a bad thing. After being the most spoiled-silly fans in sport, Edmonton fans finally found out what life was like in the bottom half of the standings.

Despite what happened the previous two seasons – the Oilers making it to the final four against all odds – the experts weren't banking on more minor miracles.

In '93-94 the pre-season publications ranked the Oilers to be, well, rank.

Todd Marchant, left, and Doug Weight. Opposite: Mark Messier celebrates his last goal as an Oiler. His loss was felt both on and off the ice.

Ted Green and Glen Sather face the media during a press conference early in the troubled 1993 season. Below: Kevin Lowe joined Messier in the Big Apple.

"No End in Sight to Oilers Skid" was the headline on the cover of *Inside Sports,* which rated "Team Fire Sale" to finish out of the playoffs. *The Sporting News* cover featured a picture of Glen Sather and the headline "Dynasty In Disarray." *The Hockey News* rated the Oilers a 'D' team, "Done Like Dinner."

Coach Ted Green said he didn't have to go to the newsstands to know what the pre-season publications were going to say.

"What do you expect?" he said. "A lot of people have been waiting a long time for us to go down. Now we're down and they're kicking us when we're down. When you have had a history like this team has, I don't think you should be surprised that people are going to trample on your back when you fall on your face."

Sather had one thing to say to the fans.

"Keep reminding yourself as you watch these kids. Whatever they accomplish, they are going to be better."

They had to remind themselves of that a lot.

The Oilers were a disastrous 1-8-1 in their first 10 games and never recovered.

The fans, who had paid for their season in advance before Sather dealt away all the names the previous season, were not buying this year. The Oilers started the season with only 9,000 season tickets sold.

The turnstiles were not clicking in the Coliseum but the revolving door kept rotating in the Oilers dressing room.

Vincent Van Goal, for example. He became Vincent Van Go. Blaming a year in Edmonton for his legal separation from his wife, Vincent Damphousse won his divorce from the Oilers after only one year. Sather gave him his wish and traded him to Montreal for Shayne Corson, Brent Gilchrist and Vladimir Vujtek.

Corson came with a reputation.

"We don't have a Crescent Street in Edmonton," said Sather of the bar capital of Canada. "And we have a coach who is tough enough to handle him."

Joe Murphy announced he wanted to be traded: "I just want out. I don't get the respect I deserve. I no longer want to play here."

But the loss that really hurt that year came when the team said goodbye to Kevin Lowe. Lowe was the last of the glory gang. He was the third musketeer with Wayne Gretzky and Mark Messier. The three of them established the Montreal Canadiens-like traditions in Edmonton from the very beginning. Nobody in the history of pro sports in Edmonton put more back into the community than Kevin Lowe. He'd played 966 games as an Oiler, more than any other player in team history.

Edmonton didn't know that day where Lowe was going, just that he was going. It took until mid-December to find out that he was joining Mark Messier with the New York Rangers.

"It's sad to think of all the fun we had with the great players but we have to start a new era," said Sather, who now had nobody left from the Oilers' first Stanley Cup-winning team. "I thought Kevin Lowe might be the one guy who was with us the whole way."

The Oilers obtained two Russians, Roman Oksiuta and Alexander Kerch, in one of Sather's more forgettable deals.

Craig MacTavish became the captain.

"MacT is the perfect choice," said Craig Simpson. "Like Mark and Kevin, he has great qualities as a person and everyone looks up to him in the same way they looked up to Kevin."

Sun hockey writer Dan Barnes tagged the season early. "The Fall of '92" he called it.

All those years of watching Firewagon Hockey and now we were watching Circle the Wagons Hockey.

On Oct. 28, after a four-game losing streak, a crowd of 12,614 showed up to watch the Minnesota North Stars. It was the lowest number in Oilers history.

On Nov. 21 the Oilers lost 9-0 in Vancouver. Three nights later they lost 8-1 at home to Chicago.

They weren't all like that. Some games weren't so bad.

"We're either good or we're gawd-awful," said goalie Bill Ranford in mid-December. "We're either good or absolutely brutal. We don't play mediocre."

On Jan. 6 Oilers lost 6-1 to St. Louis.

If his Oilers weren't a pain in the posterior, coach Green spent the season wracked with pain associated with kidney stones. Sather had to do something. He traded away Bernie Nicholls to New Jersey for Zdeno Ciger and Kevin Todd.

On Feb. 26 Sather finally moved

New kids on the block: Ryan Smyth, Tyler Wright, Jason Arnott and Steve Kelly.

Oilers forward Shjon Podein hits the ice face-first during a December '94 game against the Flames.

Murphy – to the Chicago Blackhawks for Igor Kravchuk and Dean McAmmond.

"We're putting together a stable of young guys now," the GM said of McAmmond in particular, making it obvious he was willing to ignore all the three-on-one breaks to do three-for-one deals that would give the Oilers a future if they survived the present.

The present, of course, was full of painful reminders of the past.

Lowe's turn to get the ex-Oiler-Returns-to-Town treatment came on the last day of February. Before the game the Oilers presented him with a silver stick. Then the Rangers gave the Oilers the shaft as Messier set up the winner that left the Oilers 12 games under .500.

"I feel real bad for them," said Lowe.

If the Rangers appeared to be getting the best of Sather in all the deals, along came the trade of Esa Tikkanen. With Messier, Lowe, Jeff Beuke-

boom, Adam Graves and now Tikkanen on Broadway, the Rangers had acquired 18 Stanley Cup rings.

The Oilers were in New York at the time, so Tikkanen and the kid Sather traded for simply exchanged sweaters.

The kid's name was Doug Weight.

"If our team had done better, we would not be making this kind of trade," said Sather. "But we can't flounder close to the bottom and not do something."

There was no going back now. Either Sather would be able to bottle lightning or break the bottle. The deal for Weight ensured that youth would now be served, regardless.

"Tikkanen is not a great loss in my mind," said Sather. "Realistically, he's done in four years. When this team is ready to succeed again, he won't be able to contribute. With Weight there's a huge upside."

Sather said he believed he *could* bottle lightning again.

"I think we can. I like the challenge. If you do it once, you know what the formula is and we have a lot of good young players we have to develop. It's time, patience and development. I think we can."

For the first time in 14 NHL seasons, the Oilers knew they'd be on the outside looking in when the Stanley Cup playoffs began. And the great schedule maker made sure there was a twist to it. A game before 17,503 fans at the Coliseum against the Los Angeles Kings – and with all those former Oilers in the lineup – was the one that eliminated the Oilers from the playoffs.

"I don't think that anyone would have predicted five years ago that team would miss the playoffs," observed Wayne Gretzky in the visiting dressing room. "But they've basically given up everybody for young guys."

Sather, who showed up for that game sedated, drugged up thanks to his wife Ann crashing into him in a bizarre bicycle-rollerblading accident in Palm Springs, was symbolic of the season.

"If the idea is to make the playoffs every year in history, blame me," he said. "Sure, we thought we could do it. But there was no way I was going to try it any other way. I could have acquired the players to make the playoffs. If that's all it was all about, we could have replaced people with 28- or 29-year-olds. If our ultimate goal was a short-term solution, we could have done that. But we are trying to win the Stanley Cup again."

Never did it look so far away.

The Oilers won 26, lost 50 and tied eight. Surely they'd never have fewer wins in a season.

Doug Weight topped the Oilers scoring, tied with Petr Klima, with 48 points. He only had eight of them as an Oiler. And Klima was history. The Oilers essentially traded him for a pail of pucks and a used jockstrap in the off-season.

Craig Simpson was traded to Buffalo for Jozef Cierny. Martin Gelinas was traded to the Quebec Nordiques for Scott Pearson.

But the focus was on the draft, where, after all those years of being up near the top of the league, the Oilers finally had an early pick. Selecting seventh, they picked Jason Arnott.

Fingering the Oshawa Generals star as their future franchise player, they gave him a three-year deal worth $2.1 million, including a $500,000 signing bonus.

Edmonton took to the kid right off. He was, that first year, a

Feelin' punchy: Oiler Dave Manson connects against Calgary's Joel Otto.

thrilled-to-be-in-the-NHL, unaffected, pleasant young man who was hard not to like. Funny how things change.

Arnott scored the winner in his first-ever NHL game as the Oilers opened with a 3-2 win over the San Jose Sharks.

"I had the shakes during *O Canada* but I had a chance to play and to score the winning goal ... it's just a dream come true," Arnott said that night. "It was unbelievable watching the puck dribble into the net for the win. Everything went silent. It was an unbelievable feeling."

The Oilers won their first two games. But then they lost to Vancouver. Lost to Anaheim. Tied Los Angeles. Lost to Vancouver. Lost to Winnipeg. Lost to Calgary. Lost to Boston. Lost to Washington. Lost to San Jose. Lost to Buffalo. Lost to Calgary. Lost to Ottawa. Lost to St. Louis. Lost to Chicago. Beat Detroit. Lost to Boston. Tied Hartford. Tied Toronto. Lost to Montreal. Lost to Toronto. Lost to Anaheim. Lost to Chicago.

By Nov. 24, they were 3-18-3 and dead last in the entire league.

And Green was history.

The sports pages that week were all Edmonton Eskimos. The CFL team was in a Grey Cup game. It was not the week to fire a hockey coach. But with another record-low crowd, this one 11,515, and ...

"Teddy is a helluva guy. He has more guts than Dick Tracy. But

Attendance plummeted during the Oilers' 1993-94 season.

look at the poor guy. I don't think this was doing his health any good. And it was time to fish or cut bait. We have to win some games," said Pocklington.

The replacement coach: Glen Sather.

"Nobody in the world can inspire kids like Glen," said the Oilers' owner, who admitted he forced this move. "He can get these kids going and the crowd excited again."

Green wasn't relieved about being relieved.

"I'm not happy with what happened today. I recognize the crowds were getting smaller and we were dropping lower and lower in the standings. If we had more scoring, all this would be academic. But I'm the guy who was responsible and accountable. I guess in the scope of the world events, this is probably very small. But in my world, it's very devastating. No-

body forced me into this ring. I climbed in and I couldn't go the distance."

Sather said it was a situation he couldn't really foist upon anybody else.

"I don't think I could have put this on somebody else. Under the circumstances, I was the obvious guy to do it."

The drop from penthouse to outhouse was dramatic. Since Valentine's Day, the Oilers record was 8-40-3.

It was Sather the GM, not Sather the coach, who did the best work that season, though. Forced to match an outlandish offer sheet to Dave Manson, Sather, who had been hitting and missing on deals, hit a home run. He traded Manson and his salary to Winnipeg for Boris Mironov and Mats Lindgren *plus* the Jets' first-round draft choice, which would turn out to be Jason Bonsignore.

Then, at the deadline, he did captain MacTavish a favour and shipped him to New York to join his friends and former Oiler teammates with the Rangers and a chance to win another Stanley Cup.

In return the Oilers received a kid by the name of Todd Marchant.

March 28 was the official day of elimination from the playoffs in the 1993-94 season. But it was different this time. The Oilers actually finished with fewer wins (25) than the year before. But you could see, at least, the foundation of a new team start to rise.

The year before, the Oilers lost 20 of their last 25, 11 of their last 12. This team won five and tied two of its last nine.

"This team totally quit last year," said assistant coach Ron Low. "They went through the motions. This year's team was still competing right down to the last game. It's a night and day turnaround. The whole attitude here last year was terrible. They didn't even care about the games. The last three weeks the players couldn't wait to get out of here. The fans could see it. It was obvious to everybody. I think the fans can see the difference this year. We were still working, trying right up to the end to have something to take forward to next year."

Sather had no desire to continue as a coach for the following year. But he liked the attitude of a lot of the kids he coached in the interim.

"These kids are eager, anxious to please, and they're developing," said Sather at the end of the road. "We're the youngest team in the league. We've accumulated a lot of draft picks. We've drafted some kids who will definitely play in the NHL. They're all good pieces, young pieces we can fit into the long-range puzzle."

After that season, the Oilers really believed they had something special in Arnott. Young No. 7 enjoyed one of the finest rookie seasons in Oilers history. Of all the NHL silverware Oilers collected over the years, not one player ever won the Calder but Arnott came close, leading the team in scoring with 33 goals and finishing second to Weight in points with 68. He finished second in the voting to Martin Brodeur of the New Jersey Devils. He was named to the NHL's all-rookie team along with teammate Mironov and was named rookie of the year by *The Hockey News* and *The Sporting News*.

With the fourth and sixth picks in the entry draft, Edmonton fans were drooling for two more Arnotts.

The Oilers had never before drafted higher than sixth, picking Paul Coffey in 1980. With the fourth pick, the Oilers pretty much went with Central Scouting and picked big Bonsignore. With the sixth pick, Sather went with Ryan Smyth because he felt like he knew what he was getting on the character end.

Bonsignore had been told by the Oilers they would take him if he was available at No. 4. But Smyth's selection seemed to take that player completely by surprise.

"I've known this kid since he was 10 years old," said Sather. "It wasn't that much of a guess."

Smyth was born and raised in Banff. He played with Sather's son Justin at summer hockey schools.

But the big news of the summer, of course, was the hiring of a new coach.

Glen Sather looked out over the crowd of about 4,000 season ticketholders as he prepared to make the announcement.

"When I took over this team 17 years ago, I was the same age as this guy," he said.

And with that he introduced 32-year-old George Burnett.

There was no real reaction from those fans.

Burnett had no NHL experience. He'd coached the Cape Breton farm team for two seasons.

It was clear from the crowd. He was going to have to prove himself to them. And as it turned out, the team reacted exactly the same way.

If the Oilers were hosed in the Adam Graves compensation hearing, they did much better when Steven Rice found himself in the

Top: Peter Pocklington and Glen Sather welcome new coach George Burnett. Bottom: Burnett presents Shayne Corson with the captain's 'C.'

"The last four years have been hell. But now, instead of being on the downswing, we are definitely on the upswing.

"I think we'll win the Stanley Cup again. I'm absolutely convinced of that. I think it can happen in five years. I think it's a very good prediction. The timelines aren't too difficult.

"I think you have to have seven great players, seven world-class players. I think we're going to have them. If these kids prove what I think they will, I think you'll see us in the hunt again. There are still a lot of variables, of course. One of them is what happens in the CBA negotiations. But I see that young, talented nucleus."

"CBA negotiations" would soon be translated to read "Lockout." Not long into that camp it became clear that the season wasn't going to start on schedule.

Chewing on that, the Oilers saw some positives. The Coliseum situation had been settled and millions of dollars of improvements were being put into place, including new box suites and seats. It would give the construction people time to complete the finishing touches. And the Oilers had such a young team with so many kids that the idea of maybe a 70-game schedule instead of an 82-game schedule actually might be of benefit.

It lasted until mid-January. When it was finally solved and NHL commissioner Gary Bettman and NHLPA boss Bob Goodenow were finally able to declare "Game On," the teams were left with a 48-game schedule.

You could see the change the next morning as the home boys

same position. The judge awarded Edmonton rugged defenceman Bryan Marchment.

The turnover was under control as Sather decided to hold the Oilers training camp in his off-season home of Banff. And it was there he made the Prediction.

There had previously been two great sports predictions in Edmonton's history. In the mid-'70s, Eskimos GM Norm Kimball guaranteed the team would not miss the playoffs again this century. So far, so good. And in the Oilers' first year in the NHL, owner Pocklington had proclaimed his team would do what no team had done before – win a Stanley Cup within five years of entering the league. It did.

The Oiler boss, as he watched the kids cavort at the Banff camp prior to the start of the 1994-95 season, figured he could finally see the future.

conducted their final practice prior to Training Camp II.

"Look," said the commercial league player who poked his nose into the rink for a peak at the pros. "Helmets instead of ball caps."

Weight laughed. "You know we're getting to play when we put the lids on."

Ready or not, Burnett would take his kiddie corps into the season which had turned from a marathon to a sprint.

It was a different deal as Burnett contemplated the start of his NHL coaching career (again). One reason Sather had hired him was for his patience. He wouldn't be able to have much of that over a 48-game schedule.

It was a night to remember when the season finally started at the renovated and newly renamed Edmonton Coliseum. The Oilers succeeded in making it a bit of an occasion with Hollywood-style searchlights, with

Moments of jubilation were few and far between as the Oilers struggled through the 1993-94 campaign.

bands scattered throughout the refurbished building and 500 workers who laboured on the new-look Coliseum invited to the game for a special ceremonial faceoff. The crowd cheered the opening few seconds of play. The fans showed Ranford that there were no hard feelings from the lockout when they rose out of their seats and roared after his first great save of the season.

Despite the dramatically upgraded arena, the worst crowd in team history (a record which was being broken once a month now) showed up to watch one of the worst games in Oilers history as they lost to Chicago, falling to a 1-5 start and in trouble from the git-go. The crowd of 10,492 saw the Hawks run Ranford with three goals on the first four shots for consecutive bad goals at 4:27, 5:40 and 5:52 en route to an embarrassing 7-0 loss. It was the most lopsided home shutout loss in Oiler history.

If that wasn't shocking, the move Burnett made the next day certainly was.

You just named *who* the captain of the Edmonton Oilers? The Crescent Street Carouser? Hockey's Headline Hunter? The Bar Room Brawler? The Missed Curfew Kid?

Late Night With Shayne Corson would now be in prime time. Say it ain't so, Glen Sather. Tell us your coach didn't just name the player who was previously a captain's worst nightmare as team captain?

"Yeah, we did," said Sather after he'd presented the jersey with the fresh 'C' to Corson in the Captains Room at the Coliseum.

"But look at these pictures. There's a guy up there who was worse," said Sather, pointing at a picture of Mark Messier, the player who grew up to be called perhaps the greatest leader in the history of pro sports.

There was real concern for the sanity of the Oilers brain trust when they brought in Senior Swede, the 38-year-old skating scout.

That lasted a month. Kent Nilsson played six games. Scored one goal.

Then came the night in Dallas when the Oilers rallied for a 4-4 tie, but captain Corson tried to con himself an extra assist on a goal during the comeback from a 4-1 deficit.

"A lot of stuff went on that night," remembered assistant coach Low. "It wasn't nice. What happened that night was dumb. There were seven incidents within a half-hour."

Seven games later Burnett stripped Corson of the 'C.'

The idea was to trade Corson after the Dallas incident. But Burnett snapped. And suddenly Sather, who was prepared to allow Burnett to coach from the edge of the cliff, fired his coach after 35 games.

"The dressing room was in chaos," he said. "Whether they'll play for you is the most important part. I blame myself. George is going to be a good coach, but with this group it wasn't working. He didn't communicate with this group."

Low, who some said lost the toss for the position because Pocklington figured Burnett looked better in a suit and was much more presentable to the public than the Foxwarren, Man., farmer, suddenly looked very presentable, especially to the players.

Not that they got all fired up for him after Burnett was fired. The dirty deed was done to Burnett on the road before a game in San Jose. Under new head coach Low the Oilers lost 5-0.

That's not quite the way Low had it pictured.

"You'd like to ride home on a white horse," he said.

Architect Bob Walker surveys renovations to the Coliseum.

Low had been the white knight before, riding to the rescue late in the season as a goalie traded by the Quebec Nordiques for Ron Chipperfield late in the 1980 season. The timing was almost exactly the same.

"That was likely the greatest time in my life as a hockey player," said Low.

The new coach wasn't able to salvage the season. Low was 5-7-1 – not good enough to make the playoffs as the Oilers ended up 17-27-4 for the shortened season. But Low did well enough to earn the job for the following year. And he knew, despite all the young talent on the team, how far he was away.

"We lost so much," he said when it was over. "Our pride and tradition slipped pretty bad in the last three years. Bob McCammon said it the other day. The name on the front of the uniform has to mean more than the name on the back of the uniform. That's what we lost around here."

The name 'Corson' would not be on the back of an Oilers uniform for the 1995-96 season. Corson was quickly traded to the St. Louis Blues – for Curtis Joseph and Mike Grier.

"That gives us the best goaltending tandem in the league," said Sather. Yeah, right.

Ranford and the goalie they call Cujo were both were free agents. It was Ranford Sather would sign first. Joseph, he planned to use as a poker

Left: Craig MacTavish clears his sticks out of the dressing room after being traded to the Rangers in March 1994. Middle: Kelly Buchberger assists Jason Arnott after he was cut by the puck. Above: Louie DeBrusk takes on Winnipeg Jets tough guy Tie Domi.

chip while he played for Las Vegas in the IHL.

Edmonton, for the first time since the Oilers began winning Stanley Cups, welcomed the hockey world back to town that summer. It was the year the city played host to the NHL Entry Draft.

"Doan! Doan! Doan!"

The crowd took up the chant, waiting for Sather to step to the microphone to make the Oilers' first-round pick.

"Doan! Doan! Doan!"

What a thrill for Shane Doan, the young player from Halkirk, Alberta. Until Sather stepped forward to the microphone ... and picked Steve Kelly.

Oiler fans didn't get the player they wanted. But the NHL did. When it was over, everybody in sight gave a toast to the host.

"They did great," said Ron Caron of St. Louis. "They took it over at the last minute from Winnipeg and jumped at it with enthusiasm. It was first class every which way we looked, and that was certainly a contrast to Hartford last year. It was the same first-class job they did here on the all-star game. Everything was unbelievable all weekend. The setup was sensational and the fans were knowledgeable."

NHL commissioner Gary Bettman gave the Edmonton draft the ultimate compliment.

"Everything was terrific and the fact they did this on short notice made it even more remarkable. I can't imagine how they could have made it better even if they had a year of planning."

Sather told Bettman he should hold the draft in Edmonton permanently.

The Oilers claimed a new attitude as the 1995-96 season went to the starting gate.

George Burnett was gone.

Shayne Corson was gone.

Happy days were here again?

Well, not quite. But ...

The Oilers' slogan for the season was "Get Pumped," and Low claimed for him it was a perfect fit.

"No matter what happens, I'm going to have fun," he swore. "I don't care. I'm going to make sure I enjoy this. This is the job I've wanted for a long, long time. Not just to be the head coach in the NHL. Not a job. *This* job. To be coach of the Edmonton Oilers. This is where it's at. This is what it's all about. I had a lot of fun playing in this league for 13 years. And my goal since I started in the Oilers organization in Halifax was this. I've never thought of anything else."

And so it began with much optimism. The Oilers were 7-1-1 in the pre-season. And they did look like happy campers.

But it didn't begin well.

In the opener, at home against Detroit, Jason Arnott was cut for 25 stitches over one eye and received his third concussion in two years. "It wasn't so much the concussion. It was the eye I was worried about. When I came to on the ice, that's the first thing I worried about. As soon as I regained consciousness on the ice, I started flipping out," Arnott said.

The Oilers lost the opener 3-1 to Detroit and then went to St. Louis and lost 5-3 to the Blues. The third game in Detroit the Oilers lost 9-0. And in the next outing, in Philadelphia, they lost 7-1.

Miraculously, the Oilers beat the defending Stanley Cup-champion New Jersey Devils in their own rink next time out. But the trip ended with a 4-1 loss in Buffalo. And by the end of November, all the pre-season optimism had evaporated.

Twice, in the same week, the Oilers broke their record for all-time low crowd counts – 9,384 and then 9,050 – and a Friends of the Oilers organization was being formed to get corporate Edmonton back in the game.

The Oilers weren't being much help. When 14,189 fans showed up at the Coliseum on Dec. 1 – the closest thing to a sellout so far that sea-

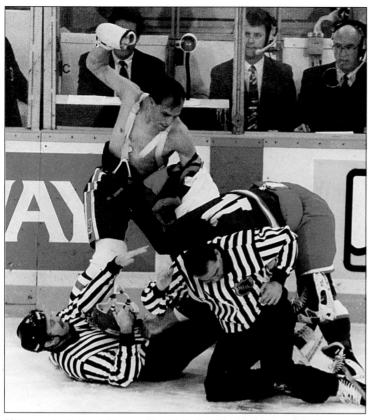

Linesmen try to break it up as Oiler Kelly Buchberger battles a Winnipeg opponent.

son – to watch the Oilers lose 8-2 to the Calgary Flames on Dec. 1, Low apologized to the fans.

"We were brutal. All I can do is apologize to the fans."

Ranford said don't blame the coach.

"This has to fall in the players' laps. The coaches are coaching their butts off. It was the players who were an absolute embarrassment. That's the bottom line. From the first minute to the 60th minute, it was an embarrassment. There was no excuse for that."

It didn't help when Arnott came up with his "I just wasn't into it" speech after one game.

Arnott was proving to be high maintenance and wasn't coming close to realizing the future everybody thought they'd seen that first season.

"The next time I wish he'd tell me that, and I'd put somebody else into the lineup who *is* into it," snapped Low, who didn't look like he was having as much fun as he had hoped.

On the night of Dec. 18, with the Colorado Avalanche in town, we learned the answer to how low it could go. The Oilers drew a crowd that would remain as the all-time attendance low – 8,419.

The season bottomed out with a 5-0 loss to Tampa Bay on Jan. 2. Tampa Bay had lost 10-0 the night before in Calgary. One fan caught the puck in the stands and threw it back on the ice as an unworthy NHL souvenir.

Sather met with the team after the game.

He claimed he was more infuriated with his team than at any point in Oilers history.

"I wasn't this mad after the game we lost 11-0 in Hartford when it looked like they'd all been drunk for a week," said Sather.

"I told the team that's the first time I'd heard a crowd boo the Oilers in 18 years here. I told them you should be embarrassed. They weren't booing because you lost. They were booing because you weren't working."

The next day there were more press people at the rink than players.

> ## 'This is the last time we won't make the playoffs in my tenure as general manager.'
> *– Glen Sather*

"I hate doing that," said Sather. "It's hard on me. It's hard on them. I had bloodshot eyes when I went home last night. It was like I'd blown a gasket. I'm sure my blood pressure was way up."

Low said he'd like to see some players traded. Sather responded. Ranford, the national netminder, to Boston for a player from Poland with 11 points and Sean Brown, the player the Bruins picked first in the entry draft in Edmonton. With Mariusz Czerkawski and Brown coming and Ranford going, new captain Kelly Buchberger was the only Oiler left who had been a part of the Stanley Cup-winning teams.

Not much of a deal?

It was only half of what happened that day. Sather signed Joseph to a three-year, $6.8-million US contract.

"The two goalies are very comparable," said Low. "But Billy has been in a position for a few years now where if he lets in a bad goal, he's not going to win. That can really wear on a goalie. I think it's probably going to be good for Billy to get away from that. The other guy is coming in here excited. He wants to play. He wants to get at it. I really like Cujo. He's a guy who, in the last three years, had a great save percentage playing for a team allowing a lot of shots. Other teams have watched Billy's save percentage decrease over time."

It was love at first sight.

At 13:50 of the second period in Joseph's first game in goal for the Oilers, the fans stood as one and chanted, "Cujo! Cujo! Cujo!"

At the end, when Weight scored the overtime winner, the Oilers' star

Bernie Nicholls, left, bids farewell to Petr Klima after Nicholls was traded to New Jersey in January 1993.

Hello Curtis Joseph, goodbye Bill Ranford.

made a beeline for the new goalie and the two threw themselves into each other's arms.

"What happened tonight really made me feel like an Oiler," said Joseph.

"To get an ovation like that, and then what happened with Weight at the end ... it's a nice way to start with a new team."

Weight said there was nothing pre-planned in it.

"Who plans on scoring the winning goal in overtime?" he said. "When I looked up, there was Cujo jumping up and down at the other end. It just felt right. It was spur of the moment, the second I saw him jumping. That was a tough thing for him to do, come into this game after being away from the NHL for so long and replace Billy Ranford in the building where he played so well for all those years."

Joseph endeared himself even more when he spent $100,000 of his new salary to create Cujo's Cloud Nine, a special skybox for sick kids.

Sather's next move didn't work as well. He plucked an ex-Oiler off the waiver wire. Glenn Anderson, hoping to end up in home-town Vancouver, wasn't thrilled.

The same week, the news broke that Arnott's poor play might have something to do with him having fathered a now five-month-old boy with a local woman he hardly knew.

The only casualty at the trade deadline was Kirk Maltby, traded to Detroit for Dan McGillis.

The turning point for the Oilers was, strange as it may sound to anyone who wasn't an Edmontonian at the time, the World Figure Skating Cham-

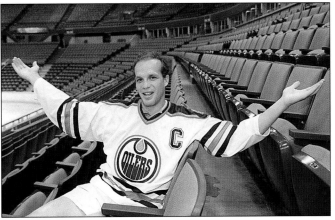

Captain Kelly Buchberger in his kingdom.

pionships.

The biggest and best Worlds ever held were held in Edmonton that year, forcing the Oilers out of the Coliseum. They won five of seven on the road and came back two points out of a playoff spot.

And things didn't just change on the ice. They changed off the ice, too.

"It's ironic that it's figure skating that got the hockey interest back," said Sather. "But it's true. I watched a lot of TV and the city looked great. And the city feels big time again and great things happen when you get enthusiasm and belief."

Sather said that's exactly what happened with his hockey club.

"The thing I think a lot of people missed is that we went away on that trip a better team. And we came back a lot better team. Before we went away we started doing some of the little things that make you win."

Off the ice Doug Piper and Eric Geddes were able to report that while the Worlds were being held in Edmonton and the Oilers were winning on the road, the Oilers passed the 9,000 mark in season tickets towards the goal of 13,000 for the following year.

"I think the Worlds were great. They reminded people how much fun a packed house is," said Piper. "It's great timing with the team playing great. Suddenly we have a little momentum going."

The Oilers made a real run for the playoffs. When they came up short, Sather offered the following short statement:

"This is the last time we won't make the playoffs in my tenure as general manager."

Chapter 18

Loud And Proud!

I t was time to bring the tough-love concept back to Edmonton. The fans were back, beating the 13,000 season-ticket base to qualify for the newly created NHL Canadian small-market subsidy. And Edmonton could see Glen Sather's endless trading of experience had created a team of young pros that should now begin to excel.

An old Oiler was back in the fold who could see it better than anybody. With a sixth Stanley Cup ring from his time as a New York Ranger, Kevin Lowe had returned to the team and, more than anybody, he endorsed a tough-love concept.

"Doug Weight is going into this season knowing he's world class now. The 100 points last year was nice. But the World Cup of Hockey proved it," Lowe said of Team USA's win over the Glen Sather-coached Canadian team, featuring Curtis Joseph as the national netminder.

"Sure, there's going to be all sorts of pressure on him now," Lowe continued. "But good players handle it."

It wasn't just one player. It was a team and a town.

"I notice a big difference here from when I left," said Lowe. "The guys are being paid on a par with the rest of the league. The guys are all getting along. That's more than half the battle right there."

What Lowe didn't say, Sather did.

The evolution of Oilers pucks through the years. Opposite: Curtis Joseph's save of the century foiled Joe Nieuwendyk and the Dallas Stars during the playoffs.

Doug Piper, centre, is the middle man as owner Peter Pocklington and Edmonton Mayor Bill Smith model the Oilers' new uniforms on May 31, 1996.

"These guys aren't just out of junior now. The fans should expect them to perform. They can't take nights off now. We've gone through the growing pains and change. Now we should be there. Now we've stepped up and paid the market value and that's part of the territory. We made a commitment to the people of Edmonton that if they supported us, we would sign the players critical to our success. The reason we were able to sign Doug to his deal, for example, was because of the NHL subsidy and because of what the Friends of the Oilers and all the people who bought season tickets did."

The Oilers spent some money, including capitulating to give Jason Arnott a $1.8-million deal. They found a solid, proven, experienced backup goaltender in Bob Essensa, the former Winnipeg Jet who was thrilled to be escaping the crowded Detroit Red Wings goaltending situation. They signed college drafts Mike Grier and Sean Brown. They drafted, with the No. 6 pick overall, slick Boyd Devereaux. During the World Cup they made a deal for Russian Andrei Kovalenko, giving up Scott Thornton to the Montreal Canadiens in trade. But being able to find the money to bring Lowe's character and experience and settling influence back to the team sent a message, too. After four years in New York, Lowe was back wearing the Oilers logo.

"I think I had to get it clear in my mind what I really wanted to do. I felt something pulling me here," he said, adding that he made the decision with his heart as much as his wallet. "Calgary did a pretty good selling job. But when it came down to it, it felt a little bit unnatural for me to go there. Once an Oiler, always an Oiler, I guess."

Tough love wasn't just a concept involving the players. Coach Ron Low qualified in that category, too. There had been no heat on the coach in his first full season. But there would be this year. And he wasn't dodging the idea.

"It's a very important point in time in my coaching career. I think my

career will go well if this year goes well. If this year goes like I think it will go, I'll be fine. If it doesn't, I won't be fine."

His goal for his team was simple.

"I want to make the playoffs," he said. "I don't care where."

The season began not only with higher expectations with the return of capacity or near-capacity crowds, it began with a whole new look and feel. The Oilers had never before understood the concept of game presentation. But they entered the '90s in 1996-97 and became a leader, not a follower, from the day Don Metz gave the fans some sizzle to go with their steak.

An oil derrick was lowered from the ceiling. Fireworks spewed from the top. Oiler logos, Maple Leafs and stars were projected onto the ice. The new scoreboard video screen showed highlights of past Stanley Cup conquests. And as the season's slogan, "The Future Is Now" flashed through dry ice and fog, the new, improved Edmonton Oilers emerged from under the derrick to start their 18th season.

Edmonton was ready to see something special this season. But nobody expected to see the Oilers hold the Buffalo Sabres to one shot in the first period.

"We went 26 minutes with one shot," raved Joseph. "That's a long time. That's the longest time for me, ever."

And it was a good time as the Oilers scored a 4-3 win. They won 2-0 over Vancouver and beat the Leafs 4-2 in Toronto to open on the road.

Three-and-oh to start the season!

By the end of October, they were 7-5, their best beginning in a decade.

If this was a year for players to step up to another level, Ryan Smyth took the first step.

By the end of October, Smyth had nine goals. Nine more than Weight, if you were scoring.

For a moment there it looked as if Cujo was going to get a goal before Weight.

"Trying to score one before I do?" joked Weight.

And Smyth . . .

"Yeah," said Weight. "Goals. Goals. Goals. That's all Smitty thinks about. Goals. Goals. Goals. He won't even talk to me any more."

He was kidding, of course. They were all kidding after Smyth scored two, including the winner, in a 4-1 win over Phoenix to complete October with a winning record.

Smyth was one goal shy of the NHL scoring lead.

"I was a little apprehensive," said the coach of starting a virtual rookie on the first line with Weight. "When you put a 20-year-old on your first line, that's not ideal. But after the first shift in the first game, when he scored his first goal, I told myself, 'I guess I don't have to worry about that.' When you play with Doug and you go to the net, you're going to get goals. It's Ryan's work ethic that's keeping him on that line. He doesn't quit. He's playing unbelievable and it's not smoke and mirrors. He wants to pay the price to score."

The Oilers won their first Battle of Alberta against the Flames 3-2 on Grey Cup Saturday night in the Coliseum, but the highlight of the night came when a fan dumped beer on the head of Calgary assistant coach Guy Lapointe, signalling to some that maybe the rivalry was going to be upgraded as well. But the rematch, three nights later in the Saddledome, doused those thoughts.

It wasn't so much that the Oilers extended their winning streak to four games and climbed back over .500 (12-11-1) with the win. It was the score.

Edmonton 10, Calgary 1.

Ten goals by 10 different goalscorers. Todd Marchant. Dan McGillis. Mats Lindgren. Bryan Marchment. Mariusz Czerkawski. Doug Weight. Dean McAmmond. Miroslav Satan. Andrei Kovalenko. And Kelly Buchberger.

And behind the score was a message that was hard to miss.

Going up. Going down.

It was the time and the place the Oilers and Flames passed each other going in different directions.

"You guys can stop writing about the Saddledome curse now," said Luke Richardson.

If 10-1 in Calgary was a score to get your attention, what about 0-0 a week and a half later in Detroit? In all of Oilers' history there had never before been a 0-0 game.

"I know in my former Oiler days we didn't much care to be in any 0-0 games," said Lowe.

Joseph and Edmonton native Chris Osgood were perfect. Osgood turned aside 21 shots. Cujo was unbelievable, stopping 52 – only seven short of the record total against an Oiler netminder.

"The goaltending tonight was better than I've ever seen," said backup Essensa.

The Oilers were leading all Canadian clubs, tied for fourth in the West with a 18-19-4 record and liking themselves a lot as they made the turn into the second half of the season.

"I see a young team getting better," said Joseph. "I see a team developing a strong belief now that we're going to be a very tough team in the playoffs."

Former teammates Kevin Lowe (4) and Mark Messier collide along the boards.

The year before, the Oilers made the turn at 13-22-6.

For the first time in six seasons the Oilers hit the all-star break at .500 (21-21-4) with a 4-0 win over the Florida Panthers.

"We're .500. We're in fourth place. And we've earned our way there," said Marchant. "Nobody handed it to us. It says we're living up to the potential of what this team can be."

Throughout Oiler history, it's remarkable the destiny and fate involved when it came to major moments and milestones. And it happened again as Lowe became the first player to hit the 1,000-game mark as an Oiler. His milestone game came in New York against the Rangers, the team stocked with ex-Oilers, where he'd played for four years and won his sixth Stanley Cup.

Only 26 players in history had played 1,000 games with the same club. Lowe became the 27th.

Midway through the second period the Madison Square Garden scoreboard flashed the information that Lowe was playing his 1,000th game as an Oiler. And the one rink in the league where you would normally bet on a response of jeers instead of cheers, erupted in applause.

"Coming from the Rangers' faithful, that's an honour," said Lowe.

It was the first game after the all-star break and the Oilers tied the Rangers 4-4, lost to the Islanders, then rattled off a five-game winning streak, lost one and won two more. The Oilers' record was 11-3-1 in their last 15 and Edmonton was 28-23-5 by mid-February.

Cujo-mania peaked when the Oilers held their Carnival of Champions in conjunction with the Eskimos. Upstairs and downstairs in the Coliseum, fans formed lineups two hours long for the chance to briefly pose pose for pictures and ask autographs of one guy.

"I've never seen anything like this," said old pro Lowe. "Cujo's popularity is incredible. He only came here at this time last year. We had Wayne Gretzky and Mark Messier here and this team has always had great goalies. But I've never seen anything quite like this."

The greatest of greats played in Edmonton and were hero-worshipped. This wasn't the same, somehow. It was more like love.

"I'm amazed," said Lowe. "I don't know what it is. It's probably that nickname, for one thing. Kids love that. But it's not just the Cujo thing. It's ability before that. He's playing great."

Defenceman Boris Mironov takes flight.

On the road Mike Grier was getting most of the attention. The first African-American to make it to the NHL after being born and trained in the U.S. and only one of 28 blacks ever to play in the league, dating back to Willie O'Ree in 1958, he was a story in every American city during his first lap around the league.

"I didn't know about all of that until a reporter telephoned me," said his dad Bobby, director of player personnel with the New England Patriots of the NFL. "It's probably not as big a deal in Canada."

In Edmonton, where every black goalie in the history of the league – Grant Fuhr, Pokey Reddick, Freddie Brathwaite and Joaquin Gage – had played, Grier's colour was almost a non-story, a fact both he and his dad appreciated more and more as the season progressed.

All was well until the Oilers made a strange move, inviting Petr Klima back to Edmonton for the remainder of the season.

It was weird. Why would they bring back the Coach Killer? They had a dressing room of guys who had developed a real rapport with each other, who were starting to show some real character. So what you needed, as the team went down the stretch in prime playoff position, was to bring in a certified case of cancer? Jason Arnott, Miroslav Satan and Mariusz Czerkawski – young talents who had yet to learn the lessons of blood, sweat and tears – and you were going to show them how to coast their way through an entire career?

The Oilers were 29-25-6 when they made that move. And suddenly there was a February free-fall. They went 1-5-2 over an eight-game stretch. Fans and media had totally given up on Arnott. Smyth had stopped scoring. Weight was playing on one leg. And Cujo was on a one-game-hot, one-game-not rotation.

Sather made a deadline deal, sending Satan to Buffalo for prospects Craig Millar, 20, and Barrie Moore, 21. But that was a futures deal, not a trade for the moment.

The spin cycle continued as the Oilers began to drop games on a regular basis and fell out of a race for fourth place.

At one point there was such panic at the morning skate, Sather had to go down to the ice and settle the players down.

This was one very fragile hockey team.

Finally, on April 5, they accomplished their minimum goal for the season. They clinched a playoff position. It wasn't pretty. They didn't win. But they were in. A 2-2 tie against Vancouver put Edmonton in the playoffs for the first time in five years.

"I think this hockey club deserves to be in the playoffs," said Low. "They've worked hard all year. It would have been a shame not to make it. Now we've just got to end up where we should be."

They didn't. The Oilers finished the season with an 8-14-4 record and gave nobody much hope for the playoffs when they tied two and then lost two as they finished with one win in the final six games.

Edmonton finished seventh with a 36-37-9 record. That earned them a date with the 48-26-8 Dallas Stars. And considering it was the Oilers' first playoff game in half a decade, Edmonton was on a down as they headed for the Big D.

Nobody was predicting the Oilers to win the series. The only debate seemed to be whether they'd be able to win a game.

Edmonton fans thought they saw a team that had collapsed and quit at the end of the regular season. They thought they saw a team that blew fourth and gassed fifth on the same night, losing 6-2 at home to Phoenix on the second-last day of the schedule. And they thought they saw a team that couldn't even conjure up the pride to at least save sixth place in the last game of the season and salvage a winning record that would have been the first in the NHL coaching career of Low.

The Oilers went into the series 0-for-their-last-seven against Dallas. They were outscored 33-12 in those seven games. And in the four losses during the season at hand, the Stars outscored the Oilers 18-6.

"I'm disappointed like everybody else," said Sather of the way the Oilers finished the regular season. "But there's no sense dwelling on what's occurred in the last three or four games. What you have to tell people, I guess, is that this is a young team. They are capable of being as good as they can be and capable of being as bad as they can be. There's no predicting which way it will come up."

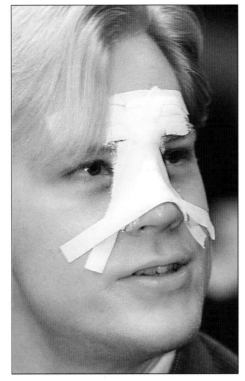

Dean McAmmond nursing a broken nose. Below: Cujo's famous goalie mask.

There were two strong local angles involved with the series. The Stars were coached by Edmonton native Ken Hitchcock. And the guy in their net was Andy Moog.

"I'm changing my name for the next two weeks," said Hitchcock. "It's us vs. them. Cities and friends are out. I'm not going to return phone calls. And I'm not going to pay any attention to messages left at hotels. I'm going to do everything I can to hate Edmonton and the Oilers. That's going to be tough. But that's the way it's going to be."

Edmonton is where he grew up. Sherwood Park is where he coached his Midget-AAA team to an incredible record of 575-69. United Cycle is where he used to sharpen Mark Messier's skates when Mess was a kid and later when he was an Oiler. Edmonton is where Hitchcock grew to be 466 pounds.

"I was let in the back door to a lot of Oilers games by security people I knew," he admitted.

"As a coach I just loved their passion, their cockiness, their abrasion. That team played the game for the right reasons. And when the playoffs came around they had another gear and they knew how to shift up to it and step up, really step it up. It was a whole other gear that nobody else played at."

A junior coach in Kamloops, Hitchcock told the story of how he drove 8½ hours from Kamloops to be at Game 7 of the Stanley Cup final between the Oilers and Philadelphia Flyers.

The last time Moog had been in the playoffs against the Oilers, it was the Stanley Cup final and he couldn't look them in the eye. He couldn't take his mask off. He always seemed to be staring at his feet and admitted it.

"It won't be like that this time," he said. "That's the Oilers jersey but that's not a team I'm familiar with. That's not what it was like the last time. That was a team I was familiar with – there were quite a few guys still on that team. I'd only been out of there a year or two. That was so tough it's still hard to explain. I've never been real good at communication with teammates who have gone to other teams. I guess I did keep my head down all the time. I never looked up."

Moog said he didn't think there was a "thing" between him and the Oilers.

"I've got a pretty darn good record against them," he pointed out. Indeed. His career record against the Oilers, at least in the regular season, was 15-3-2.

In Game 1 Todd Marchant scored the Oilers' first playoff goal in five years on a weak wrist shot which beat Moog for the first lead the Oilers had enjoyed against the Stars all season. But Dallas scored a 5-3 win after Mike Modano broke up a 3-3 tie at 17:29 of the third period.

It was tough to decide if it was a glass half full or a glass half empty game for the Oilers. They were in it. It was a great game to watch. It went down to the last two minutes. Most of the team came to compete. And they certainly didn't embarrass Edmonton.

Three Oilers were fingered for being Larry, Curly and Moe in Game 1 – Mariusz, Kovie and Bo.

"Everybody else played well," said Sather. "Everybody else on the team competed. We were short three guys."

Kovalenko, who had been a disappearing act in the playoffs in Montreal the year before, was minus-two. Both he and Czerkawski were benched for the third period. Mironov, playing in his first playoff game, was minus-three.

"Ninety-five per cent of our guys came to play for each other," said Sather. "But we had some passengers. And it's the responsibility of everybody, from myself to the coaches to the players to the trainers, the media, everybody, to give them a swift kick on the rump."

The media? Hey, no problem, Slats. Give us a call when you think Jason Arnottski deserves a boot in the butt, too, huh?

They all answered the bell in Game 2. It was awesome. It was probably as good a first period as the Oilers had played in the last five years and certainly as big a character game as this group – with 11 of them playing in only their second playoff game – had ever played, as they scored a 4-0 win to square the series. And what perhaps said the most was that they did it despite the sight of Bryan Marchment convulsing on the ice and leaving the arena with serious questions about his health.

It was one of the scariest sights you'll ever see in sport when Marchment tripped in front of the penalty box as Guy Carboneau was leaving and went head-first into the hinges of the open gate. He immediately went into convulsions and it was instantly recognized by everybody as a life-threatening situation. The look on the faces of Ryan Smyth and others on the Oilers bench was almost as disturbing as the frightening sight of Marchment writhing for more than a minute.

Kelly Buchberger and Doug Weight.

"We had a little meeting at the bench," said Low. "Everybody looked devastated. Like they were in shock."

Sather said his coach handled the situation perfectly.

"Ron did the right thing," he said. "He got them over to the bench and settled them right down."

Low said they all took the same attitude.

"They didn't change their game. They battled hard and won the game for Mush."

Joseph probably put it best.

"There was nothing we could do for him but say a little prayer to ourselves and a lot of us did that."

It was a 1-1 Stanley Cup series, and one which already had plenty of substance, as the scene switched back to Edmonton.

It had been exactly 1,792 days since the last Stanley Cup playoff game in the building. And only Kelly Buchberger and an injured Kevin Lowe were in that game. For the rest of the team this was going to be a first.

"I'm really intrigued to see what it'll be like," said Weight. "I've heard the guys talk about how good the fans are in the playoffs and I'm kinda excited to experience all that. We don't have a lot of playoff experience, but our fans sure do."

Games 3 and 4 in the Coliseum were the 99th and 100th Stanley Cup playoff home games in Edmonton Oilers history. And like the player who wore the number, Game No. 99 was unforgettable.

Pictures of Wayne Gretzky and Paul Coffey ('84), Gretzky again ('85),

Lowe ('87), Messier ('88) and Bill Ranford and Craig Simpson ('90) on huge banners hoisting Stanley Cups over their heads were unveiled just prior to the opening faceoff, a sign that the Oilers were finally ready to honour their past as they forged towards their future.

When it was over the phone rang in the back of the Oilers dressing room. It was Messier calling from New York to talk to Buchberger.

The captain babbled about it being the most incredible playoff comeback in which he'd ever been involved. And Messier, on the other end of the line, was telling him how he'd watched the end of it on television after the Rangers game.

"What an unbelievable feeling," Buchberger told his old teammate.

Lowe told Messier he couldn't remember any comeback like that in the Oilers' previous 178 playoff games.

The Stars led 3-0 with less than five minutes to go. Buchberger won it at 9:15 of overtime.

When the night began the fans created a special scene, playing their part in the "You Drive Us Wild – We'll Drive You Crazy" theme. But Dallas had taken the crowd more or less out of it by the end of the second period. Who knew they hadn't taken the Oilers out of it, too?

"It might as well be the fearless leader who gets it. He bleeds Oilers hockey," said Todd Marchant of Buchberger's OT winner.

There were plenty of other heroes. Weight beat Moog with a backhand to begin the comeback. Marchant set up Kovalenko to make it 3-2. Grier tipped a Dan McGillis shot to make it 3-3. All in a span of one minute and 56 seconds.

"What that does for your team is indescribable ... you couldn't write a better script than that," said Weight.

There was even the feeling that they might manage to repeat the feat in Game 4 when a Smyth shot found the back of Moog's net with 1:13 left, to reduce the Dallas lead to 4-3. But it stayed that way.

Like a couple of Edmonton-Calgary series in the previous era, it was obvious by Game 4 that this was well on its way to being another classic. There wasn't another series out there that could compare. And when both coaches, every night, start their post-game interview-room sessions with the word "wow" ...

"What a great game," said Low after Game 4. "You couldn't leave the building and not be happy with both clubs. It was a war down there."

Hitchcock was saying wow, too.

"It was just a great game and it's just a great series. The only thing wrong with it is the real winner of this series might be the team who gets to play the winner in the next series."

Hitchcock made several profound statements in a one-on-one interview with me between games.

"The Oilers are going to change the game," he predicted. "Again.

"You can see it in this series. The re-emphasizing of speed with size and pressure as the Oilers play through the next few years . . .

"This Edmonton team will become the measuring stick to judge your game by. If you are going to play Edmonton in the coming years, you are

Todd Marchant was an unlikely overtime hero during the playoff series against Dallas.

going to have to bring some of their elements into your own game. As the Oilers mature, their emotional levels will become more consistent. When that happens, when they mature a little bit more, they'll become the measuring stick. Speed is going to become a tremendous part of the game again. But physical play plus speed is a dangerous combination, and the Stanley Cup finals in the future for that team are realistic."

As good as the series had been to that point, it became even better when Game 5 required double OT to break a 0-0 tie.

Joseph's stated aim at the start of the series was to steal a game. And this was the one. Normally the hero would be the guy who got the goal. But Smyth, who scored on a slapper at the 22-second mark of the second overtime session, refused the honour.

"Cujo won that one," said Smyth of the second straight shutout on Dallas ice. "It feels unbelievable but if it wasn't for Cujo ..."

All the guy did was stop 43 shots. Grant Fuhr, Andy Moog and Bill Ranford all had great Stanley Cup playoff games for the Oilers. But did any of them ever play any better than that?

"When he gets in the zone like he did tonight, they could play until 3 a.m. and they are not going to score," said assistant coach Bob Mc-Cammon. "He played out of his mind."

Game 6 started at noon in Edmonton because of the NHL's Fox-TV contract. But the way this series was going they could have started it at 5 a.m. and nobody would have complained.

"I've never seen a series like this," said Sather. "This is the most unusual Stanley Cup playoff series I've ever seen. Give a young, talented team like this a light at the end of the tunnel and the bigger it looks to

them and the harder they are going to go."

The statistics suggested they ought not to be up three games to two. The team had only managed to win 143 of the 352 faceoffs in the series so far, only 29 of 91 in Game 5 and only two of 20 in the offensive zone. They were two-for-29 on the power play for a pathetic 6.9 per cent. But Joseph had a .935 save percentage with a goals-against average of 1.56.

It was hardly a shock, or even a disappointment, when Mike Modano scored with 5:18 left in Game 6 to give the Stars a 3-2 win. Great series go seven games. And this was a great series.

"I've always wanted to play in a Game 7 and I'm sure we'll be excited about it when we get there," said Marchant as the Oilers looked forward, not backward, in the dressing room after the Game 6 loss.

"Everyone dreams of being a Game 7 hero," said Smyth, the overtime hero in Game 5. "To be in a Game 7 ... it's just ... well, it's just so ... it's so neat!"

Eleven players had never played a Stanley Cup playoff game, much less a Game 7.

They'd remember it the rest of their lives.

Cujo made the save of all saves on Joe Nieuwendyk. Weight dug the puck out of the Oiler zone and hit Marchant on the fly. Grant Ledyard stumbled. Marchant went in on Moog alone. And at 12:26 of overtime ...

Todd Marchant? Are you kidding me?

And Cujo? On his birthday? Does the name Steve Smith ring a bell?

"Oh thank you, thank you, thank you," said Joseph of me not re-

Stars in their eyes: The underdog Oilers did the unthinkable – they got past Dallas.

minding him of that fact until after the game.

What a scene it was in the basement of Reunion Arena after the 4-3 win that gave the Oilers the series. The Oilers came off the ice sky-high, shouting in the corridors before they even entered the cramped visitors dressing room.

"I love playing with fast wingers!" raved Weight as he entered the room.

"When we needed it, Toddy comes through!" Grier shouted at his teammates inside the dressing room. "Come in here, Mighty Mouse!"

"Toddy! Of all guys!" shouted Smyth. "Only do it when it counts, Toddy!"

"Way to go, Toad!" rasped Rem Murray.

"Who said I can't put it in the ocean?" said Marchant when he entered the room.

Then somebody started it and they all picked up on it.

"Happy birthday to you. Happy birthday to you. Happy birthday, dear Cujo. Happy birthday to you!"

"Awesome! Absolutely awesome," raved Grier. "Cujo was awesome again."

"Amazing," said Sather. "Absolutely amazing. There's probably no adjective to describe how they played. Have there ever been that many rookies in that kind of a game?"

Eight rookies. Nine if you counted Smyth.

"I couldn't be more proud," said Sather.

What a perfect ending. Except they have this quirky rule in the Stanley Cup playoffs. If you win a series, you must advance and play another one.

DENVER – It's 10 a.m. and you're in a new town, in a new rink and there's a new team out there at practice. And the bleary-eyed sportswriter, just to be sure all of this really transpired the night before, gazes out at their faces.

Patrick Roy. Check.
Joe Sakic. Check.
Peter Forsberg. Check.
Claude Lemieux. Check.
Sandis Ozolinsh. Check.
Mike Ricci. Check.
Adam Foote. Check.
Valeri Kamensky. Check.
Adam Deadmarsh. Check.

Yup. These are the guys. The Colorado Avalanche. The defending Stanley Cup-champion Colorado Avalanche.

Oh, my gawd, what have the Edmonton Oilers gone and done?

"It's an honour to play the Stanley Cup champions," says Smyth. "That's how I look at it. It's an honour."

An honour?

There's no "It's an honour" in the Stanley Cup playoffs.

"It's tough to sleep," said Grier. "Just thinking of everything that's happened over the last couple of weeks ... it's hard to fall asleep."

The Oilers were Canada's Team, the only Canadian team left playing, when they stepped on the ice at McNichols Arena for Game 1. And for openers it didn't look like they deserved to be on the same ice.

It was men vs. boys. Or Roy vs. boys. Either way, there was no Mile-High miracle in Game 1 as the Oilers lost 5-1.

"Obviously, we were flat," said Sather. "And we were flat for a lot of reasons. I had a suspicion after what happened the other night that we'd be like that. We have to let them recover. We have to let them suffer a little bit with the humiliation, deal with it and get them up again."

If there was one guy who definitely wasn't down after the Game 1 drubbing, it was Sather. Eight games into his first Stanley Cup playoffs in five years, he was a study. It was like he'd been reborn. And nobody – not the players, not the coaches, not the fans – was enjoying this ex-

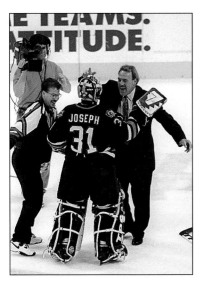

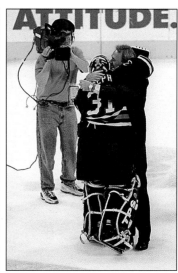

Oilers coach Ron Low has a huge playoff hug for goalie Curtis Joseph, who stood on his head in the Dallas series.

perience more than the Oilers GM.

"The guy should be having fun," said Low. "He put these guys together. He's spent a long time waiting to see the light at the end of the tunnel. It looked like a rock pile for a long time."

But you can't will a team to win. And when the Oilers left McNichols Arena, losing Game 2 by a 4-1 score, it was quite clear to everybody involved that they weren't going to win. In fact, Low was suggesting the inspiration that remained for the Oilers was to not be a mere speed bump on the road for the defending champions.

Speed bump?

They'd been roadkill.

But it was a team that had little left, especially emotionally after the first-round series, against a team that was doing this sort of thing not just to the Oilers but to everybody.

In six home playoff games to that point, Colorado had outscored the visitors by a grand total of 25-3.

The Oilers arrived home and found a loud and proud crowd.

During Game 3, in the building which was once known as "the Library" and "the Morgue," people who had been everywhere in the hockey world were asking a question they never dreamed they'd ask about an Edmonton crowd.

Has there ever been a crowd so loud?

"I always said there's never been a crowd as loud as Chicago Stadium," said Harry Neale of *Hockey Night In Canada*. "I've always said it was worth the price of admission to go to Chicago Stadium to watch the warm-up, listen to the national anthem and leave. When they played the last game in Chicago Stadium I took my 10-year-old boy because I figured a young hockey fan, just once, had to experience that. But I don't know if I've ever heard a crowd any louder anywhere than the crowd in the Coliseum for Game 3."

The Oilers gave them one more miracle and one more memory as Buchberger and Smyth brought them back from the dead again.

Again, it was storybook stuff.

Smyth insisted it was Buchberger, who scored two minutes and 18 sec-

Ryan Smyth fired the game-winning goal in a 4-3 playoff victory over the Colorado Avalanche.

onds before his 4-3 winner with 3:45 left on the clock, who was the real hero.

"That's why he's captain. He's a great example for everybody because he works so hard."

Joseph said he finally had the same team in front of him that he'd had in Dallas. And the team had the same Cujo behind it.

"That's a great comeback," he said. "That might even be the best start-to-finish game we've played in the playoffs And those were just huge goals from Bucky and Ryan."

It meant that these kids ended up with 12 games of Stanley Cup experience, not 11.

Claude Lemieux, a playoff legend, had 11 shots on goal in Game 4 and scored his third overtime winner of the playoffs as the Oilers lost the swing game, 3-2. But even Lemieux was talking about the crowd more than the game and his own heroics when it was over.

"What a great place to play," bubbled Lemieux after explaining how he squeezed the puck past Joseph and one inch over the goal line to win the game.

"I've never experienced playoffs in Edmonton before. I only watched the games on TV when they were winning the Stanley Cups in the '80s. This was my first opportunity to come in here. It's very exciting. The fans are very supportive of that team. But they also love good hockey."

They'd seen the last of it for the season. A 4-3 loss back in Colorado and the magic carpet ride had come to an end.

But there was one last moment, one final freeze-frame from a mountain of memories from the spring of '97.

The game was over. The series was over. And the defending Stanley Cup champions were waiting at centre ice to shake the hands of the whiz-kid Edmonton Oilers. But there they were, standing in front of their bench, hugging each other.

"Cujo was on the bench because the game ended with an empty net," said Weight. "We went to Cujo. Then we just started hugging each other. Guys had tears. We found out how much it hurt to have it over."

Chapter 19

Rocky Mountain High

If the Edmonton Oilers could accomplish what they did in the playoffs in 1997, think what they might be able to do in the 1997-98 regular season.

There was that.

On the other hand, this was a team which had gone 1-15-2 against the top teams in the league the previous season.

There was that, too.

Credibility games were back.

If the Oilers were to prove they were the real deal, they had to prove they could beat the best.

"It's important to beat everybody, but it's more important to beat the best teams because if you can beat them then you're going to be one of them," said GM Glen Sather before the season started.

"Last year I didn't talk to the team about expectations. This year, I've talked to them. I think they are ready to accept expectations. They weren't ready to do that at the start of last year. They were at the end of the year. I expect them to be better. They expect themselves to be better."

The Oilers lost Luke Richardson as an unrestricted free agent to the Philadelphia Flyers, which paid a staggering $12.6 million over five years for the services of a stay-at-home defenceman who scored one goal and 11 assists the year before. Nobody in Edmonton was suggesting Sather should have tried to match it. But the big concern was for Curtis Joseph. The goalie would be in exactly the same unrestricted situation at the end of the season.

Rod Phillips and Murray Promislow have alpaca fun on the golf course. Opposite: Kelly Buchberger seems to be having an identity crisis.

There were confirmed reports that Sather had offered Jason Arnott for trade at the draft where the Oilers chose Switzerland's Michel Riesen as their 14th pick. Ted Green returned as an assistant coach to replace Kevin Primeau, who took a head coaching job in Europe. And Ron Low signed a new contract as coach.

There are many cases in hockey history where a coach takes a young team so far, hits a bump in the road and then somebody else moves in to take the team to its greatest glory. But now Low would have a chance to go all the way.

"I think it was, 'Fire him if he doesn't make the playoffs – give him a new contract if he does,' " said Low. "I imagine there was a huge amount of pressure there. I imagine there was a whole lot to lose and not a whole lot to gain."

In a sports city like Edmonton, it doesn't take long to get down to the old, "What have you done for us lately?" routine. And in 1997-98 the glow was gone on opening night in the Edmonton Coliseum.

It was the worst home opener in the city since six inmates escaped in three different jail breaks from the brand new Edmonton Institute for Women back in the spring of '96. It was by far the worst home-opening loss in 19 NHL seasons for the Oilers. Even in its worst year, Edmonton had not been so humbled for home openers as it was on the night of Oct. 3.

"I haven't seen all of them," said Low of the 8-2 loss to Detroit. "But that was pretty rotten. We got our asses beat by a club which came in here and decided they wanted to kick our asses. We were horsebleep. We were totally horsebleep."

The Oilers were 3-6-1 for their first 10 games and the struggle didn't stop.

After the 8-2 loss to Detroit, the Oilers lost 3-0 and 6-2 to the Colorado Avalanche. So far so bad when it came to credibility games.

By mid-November the Oilers were 5-12-5.

"Maybe the focus of our attention is being focused somewhere else," said Sather. "Maybe it's the distraction of the sale of the team. I don't know."

Owner Peter Pocklington had announced the team was for sale. Les Alexander, owner of the Houston Rockets NBA team, had announced he wanted to move the team to Texas. A local ownership group had a deadline to meet to raise the capital to keep the team in town. The storyline involving the Edmonton Oilers was definitely not on the ice and wouldn't be until spring.

Opposite: Fireworks light up the Coliseum. Right: Curtis Joseph.

Bill Guerin taps Andrei Kovalenko on the helmet after accidentally swatting him in practice.

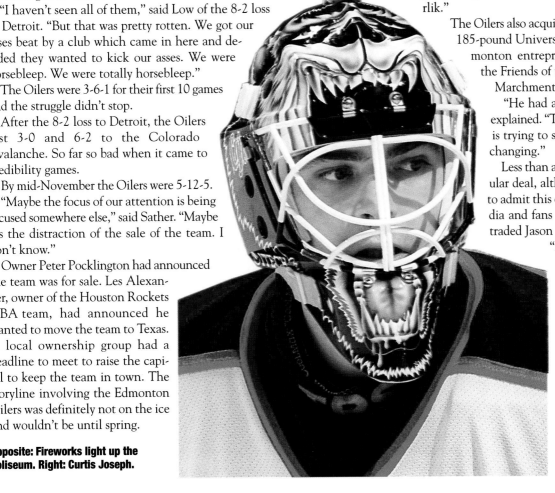

When the Oilers lost 5-1 to the Avalanche on Dec. 27, it was clearly time for Sather to take note that the fat elf had fled, the peace on earth and goodwill season was gone, the turkey had been carved and it was time to carve up the Oilers. Whatever Sather had learned from a positive point of view in the playoffs, he had an equal eyeful from the negative end in the front end of the season. It was time to make a mid-course correction. It was time to reconstruct significant parts of his hockey club.

Sather pulled the trigger. And he pulled it again. And again. In all of hockey history, it is debatable whether anybody ever pulled off better bang-bang-bang deals to help his club.

First he did a deal with Phil Esposito in Tampa Bay to acquire former first-round first pick Roman Hamrlik in a trade that sent Bryan Marchment, Steve Kelly and forgotten first-round flop Jason Bonsignore to Tampa Bay.

"You might go five, 10 years in this league running a hockey team and never have an opportunity to get a player like this," said Sather. "Hamrlik has all the credentials in the world. He's exactly the player to move the puck out of our end in one pass. He can be a world-class hockey player. These guys don't come around. We have a lot of prospects like Kelly in our organization. But we don't have anybody like Hamrlik."

The Oilers also acquired Paul Comrie, the five-foot-10, 185-pound University of Denver star and son of Edmonton entrepreneur Bill Comrie, who started the Friends of the Oilers project.

Marchment had been a fan favourite.

"He had a lot of suspensions here," Sather explained. "The referees watch him. The league is trying to stop his kind of play. The game is changing."

Less than a week later he made his most popular deal, although Sather was candid enough to admit this one was made as much by the media and fans as any deal in Oilers history. He traded Jason Arnott.

"I can't believe it," said agent Mike Barnett of the deal that brought Bill Guerin from the New Jersey Devils instead of the pail of pucks the fans would have dealt to rid the team of their favourite whipping boy. "How does Glen Sather make that trade? He should have worn a mask. He's getting a character guy. The biggest thing about this trade is that Bill Guerin is going to make Doug Weight a better hockey player. And Doug Weight is the key to the Edmonton Oilers."

Low said it got to the point where the fans left the Oilers with no option on that one. Nothing like the Arnott scenario had happened before with a player in Edmonton.

"Before he even skated a shift he was getting booed," he said. "When you're getting booed before you even play ...

"Glen liked Jason a lot. But in the end he had to trade him because Jason couldn't stay here and play like that."

Sather agreed.

"We had to do it. The pressure from the crowd, the media and himself left him trapped in a situation he couldn't get out of here."

Kevin Lowe might have been the most excited about getting Guerin. He knew, from playing against him in New Jersey, what the Oilers were getting.

"I played against him a lot and I thought he was maybe the best player on that team when they won the Stanley Cup," he said.

Arnott, when he returned to Edmonton as a New Jersey Devil, was booed beyond belief.

"They were doing that when he played for us," said Low. "Why should I be surprised if they do that when he's playing for them? That's the way people felt about him."

The Oilers season turned with the Hamrlik and Guerin deals. Edmonton won six in a row in early January. They won six out of seven from late February to early March.

The deal that settled it as Sather's greatest swapping season came at the trade deadline when he traded Dan McGillis to Philadelphia for 22-year-old Janne Niinimaa. When an Edmonton deal really raises the ire of the folks with the Flames franchise, you know it's something special.

"I don't understand," said Flames GM Al Coates. "It makes no sense to us why Philadelphia would make that trade. We think Niinimaa is a great young player. We don't understand it. There must be something more to it. We certainly didn't know he was available. And we're not happy to see him going to Edmonton. They're going to have the same kind of thing going now that St. Louis has with Al McInnis, Steve Duchesne and Chris Pronger."

Sather agreed.

"We think we've got three of the best defencemen in the game," he said, counting Boris Mironov and Hamrlik.

In the end, the Oilers won their way in. They won seven of their last nine games of the season, including the final four.

It was the exact opposite of the way it worked the year before.

Kelly Buchberger with his three-year-old son, Keaton.

Roman Hamrlik, accompanied by his girlfriend Nikol Nedabylkova, shows off his gold medal from the 1998 Nagano Olympics.

"Last year we went into the playoffs with our tail between our legs," said Weight, who was the Oilers MVP with 26 goals and 44 assists for 70 points.

"We were 13 games below .500 and we ended up two below," said Low.

The Oilers would get a post-season do-over against the Colorado Avalanche. And forget stealth and scratch surprise.

"I think Dallas last year was surprised by us," said Sather. "I don't think they expected us to be so gritty or determined. This time whoever we play will be aware of us. We're going to get a lot more respect than last year."

If the Avs read the year-end standings they'd still see a sub-.500 team. But if you read the second-half standings, if you read the post-Winter Olympics standings, if you analysed any new year numbers, you'd see a different squad.

The Oilers were 23rd overall in the first half and fourth in the second half — tied for first in wins with Dallas at 23. Fourth overall since the debut of NHL players in the Olympics, the Oilers were also first in wins since Nagano.

And remember the credibility games thing? In the second half of the schedule the Oilers were 11-5-1 against the over-.500 teams. The Avs, on the other hand, skidded into the post-season with a 3-6-1 run.

Sather was in fine form in the pre-series posturing, making headlines for referees to read about the "Flying Crawford."

"Colorado has two or three set plays off the faceoff that they do more than any team in the league on faceoffs. It depends how the league is going to call it," said Sather of the obstruction coaching strategies of his World Cup of Hockey assistant Marc Crawford. "It's a set play. It's the Flying Crawford. We used it in the World Cup."

But fear of heights was more of a factor in the Oilers' minds than the Flying Crawford. And the Avalanche worked hard with that fear. It was the very first page of their fact book. Full colour. Advertising agency sort of stuff featuring a road sign: "One Mile Above Sea Level. Elevation 5,280 Feet."

The Oilers knew the feeling from games 1, 2 and 5 in the playoffs the year before.

Low, for one, had come to the conclusion that you have to coach differently in Denver.

"You can't have shifts longer than 35-40 seconds. There's no recovery time. You won't recover. Guys can't spend a minute-and-a-half out there on the power play. If you stay out there too long, you won't get it back."

Weight said it did in the Oilers the year before.

"I think it makes it easier to handle when you play here in the first round and you're fresh," he said.

The night before the series opened, the Oilers gathered at the Denver Chop House for Sather's "First Supper." With the Oilers having a 30-9 playoff series record and having lost only one first-round series since 1982, the significance of the team meal was beginning to demand investigation.

"It's done out of tradition," said assistant coach Ted Green of the team-building event which goes back to Edmonton's first playoff series and an evening at the famed Bookbinders restaurant in Philadelphia 19 years earlier.

"It's another fibre in the fabric. It's something, the way we do it, I think, that pulls a team together in the playoffs. It has nothing to do with strategy. It has a lot to do with being one."

It worked in Game 1.

"ONE-DERFUL"

That was *The Edmonton Sun*'s headline on the classic comeback and furious finish of the opener.

The Oilers' go-go-go skating game was great. But it was the goal-goal-goal that made it memorable. The true grit and don't quit formula that created the miracle comeback in Game 3 the year before against Dallas worked again for openers in Denver as the Oilers scored three goals in three minutes and 49 seconds to turn a 2-0 loss into a 3-2 win.

"Roy happened?" asked a Denver press room wag, using the correct French pronunciation of the name of the Avalanche goalie who had specialized in shutting down the Oilers.

Indeed. How does Patrick Roy give up three goals in a span of 229 seconds?

It was sensational stuff as Bill Guerin, playing like the playoff player he was in New Jersey, finally broke Roy's seal. The speed-kills philosophy of the Oilers paid off again as Todd Marchant raced into a corner and passed the puck to Dean McAmmond, who sped into perfect position from the other wing for his first goal in his first playoff game, having been out with an injury the year before. Then there was Boris Mironov, much maligned for not shooting when he should, who shot when he should and scored the winner.

As memorable as that was, it was the frantic final few seconds which most people would remember best about the game. And it was a good thing the referees took the clock down from 31.8 seconds to 24.8.

"It was incredible. Everybody was going everywhere," said Cujo of the excruciating end to it all in his goal crease. "Everybody was hacking and whacking. There had to be six or seven broken sticks. It was ferocious."

The Avalanche was playing without Joe Sakic, out on a one-game suspension for a late-season incident. But it was still a huge upset for a

Drew Bannister and Kelly Buchberger rejoice.

team with a 16-4 home-ice playoff record in the past two years, with a for-against total of 87-38.

Roy went into the series 21-5-2 lifetime against the Oilers and maybe the best part of it all for Edmonton was beating him. Now if they could only do something about Peter Forsberg ...

The Fors was still with them. He scored the first two goals for the Avalanche and Colorado was 17-0-6 in games in which Forsberg scored goals during the regular season. And Forsberg, cut for nine stitches by a high stick by Bill Guerin – earning him the nickname "The Butcher" from one of Denver's columnists – picked up right where he left off in Game 2.

He scored two more goals and had a point on all seven Avalanche goals in the series as Colorado bounced back to win 5-2 on a night when it was written that Cujo bites.

The Oilers netminder got the hook at 13:23 with the score 4-1. He allowed two soft goals within seconds at the start of the game. Or, at least, that's how I saw the game. A Denver writer saw a different one.

IT'S ALL OVER
FOR IMPOSTERS
FROM CANADA

That was the headline above the words penned by Mark Kiszla, the *Denver Post*'s starting columnist for Game 2.

"The best-of-seven series is officially tied 1-1. But the truth is: It's over. Edmonton can't beat Colorado. The Oilers are irrelevant. Edmonton's only remaining purpose is to serve as the Avs' tune-up for a post-season rematch against Detroit," he wrote.

The indelible memory from Game 3 back in Edmonton was a sight you don't want to see in overtime in the playoffs.

Mats Lindgren fell down.

Kelly Buchberger fell down.

Drake Berehowsky was back.

And Joe Sakic had the puck.

That pretty much left one option for Curtis Joseph. "Yea, though I walk through the valley of the shadow of death ..." But he didn't have time to go upstairs. And the only religious sort of sign in the building read: "Roy: 3:49."

You could hear Foster Hewitt shouting, "He shoots! He scores!" on Sakic's backswing.

Hamrlik had played 38 minutes, Niinimaa 32:02 and Mironov 31:41 when Sakic scored the 5-4 winner 15 minutes and 25 seconds into overtime.

"I don't know what happened," said Lindgren.

"I was just turning. I lost an edge. I looked up and I saw Bucky. The same thing happened to him."

Buchberger blamed himself.

"I went to cut sharp to come back. I should have stopped to come back. It's not a great feeling. It's pretty hard to swal-

Defenceman Bryan Marchment tests a new helmet after his concussion in Dallas.

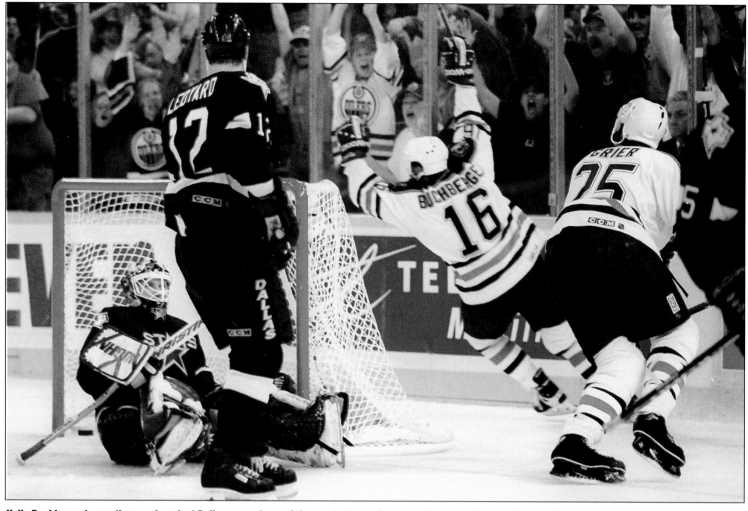

Kelly Buchberger's overtime goal against Dallas capped one of the greatest comebacks in NHL playoff history. Below: Bill Guerin.

low. You can't make those mistakes. That was a big one."

For the third game in a row the Oilers gave the Avalanche a 2-0 lead. For the third game in a row it was a goal by Guerin that brought them back. And it was Buchberger who tied it 4-4 midway through the third period. Joseph still wasn't giving the Oilers the goaltending he'd supplied in the previous playoffs. And the big boys were still killing the Oilers. After three games Forsberg (4-4-8), Sakic (2-3-5), Sandis Ozolinsh (0-8-8) and Claude Lemieux (2-2-4) were feasting on the young Edmonton team. And Lemieux was just warming up. He hadn't really struck yet.

He did in Game 4.

The prototype playoff player scored his 19th post-season game-winner as the Avalanche took a 3-1 lead in the series with a 3-1 win. And none of them had come easier.

Greg de Vries and Rem Murray so spectacularly screwed up their communication as to leave Lemieux alone on one side of the ice, and Joseph gave him so much net to shoot at, it was suggested that of all those notches on Lemieux's playoff belt, No. 19 would be smaller than the other 18.

Ron Low and the Oilers brain trust came unbelievably close to sitting Cujo in Game 5 in favour of Bob Essensa.

"I don't think he's playing poorly," said Sather. "But he's come up with bad goals at the wrong time in every game. In the playoffs, you can't do that."

At midnight, Low had made up his mind that he was definitely

going with Essensa. When he woke up in the morning he changed his mind.

Well, actually, it was even later than that.

"It wasn't until I got to the rink," said the coach.

"I know John Muckler was close to switching Billy Ranford in Game 5 of that series against Winnipeg when we were down three games to one and came back. But you get to the moment and you can think all you want about the change and it gets real simple. Curtis Joseph is one of the best. He's our goalie. He's the guy you've got to go with. When all is said and done, he's the guy who brought you. And maybe the players would never forgive you. If you don't go with the best, it's not fair to anybody."

As was the case with Muckler, sometimes your best moves are the ones you don't make.

Joseph was brilliant.

"There was a little fighting there early," said Low. "But then ... I think it was when the two goal posts on that shot by Ewe Krupp bailed him out. After that ..."

But it wasn't just Cujo. More than anybody it was Guerin who brought the Oilers back to life.

Oh, Mike Grier was a 24-karat Stanley Cup hero, the unlikely scorer of both the winning and game-over goals for the Oilers in the 3-1 win in Game 5. But Guerin was the guy. Again.

He brought the Oilers back from a 2-0 deficit in their Game 1 win. He tried to do the same when they trailed 2-0 in Game 2, scoring his first of two on the night. He brought them back from 4-2 with a goal to set up overtime in Game 3. And when

Doug Weight moves in on Stars netminder Eddie Belfour.

Goalies Ed Belfour and Curtis Joseph shake hands after the series.

it looked like we were watching the series walkout bout, he did it again in Game 5.

"Billy Guerin is our MVP in the first five games," said Buchberger. "He's our Craig Simpson. Remember that first-round series Simpson had in '90? He had 16 goals that series."

Buchberger was in charge of all "Remember 1990" facts and figures. He started selling the idea, immediately after they lost to go down three games to one, that the Oilers, who had done it before against Winnipeg, could become the 14th team in Stanley Cup history to get down by that count and bounce back.

And they started listening.

"Going out there for the third period, everybody was saying, 'It's too damn early to golf yet,' " said Low.

The problem with Game 6 was that it was at home. The Oilers crowd was wonderful in the first two games, every bit as loud as the year before. But the Oilers were proving themselves to be a better team on the road in the playoffs than at home. They were 5-5 on the road in these past two playoff years to this point and two for seven at home.

"Maybe we get too excited," said Marchant, the Game 7 overtime hero in Dallas the year before. "Maybe we get too pumped up at home."

"It makes no sense," said Buchberger. "You can't find a better place to play. With that crowd and that ice, there's just nowhere any better."

The crowd, for Game 6, went crazy in the Coliseum. Joseph played out of his gourd in goal. And the Oilers played refuse-to-lose hockey to take their stairway to seven with a 2-0 win.

There was an amazing atmosphere in the

Defenceman Janne Niinimaa.

building, with a flavour that ought to have been bottled to savour like a fine wine. And you wouldn't have to distil it. This crowd had had a few. An hour before game time it sounded like the Grey Cup was back in town from within the walls of the Coliseum.

And Edmonton fans don't get any louder or act any prouder than they did when Mironov took the shot that sent the series back to Denver.

"That's as loud a crowd as I've ever heard," said Cujo. "It was great to win that for the fans. What a great hockey town!

"It's been a great series. And it's going to be a great Game 7," said the goalie who had found his first-round form from the year before, stopping 31 shots for his third playoff shutout.

"Cujo was unbelievable," said Low. "And the crowd was phenomenal. That's the best crowd I've ever seen or heard. Period. I didn't think it could get any better than it was last year. But it did."

Assistant coach Green refers to the building of a young team as "forging steel" and it hit everybody on this young team that, if nothing else, they were certainly in an excellent environment.

A fuzzy-faced collection of kids would, for the most part, be playing their 19th playoff game back in Denver. And their second Game 7!

Like Marchant. The kid figured he'd never have a chance to top his moment from the year before when he scored the winner in double overtime of Game 7 against Dallas. But one year later and ...

"I love it," he said. "It's great. I thought that until I won a Stanley Cup I wasn't going to have a chance to top it. But I can top it *now*."

Game 7 was the Oilers' 201st playoff game. It would leave Edmonton with a 31-9 record for series won and lost.

The Oilers, at Mile High Denver, ran the Avalanche into their own ice. In the end, the pace the Oilers played at left the team, that two years earlier had won the Stanley Cup, skating in sand.

Well, that and Cujo.

In the end the Avs couldn't score on the netminder for an amazing Oilers team-record 163 minutes and 40 seconds over the last three games. The Oilers didn't edge the Avalanche. They won going away. In the end it was 4-0 on the scoreboard and the McNichols Arena fans, who had been challenged to match the Edmonton noise level, sent their team into the off-season serenading them with the *Na-na-na-na Kiss Him Goodbye* song.

Led by Joseph the Oilers came off the ice and their grins were just as gigantic as they'd been a year ago. They hugged each other just as hard.

Low, who this night got the right finger in the air (he'd saluted Crawford with the middle one late in Game 6 after he put a lineup of thugs on the ice), came off the ice bouncing like he was on a pogo stick.

"The Fat Man wants us! He's got us!" he shouted at his team.

The Oilers had their Reunion at Reunion Arena with Ken Hitchcock and the Dallas Stars.

Sather had a great grin punctuated by a cigar.

"They played as a team," he said as he stood watching them dance with each other through the dressing-room door.

"That's the way a team is built right there! You keep winning!"

Never in Colorado Avalanche (Quebec Nordique) history had the team been shut out in back-to-back games, regular season or playoffs.

"I think we all feel best for Cujo because he exorcised the Patrick Roy demons," said Lowe.

"We wore 'em down," said Buchberger. "We could see we were wearing them out as the series went along. We wore them out."

Low had clearly outcoached Crawford in the series.

"The turning point of this series was when Ronnie changed the lines," said Sather. "They didn't do anything to counter them. Ronnie did a great coaching job."

Struggling to become a winning coach in the regular season, Low again won where it matters most.

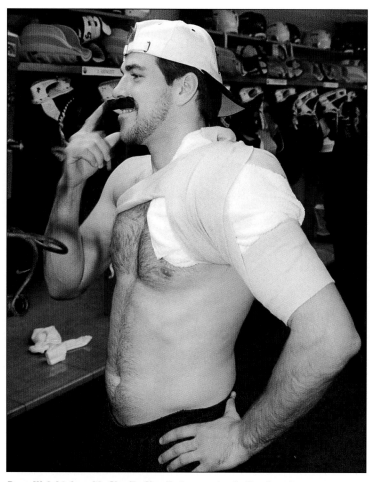

Doug Weight does his Charlie Chaplin impression in the dressing room.

"He took a real slap at me and Jonesy," said the now only pleasantly plump Dallas Stars coach of this not-so-svelte scribe, reacting to Low's "The Fat Man wants us! He's got us!" quote.

Low was beginning to get a profile.

Using the four-letter friend-getter on a live post-game radio show in Edmonton; giving Marc Crawford the finger, and his easy-to-lip-read curses at the Colorado coach, not to mention the fact he'd outcoached the coach of Canada's Olympic team, made him much less anonymous.

And Low was getting rave reviews from the Stars room.

"His players love him and they feed off him," said Mike Modano, who suggested it was a similar situation with Dallas and Hitchcock.

The Fat Man sidebar continued to the morning of Game 1. In shoot-the-messenger damage control for something he wished he hadn't said, Low claimed it was "bush league" to use the quote and had a heart-to-heart with Hitchcock before the game.

And Hitchcock, as a joke, listed a 21st player on his starting lineup card which went to Low. The 21st player: Terry Jones.

For Hitchcock, the series wasn't a matter of revenge from the year before.

"I look at this as a second chance," he said.

For the Oilers, it should have been a second chance to remember to leave the previous series behind when they started the next one. But it was clear for the second year in a row they hadn't been able to do that.

"In the first 10 or 12 minutes of the game we were still in Denver and enjoying ourselves," said Low. "A lot of guys weren't there."

The Oilers gave the Stars two early power plays, then screened

"I'm elated," he said. "What a tremendous feeling of pride to see what our hockey team accomplished. It's something that very few teams have done. I can't be more proud of those 20 guys in our dressing room right now."

Not only had the Oilers become the 14th team to come back from down 3-1, they were the lowest-ranked team to do it, being 16 points poorer than Colorado in the standings.

Tired of hearing about the history of the team that had won five Stanley Cups, this young team was beginning to write its own history and contribute to the overall history.

It was the eighth time the Oilers were in a Game 7 and the win gave them a 6-2 record. Their 1990s Game 7 record became 4-0. And the Oilers' first-round record was now 12-3 with a win-loss record of 48-26 in those games.

So it was on to Dallas, where Hitchcock waited with a smile on his face.

He'd seen the quote.

> '**It was a five-game series, but one of our players said it felt like 12 games.**'
>
> – *Ken Hitchcock, Dallas Stars coach*

192

Banner years: The Oilers have won their share of championships.

Joseph so he couldn't see the shots. Add a ghastly giveaway by Hamrlik and there's your game story. Dallas 3, Edmonton 1.

The scene in the press box during Game 2 was more entertaining that what we were watching on the Slurpee-like ice surface.

"Don't worry, boys, we're calling our soccer writer to see what he does," said a *Dallas Morning News* columnist late in the second period with the score nil-nil.

Who knew? Boring can be beautiful.

"Maybe you guys didn't think it was a great game to watch but it was a great game from where I was sitting," said Weight of the Oilers' 2-0 empty-net win.

"There are not many times you can shut the best team in the league down in their own building," said Sather.

"How many times are you going to play in a playoff game when there isn't a shot on goal?" said Buchberger.

The correct answer was one.

Only once since 1968 had it happened. The Stars didn't get a single shot on goal in the first period. The Stars had four shots in the second.

In Edmonton, the two teams were 0-0 after regulation time with a major mismatch in favour of the Oilers in speed.

What happened next, Sather called "the pivotal moment" of the series.

Janne Niinimaa didn't pull a Steve Smith and score on his own net. But he blew it. He gassed it and he gaffed it. And not once, but twice.

The Oilers' best man at getting the puck out of his own end, he'd been brilliant throughout the playoffs. But after playing near-perfect through 27 minutes of ice time in Game 3, he managed to mangle his

Sparky Kulchisky applies a sticker signifying another Stanley Cup playoff victory to the team's dressing room door.

Coaches Kevin Lowe, Ron Low, Ted Green.

last seven seconds.

"Everybody saw," he said. "I had lots of time. I tried to flip the puck up high. I should have hit it off the glass. It was a stupid play."

Joseph had played 149 minutes and 35 seconds of shutout goal against the Stars and this was a goaltending duel for the ages in overtime against Eddie Belfour.

"Somebody is going to make a mistake," said Low. "What the hell. It was a great game. That's just life."

Benoit Hogue scored the winner at 13:07 of overtime. And it was Hogue who scored two more to lead the Stars to a 3-1 win and a 3-1 series lead in Game 4.

And that's when it was obvious what had happened here.

The Oilers had run Colorado out of gas in the first round. And they'd run themselves out of gas now.

"They trap a lot," said Guerin. "They conserve energy that way. I know. I played six years for the New Jersey Devils."

No team in the history of hockey had ever come from behind three games to one twice in the same playoff year. And the Oilers' body language said they weren't going to be the first.

"That looked like a 109-point hockey team against an 80-point hockey team," said Low.

In the end, as the Oilers lost 2-1 in Dallas, there was no conspiracy theory and no need to check a grassy knoll. The Oilers died of suffocation and assault with an empty weapon. Five goals in five games told their story.

But a final quote out of the Dallas dressing room told another story.

"It was a five-game series," said Hitchcock. "But one of our players said it felt like 12 games."

Chapter 20
Forward With A Future

NATIONAL HOCKEY LEAGUE

98
M E D

Rob Tychowski
Edmonton Sun

MEDIA

OILERS

MARIO ANNICCHIARICO

98/99

I n Winnipeg there were strippers donating their tips and kids with coins, including one little girl who came with exactly $5.31 in her actual piggy bank. A travelling salesman dropped off $3,000, part of $1.5 million collected at a radio station. A social was held at the convention centre and 2,500 people paid $100 just to be there. In all, $10 million was raised dime by dime and dollar by dollar. And it wasn't nearly enough. The Winnipeg Jets were gone.

Gone, too, were the Quebec Nordiques, to painfully win a Stanley Cup in their first season as the Colorado Avalanche. And the Hartford Whalers were relocated to North Carolina.

The Edmonton Oilers were left as the sole survivors of the WHA. And the betting outside of Edmonton was against their survival.

Peter Pocklington had sold and Glen Sather had traded all the star players. And with every season the season-ticket numbers had dropped. Rumours were running rampant. It was obvious that the five-time Stanley Cup Oilers franchise was on the endangered species list in 1992.

If Edmonton wasn't worried, Calgary Flames president Bill Hay told me three days before Christmas that he was.

"Sure, we've heard the rumours. And, yes, we've been monitoring it. I know Peter has been talking. We've visited with Pocklington. We're concerned. I don't know Peter very well but I'd say he could be serious about relocating the team. I'm afraid. We're afraid. Sure we are," said Hay.

Opposite: Jim Hole, left, and Cal Nichols were instrumental in keeping the Oilers in Edmonton.

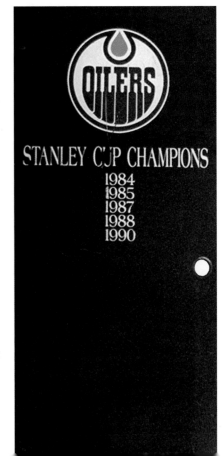

STANLEY CUP CHAMPIONS
1984
1985
1987
1988
1990

There was a scare story virtually every day. By the middle of January Glen Sather had something to say.

"I don't plan to go anywhere. Edmonton is my home. I'm not the kind of guy to walk away from a fight. I'm in here fighting for Edmonton. I'm not doing all this work to pick up in the middle of the night and just leave. I'm loyal. I'm trying to rebuild this thing with youth. I'm not doing that so the fans of Edmonton won't see the results when we're done."

Pocklington said he wanted to stay, too. And four days later he tipped his hand.

He'd just climbed off his chair, his talk-to-the-town *Face-Off Show* on TV over, when he put some papers on the table.

"We can't keep feeding Edmonton Northlands," he said, finally getting to the short-term point of the frightening situation that could have conceivably had the Oilers, at the end of the season, loading the trucks in the middle of the night and leaving town.

The plot thickened when Pocklington produced an arena lease for Copps Coliseum in Hamilton.

On April 27, Pocklington took Edmonton hostage. If there was one guy in town who knew about being held hostage, it was the Oilers' owner. On April 20, 1982, Mirko Petrovic held him hostage for 11 hours. He suffered a gunshot wound and Petrovic received a 15-year jail sentence. Now claiming to be held hostage by the lousy Northlands lease he'd signed in 1989, Pocklington that day made all of Edmonton an emotional hostage. Give him the deal by May 14 or he'd move the team to Hamilton.

The next day Rick LeLacheur of Economic Development Edmonton stepped forward to dedicate himself full time until May 14 to get all parties talking.

Ten days before the deadline, Northlands called a press conference under the scoreclock at the Coliseum.

Northlands general manager Colin Forbes, sounding like Jack Nicholson in *A Few Good Men*, with appalling arrogance said Northlands could bring in "other things" which would "generate just as much money and a whole lot less heartache than the Oilers staying here" and then blurted out that if Pocklington "wants to play hardball, I'm ready to go right now."

On May 5, Jack Ramsey entered the picture. As the president of the Edmonton Eskimos, the head of EDE, a Northlands board member, a business partner of Gerry Yuen and Mayor Jan Reimer's travelling companion on a recent trip to the Orient, he was perfectly positioned to make the big save.

"We've had enough pushing. Now we need to try to row together to the same destination," he said.

Ramsey and LeLacheur talked to 42 different parties around the world of sport, looked at very private documents which had to be shredded, and on D-Day announced a deal.

The press conference was first planned for 7 p.m. Then 8. Then 9. Finally at 9:30 Ramsey, with tears in his eyes, announced a deal in which Northlands would head-lease the Coliseum to EDE, which would sublet it to the Oilers.

That kept the Oilers in Edmonton for the next year and took Hamilton out of the picture. But on June 24, Northlands voted to "resume the operation of its business in the status quo

It was the end of an era when Peter Pocklington relinquished control of the NHL's Edmonton Oilers in 1998.

mode."

They reneged on the deal.

"We're as good as gone," said Pocklington. "Looking at this I'd say Edmonton has probably lost the Oilers. Last one out of Edmonton, turn out the lights."

On Sept. 17, Pocklington filed "Intention To Relocate" papers with the NHL.

"Pursuant to the Constitution and the Bylaws of the National Hockey League, please consider this a formal request by the Edmonton Oilers Hockey Club to relocate its franchise for the 1994-95 hockey season."

The Sun staged a "Stay Oilers Stay" rally on the steps of Edmonton City Hall. And as the 1993-94 hockey season began, the next news was out of Minnesota. The town which had lost its team to Dallas was allegedly prepared to give Pocklington "everything I want" to move the team to the Target Centre in Minneapolis.

If that wasn't ugly enough, at the NHL board of governors meeting in Laguna Niguel, California, Pocklington told the owners that Edmonton was no longer a major-league city in any way, shape or form.

On Dec. 21, a Calgary judge gave Edmonton another year. The judge barred Pocklington from taking any further action to move the team until there was a trial to decide whether he could break his lease with Northlands. Chief Justice Kenneth Moore of the Alberta Court of Queen's Bench ruled to keep an injunction in place, preventing Pocklington from taking action to move the team.

"I am of the view that without the injunction the relative positions of the parties will shift so radically that a trial judge could not reverse the situation," Judge Moore wrote.

NHL commissioner Gary Bettman decided to come to town.

In a single day he managed to get major movement.

"When I got up this morning, I didn't plan to have us at this point by the end of the day," said Bettman.

Not long later, they had a deal. Northlands, in exchange for $2.8 million of ticket-tax user-fee money, gave up the building. Using federal government infrastructure money, major renovations were made to the Coliseum. Thanks to the NHL lockout, it was ready in time for the first game of the delayed season. And the key part of the deal was a 2004 relocation agreement.

The war between Pocklington and Northlands resulted in heavy casualties. As impressive as the improvements to the Coliseum were, corporate Edmonton had stopped buying Oilers tickets.

And with the franchise back on the agenda at the board of governors meeting in Palm Beach, Florida, Pocklington tried to put the gun back to the head of Edmonton.

Support his team. Or else.

The or else?

"Unfortunately, I guess they're going to get to watch junior," Pocklington said.

The league, however, was now fighting for Edmonton. The NHL had signed off on the 2004 relocation agreement as well as the owner. And to illustrate that the league did not want to lose any more Canadian content, Bettman's bunch created a small-market subsidy. Edmonton would be eligible for the money if the Oilers could sell all the advertising board signs, rent all the sky suites and sell a minimum of 13,000 season tickets.

That was the turning point.

Brick Warehouse owner Bill Comrie called a meeting of Edmonton's movers and shakers at the Mayfair Golf and Country Club.

"We're going to talk about getting more support from the business community. We don't want to see them leave," said Comrie. "It's very informal. It's not a commitment to do anything alone by myself. It's an attempt to do whatever it is business people have to do to help keep the team here. That's the goal."

Finally, Edmonton was going to fight for its franchise.

Ten years earlier Sather had tried to convince Pocklington to put together a group of highly placed businessmen as a board of directors for the Oilers. Pocklington wanted no part of it. It was his baby, his team. But on Dec. 19, 1995, thanks to the Mayfair Accord, he had a board of directors, like it or not. Dennis Erker headed the creation of the Friends of the Oilers committee.

"I'm walking away from here today convinced it's going to be done," said Sather. "Today is the most positive thing that's happened to the team in the last five years."

New Mayor Bill Smith was part of the proceedings.

"I just came out of a meeting so positive it's hard to be anything but excited," said Smith.

The new Mayor had stood up in the meeting and told the business boys where he was at.

"I talked to Susan Thompson, the mayor of Winnipeg, and she told me that I don't want to be in that position – that the last thing we want to do in Edmonton is lose the Oilers."

The movers started to move. And the shakers started to shake.

Gasland president Cal Nichols took up the fight on his own, forming a group called SEATS ("Shrewd Eleven Aggressive Ticket Salesmen, or Save Edmonton, Acquire Tickets Soon," he laughed.).

"I don't want to create the impression we're doing it for Peter Pocklington," said Nichols. "We're doing it for the whole community."

Eric Geddes came on board as the new Friends chairman.

"I'm thrilled at the prospect of what is happening in Edmonton," said Bettman from New York. "I don't want people in Edmonton to get too confident yet, but it's going great."

Edmonton pulled off the great save.

As the deadline expired, Bettman made the announcement:

"We have been able to ensure that we don't lose another franchise in Canada. We're done moving Canadian franchises."

Oils well that ends well?

It turned out that everything Edmonton had gone through to this point was merely the undercard for the really big fight.

Peter Puck appears to be yawning during this team photo, but building championship NHL teams was never boring.

Pocklington was drowning in debt. And the Alberta Treasury Branches wanted their money.

Al Strachan filed the Sun Media scoop on the story:

"Fans of the Edmonton Oilers are close to getting exactly what they want – a resurgent team without Peter Pocklington as owner," was his first paragraph.

Pocklington, a week later, in a *Sun* exclusive under my byline, confirmed that the rumours were true and provided details.

It would be a supervised sale. The NHL and the ATB would be involved. Sather would run the team in the interim.

"The bank has said to me that they'd like me to pay them down or pay them off," said Pocklington. "I've done everything I can do. I've kept the team in Edmonton. I wasn't like the guy in Quebec and the guy in Winnipeg, and make what was probably the best business decision and sell the team south and put the money in my pocket. We're the last WHA team left. Gary Bettman obviously wants the team to stay in Edmonton. And that's what would happen. I haven't worked this long and hard to see the team leave the city."

The next day, June 5, 1997, Pocklington called a press conference and made it official. He was selling the team.

In 1971, Peter Pocklington, at the age of 29, had moved to Edmonton from London, Ont., and purchased a local Ford dealership. Five years later he bought a 40 per cent interest in the Oilers, later acquiring the remainder from Nelson Skalbania. Involved in the deal was a Renoir painting, his wife's 12-carat diamond ring and the takeover of a $1.4-million loan.

Peter Puck attempted to win the leadership of the Progressive Conservative party in 1983. But that was the year his fortunes turned for the worse and his image began to become soiled and spoiled. That was the year of the collapse of Pocklington's Fidelity Trust Co., which cost taxpayers $359 million.

In 1986, 1,080 employees at Pocklington's Gainers meat-packing plant began one of the most violent strikes in western Canadian history. Six and a half months later it was settled but Pocklington had lost the support of a large percentage of the blue-collar crowd, which is the essence of Edmonton's sports scene.

Then he sold Gretzky ...

"It's tough to part with something like this," said the emotional Pocklington at a press conference where he announced he was selling the Oilers. "It's like losing the most fabulous wife in the world."

Would-be owner Michael Largue provided some timely comic relief when the Oilers hung out the 'for sale' sign.

Pocklington was asked at the press conference how he'd like to be remembered.

"I hope I'll be remembered for bringing NHL hockey to Edmonton," he said.

The headline on my column the next day was "Good Buy Or Goodbye?"

"FOR SALE: One NHL hockey team. Reasonably good condition. Call 403-474-8561. No tire kickers please.

"How do you sell a hockey club. And who do you sell it to?

"Bruce Saville? Ed Bean? Jim Hole? Cal Nichols? Cam Allard? Jim Shaw? Don Wheaton? Al Owen? Denny Andrews? Stan Milner? Ken Webb? Al Purves? Hugh McColl? Glen Sather?"

I talked to Hole that day.

"This isn't a no-emotion, straight capitalist deal," he said. "It's what it means to the community. It means an awful lot to the ordinary guy. It's part of the fabric of the city. As a longtime resident who cares about the city, you'd have to hope that something could be worked out so it could operate on a viable basis. We have a lot of good guys in this city."

Ramsey agreed to act as temporary CEO, bridging the bank and the Oilers.

And so it began. The search for $70 million US and the corporate support that would give the Oilers a fighting chance to compete if they found it.

Wayne Gretzky endorsed the idea of local ownership and suggested he wouldn't think twice about putting money into the team himself if

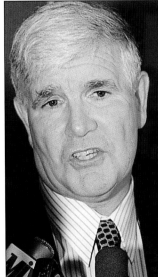

John Ramsey, left, and Rick LeLacheur.

he could. He said if Pocklington had held on for a few more years, he'd probably be one of the members of a new ownership group.

"Absolutely. Edmonton is a great hockey city. My heart is still in Edmonton. Glen Sather is a tremendous operator. And I'd love to be involved in a team with Glen Sather. Obviously it's difficult now in a small market. But if there is a city which can make it, that city is Edmonton."

With one save of the franchise already credited to his work with the Friends of the Oilers, Cal Nichols was back on the mound trying to round up support.

"It's a big task," he said. "It's starting to make the ticket drive look very simple by comparison. With the tickets you were talking hundreds or thousands. Now we're talking millions. It's a completely different audience. I doubt if there is any single person who will buy the Oilers now. They may be able to buy the team, but I don't see one person taking that kind of risk given the size of the market and the kinds of salary demands that are going on."

Ramsey, for his part, tried to settle a community which, thanks to some panic-mode reporting, was getting a daily dose of sky-is-falling stories.

"It will get done," he said. "Why are we panicking about it? I'm not panicked. It'll be done. It will get done. I wouldn't be sitting here if this was not going to get done and I think everybody knows that."

It didn't work. Because of Winnipeg and Quebec, Edmontonians were scared stiff the hockey team was going, going ... and by mid-June they figured they knew where it was going to: Houston.

NBA Houston Rockets' owner Les Alexander had entered the picture.

"I told him it's available, but I simply stated I want the team to stay here in Edmonton and if no one makes an offer we'll look at outside buyers later," said Pocklington. "He immediately leaked it. I've had calls from various Houston news organizations. The timeline is this: If by next January we haven't got an offer from here in Edmonton, it's not looking good. I'm in a real tough spot. The aim at the end of the day is to sell it but the aim is also to keep it here."

In early September Pocklington turned up the heat. He said he was now asking brokers Midland Walwyn to invite external bidders for the team.

"We've waited two or three months. We said we'd give the locals until now for the bids to be in. There aren't any in. So let's bring in interested people from outside the city. You know as well as I do that the people in Edmonton have 30 days after any external bid is selected to buy the team and keep it in town. Unfortunately, there is no serious bidder that I know."

Every TV station and half the radio stations in town were live for the announcement that a bid proposal had been put in an envelope.

It was Sept. 17 now and the bid group, the nucleus of which was known to anybody who was anybody in Edmonton, was still attempting to remain anonymous. It was as if the media figured there would be a photo opportunity of the members of the local bid group assembled on a stage, posed together like a painting of the Last Supper, introducing themselves, telling their life stories and telling everybody in Edmonton they could live happily ever after.

"What we're dealing with here is about stage 14 in a 25-stage process," Hole whispered at the time.

"This is a serious proposal," said group lawyer John Butler, whose law firm donated his time and services to the cause.

"I can assure you and all Edmontonians that this group is credible in all respects. Is there a lot of work to be done? Absolutely. It's not going to happen overnight. And not in the media."

There was news of a second local bid from bar owner Robert Proznik. But it came and went away, never really regarded as anything serious.

Then came the World War III-sized headline on the front page of the *Edmonton Journal*:

"SOLD"

"The Edmonton Oilers are expected to call a news conference today

Top: Michael Largue faces a skeptical Edmonton media. Above: Houston Rockets' owner Les Alexander arrives in Edmonton.

Bob Turner, John Butler, Cal Nichols, Jim Hole and Gordon Buchanan.

to announce that the team has been purchased by Les Alexander, owner of the NBA Houston Rockets."

"Kiss Oilers Goodbye" was the headline above the Cam Cole column on the sports pages.

"It's A Done Deal – Puck" was the headline on the *Journal* front the next day after there was no press conference.

"SOLD" wasn't the story. "Kiss the Oilers Goodbye" wasn't the story either. But there was a story behind those non-scoops.

There was every evidence now to suggest that the NHL, rightly or wrongly, had come to the conclusion that the would-be local owners weren't going to get $70 million US on the table to buy the Oilers now or any time soon. And there was every evidence that Alexander was an NHL-endorsed legitimate Plan B-going-on-Plan A.

And any chance of Pocklington coming away from this without another hit to his image in Edmonton was out the window. Despite his claim to want to keep the team in town, from the beginning it was very visible to the ownership group members that he was trying every trick to scare them away.

Alexander had offered a three-year guarantee that the team would stay in town. It was down to two years by the time he hit town.

Saville, Hole, Nichols, Bean and Co. were beginning to get more committed and more company.

"I can tell you that after what I've seen in the last couple of days, the local group has not only not thrown in the towel, they now have an excitement level higher than I've seen from them before," said LeLacheur at the end of October.

"I think I could probably characterize them as looking at this now as being a race and now they're getting warmed up and ready to run it. They are not giving up. In fact, it's just the opposite. I've talked to a fair number of the local guys and I've heard more interest from other members of the business community who now want to be a part of the group than there were a month ago. I really see things crystallizing with the local group. Right now I can tell you they are hell-bent for leather to try to get this done. I haven't seen some of these guys with their adrenalin flaming so much in all the time I've known them."

On Nov. 3 Les Alexander and a pack of press people from Houston arrived in Edmonton.

Bernie Pilon, the *Sun* news writer who followed the story on a daily basis, wrote the lead:

"Peter Pocklington's so-called done deal to sell the Oilers to junk-bond tycoon Les Alexander has failed to score."

What a great day in Edmonton sports history, although one loud-mouthed radio sportscaster and a surprising number of hockey writers thought it was just the opposite at the time.

My first paragraph the next morning:

"Less Alexander."

Alexander had left town in a huff, suggesting he'd been sold a bill of goods and led down the garden path by our old south-side used-car salesman. He suggested our man Pocklington had convinced him that the City of Edmonton, Economic Development Edmonton and Edmonton Northlands would all be on board, happy to see him riding in to the rescue on his white horse with his white hat, ready to rip off their cute little 2004 agreement.

"My idea was to come here, be a white knight and keep the team in Edmonton," Alexander told his Houston media entourage. "It was almost like I was an enemy from another planet."

Alexander also told the Houston media that he should have known the minute he jumped in Pocklington's car at the airport and asked if everybody was on board and everything lined up and Pocklington said, "Well ..."

The Pocklington press conference the next morning was memorable as the Oilers owner-in-limbo was forced to stand there and tell everybody Alexander had decided to return to Houston.

"I told Alexander that as CEO I was not prepared to recommend removing the 2004 location agreement," said LeLacheur of the meeting in the mayor's office at City Hall the night before.

Northlands boss Alan Skoreyko informed him of the same thing.

Mayor Smith said he was blown away by the way in which Alexander blew into his office and announced, "I'm not here to negotiate."

LeLacheur said he couldn't believe the look on Alexander's face.

"My view is that there was some surprise," he said. "When he asked our position, I believe there was some surprise when we gave him our answer."

Skoreyko made the point.

"This deal was announced 10 days ago as a done deal. The 2004 location agreement is the real deal. Why do people doubt that? Maybe the location agreement has just worked to keep the team in town."

No maybe about it.

The Edmonton hockey knights had trumped the self-styled white knight from Houston. But the local group knew it had made a mistake by not showing more of its hand to the NHL. It immediately took a significant step closer to local ownership when Saville, Hole, Nichols and Butler visited with Bettman in New York.

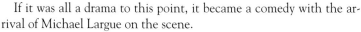

Glen Sather toasts the new owners via the miracle of video technology.

"It was the right thing to do," reported Nichols. "It went very well."

In late December the local group swelled to nine with the addition of Gordon Buchanan, Gary Gregg and Art Mihalcheon. And the next story out of Houston was how Chuck Watson, IHL franchisee and Summit Arena owner, was willing to loan the locals half the $70 million.

"In turn, the NHL would look favourably on a franchise for me in Houston," he said.

On Feb. 11, with everybody in the NHL in Nagano at the Winter Olympics, Alexander was back in the picture. He'd ended months of speculation by offering $82.5 million US, backed by a non-refundable $5-million deposit for the team.

The clock started ticking. The local group had until Friday the 13th of March to find the $70 million and put it on the table.

"This will be a motivator," said Nichols. "Let's face it. There has been a lot of fence-sitting. Those on the fence are now going to have to fall off or jump in with us."

If it was all a drama to this point, it became a comedy with the arrival of Michael Largue on the scene.

The Sun broke the story.

Largue, supposedly a former player in the Swiss Hockey League representing the alleged former owner of the Bern Bears, one Lester Mittendorf, said he was going to buy the Oilers and keep them in Edmonton.

I wrote the column:

"Michael Largue. First impressions. Thumbnail sketch:

"Nervous. Thin-skinned. No sense of humour. Snaps. Confrontational. Hero complex. Zero media savvy. Didn't take Dale Carnegie course on how to make friends and influence people ...

"Maybe it was that front page picture in *The Sunday Sun*. Maybe it's just that you don't expect a $100-million man to grab a disposable camera and have his picture taken in what looks like a basement suite or a trailer with cheap wood panelling, plug-ins sticking out of the wall, bottles of pills on the table and a 'Happy St. Patrick's Day' tablecloth. The only thing missing was the hot plate."

He wasn't happy with the press he'd received before we were given those first impressions. He

A new beginning: The Edmonton Oilers ownership group.

especially didn't like being called Michael Largesse, Joe Large and Michael Lark in my column, nor my writing "I don't care if he moves in as my next door neighbour, he's an outsider."

He snapped at the press conference when I identified myself as the guy who wrote that stuff.

En route to Edmonton, C.R. Nichols of CHED tracked him down at the Toronto airport.

"I can always turn around and go home," Largue told Nichols. "What would they like, my blood? You can quote me on that. I'm getting insulted. I'm getting sick of it. I may walk into town and buy the whole thing. What would you people do then? It seems to me you have two options. Actually three. Mr. Alexander moves the team to Houston. You guys squirrel away your nickels and dimes and try to keep the team here. Then you have me. References. Stand-up guy. Has walked in with his head held high. Has walked in answering every question I could. And frankly, you're not treating me too well."

Edmonton exposed the guy.

Largue had pulled his act previously with four different NHL teams – Hartford, Buffalo, Tampa Bay and even the Montreal Canadiens – without being exposed.

But he was found out to be a fraud in Edmonton.

He left town in tears.

"Outside the ITV studio he was welling up, starting to cry," reported ITV's Graham Richardson.

The Sun's story carried the triple byline of Bart Johnson, Tony Blais and Jeremy Loome under the headline "Largue Doesn't Cheque Out."

Swiss league hockey officials said their records showed no player by the name of Largue and no Bern owner by the name of Lester Mittendorf.

The Sun had Martin Bienz, counsel at the Swiss Embassy in Ottawa, run the name Lester Mittendorf through all Swiss databases and found no record of him.

Largue had boasted of a bachelor's degree from Northeastern University, saying he attended on a scholarship and played hockey for the Huskies while he was there. Northeastern was unable to find Largue's name anywhere after poring through its hockey records.

Largue, *The Sun* revealed, had been convicted of fraud four months earlier, pleaded guilty and was given five years probation.

Reporter Johnson went to Largue's home in Long Island, New York, and found out that Jeanette Largue, in a 1995 affidavit that led to a restraining order against her now estranged husband, claimed he harassed and assaulted her and once threatened to have her bumped off by "his connections."

It was terrific stuff. Excellent entertainment. And a great diversion while the local ownership group worked away.

"We didn't take our eye off the ball," said Butler. "We continued to make progress every day."

With a week to go to the very scary Friday the 13th deadline, things weren't looking so scary any more.

"We're at the 10-yard line now," said Nichols.

This was becoming a helluva story. The Small-Market Franchise That Could.

That night Glen Sather stood in front of sponsors, staff, players and media at the Hockey Hall of Fame in Toronto and made the following statement: "I'm confident the local people will complete the deal and we'll be the first small-market team to win the Stanley Cup."

Funny. Edmonton didn't see itself as a small market when the Oilers won their first five Stanley Cups.

The new owners were all on their way to the final-writing-of-the-offer session on March 12 when they spoke to the subject. It was a slam dunk now and they were all going to be home-town heroes when they put the money down the next day. But, to a man, they went on the

record for my column in *The Sun* about the man who got it done.

"Cal Nichols was the key player," said Hole. "Cal Nichols saved the deal with the tickets and he was the key player in this effort to keep the team here. He kept his objectives clear – to see that the team stayed here. He's a very dedicated Edmontonian."

Ed Bean, the first ownership candidate Nichols approached, said the man was amazing.

"He had the patience of a saint. And the intestinal fortitude to go with it. I don't know how he managed to keep going. I don't think it would have come together without him."

The second guy Nichols talked to was Bruce Saville. He'd never met the man.

"He said, 'Listen, we've got to do something about the Oilers.' I told him I was in, that I owed something to the community. And he ran with it. I don't know if it would ever have got done without Cal Nichols. I think everybody owes him a debt of gratitude. Every time something went wrong, he bounced back," Saville said.

Lawyer Butler spoke to the subject as well.

"It's taken a lot of people. A lot of unnamed unseen people. But if Cal Nichols hadn't stepped up ... Maybe somebody else would have. But I have my doubts."

Nichols himself said while every major player played a huge part, the turning point player was Larry Makelki of Lloydminster.

"Having Larry come on board was a huge emotional lift. He was the first guy out of the oilpatch. And the timing of him coming on board was what we needed."

"The Oilers wouldn't be in Edmonton if it weren't for Larry Makelki," said Nichols.

"Larry made it happen. If he hadn't stepped up when he did and if his friends from Lloydminster hadn't decided to join him, the Oilers wouldn't

Cal Nichols, right, and the Lloydminster contingent of the Oilers ownership group.

be in Edmonton.

"Lloydminster is responsible for 25 per cent of the ownership of the team. The guys from here are responsible for 12½ per cent. And they rounded up another 12½ per cent."

The next day they held the big press conference. They'd raised more than $60 million Cdn and found Canadian bank financing for the rest. But there was one reason more than any other why the team was still in Edmonton, they all agreed, and that was Bob Turner's 2004 location agreement.

"If we hadn't put that location agreement together I don't think it would have happened today," said LeLacheur.

He said the owners had their last laugh at the loud-mouthed local sportscaster and the hockey writers who kept telling this town they'd rue the day they first sent Les Alexander away.

"I betcha those guys are happy now that we did what we did," he said.

In the end there were 37 Edmonton owners. And there were other companies, such as *The Sun*, the *Journal*, Denny Andrews Inc. and Hughes Petroleum, who jointly announced that they were putting up $2.2 million of advertising product over the next three years.

"We have to prove we can make this thing work beyond next year," said Nichols.

Backing from the community: Members of the local ownership group assemble in the Coliseum, recently renamed Skyreach Centre.

While it was starting to be quite clear that the Oilers would lose goaltender Curtis Joseph (he went to Toronto for $6 million a year) as a free agent, the No. 1 priority was to sign Sather.

The Oilers, at this point, were in Denver in the playoffs. And Sather invited Pocklington to attend his last game as Oilers owner.

"If he'd used silk instead of a sledgehammer, if he'd put together a board of directors from community leaders like I'd suggested ... this is all the stuff Peter tried to do from the beginning," said Sather of what was now happening in Edmonton.

That day city council had voted 7-4 to play its part financially in replacing the $2.8-million-a-year payment to Northlands. And the creation of a sports bond lottery was in the works.

"All these guys are getting the stuff Peter was trying to get," Sather said. "These guys haven't done anything different than Peter wanted to do."

The next day the NHL voted on approving the only 37-man ownership group the league would ever see, with very little question as to the outcome.

As William Daly, the NHL's due diligence man put it, "I think we're a little pregnant on this one. We've told them we can live with this. But I don't think the league or the owners would ever consider anything but this exact situation again. In any other case, I think it would be a non-starter."

Sather said it was an emotional farewell for Pocklington.

"It's tough for Peter. The guy loved this game just for the purity of it. When he left it was pretty sad. At breakfast with the coaches and the staff he started talking about how much he was going to miss it. He had tears in his eyes. I felt bad for him."

A two-paragraph press release arrived on a fax machine the next day. Twenty-two of the new Oilers owners sat in the second-floor boardroom of Hole's Beaufort Building, holding a scheduled ownership meeting when it was interrupted, if ever so briefly, by Hole.

"The NHL news release was passed around at the meeting," said Nichols.

The only word they looked for in the press release was "unanimous." It was there.

"We're very proud of the unanimous part," said Hole. "It was nice to get that from our other league members. We hope for the foreseeable future this removes the stigma that this hockey team will leave town."

Sather – there was never really any doubt – decided to stay.

"He's the key to the puzzle," said Hole.

Ownership group member Barry Weaver of St. Albert later stepped up for an extra $1 million a year to buy the right to rename the Coliseum after his business. Skyreach Centre would be the home of the Oil-

ers for their 20th season in the NHL.

It would be a season not just to celebrate the Oilers history and the future of a team staying in town, but a season to celebrate ulcer-free hockey. At last, a year to keep your eye on the puck, not the buck or the moving truck.

"Keep the seats full and sit back and enjoy the ride," suggested Hole.

"This looks like it's really going to work," said Weaver, who got Pocklington's box as part of the Skyreach Centre package. "You can feel the excitement. The focus is finally back on hockey. And the best part is that this looks like it's going to be a pretty good hockey team again."

Sather found a new goaltender in Mikhail Shtalenkov, added Joseph Beranek and Pat Falloon, brought back Marty McSorley, introduced rookie defenceman Tom Poti, added even more speed and youth to the lineup and even took the team to Lloydminster during training camp for a practice. There, a capacity crowd of 2,800 people sat in the stands for two hours before the team arrived and made it a love-in with the town which had contributed between an eighth and a quarter to the Oilers' ownership.

And when Sather signed Doug Weight to a two-year, $7.8-million US contract with another $500,000 in bonuses kicking in at about 80 points, none of the owners had the big one. And they passed the test.

"How much?" said one of the owners.

He was informed of the deal.

"That much."

Pause.

"Nobody's worth that much money."

Pause. Breath.

"Well, that's up to Slats. If he had that in his budget he can spend it. He's running the hockey club. As a fan I'm saying nobody is worth that kind of money. But as an owner I'm saying that's up to Slats. He has the budget. We know he knows what he's doing."

Doug Weight's signing, and Ryan Smyth's a few days before his, telegraphed to the hockey world that the Edmonton Oilers planned to compete as the closest thing in the NHL to a community-owned club.

And for the first time in six years, the only stories about the Oilers would be game stories.

"There's the feeling that maybe we're on the verge of something great," said Bob Essensa.

And so it began, the Oilers' celebration of their 20th season in the National Hockey League.

There's a lot of history packed into these 20 years, a lot more than most pro sports franchises manage to manufacture in 50 years. And as the Edmonton Oilers forge forward to a new future, there's definitely the sense that there's more, much more, to come.

KEVIN LOWE

Edmonton Oilers
First Goal
Oct.10/79
at Chicago

Most Games
1,037 games

Most Games
including
playoffs
1,201 games

Chapter 21

Rosters and Records

Most Goals, One Season (80 GP)
446 – Edmonton, '83-84
426 – Edmonton, '85-86
424 – Edmonton, '82-83
417 – Edmonton, '81-82
401 – Edmonton, '84-85

1979-80 SEASON

COACH	GP	W	L	T	PTS	GF	GA
			Regular Season				
Glen Sather	80	28	39	13	69	301	322

	GP	W	L	GF	GA
Playoffs	3	0	3	6	12

4th Smythe Division, 16th Overall. Playoffs: Lost Preliminary Round 3-0 vs Philadelphia.

PLAYER	REGULAR SEASON					PLAYOFFS				
	GP	G	A	PTS	PIM	GP	G	A	PTS	PIM
Wayne Gretzky	79	51	86	137	21	3	2	1	3	0
Blair MacDonald	80	46	48	94	6	3	0	3	3	0
Stan Weir	79	33	33	66	40	3	0	0	0	2
Brett Callighen	59	23	35	58	72	3	0	2	2	0
Dave Lumley	80	20	38	58	138	3	1	0	1	12
Don Murdoch (EDM)	10	5	2	7	4	3	2	0	2	0
Dave Hunter	80	12	31	43	103	3	0	0	0	7
Doug Hicks	78	9	31	40	52	3	0	0	0	2
Ron Chipperfield	67	18	19	37	24	–	–	–	–	–
Risto Siltanen	64	6	29	35	26	2	0	0	0	2
Mark Messier	75	12	21	33	120	3	1	2	3	2
Pat Price	75	11	21	32	134	3	0	0	0	11
Kevin Lowe	64	2	19	21	70	3	0	1	1	0
Don Ashby (EDM)	18	10	9	19	0	3	0	0	0	0
Cam Connor	38	7	13	20	136	–	–	–	–	–
Al Hamilton	31	4	15	19	20	1	0	0	0	0
Lee Fogolin	80	5	10	15	104	3	0	0	0	4
Dave Semenko	67	6	7	13	135	3	0	0	0	2
Colin Campbell	72	2	11	13	196	3	0	0	0	11
Bill Flett	20	5	2	7	2	–	–	–	–	–
Peter Driscoll	39	1	5	6	54	3	0	0	0	0
Dan Newman	10	3	1	4	0	–	–	–	–	–
Kari Makkonen	9	2	2	4	0	–	–	–	–	–
Ron Low (EDM)	11	0	1	1	0	3	0	0	0	0
Jim Corsi	26	0	3	3	6	–	–	–	–	–
Ed Mio	34	0	1	1	4	–	–	–	–	–
John Bednarski	1	0	0	0	0	–	–	–	–	–
Bob Dupuis	1	0	0	0	0	–	–	–	–	–
Ron Carter	2	0	0	0	0	–	–	–	–	–
Mike Forbes	2	0	0	0	0	–	–	–	–	–
Bryon Baltimore	2	0	0	0	0	–	–	–	–	–
Jim Harrison	3	0	0	0	0	–	–	–	–	–
Mike Toal	3	0	0	0	0	–	–	–	–	–
Ron Areshenkoff	4	0	0	0	0	–	–	–	–	–
Alex Tidey	5	0	0	0	8	–	–	–	–	–
Don Cutts	6	0	0	0	6	–	–	–	–	–
Poul Popiel	10	0	0	0	0	–	–	–	–	–
Wayne Bianchin	11	0	0	0	7	–	–	–	–	–
Dave Dryden	14	0	0	0	0	–	–	–	–	–

GOALTENDER	REGULAR SEASON						PLAYOFFS				
	GP	MINS	GA	SO	GAA.	W-L-T	GP	MIN	GA	GAA.	W-L
Ron Low(EDM)	11	650	37	0	3.42	8-2-1	3	212	12	3.40	0-3
Don Cutts	6	269	16	0	3.57	1-2-1	–	–	–	–	–
Jim Corsi	26	1366	83	0	3.65	8-14-3	–	–	–	–	–
Bob Dupuis	1	60	4	0	4.00	0-1-0	–	–	–	–	–
Ed Mio	34	1711	120	1	4.21	9-13-5	–	–	–	–	–
Dave Dryden	14	744	53	0	4.27	2-7-3	–	–	–	–	–

1980-81 SEASON

COACH	GP	W	L	T	PTS	GF	GA
			Regular Season				
Brian Watson(4-9-5)	80	29	35	16	74	328	327
Glen Sather(25-26-11)							

	GP	W	L	GF	GA
Playoffs	9	5	4	35	35

4th Smythe Division, 14th Overall. Playoffs: Won Preliminary Round 3-0 vs Montreal, Lost Quarter-Final 4-2 vs NY Islanders.

PLAYER	REGULAR SEASON					PLAYOFFS				
	GP	G	A	PTS	PIM	GP	G	A	PTS	PIM
Wayne Gretzky	80	55	109	164	28	9	7	14	21	4
Jari Kurri	75	32	43	75	40	9	5	7	12	4
Mark Messier	72	23	40	63	102	9	2	5	7	13
Brett Callighen	55	25	35	60	32	9	4	4	8	6
Glenn Anderson	58	30	23	53	24	9	5	7	12	12
Matti Hagman	75	20	33	53	16	9	4	1	5	6
Risto Siltanen	79	17	36	53	54	9	2	0	2	8
Blair MacDonald	51	19	24	43	27	–	–	–	–	–
Kevin Lowe	79	10	24	34	94	9	0	2	2	11
Stan Weir	70	12	20	32	40	5	0	0	0	2
Paul Coffey	74	9	23	32	130	9	4	3	7	22
Pat Price	59	8	24	32	193	–	–	–	–	–
Lee Fogolin	80	13	17	30	137	9	0	0	0	12
Dave Hunter	78	12	16	28	98	9	0	0	0	28
Doug Hicks	59	5	16	21	76	9	1	1	2	4
Garry Unger(EDM)	13	0	0	0	6	8	0	0	0	2
Dave Semenko	58	11	8	19	80	9	0	0	0	5
Don Murdoch	40	10	9	19	18	–	–	–	–	–
Pat Hughes(EDM)	2	0	0	0	0	5	0	0	0	2
Garry Lariviere(EDM)	13	0	2	2	6	9	0	3	3	4
Dave Lumley	53	7	9	16	74	7	1	0	1	4
Curt Brackenbury	58	2	7	9	153	2	0	0	0	0
Charlie Huddy	12	2	5	7	6	–	–	–	–	–
Don Ashby	6	2	3	5	2	–	–	–	–	–
Peter Driscoll	21	2	3	5	43	–	–	–	–	–
Eddie Mio	43	0	5	5	6	–	–	–	–	–
John Hughes	18	0	3	3	18	–	–	–	–	–
Ron Low	24	0	3	3	0	–	–	–	–	–
Tom Roulston	11	1	1	2	2	–	–	–	–	–
Gary Edwards	15	0	2	2	0	1	0	0	0	0
Roy Sommer	3	1	0	1	7	–	–	–	–	–
Andy Moog	7	0	1	1	0	9	0	0	0	0
Tom Bladon	1	0	0	0	0	–	–	–	–	–
Peter LoPresti	2	0	0	0	0	–	–	–	–	–

GOALTENDER	REGULAR SEASON						PLAYOFFS				
	GP	MINS	GA	SO	GAA.	W-L-T	GP	MIN	GA	GAA.	W-L
Gary Edwards	15	729	44	0	3.62	5-3-4	1	20	2	6.00	0-0
Andy Moog	7	313	20	0	3.83	3-3-0	9	526	32	3.65	5-4
Eddie Mio	43	2393	155	0	3.89	16-15-9	–	–	–	–	–
Ron Low	24	1260	93	0	4.43	5-13-3	–	–	–	–	–
Pete LoPresti	2	105	8	0	4.57	0-1-0	–	–	–	–	–

1981-82 SEASON

COACH	GP	W	L	T	PTS	GF	GA
			Regular Season				
Glen Sather	80	48	17	15	111	417	295

	GP	W	L	GF	GA
Playoffs	5	2	3	23	27

1st Smythe Division, 2nd Overall. Playoffs: Lost Smythe Division Semi-Final 3-2 vs Los Angeles.

PLAYER	REGULAR SEASON					PLAYOFFS				
	GP	G	A	PTS	PIM	GP	G	A	PTS	PIM
Wayne Gretzky	80	92	120	212	26	5	5	7	12	8
Glenn Anderson	80	38	67	105	71	5	2	5	7	8
Paul Coffey	80	29	60	89	106	5	1	1	2	6
Mark Messier	78	50	38	88	119	5	1	2	3	8
Jari Kurri	71	32	54	86	32	5	2	5	7	10
Dave Lumley	66	32	42	74	96	5	2	1	3	21
Risto Siltanen	63	15	48	63	24	5	3	2	5	10
Matti Hagman	72	21	38	59	18	3	1	0	1	0
Pat Hughes	68	24	22	46	99	5	2	1	3	6
Kevin Lowe	80	9	31	40	63	5	0	3	3	0
Dave Hunter	63	16	22	38	63	5	0	1	1	26
Laurie Boschman(EDM)	11	2	3	5	37	3	0	1	1	4
Lee Fogolin	80	4	25	29	154	5	1	1	2	14
Brett Callighen	46	8	19	27	28	2	0	0	0	2
Dave Semenko	59	12	12	24	194	4	0	0	0	2
Doug Hicks	49	3	20	23	55	–	–	–	–	–
Garry Lariviere	62	1	21	22	41	4	0	1	1	0
Garry Unger	46	7	13	20	69	4	1	0	1	23
Stan Weir	51	3	13	16	13	–	–	–	–	–
Charlie Huddy	41	4	11	15	48	5	1	2	3	14
Tom Roulston	35	11	3	14	22	5	1	0	1	2
Mike Forbes	16	1	7	8	26	–	–	–	–	–
Grant Fuhr	48	0	6	6	6	5	0	1	1	0
Ken Berry	15	2	3	5	9	–	–	–	–	–
Marc Habscheid	7	1	3	4	2	–	–	–	–	–
Lance Nethery(EDM)	3	0	2	2	2	–	–	–	–	–
Curt Brackenbury	14	0	2	2	12	–	–	–	–	–
Andy Moog	8	0	1	1	2	–	–	–	–	–
Todd Strueby	3	0	0	0	0	–	–	–	–	–
Walt Poddubny	4	0	0	0	0	–	–	–	–	–
Don Jackson	8	0	0	0	18	–	–	–	–	–
Ron Low	29	0	0	0	2	–	–	–	–	–
Randy Gregg	–	–	–	–	–	4	0	2	2	12

GOALTENDER	REGULAR SEASON						PLAYOFFS				
	GP	MINS	GA	SO	GAA.	W-L-T	GP	MIN	GA	GAA.	W-L
Grant Fuhr	48	2847	157	0	3.31	28-5-14	5	309	26	5.05	2-3
Ron Low	29	1554	100	0	3.85	17-7-1	–	–	–	–	–
Andy Moog	8	399	32	0	4.81	3-5-0	–	–	–	–	–

Most Scoring Points, One Season

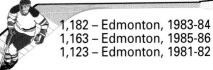

1,182 – Edmonton, 1983-84
1,163 – Edmonton, 1985-86
1,123 – Edmonton, 1981-82

1982-83 SEASON

Regular Season

COACH	GP	W	L	T	PTS	GF	GA
Glen Sather	80	47	21	12	106	424	315

Playoffs

GP	W	L	GF	GA
16	11	5	80	50

1st Smythe Division, 3rd Overall.
Playoffs: Stanley Cup Finalists;
Won Smythe Division Semi-Final 3-0 vs Winnipeg,
Won Smythe Division Final 4-1 vs Calgary,
Won Campbell Conference Final 4-0 vs Chicago,
Lost Stanley Cup Final 4-0 vs NY Islanders.

	REGULAR SEASON					PLAYOFFS				
PLAYER	GP	G	A	PTS	PIM	GP	G	A	PTS	PIM
Wayne Gretzky	80	71	125	196	59	16	12	26	38	4
Mark Messier	77	48	58	106	72	15	15	6	21	14
Glenn Anderson	72	48	56	104	70	16	10	10	20	32
Jari Kurri	80	45	59	104	22	16	8	15	23	8
Paul Coffey	80	29	67	96	87	16	7	7	14	14
Ken Linseman	72	33	42	75	181	16	6	8	14	22
Charlie Huddy	76	20	37	57	58	15	1	6	7	10
Willy Lindstrom (EDM)	10	6	5	11	2	16	2	11	13	4
Pat Hughes	80	25	20	45	85	16	2	5	7	14
Tom Roulston	67	19	21	40	24	16	1	2	3	0
Kevin Lowe	80	6	34	40	43	16	1	8	9	10
Dave Lumley	72	13	24	37	158	16	0	0	0	19
Jaroslav Pouzar	74	15	18	33	57	1	2	0	2	0
Dave Hunter	80	13	18	31	120	16	4	7	11	60
Randy Gregg	80	6	22	28	54	16	2	4	6	13
Dave Semenko	75	12	15	27	141	15	1	1	2	69
Laurie Boschman	62	8	12	20	183	–	–	–	–	–
Lee Fogolin	72	0	18	18	92	16	0	5	5	36
Marc Habscheid	32	3	10	13	14	–	–	–	–	–
Don Jackson	71	2	8	10	136	16	3	3	6	30
Andy Moog	50	0	4	4	16	16	0	1	1	2
John Blum	5	0	3	3	24	–	–	–	–	–
Garry Unger	16	2	0	2	8	1	0	0	0	0
Garry Lariviere	17	0	2	2	14	1	0	1	1	2
L. Middlebrook(EDM)	1	0	0	0	0	–	–	–	–	–
Todd Strueby	1	0	0	0	0	–	–	–	–	–
Ron Low	3	0	0	0	0	–	–	–	–	–
Don Nachbaur	4	0	0	0	17	2	0	0	0	7
Grant Fuhr	32	0	0	0	6	1	0	0	0	0
Ray Cote	–	–	–	–	–	14	3	2	5	4

	REGULAR SEASON						PLAYOFFS				
GOALTENDER	GP	MINS	GA	SO	GAA.	W-L-T	GP	MIN	GA	GAA.	W-L
L. Middlebrook	1	60	3	0	3.00	1-0-0	–	–	–	–	–
Andy Moog	50	2833	167	1	3.54	33-8-7	16	949	48	3.03	11-5
Grant Fuhr	32	1803	129	0	4.29	13-12-5	1	11	0	0.00	0-0

1983-84 SEASON

Regular Season

COACH	GP	W	L	T	PTS	GF	GA
Glen Sather	80	57	18	5	119	446	314

Playoffs

GP	W	L	GF	GA
19	15	4	94	56

STANLEY CUP CHAMPIONS, 1st Smythe Division, 1st Overall. Playoffs: Won Smythe Division Semi-Final 3-0 vs Winnipeg, Won Smythe Division Final 4-3 vs Calgary, Won Campbell Conference Final 4-0 vs Minnesota, Won Stanley Cup Final 4-1 vs NY Islanders.

	REGULAR SEASON					PLAYOFFS				
PLAYER	GP	G	A	PTS	PIM	GP	G	A	PTS	PIM
Wayne Gretzky	74	87	118	205	39	19	13	22	35	12
Paul Coffey	80	40	86	126	104	19	8	14	22	21
Jari Kurri	64	52	61	113	14	19	14	14	28	13
Mark Messier	73	37	64	101	165	19	8	18	26	19
Glenn Anderson	80	54	45	99	65	19	6	11	17	33
Ken Linseman	72	18	49	67	119	19	10	4	14	65
Pat Hughes	77	27	28	56	61	19	2	11	13	12
Dave Hunter	80	22	26	48	90	17	5	5	10	14
Kevin Lowe	80	4	42	46	59	19	3	7	10	16
Charlie Huddy	75	8	34	42	43	12	1	9	10	8
Randy Gregg	80	13	27	40	56	19	3	7	10	21
Willy Lindstrom	73	22	16	38	38	19	5	5	10	10
Kevin McClelland(EDM)	52	8	20	28	127	18	4	6	10	42
Jaroslav Pouzar	67	13	19	32	44	14	1	2	3	12
Dave Lumley	56	6	15	21	68	19	2	5	7	44
Lee Fogolin	80	5	16	21	125	19	1	4	5	23
Don Jackson	64	8	12	20	120	19	1	2	3	32
Dave Semenko	52	6	11	17	118	19	5	5	10	44
Grant Fuhr	45	0	14	14	6	16	0	3	3	4
Tom Roulston	24	5	7	12	16	–	–	–	–	–
Pat Conacher	45	2	8	10	31	3	1	0	1	2
Rick Chartraw(EDM)	24	2	6	8	21	1	0	0	0	2
Ken Berry	13	2	3	5	10	–	–	–	–	–
Raimo Summanen	2	1	4	5	2	5	1	4	5	0
Kari Jalonen(EDM)	3	0	0	0	0	–	–	–	–	–
Jim Playfair	2	1	1	2	2	–	–	–	–	–
Tom Gorence	12	1	1	2	0	–	–	–	–	–
Gord Sherven	2	1	0	1	0	–	–	–	–	–
Marc Habscheid	9	1	0	1	6	–	–	–	–	–
Todd Strueby	1	0	1	1	2	–	–	–	–	–
John Blum	4	0	1	1	2	–	–	–	–	–
Andy Moog	38	0	1	1	4	7	0	0	0	2
Dean Clark	1	0	0	0	0	–	–	–	–	–
Steve Graves	2	0	0	0	0	–	–	–	–	–
Reg Kerr	3	0	0	0	0	–	–	–	–	–
Ray Cote	13	0	0	0	2	–	–	–	–	–
Larry Melnyk	–	–	–	–	–	6	0	1	1	2

	REGULAR SEASON						PLAYOFFS				
GOALTENDER	GP	MINS	GA	SO	GAA.	W-L-T	GP	MIN	GA	GAA.	W-L
Andy Moog	38	2212	139	1	3.77	27-8-1	7	263	12	2.74	4-0
Grant Fuhr	45	2625	171	1	3.91	30-10-4	16	883	44	2.99	11-4

Most Assists, One Season (80 GP)

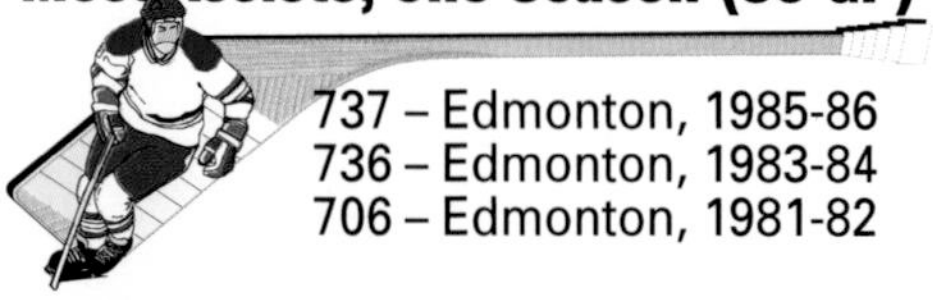

737 – Edmonton, 1985-86
736 – Edmonton, 1983-84
706 – Edmonton, 1981-82

1984-85 SEASON

Regular Season

COACH	GP	W	L	T	PTS	GF	GA
Glen Sather	80	49	20	11	109	401	298

Playoffs

GP	W	L	GF	GA
18	15	3	98	57

STANLEY CUP CHAMPIONS, 1st Smythe Division, 2nd Overall. Playoffs: Won Smythe Division Semi-Final 3-0 vs Los Angeles, Won Smythe Division Final 4-0 vs Winnipeg, Won Campbell Conference Final 4-2 vs Chicago, Won Stanley Cup Final 4-1 vs Philadelphia.

	REGULAR SEASON					PLAYOFFS				
PLAYER	GP	G	A	PTS	PIM	GP	G	A	PTS	PIM
Wayne Gretzky	80	73	135	208	52	18	17	30	47	4
Jari Kurri	73	71	64	135	30	18	19	12	31	6
Paul Coffey	80	37	84	121	97	18	12	25	37	44
Mike Krushelnyski	80	43	45	88	60	18	5	8	13	22
Glenn Anderson	80	42	39	81	69	18	10	16	26	38
Mark Napier(EDM)	33	9	26	35	19	18	5	5	10	7
Mark Messier	55	23	31	54	57	18	12	13	25	12
Charlie Huddy	80	7	44	51	46	18	3	17	20	17
Dave Hunter	80	17	19	36	122	18	2	5	7	33
Willy Lindstrom	80	12	20	32	18	18	5	1	6	8
Dave Lumley (EDM)	12	1	3	4	13	8	0	0	0	29
Pat Hughes	73	12	13	25	85	10	1	1	2	4
Kevin Lowe	80	4	21	25	104	16	0	5	5	8
Kevin McClelland	62	8	15	23	212	18	1	3	4	75
Randy Gregg	57	3	20	23	32	17	0	6	6	12
Don Jackson	78	3	17	20	141	9	0	0	0	64
Dave Semenko	69	6	12	18	167	14	0	0	0	39
Bill Carroll	65	8	9	17	22	9	0	0	0	4
Lee Fogolin	79	4	13	17	126	18	3	1	4	16
Gord Sherven	37	9	7	16	10	–	–	–	–	–
Jaroslav Pouzar	33	4	8	12	28	9	2	1	3	2
Larry Melnyk	28	0	11	11	25	12	1	3	4	26
Marc Habscheid	26	5	3	8	4	–	–	–	–	–
Raimo Summanen	9	0	4	4	0	–	–	–	–	–
Grant Fuhr	46	0	3	3	6	18	0	3	3	2
Marco Baron	1	0	0	0	0	–	–	–	–	–
Daryl Reaugh	1	0	0	0	0	–	–	–	–	–
Ray Cote	2	0	0	0	2	–	–	–	–	–
Steve Smith	2	0	0	0	2	–	–	–	–	–
Mike Zanier	3	0	0	0	0	–	–	–	–	–
Andy Moog	39	0	0	0	8	2	0	0	0	0
Esa Tikkanen	–	–	–	–	–	3	0	0	0	2

	REGULAR SEASON						PLAYOFFS				
GOALTENDER	GP	MINS	GA	SO	GAA.	W-L-T	GP	MIN	GA	GAA.	W-L
Andy Moog	39	2019	111	1	3.30	22-9-3	2	20	0	0.00	0-0
Marco Baron	1	33	2	0	3.64	0-1-0	–	–	–	–	–
Grant Fuhr	46	2559	165	1	3.87	26-8-7	18	1064	55	3.10	15-3
Mike Zanier	3	185	12	0	3.89	1-1-1	–	–	–	–	–
Daryl Reaugh	1	60	5	0	5.00	0-1-0	–	–	–	–	–

Goals Galore ...
6050
6000
5950
5900
5850
5800
5750
5700
5650
5600
6031
Edmonton
5810
Calgary
5641
Pittsburgh
Goals-per-game averages
4.5
4.0
3.5
3.0
2.5
2.0
1.5
1.0
0.5
0.0
4.02
3.87
3.78
Edmonton
Calgary
Pittsburgh

Since joining the league, Edmonton has scored more times than any other team.

1985-86 SEASON

Regular Season

COACH	GP	W	L	T	PTS	GF	GA
Glen Sather	80	56	17	7	119	426	310

Playoffs

GP	W	L	GF	GA
10	6	4	41	30

1st Smythe Division, 1st Overall.
Playoffs: Won Smythe Division Semi-Final 3-0 vs Vancouver,
Lost Smythe Division Final 4-3 vs Calgary.

	REGULAR SEASON					PLAYOFFS				
PLAYER	GP	G	A	PTS	PIM	GP	G	A	PTS	PIM
Wayne Gretzky	80	52	163	215	46	10	8	11	19	2
Paul Coffey	79	48	90	138	120	10	1	9	10	30
Jari Kurri	78	68	63	131	22	10	2	10	12	4
Glenn Anderson	72	54	48	102	90	10	8	3	11	14
Mark Messier	63	35	49	84	68	10	4	6	10	18
Mark Napier	80	24	32	56	14	10	1	4	5	0
Craig MacTavish	74	23	24	47	70	10	4	4	8	11
Charlie Huddy	76	6	35	41	55	7	0	2	2	0
Mike Krushelnyski	54	16	24	40	22	10	4	5	9	16
Raimo Summanen	73	19	18	37	16	5	1	1	2	0
Dave Hunter	62	15	22	37	77	10	2	3	5	23
Kevin McClelland	79	11	25	36	266	10	1	0	1	32
Randy Gregg	64	2	26	28	47	10	1	0	1	12
Lee Fogolin	80	4	22	26	129	8	0	2	2	10
Steve Smith	55	4	20	24	166	6	0	1	1	14
Marty McSorley	59	11	12	23	265	8	0	2	2	50
Dave Lumley	46	11	9	20	35	3	0	2	2	2
Dave Semenko	69	6	12	18	141	6	0	0	0	32
Kevin Lowe	74	2	16	18	90	10	1	3	4	15
Esa Tikkanen	35	7	6	13	28	8	3	2	5	7
Don Jackson	45	2	8	10	93	8	0	0	0	21
Mike Rogers (EDM)	8	1	0	1	0	–	–	–	–	–
Gord Sherven(EDM)	5	1	1	2	4	–	–	–	–	–
Risto Jalo	3	0	3	3	0	–	–	–	–	–
Grant Fuhr	40	0	2	2	0	9	0	1	1	0
Andy Moog	47	0	2	2	8	1	0	0	0	0
Ken Solheim	6	1	0	1	5	–	–	–	–	–
Jeff Brubaker(EDM)	4	1	0	1	12	–	–	–	–	–
Dean Hopkins	1	0	0	0	0	–	–	–	–	–
Mike Moller	1	0	0	0	0	–	–	–	–	–
Selmar Odelein	4	0	0	0	0	–	–	–	–	–
Jeff Beukeboom	–	–	–	–	–	1	0	0	0	4

	REGULAR SEASON						PLAYOFFS				
GOALTENDER	GP	MINS	GA	SO	GAA.	W-L-T	GP	MIN	GA	GAA.	W-L
Andy Moog	47	2664	164	1	3.69	27-9-7	1	60	1	1.00	1-0
Grant Fuhr	40	2184	143	0	3.93	29-8-0	9	541	28	3.11	5-4

Most Shorthanded Goals, One Season (80 GP)

36 – Edmonton, 1983-84
28 – Edmonton, 1986-87
27 – Edmonton, 1985-86
– Edmonton, 1988-89

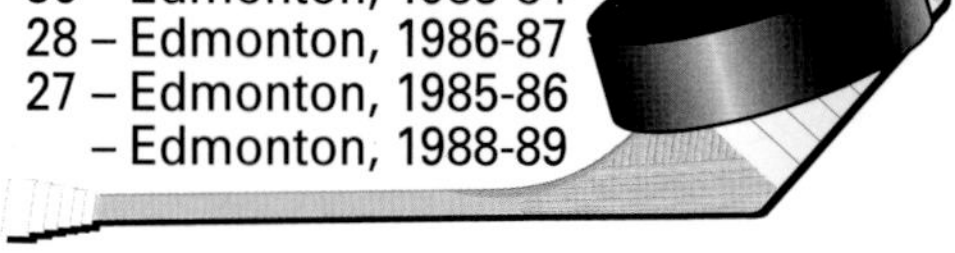

1986-87 SEASON

Regular Season

COACH	GP	W	L	T	PTS	GF	GA
Glen Sather	80	50	24	6	106	372	284

Playoffs

GP	W	L	GF	GA
21	16	5	87	57

STANLEY CUP CHAMPIONS, 1st Smythe Division, 1st Overall. Playoffs: Won Smythe Division Semi-Final 4-1 vs Los Angeles, Won Smythe Division Final 4-0 vs Winnipeg, Won Campbell Conference Final 4-1 vs Detroit, Won Stanley Cup Final 4-3 vs Philadelphia.

	REGULAR SEASON					PLAYOFFS				
PLAYER	GP	G	A	PTS	PIM	GP	G	A	PTS	PIM
Wayne Gretzky	79	62	121	183	28	21	5	29	34	6
Jari Kurri	79	54	54	108	41	21	15	10	25	20
Mark Messier	77	37	70	107	73	21	12	16	28	16
Esa Tikkanen	76	34	44	78	120	21	7	2	9	20
Glenn Anderson	80	35	38	73	65	21	14	13	27	59
Paul Coffey	59	17	50	67	49	17	3	8	11	30
Kent Nilsson(EDM)	17	5	12	17	4	21	6	13	19	6
Mike Krushelnyski	80	16	35	51	67	21	3	4	7	18
Craig MacTavish	79	20	19	39	55	21	1	9	10	16
Kevin Lowe	77	8	29	37	94	21	2	4	6	22
Moe Lemay(EDM)	10	1	2	3	36	9	2	1	3	11
Craig Muni	79	7	22	29	85	14	0	2	2	17
Kevin McClelland	72	12	13	25	238	21	2	3	5	43
Randy Gregg	52	8	16	24	42	18	3	6	9	17
Steve Smith	62	7	15	22	165	15	1	3	4	45
Mark Napier	62	8	13	21	2	–	–	–	–	–
Charlie Huddy	58	4	15	19	35	21	1	7	8	21
Raimo Summanen	48	10	7	17	15	–	–	–	–	–
Dave Hunter	77	6	9	15	75	21	3	3	6	20
Reijo Ruotsalainen	16	5	8	13	6	21	2	5	7	10
Normand Lacombe(EDM)	1	0	0	0	2	–	–	–	–	–
Jeff Beukeboom	44	3	8	11	124	–	–	–	–	–
Marty McSorley	41	2	4	6	159	21	4	3	7	65
Jaroslav Pouzar	12	2	3	5	6	5	1	1	2	2
Stu Kulak	23	3	1	4	41	–	–	–	–	–
Danny Gare	18	1	3	4	6	–	–	–	–	–
Lee Fogolin	35	1	3	4	17	–	–	–	–	–
Mike Moller	6	2	1	3	0	–	–	–	–	–
Steve Graves	12	2	0	2	0	–	–	–	–	–
Grant Fuhr	44	0	2	2	6	19	0	1	1	0
Andy Moog	46	0	2	2	8	2	0	0	0	0
Dave Lumley	1	0	0	0	0	–	–	–	–	–
Wayne Van Dorp	3	0	0	0	25	3	0	0	0	2
Dave Semenko	5	0	0	0	0	–	–	–	–	–
Kelly Buchberger	–	–	–	–	–	3	0	1	1	5

	REGULAR SEASON						PLAYOFFS				
GOALTENDER	GP	MINS	GA	SO	GAA.	W-L-T	GP	MIN	GA	GAA.	W-L
Grant Fuhr	44	2388	137	0	3.44	22-13-3	19	1148	47	2.46	14-5
Andy Moog	46	2461	144	0	3.51	28-11-3	2	120	8	4.00	2-0

1987-88 SEASON

Regular Season

COACH	GP	W	L	T	PTS	GF	GA
Glen Sather	80	44	25	11	99	363	288

Playoffs

GP	W	L	GF	GA
18	16	2	84	53

STANLEY CUP CHAMPIONS, 2nd Smyth Division, 3rd Overall. Playoffs: Won Smythe Division Semi-Final 4-1 vs Winnipeg, Won Smythe Division Final 4-0 vs Calgary, Won Campbell Conference Final 4-1 vs Detroit, Won Stanley Cup Final 4-0 vs Boston.

	REGULAR SEASON					PLAYOFFS				
PLAYER	GP	G	A	PTS	PIM	GP	G	A	PTS	PIM
Wayne Gretzky	64	40	109	149	24	19	12	31	43	16
Mark Messier	77	37	74	111	103	19	11	23	34	29
Jari Kurri	80	43	53	96	30	19	14	17	31	12
Craig Simpson(EDM)	59	43	21	64	43	19	13	6	19	26
Glenn Anderson	80	38	50	88	58	19	9	16	25	49
Esa Tikkanen	80	23	51	74	153	19	10	17	27	72
Geoff Courtnall(EDM)	12	4	4	8	15	19	0	3	3	23
Steve Smith	79	12	43	55	286	19	1	11	12	55
Mike Krushelnyski	76	20	27	47	64	19	4	6	10	12
Charlie Huddy	77	13	28	41	71	13	4	5	9	10
Craig MacTavish	80	15	17	32	47	19	0	1	1	31
Keith Acton(EDM)	26	3	6	9	21	7	2	0	2	16
Dave Hannan(EDM)	51	9	11	20	43	12	1	1	2	8
Marty McSorley	60	9	17	26	223	16	0	3	3	67
Jeff Beukeboom	73	5	20	25	201	7	0	0	0	16
Kevin Lowe	70	9	15	24	89	19	0	2	2	26
Craig Muni	72	4	15	19	77	19	0	4	4	31
Normand Lacombe	53	8	9	17	36	19	3	0	3	28
Kevin McClelland	74	10	6	16	281	19	2	3	5	68
Chris Joseph(EDM)	7	0	4	4	6	–	–	–	–	–
Grant Fuhr	75	0	8	8	16	19	0	1	1	6
Steve Graves	21	3	4	7	10	–	–	–	–	–
Steve Dykstra(EDM)	15	2	3	5	39	–	–	–	–	–
Dave Hunter	21	3	3	6	6	–	–	–	–	–
Moe Mantha	25	0	6	6	26	–	–	–	–	–
Tom McMurchy	9	4	1	5	8	–	–	–	–	–
John Miner	14	2	3	5	16	–	–	–	–	–
Ron Shudra	10	0	5	5	6	–	–	–	–	–
Jim Wiemer	12	1	2	3	15	2	0	0	0	2
Randy Gregg	15	1	2	3	8	19	1	8	9	24
Bill Ranford	6	0	2	2	0	–	–	–	–	–
Selmar Odelein	12	0	2	2	33	–	–	–	–	–
Jim Ennis	5	1	0	1	10	–	–	–	–	–
Kelly Buchberger	19	1	0	1	81	–	–	–	–	–
Scott Metcalfe	2	0	0	0	0	–	–	–	–	–
Warren Skorodenski	3	0	0	0	0	–	–	–	–	–
Moe Lemay	4	0	0	0	2	–	–	–	–	–
Dave Donnelly	4	0	0	0	4	–	–	–	–	–
Daryl Reaugh	6	0	0	0	0	–	–	–	–	–

	REGULAR SEASON						PLAYOFFS				
GOALTENDER	GP	MINS	GA	SO	GAA.	W-L-T	GP	MIN	GA	GAA.	W-L
Bill Ranford	6	325	16	0	2.95	3-0-2	–	–	–	–	–
Grant Fuhr	75	4304	246	4	3.43	40-24-9	19	1136	55	2.90	16-2
Daryl Reaugh	6	176	14	0	4.77	1-1-0	–	–	–	–	–
Warren Skorodenski	3	61	7	0	6.89	0-0-0	–	–	–	–	–

1988-89 SEASON

Regular Season

COACH	GP	W	L	T	PTS	GF	GA
Glen Sather	80	38	34	8	84	325	306

Playoffs

GP	W	L	GF	GA
7	3	4	20	25

3rd Smythe Division, 7th Overall.
Playoffs: Lost Smythe Division Semi-Final 4-3 vs Los Angeles.

	REGULAR SEASON					PLAYOFFS				
PLAYER	GP	G	A	PTS	PIM	GP	G	A	PTS	PIM
Jari Kurri	76	44	58	102	69	7	3	5	8	6
Jimmy Carson	80	49	51	100	36	7	2	1	3	6
Mark Messier	72	33	61	94	130	7	1	11	12	8
Esa Tikkanen	67	31	47	78	92	7	1	3	4	12
Craig Simpson	66	35	41	76	80	7	2	0	2	10
Glenn Anderson	79	16	48	64	93	7	1	2	3	8
Craig MacTavish	80	21	31	52	55	7	0	1	1	8
Charlie Huddy	76	11	33	44	52	7	2	0	2	4
Tomas Jonsson(EDM)	20	1	10	11	22	4	2	0	2	6
Normand Lacombe	64	17	11	28	57	7	2	1	3	21
Keith Acton	46	11	15	26	47	–	–	–	–	–
Miroslav Frycer(EDM)	14	5	5	10	18	–	–	–	–	–
Kevin Lowe	76	7	18	25	98	7	1	2	3	4
Steve Smith	35	3	19	22	97	7	2	2	4	20
Kevin McClelland	79	6	14	20	161	7	0	2	2	16
Craig Muni	69	5	13	18	71	7	0	3	3	8
Randy Gregg	57	3	15	18	28	7	1	0	1	6
Kelly Buchberger	66	5	9	14	234	–	–	–	–	–
Craig Redmond	21	3	10	13	12	–	–	–	–	–
Dave Hunter(EDM)	32	3	5	8	22	6	0	0	0	0
Mark Lamb	20	2	8	10	14	6	0	2	2	8
Chris Joseph	44	4	5	9	54	–	–	–	–	–
Greg Adams	49	4	5	9	72	–	–	–	–	–
Reed Larson	10	2	7	9	15	–	–	–	–	–
Doug Halward(EDM)	24	0	7	7	25	2	0	0	0	0
Jeff Beukeboom	36	0	5	5	94	1	0	0	0	2
Dave Brown(EDM)	22	0	2	2	66	7	0	0	0	6
Martin Gelinas	6	1	2	3	0	–	–	–	–	–
Doug Smith	19	1	1	2	9	–	–	–	–	–
John LeBlanc	2	1	0	1	0	1	0	0	0	0
Alan May	3	1	0	1	7	–	–	–	–	–
Mike Ware	2	0	1	1	11	–	–	–	–	–
Ken Hammond	5	0	1	1	8	–	–	–	–	–
Grant Fuhr	59	0	1	1	6	7	0	0	0	0
Nick Fotiu	1	0	0	0	0	–	–	–	–	–
Francois Leroux	2	0	0	0	0	–	–	–	–	–
Selmar Odelein	2	0	0	0	2	–	–	–	–	–
Kim Issel	4	0	0	0	0	–	–	–	–	–
Glen Cochrane(EDM)	12	0	0	0	52	–	–	–	–	–
Bill Ranford	29	0	0	0	2	–	–	–	–	–

	REGULAR SEASON						PLAYOFFS				
GOALTENDER	GP	MINS	GA	SO	GAA.	W-L-T	GP	MIN	GA	GAA.	W-L
Bill Ranford	29	1509	88	1	3.50	15-8-2	–	–	–	–	–
Grant Fuhr	59	3341	213	1	3.83	23-26-6	7	417	24	3.45	3-4

1989-90 SEASON

Regular Season

COACH	GP	W	L	T	PTS	GF	GA
John Muckler	80	38	28	14	90	315	283

Playoffs

GP	W	L	GF	GA
22	16	6	93	60

STANLEY CUP CHAMPIONS, 2nd Smyth Division, 5th Overall. Playoffs: Won Smythe Division Semi-Final 4-3 vs Winnipeg, Won Smythe Division Final 4-0 vs Los Angeles, Won Campbell Conference Final 4-2 vs Chicago, Won Stanley Cup 4-1 vs. Boston.

	REGULAR SEASON					PLAYOFFS				
PLAYER	GP	G	A	PTS	PIM	GP	G	A	PTS	PIM
Mark Messier	79	45	84	129	79	22	9	22	31	20
Jari Kurri	78	33	60	93	48	22	10	15	25	18
Glenn Anderson	73	34	38	72	107	22	10	12	22	20
Petr Klima(EDM)	63	25	28	53	66	21	5	0	5	8
Esa Tikkanen	79	30	33	63	161	22	13	11	24	26
Craig Simpson	80	29	32	61	180	22	16	15	31	8
Craig MacTavish	80	21	22	43	89	22	2	6	8	29
Steve Smith	75	7	34	41	171	22	5	10	15	37
Kevin Lowe	78	7	26	33	140	20	0	2	2	10
Joe Murphy(EDM)	62	7	18	25	56	22	6	8	14	16
Mark Lamb	58	12	16	28	42	22	6	11	17	2
Martin Gelinas	46	17	8	25	30	20	2	3	5	6
Randy Gregg	48	4	20	24	42	20	2	6	8	16
Charlie Huddy	70	1	23	24	56	22	0	6	6	10
Adam Graves(EDM)	63	9	12	21	123	22	5	6	11	17
Vladimir Ruzicka	25	11	6	17	10	–	–	–	–	–
Craig Muni	71	5	12	17	81	22	0	3	3	16
Geoff Smith	74	4	11	15	52	3	0	0	0	0
Reijo Ruotsalainen(EDM)	10	1	7	8	6	22	2	11	13	12
Jeff Beukeboom	46	1	12	13	86	2	0	0	0	0
Kelly Buchberger	55	2	6	8	168	19	0	5	5	13
Normand Lacombe	15	5	2	7	21	–	–	–	–	–
Peter Eriksson	20	3	3	6	24	–	–	–	–	–
Dave Brown	60	0	6	6	145	3	0	0	0	0
Jimmy Carson	4	1	2	3	0	–	–	–	–	–
Kevin McClelland	10	1	1	2	13	–	–	–	–	–
Chris Joseph	4	0	2	2	2	–	–	–	–	–
Bill Ranford	56	0	2	2	18	22	0	2	2	4
Mike Greenlay	2	0	1	1	0	–	–	–	–	–
Francois Leroux	3	0	1	1	0	–	–	–	–	–
Trevor Sim	3	0	1	1	2	–	–	–	–	–
Bruce Bell	1	0	0	0	0	–	–	–	–	–
Randy Exelby	1	0	0	0	0	–	–	–	–	–
Tom Lehmann	1	0	0	0	0	–	–	–	–	–
Norm Maciver	1	0	0	0	0	–	–	–	–	–
Mike Ware	3	0	0	0	4	–	–	–	–	–
Eldon Reddick	11	0	0	0	0	1	0	0	0	0
Grant Fuhr	21	0	0	0	2	–	–	–	–	–
Anatoli Semenov	–	–	–	–	–	2	0	0	0	0

	REGULAR SEASON						PLAYOFFS				
GOALTENDER	GP	MINS	GA	SO	GAA.	W-L-T	GP	MIN	GA	GAA.	W-L
Eldon Reddick	11	604	31	0	2.08	5-4-2	1	2	0	0.00	0-0
Bill Ranford	56	3107	165	1	3.19	24-16-9	22	1401	59	2.53	16-6
Grant Fuhr	21	1081	70	1	3.89	9-7-3	–	–	–	–	–
Randy Exelby	1	60	5	0	5.00	0-1-0	–	–	–	–	–
Mike Greenlay	1	20	4	0	12.00	0-0-0	–	–	–	–	–

Most 50 Goal Scorers, One Season

3 – Edmonton, '83-84
(Wayne Gretzky, 87; Glenn Anderson, 54; Jari Kurri, 52. 80 GP)

3 – Edmonton, '85-86
(Jari Kurri, 68; Glenn Anderson, 54; Wayne Gretzky, 52. 80 GP)

1990-91 SEASON

Regular Season

COACH	GP	W	L	T	PTS	GF	GA
John Muckler	80	37	37	6	80	272	272

Playoffs

GP	W	L	GF	GA
18	9	9	57	60

3rd Smythe Division, 11th Overall.
Playoffs: Won Smythe Division Semi-Final 4-3 vs Calgary, Won Smythe Division Final 4-2 vs Los Angeles, Lost Campbell Conference Final 4-1 vs Minnesota.

1990-91 Season cont.

PLAYER	REGULAR SEASON GP	G	A	PTS	PIM	PLAYOFFS GP	G	A	PTS	PIM
Esa Tikkanen	79	27	42	69	85	18	12	8	20	24
Petr Klima	70	40	28	68	113	18	7	6	13	16
Mark Messier	53	12	52	64	34	18	4	11	15	16
Joe Murphy	80	27	35	62	35	15	2	5	7	14
Craig Simpson	75	30	27	57	66	18	5	11	16	12
Glenn Anderson	74	24	31	55	59	18	6	7	13	41
Steve Smith	77	13	41	54	193	18	1	2	3	45
Martin Gelinas	73	20	20	40	34	18	3	6	9	25
Ken Linseman	56	7	29	36	94	2	0	1	1	0
Craig MacTavish	80	17	15	32	76	18	3	3	6	20
Anatoli Semenov	57	15	16	31	26	12	5	5	10	6
Charlie Huddy	53	5	22	27	32	18	3	7	10	10
Adam Graves	76	7	18	25	127	18	2	4	6	22
Chris Joseph	49	5	17	22	59	-	-	-	-	-
Kevin Lowe	73	3	13	16	113	14	1	1	2	14
Geoff Smith	59	1	12	13	55	4	0	0	0	0
Mark Lamb	37	4	8	12	25	15	0	5	5	20
Jeff Beukeboom	67	3	7	10	150	18	1	3	4	28
Craig Muni	76	1	9	10	77	18	0	3	3	20
Dave Brown	58	3	4	7	160	16	0	1	1	30
Norm Maciver	21	2	5	7	14	18	0	4	4	8
Kelly Buchberger	64	3	1	4	160	12	2	1	3	25
Bill Ranford	60	0	4	4	6	3	0	0	0	0
Francois Leroux	1	0	2	2	0	-	-	-	-	-
Brad Aitken(EDM)	3	0	1	1	0	-	-	-	-	-
Max Middendorf	3	1	0	1	2	-	-	-	-	-
Igor Vyazmikin	4	1	0	1	0	-	-	-	-	-
David Haas	5	1	0	1	0	-	-	-	-	-
Greg Hawgood	6	0	1	1	6	-	-	-	-	-
Kari Takko(EDM)	11	0	1	1	0	-	-	-	-	-
Eldon Reddick	2	0	0	0	0	-	-	-	-	-
Tomas Srsen	2	0	0	0	0	-	-	-	-	-
Shaun Van Allen	2	0	0	0	0	-	-	-	-	-
Dan Currie	5	0	0	0	0	-	-	-	-	-
Grant Fuhr	13	0	0	0	0	17	0	2	2	2

GOALTENDER	REGULAR SEASON GP	MINS	GA	SO	GAA.	W-L-T	PLAYOFFS GP	MIN	GA	GAA.	W-L
Grant Fuhr	13	778	39	1	3.01	6-4-3	17	1019	51	3.00	8-7
Bill Ranford	60	3415	182	0	3.20	27-27-3	3	135	8	3.56	1-2
Kari Takko	11	529	37	0	4.20	4-4-0	-	-	-	-	-
Eldon Reddick	2	120	9	0	4.50	0-2-0	-	-	-	-	-

1991-92 SEASON

COACH	Regular Season GP	W	L	T	PTS	GF	GA
Ted Green	80	36	34	10	82	295	297

Playoffs GP	W	L	GF	GA
16	8	8	49	54

3rd Smythe Division, 12th Overall.
Playoffs: Won Smythe Division Semi-Final 4-2 vs Los Angeles, Won Smythe Division Final 4-2 vs Vancouver, Lost Campbell Conference Final 4-0 vs Chicago.

PLAYER	REGULAR SEASON GP	G	A	PTS	PIM	PLAYOFFS GP	G	A	PTS	PIM
Vincent Damphousse	80	38	51	89	53	16	6	8	14	8
Joe Murphy	80	35	47	82	52	16	8	16	24	12
Craig Simpson	79	24	37	61	80	1	0	0	0	0
Scott Mellanby	80	23	27	50	197	16	2	1	3	29
Bernie Nicholls(EDM)	49	20	29	49	40	16	8	11	19	25
Dave Manson	79	15	32	47	220	16	3	9	12	44
Kelly Buchberger	79	20	24	44	157	16	1	4	5	32
Anatoli Semenov	59	20	22	42	16	8	1	1	2	6
Norm Maciver	57	6	34	40	38	13	1	2	3	10
Petr Klima	57	21	13	34	52	15	1	4	5	8
Craig MacTavish	80	12	18	30	98	16	3	0	3	28
Martin Gelinas	68	11	18	29	62	15	1	3	4	10
Esa Tikkanen	40	12	16	28	44	16	5	3	8	8
Josef Beranek	58	12	16	28	18	12	2	1	3	0
Mark Lamb	59	6	22	28	46	16	1	1	2	10
David Maley(EDM)	23	3	6	9	46	10	1	1	2	4
Brian Glynn(EDM)	25	2	6	8	6	16	4	1	5	12
Luke Richardson	75	2	19	21	118	16	0	5	5	45
Geoff Smith	74	2	16	18	43	5	0	1	1	6
Greg Hawgood	20	2	11	13	22	13	0	3	3	23
Kevin Lowe	55	2	7	9	107	11	0	3	3	16
Craig Muni	54	2	5	7	34	3	0	0	0	2
Jeff Beukeboom	18	0	5	5	78	-	-	-	-	-
Troy Mallette	15	1	3	4	36	-	-	-	-	-
Louie DeBrusk	25	2	1	3	124	-	-	-	-	-
Peter Ing	12	0	3	3	0	-	-	-	-	-
Bill Ranford	67	0	3	3	4	16	0	0	0	0
David Shaw	12	1	1	2	8	-	-	-	-	-
Dan Currie	7	1	0	1	0	-	-	-	-	-
Scott Thornton	15	0	1	1	43	1	0	0	0	0
Martin Rucinsky	2	0	0	0	0	-	-	-	-	-
Steven Rice	3	0	0	0	2	-	-	-	-	-
Francois Leroux	4	0	0	0	7	-	-	-	-	-
Chris Joseph	7	0	0	0	8	5	1	3	4	2
Norm Foster	10	0	0	0	2	-	-	-	-	-
Ron Tugnutt(EDM)	3	0	0	0	2	2	0	0	0	0

GOALTENDER	REGULAR SEASON GP	MINS	GA	SO	GAA.	W-L-T	PLAYOFFS GP	MIN	GA	GAA.	W-L
Norm Foster	10	439	20	0	2.73	5-3-0	-	-	-	-	-
Bill Ranford	67	3822	228	1	3.58	27-26-10	16	909	51	3.37	8-8
Peter Ing	12	463	33	0	4.28	3-4-0	-	-	-	-	-
Ron Tugnutt	3	124	10	0	4.84	1-1-0	2	60	3	3.00	0-0

Longest Undefeated Streak From Start of Season

15 Games – Edmonton, 1984-85 (12 W, 3 T)
14 Games – Montreal, 1943-44 (11 W, 3 T)
13 Games – Montreal, 1972-73 (9 W, 4 T)
– Pittsburgh, 1994-95 (12 W, 1 T)

1992-93 SEASON

COACH	Regular Season GP	W	L	T	PTS	GF	GA
Ted Green	84	26	50	8	60	242	337

Playoffs GP	W	L	GF	GA
–	–	–	–	–

5th Smythe Division, 20th Overall. Playoffs: Did not qualify.

PLAYER	REGULAR SEASON GP	G	A	PTS	PIM	PLAYOFFS GP	G	A	PTS	PIM
Petr Klima	68	32	16	48	100	-	-	-	-	-
Doug Weight(EDM)	13	2	6	8	10	-	-	-	-	-
Shayne Corson	80	16	31	47	209	-	-	-	-	-
Craig Simpson	60	24	22	46	36	-	-	-	-	-
Dave Manson	83	15	30	45	210	-	-	-	-	-
Todd Elik(EDM)	14	1	9	10	8	-	-	-	-	-
Bernie Nicholls	46	8	32	40	40	-	-	-	-	-
Zdeno Ciger(EDM)	37	9	15	24	6	-	-	-	-	-
Brian Benning(EDM)	18	1	7	8	59	-	-	-	-	-
Esa Tikkanen	66	14	19	33	76	-	-	-	-	-
Scott Mellanby	69	15	17	32	147	-	-	-	-	-
Kelly Buchberger	83	12	18	30	133	-	-	-	-	-
Craig MacTavish	82	10	20	30	110	-	-	-	-	-
Igor Kravchuk(EDM)	17	4	8	12	2	-	-	-	-	-
Martin Gelinas	65	11	12	23	30	-	-	-	-	-
Kevin Todd(EDM)	25	4	9	13	10	-	-	-	-	-
Brent Gilchrist	60	10	10	20	47	-	-	-	-	-
Shjon Podein	40	13	6	19	25	-	-	-	-	-
Greg Hawgood	29	5	13	18	35	-	-	-	-	-
Geoff Smith	78	4	14	18	30	-	-	-	-	-
Brian Glynn	64	4	12	16	60	-	-	-	-	-
Luke Richardson	82	3	10	13	142	-	-	-	-	-
Chris Joseph	33	2	10	12	48	-	-	-	-	-
Vladimir Vujtek	30	1	10	11	8	-	-	-	-	-
Craig Muni	72	0	11	11	67	-	-	-	-	-
Louie DeBrusk	51	8	2	10	205	-	-	-	-	-
Brad Werenka	27	5	4	9	24	-	-	-	-	-
Josef Beranek	26	2	6	8	28	-	-	-	-	-
Mike Hudson(EDM)	5	0	1	1	2	-	-	-	-	-
Steven Rice	28	2	5	7	28	-	-	-	-	-
Shaun Van Allen	21	1	4	5	6	-	-	-	-	-
Bill McDougall	4	2	1	3	4	-	-	-	-	-
Bill Ranford	67	0	3	3	10	-	-	-	-	-
Tyler Wright	7	1	1	2	19	-	-	-	-	-
David Maley	13	1	1	2	29	-	-	-	-	-
Scott Thornton	9	0	1	1	0	-	-	-	-	-
Francois Leroux	1	0	0	0	0	-	-	-	-	-
Dan Currie	5	0	0	0	4	-	-	-	-	-
Ron Tugnutt	26	0	0	0	2	-	-	-	-	-

GOALTENDER	REGULAR SEASON GP	MINS	GA	SO	GAA.	W-L-T	PLAYOFFS GP	MIN	GA	GAA.	W-L
Bill Ranford	67	3753	240	1	3.84	17-38-6	-	-	-	-	-
Ron Tugnutt	26	1338	93	0	4.17	9-12-2	-	-	-	-	-

1993-94 SEASON

COACH	Regular Season GP	W	L	T	PTS	GF	GA
Ted Green(3-18-3)	84	25	45	14	64	261	305
Glen Sather(22-27-11)							

Playoffs GP	W	L	GF	GA
–	–	–	–	–

6th Pacific Division, 23rd Overall. Playoffs: Did not qualify.

PLAYER	REGULAR SEASON GP	G	A	PTS	PIM	PLAYOFFS GP	G	A	PTS	PIM
Doug Weight	84	24	50	74	47	-	-	-	-	-
Jason Arnott	78	33	35	68	104	-	-	-	-	-
Zdeno Ciger	84	22	35	57	8	-	-	-	-	-
Shayne Corson	64	25	29	54	118	-	-	-	-	-
Igor Kravchuk	81	12	38	50	16	-	-	-	-	-
Bob Beers(EDM)	66	10	27	37	74	-	-	-	-	-
Scott Pearson	72	19	18	37	165	-	-	-	-	-
Fredrik Olausson(EDM)	55	9	19	28	20	-	-	-	-	-
Steven Rice	63	17	15	32	36	-	-	-	-	-
Boris Mironov(EDM)	14	0	2	2	14	-	-	-	-	-
Ilya Byakin	44	8	20	28	30	-	-	-	-	-
Dean McAmmond	45	6	21	27	16	-	-	-	-	-
Craig MacTavish	66	16	10	26	80	-	-	-	-	-
Mike Stapleton(EDM)	23	5	9	14	28	-	-	-	-	-
Kelly Buchberger	84	3	18	21	199	-	-	-	-	-
Kirk Maltby	68	11	8	19	74	-	-	-	-	-
Vladimir Vujtek	40	4	15	19	14	-	-	-	-	-
Brent Grieve(EDM)	24	13	5	18	14	-	-	-	-	-
Dave Manson	57	3	13	16	140	-	-	-	-	-
Scott Thornton	61	4	7	11	104	-	-	-	-	-
Louie DeBrusk	48	4	6	10	185	-	-	-	-	-
Adam Bennett	48	3	6	9	49	-	-	-	-	-
Peter White	26	3	5	8	2	-	-	-	-	-
Shjon Podein	28	3	5	8	8	-	-	-	-	-
Luke Richardson	69	2	6	8	131	-	-	-	-	-
Brad Werenka	15	0	4	4	14	-	-	-	-	-
Roman Oksiuta	10	1	2	3	4	-	-	-	-	-
Geoff Smith	21	0	3	3	12	-	-	-	-	-
Chris Joseph	10	1	1	2	28	-	-	-	-	-
Ian Herbers	22	0	2	2	32	-	-	-	-	-
Bill Ranford	71	0	2	2	2	-	-	-	-	-
Todd Marchant(EDM)	3	0	1	1	2	-	-	-	-	-
Gord Mark	12	0	1	1	43	-	-	-	-	-
Jozef Cierny	1	0	0	0	0	-	-	-	-	-
Wayne Cowley	1	0	0	0	0	-	-	-	-	-
Jeff Chychrun	2	0	0	0	0	-	-	-	-	-
Darcy Martini	2	0	0	0	0	-	-	-	-	-
Brad Zavisha	2	0	0	0	0	-	-	-	-	-
Todd Elik	4	0	0	0	6	-	-	-	-	-
Alexander Kerch	5	0	0	0	2	-	-	-	-	-
Tyler Wright	5	0	0	0	4	-	-	-	-	-
Marc Laforge	5	0	0	0	21	-	-	-	-	-
Fred Brathwaite	19	0	0	0	0	-	-	-	-	-

GOALTENDER	REGULAR SEASON GP	MINS	GA	SO	GAA.	W-L-T	PLAYOFFS GP	MIN	GA	GAA.	W-L
Wayne Cowley	1	57	3	0	3.16	0-1-0	-	-	-	-	-
Bill Ranford	71	4070	236	1	3.48	22-34-11	-	-	-	-	-
Fred Brathwaite	19	982	58	0	3.54	3-10-3	-	-	-	-	-

1994-95 SEASON

COACH	Regular Season GP	W	L	T	PTS	GF	GA
George Burnett(12-20-3)	48	17	27	4	38	136	183
Ron Low(5-7-1)							

Playoffs GP	W	L	GF	GA
–	–	–	–	–

5th Pacific Division, 22nd Overall. Playoffs: Did not qualify.

PLAYER	REGULAR SEASON GP	G	A	PTS	PIM	PLAYOFFS GP	G	A	PTS	PIM
Doug Weight	48	7	33	40	69	-	-	-	-	-
Jason Arnott	42	15	22	37	128	-	-	-	-	-
Shayne Corson	48	12	24	36	86	-	-	-	-	-
David Oliver	44	16	14	30	20	-	-	-	-	-
Todd Marchant	45	13	14	27	32	-	-	-	-	-
Kelly Buchberger	48	7	17	24	82	-	-	-	-	-
Scott Thornton	47	10	12	22	89	-	-	-	-	-
Igor Kravchuk	36	7	11	18	29	-	-	-	-	-
Mike Stapleton	46	6	11	17	21	-	-	-	-	-
Roman Oksiuta	26	11	2	13	8	-	-	-	-	-
Luke Richardson	46	3	10	13	40	-	-	-	-	-
Jiri Slegr(EDM)	12	1	5	6	14	-	-	-	-	-
Kirk Maltby	47	8	3	11	49	-	-	-	-	-

Dean Kennedy	40	2	8	10	25	–	–	–	–	–
Fredrik Olausson	33	0	10	10	10	–	–	–	–	–
Boris Mironov	29	1	7	8	40	–	–	–	–	–
Ken Sutton(EDM)	12	3	1	4	12	–	–	–	–	–
Peter White	9	2	4	6	0	–	–	–	–	–
Bryan Marchment	40	1	5	6	184	–	–	–	–	–
Len Esau	14	0	6	6	15	–	–	–	–	–
Scott Pearson	28	1	4	5	54	–	–	–	–	–
Zdeno Ciger	5	2	2	4	0	–	–	–	–	–
Iain Fraser(EDM)	9	3	0	3	0	–	–	–	–	–
Louie DeBrusk	34	2	0	2	93	–	–	–	–	–
Gord Mark	18	0	2	2	35	–	–	–	–	–
Bill Ranford	40	0	2	2	2	–	–	–	–	–
Jason Bonsignore	1	1	0	1	0	–	–	–	–	–
Kent Nilsson	6	1	0	1	0	–	–	–	–	–
Tyler Wright	6	1	0	1	14	–	–	–	–	–
Ralph Intranuovo	1	0	1	1	0	–	–	–	–	–
Joaquin Gage	2	0	1	1	0	–	–	–	–	–
Micah Aivazoff	21	0	1	1	2	–	–	–	–	–
Dennis Bonvie	2	0	0	0	0	–	–	–	–	–
Ryan Smyth	3	0	0	0	0	–	–	–	–	–
Marko Tuomainen	4	0	0	0	0	–	–	–	–	–
Dean McAmmond	6	0	0	0	0	–	–	–	–	–
Fred Brathwaite	14	0	0	0	0	–	–	–	–	–
Ryan McGill(EDM)	8	0	0	0	8	–	–	–	–	–

	REGULAR SEASON						PLAYOFFS				
GOALTENDER	GP	MINS	GA	S0	GAA.	W-L-T	GP	MIN	GA	GAA.	W-L
Bill Ranford	40	2203	133	2	3.62	15-20-3	–	–	–	–	–
Fred Brathwaite	14	601	40	0	3.99	2-5-1	–	–	–	–	–
Joaquin Gage	2	99	7	0	4.24	0-2-0	–	–	–	–	–

Highest Goals-Per-Game Average, One Season

5.58 – Edmonton, 1983-84, 446 goals in 80 games.
5.38 – Montreal, 1919-1920, 129 goals in 24 games.
5.33 – Edmonton, 1985-86, 426 goals in 80 games.
5.30 – Edmonton, 1982-83, 424 goals in 1980.

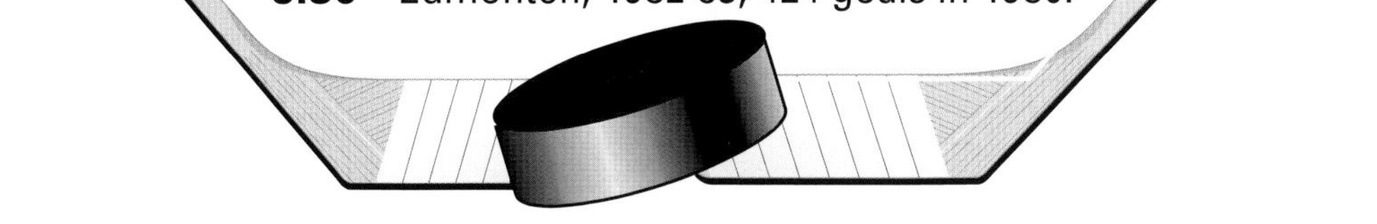

Fastest Two Goals From Start of Game

Edmonton, March 28, 1982 at Los Angeles. (Mark Messier at 0:14 and Dave Lumley at 0:24.) Edmonton won 6-2.

1995-96 SEASON

Regular Season

COACH	GP	W	L	T	PTS	GF	GA
Ron Low	82	30	44	8	68	240	304

Playoffs

GP	W	L	GF	GA
–	–	–	–	–

5th Pacific Division, 21st Overall. Playoffs: Did not qualify.

	REGULAR SEASON					PLAYOFFS				
PLAYER	GP	G	A	PTS	PIM	GP	G	A	PTS	PIM
Doug Weight	82	25	79	104	95	–	–	–	–	–
Zdeno Ciger	78	31	39	70	41	–	–	–	–	–
Jason Arnott	64	28	31	59	87	–	–	–	–	–
M.Czerkawski(EDM)	37	12	17	29	8	–	–	–	–	–
David Oliver	80	20	19	39	34	–	–	–	–	–
Todd Marchant	81	19	19	38	66	–	–	–	–	–
Miroslav Satan	62	18	17	35	22	–	–	–	–	–
Boris Mironov	78	8	24	32	101	–	–	–	–	–
Jeff Norton(EDM)	30	4	16	20	16	–	–	–	–	–
Dean McAmmond	53	15	15	30	23	–	–	–	–	–
Kelly Buchberger	82	11	14	25	184	–	–	–	–	–
Scott Thornton	77	9	9	18	149	–	–	–	–	–
Bryan Marchment	78	3	15	18	202	–	–	–	–	–
Jiri Slegr	57	4	13	17	74	–	–	–	–	–
David Roberts(EDM)	6	2	4	6	6	–	–	–	–	–
Ryan Smyth	48	2	9	11	28	–	–	–	–	–
Luke Richardson	82	2	9	11	108	–	–	–	–	–
Glenn Anderson	17	4	6	10	27	–	–	–	–	–
Igor Kravchuk	26	4	4	8	10	–	–	–	–	–
Peter White	26	5	3	8	0	–	–	–	–	–
Kent Manderville	37	3	5	8	38	–	–	–	–	–
Kirk Maltby	49	2	6	8	61	–	–	–	–	–
Ken Sutton	32	0	8	8	39	–	–	–	–	–
Donald Dufresne(EDM)	42	1	6	7	16	–	–	–	–	–
Brett Hauer	29	4	2	6	30	–	–	–	–	–
Fredrik Olausson	20	0	6	6	14	–	–	–	–	–
Louie DeBrusk	38	1	3	4	96	–	–	–	–	–
Ralph Intranuovo	13	1	2	3	4	–	–	–	–	–
Greg de Vries	13	1	1	2	12	–	–	–	–	–
Jason Bonsignore	20	0	2	2	4	–	–	–	–	–

Tyler Wright	23	1	0	1	33	–	–	–	–	–
Curtis Joseph	34	0	1	1	4	–	–	–	–	–
Bill Ranford	37	0	1	1	2	–	–	–	–	–
Nick Stajduhar	2	0	0	0	4	–	–	–	–	–
Bryan Muir	5	0	0	0	6	–	–	–	–	–
Fred Brathwaite	7	0	0	0	2	–	–	–	–	–
Dennis Bonvie	8	0	0	0	47	–	–	–	–	–
Joaquin Gage	16	0	0	0	4	–	–	–	–	–

	REGULAR SEASON						PLAYOFFS				
GOALTENDER	GP	MINS	GA	S0	GAA.	W-L-T	GP	MIN	GA	GAA.	W-L
Fred Brathwaite	7	293	12	0	2.46	0-2-0	–	–	–	–	–
Curtis Joseph	34	1936	111	0	3.44	15-16-2	–	–	–	–	–
Joaquin Gage	16	717	45	0	3.77	2-8-1	–	–	–	–	–
Bill Ranford	37	2015	128	1	3.81	13-18-5	–	–	–	–	–

1996-97 SEASON

Regular Season

COACH	GP	W	L	T	PTS	GF	GA
Ron Low	82	36	37	9	81	252	247

Playoffs

GP	W	L	GF	GA
12	5	7	32	37

3rd Pacific Division, 13th Overall.
Playoffs: Won Western Conference Quarter-Final 4-3 vs Dallas, Lost Western Conference Semi-Final 4-1 vs Colorado.

	REGULAR SEASON					PLAYOFFS				
PLAYER	GP	G	A	PTS	PIM	GP	G	A	PTS	PIM
Doug Weight	80	21	61	82	80	12	3	8	11	8
Ryan Smyth	82	39	22	61	76	12	5	5	10	12
Andrei Kovalenko	74	32	27	59	81	12	4	3	7	6
Jason Arnott	67	19	38	57	92	12	3	6	9	18
Mariusz Czerkawski	76	26	21	47	16	12	2	1	3	10
Kelly Buchberger	81	8	30	38	159	12	5	2	7	16
Todd Marchant	79	14	19	33	44	12	4	2	6	12
Mike Grier	79	15	17	32	45	12	3	1	4	4
Boris Mironov	55	6	26	32	85	12	2	8	10	16
Rem Murray	82	11	20	31	16	12	1	2	3	4
Dean McAmmond	57	12	17	29	28	–	–	–	–	–
Miroslav Satan	64	17	11	28	22	–	–	–	–	–
Mats Lindgren	69	11	14	25	12	12	0	4	4	0
Dan McGillis	73	6	16	22	52	12	0	5	5	24
Drew Bannister(EDM)	1	0	1	1	0	12	0	0	0	30
Bryan Marchment	71	3	13	16	132	3	0	0	0	4
Petr Klima(EDM)	16	1	5	6	6	6	0	0	0	4
Kevin Lowe	64	1	13	14	50	1	0	0	0	0
Jeff Norton	62	2	11	13	42	–	–	–	–	–
Luke Richardson	82	1	11	12	91	12	0	2	2	14
Barrie Moore(EDM)	4	0	0	0	0	–	–	–	–	–
Michel Petit	18	2	4	6	20	–	–	–	–	–
Greg de Vries	37	0	4	4	52	12	0	1	1	8
David Oliver	17	1	2	3	4	–	–	–	–	–
Louie DeBrusk	32	2	0	2	94	6	0	0	0	4
Ralph Intranuovo(EDM)	5	1	0	1	0	–	–	–	–	–
Curtis Joseph	72	0	2	2	20	12	0	0	0	2
Steve Kelly	8	1	0	1	6	6	0	0	0	2
Donald Dufresne	22	0	1	1	15	3	0	0	0	0
Craig Millar	1	0	0	0	2	–	–	–	–	–
Sean Brown	5	0	0	0	4	–	–	–	–	–
Jesse Belanger	6	0	0	0	0	–	–	–	–	–
Joe Hulbig	6	0	0	0	0	6	0	1	1	2
Bob Essensa	19	0	0	0	4	–	–	–	–	–
Bryan Muir	–	–	–	–	–	5	0	0	0	4

	REGULAR SEASON						PLAYOFFS				
GOALTENDER	GP	MINS	GA	S0	GAA.	W-L-T	GP	MIN	GA	GAA.	W-L
Bob Essensa	19	869	41	1	2.83	4-8-0	–	–	–	–	–
Curtis Joseph	72	4100	200	6	2.93	32-29-9	12	767	36	2.82	5-7

1997-98 SEASON

Regular Season

COACH	GP	W	L	T	PTS	GF	GA
Ron Low	82	00	00	0	00	000	000

Playoffs

GP	W	L	GF	GA
00	0	0	00	00

	REGULAR SEASON					PLAYOFFS				
PLAYER	GP	G	A	PTS	PIM	GP	G	A	PTS	PIM
Doug Weight	79	26	44	70	69	12	2	7	9	14
Dean McAmmond	77	19	31	50	46	12	1	4	5	12
Boris Mironov	81	16	30	46	100	12	3	3	6	27
Janne Niinimaa (EDM)	11	1	8	9	6	11	1	1	2	13
Roman Hamrlik(EDM)	41	6	20	26	48	12	0	6	6	12
Bill Guerin (EDM)	40	13	16	29	80	12	7	1	8	17
Todd Marchant	76	14	21	35	71	12	1	1	2	12
Ryan Smyth	65	20	12	33	44	12	1	3	4	16
Tony Hrkac (EDM)	36	8	11	19	10	12	0	3	3	2
Mats Lindgren	82	13	13	26	42	12	1	1	2	10
Dan McGillis	67	10	15	25	74	-	-	-	-	-
Scott Fraser	29	12	11	23	6	11	1	1	2	0
Andrei Kovalenko	59	6	17	23	28	-	-	-	-	-
Kelly Buchberger	82	6	17	23	122	12	1	2	3	25
Valeri Zelepukin (EDM)	33	2	10	12	57	8	1	2	3	2
Rem Murray	61	9	9	18	39	11	1	4	5	2
Jason Arnott	35	5	13	18	78	-	-	-	-	-
Mike Grier	66	9	6	15	73	12	2	2	4	13
Greg de Vries	65	7	4	11	80	7	0	0	0	21
Bobby Dollas (EDM)	30	2	5	7	22	11	0	0	0	16
Drake Berehowsky	67	1	6	7	169	12	1	2	3	14
Boyd Devereaux	38	1	4	5	6	-	-	-	-	-
Craig Millar	11	4	0	4	8	-	-	-	-	-
Joe Hulbig	17	2	2	4	2	-	-	-	-	-
Ray Whitney	9	1	3	4	0	-	-	-	-	-
Bryan Marchment	27	0	4	4	58	-	-	-	-	-
Mike Watt	14	1	2	3	4	-	-	-	-	-
Frank Musil	17	1	2	3	8	7	0	0	0	6
Steve Kelly	19	0	2	2	8	-	-	-	-	-
Drew Bannister	34	0	2	2	42	-	-	-	-	-
Curtis Joseph	71	0	2	2	4	11	-	-	-	-
Sean Brown	18	0	1	1	43	-	-	-	-	-
Bill Huard	30	0	1	1	72	-	-	-	-	-
Scott Ferguson	1	0	0	0	0	-	-	-	-	-
Ladislav Benysek	2	0	0	0	0	-	-	-	-	-
Jason Bowen	4	0	0	0	0	-	-	-	-	-
Dennis Bonvie	4	0	0	0	27	-	-	-	-	-
Bryan Muir	7	0	0	0	17	-	-	-	-	-
Terran Sandwith	8	0	0	0	6	-	-	-	-	-
Georges Laraque	11	0	0	0	59	-	-	-	-	-
Bob Essensa	16	0	0	0	0	1	-	-	-	-
Doug Friedman	16	0	0	0	0	-	-	-	-	-

	REGULAR SEASON						PLAYOFFS				
GOALTENDER	GP	MINS	GA	S0	GAA.	W-L-T	GP	MIN	GA	GAA.	W-L
Curtis Joseph	71	4132	181	8	2.63	29-31-9	11	716	23	1.93	5-7
Bob Essensa	16	825	35	0	2.55	6-6-1	1	27	1	2.22	0-0

Most 40 Goal Scorers, One Season

4 – Edmonton, '82-83
(Wayne Gretzky, 71; Glenn Anderson, 48; Mark Messier, 48; Jari Kurri, 45. 80 GP)

4 – Edmonton, '83-84
(Wayne Gretzky, 87; Glenn Anderson, 54, Jari Kurri, 52; Paul Coffey, 40. 80 GP)

4 – Edmonton, '84-85
(Wayne Gretzky, 73; Jari Kurri, 71; Mike Krushelnyski, 43; Glenn Anderson, 42. 80 GP)

4 – Edmonton, '85-86
(Jari Kurri, 68; Glenn Anderson, 54; Wayne Gretzky, 52; Paul Coffey, 48. 80 GP)

Award Winners

Hart Memorial
(Most Valuable Player)

1990 – Mark Messier
1987 – Wayne Gretzky
1986 – Wayne Gretzky
1985 – Wayne Gretzky
1984 – Wayne Gretzky
1983 – Wayne Gretzky
1982 – Wayne Gretzky
1981 – Wayne Gretzky
1980 – Wayne Gretzky

Art Ross
(Leading Scorer)

1987 – Wayne Gretzky
1986 – Wayne Gretzky
1985 – Wayne Gretzky
1984 – Wayne Gretzky
1983 – Wayne Gretzky
1982 – Wayne Gretzky
1981 – Wayne Gretzky

Lady Byng
(Most Gentlemanly Player)

1985 – Jari Kurri
1980 – Wayne Gretzky

Jack Adams
(Coach of the Year)

1986 – Glen Sather

Conn Smythe
(Stanley Cup MVP)

1990 – Bill Ranford
1988 – Wayne Gretzky
1985 – Wayne Gretzky
1984 – Mark Messier

James Norris
(Outstanding Defenceman)

1986 – Paul Coffey
1985 – Paul Coffey

Vezina Trophy
(Outstanding Goaltender)

1988 – Grant Fuhr

Emery Edge
(Plus-Minus leader)

1986-87- Wayne Gretzky
1984-85- Wayne Gretzky
1983-84- Wayne Gretzky
1982-83- Charlie Huddy

Lester B. Pearson
(Outstanding player as selected by the NHLPA)

1989-90- Mark Messier
1986-87- Wayne Gretzky
1984-85- Wayne Gretzky
1983-84- Wayne Gretzky
1982-83- Wayne Gretzky

All-Time Standings of NHL Teams

Active clubs ranked by percentage through 96-97 season

	Games Played	Wins	Losses	Ties	Goals For	Goals Against	Points	Winning %	First Season
Montreal	4972	2610	1593	769	16843	13308	5989	.602	1917-18
Philadelphia	2358	1174	818	366	8407	7238	2714	.575	1967-68
Boston	4812	2306	1800	706	15891	14391	5318	.553	1924-25
Edmonton	1420	691	552	177	5816	5287	1559	.549	1979-80
Buffalo	2132	1004	797	331	7604	6862	2339	.549	1970-71
Calgary	1976	925	756	295	7368	6709	2145	.543	1972-73
NY Islanders	1976	898	798	280	7104	6504	2076	.525	1972-73
Florida	296	129	115	52	823	795	310	.524	1993-94
Detroit	4746	2028	1975	743	14736	14585	4799	.506	1926-27
NY Rangers	4746	2016	1989	741	14952	14983	4773	.503	1926-27
Toronto	4972	2129	2121	722	15526	15535	4980	.501	1917-18
St. Louis	2358	989	1011	358	7691	7935	2336	.495	1967-68
Chicago	4746	1964	2048	734	14386	14505	4662	.491	1926-27
Colorado	1420	593	648	179	5228	5328	1365	.481	1979-80
Washington	1820	757	829	234	6140	6473	1748	.480	1974-75
Pittsburgh	2358	964	1082	312	8369	8847	2240	.475	1967-68
Los Angeles	2358	913	1095	350	8203	8836	2176	.461	1967-68
Dallas	2358	891	1090	377	7591	8251	2159	.458	1967-68
Anaheim	296	120	145	31	833	895	271	.458	1993-94
Phoenix (Winnipeg)	1420	544	697	179	5002	5590	1267	.446	1979-80
Hartford (Carolina)	1420	534	709	177	4704	5345	1245	.438	1979-80
Vancouver	2132	780	1043	309	7023	7909	1869	.438	1970-71
Tampa Bay	380	140	197	43	1044	1222	323	.425	1992-93
New Jersey	1820	616	949	255	5746	6870	1487	.409	1974-75
San Jose	460	127	291	42	1281	1834	296	.322	1991-92
Ottawa	380	82	260	38	937	1491	202	.266	1992-93

Calgary totals include Atlanta, 1972-73 to 1979-80
Colorado totals include Quebec, 1979-80 to 1994-95
Dallas totals include Minnesota, 1967-68 to 1992-93
Detroit totals include Cougars, 1926-27 to 1928-29, and Falcons, 1929-30 to 1931-32
New Jersey totals include Kansas City, 1974-75 and Colorado Rockies, 1976-77 to 1981-82
Toronto toals include Arenas, 1917-18 to 1918-19 and St. Patricks, 1919-20 to 1925-56

All-time leaders

GAMES PLAYED
1. Kevin Lowe — 1037
2. Mark Messier — 851
3. Glenn Anderson — 845
4. Jari Kurri — 754
5. Craig MacTavish — 701

GOALS
1. Wayne Gretzky — 583
2. Jari Kurri — 474
3. Glenn Anderson — 417
4. Mark Messier — 392
5. Paul Coffey — 209

ASSISTS
1. Wayne Gretzky — 1086
2. Mark Messier — 642
3. Jari Kurri — 569
4. Glenn Anderson — 489
5. Paul Coffey — 460

POINTS
1. Wyane Gretzky — 1669
2. Jari Kurri — 1043
3. Mark Messier — 1034
4. Glenn Anderson — 906
5. Paul Coffey — 669

PENALTIES
1. Kelly Buchberger — 1557
2. Kevin McClelland — 1298
3. Kevin Lowe — 1214
4. Mark Messier — 1122
5. Steve Smith — 1080

HAT TRICKS
1. Wayne Gretzky — 43
2. Glenn Anderson — 20
   Jari Kurri — 20
4. Mark Messier — 13
5. Esa Tikkanen — 5

POWERPLAY GOALS
1. Glenn Anderson — 126
2. Wayne Gretzky — 125
3. Jari Kurri — 107
4. Mark Messier — 89
5. Craig Simpson — 75

SHORTHANDED GOALS
1. Wayne Gretzky — 55
2. Mark Messier — 36
3. Jari Kurri — 31
4. Craig MacTavish — 29
5. Esa Tikkanen — 21

GAME WINNING GOALS
1. Glenn Anderson — 73
2. Wayne Gretzky — 61
3. Jari Kurri — 60
4. Mark Messier — 43
5. Esa Tikkanen — 30

ROOKIE RECORDS

SCORING

	GP	G	A	PTS	PIM	SEASON
1. Jari Kurri	75	32	43	75	40	80-81
2. Jason Arnott	78	33	35	68	104	94-95
3. Dave Lumley	80	30	28	58	138	79-80
4. Glenn Anderson	58	30	23	53	24	80-81
5. Raimo Summanen	73	19	18	37	16	85-86

GAMES PLAYED
1. Remy Murray — 82 — 96-97
2. Dave Lumley — 80 — 79-80
3. Randy Gregg — 80 — 82-83
4. Mike Grier — 79 — 96-97
5. Jason Arnott — 78 — 93-94

GOALS
1. Jason Arnott — 33 — 93-94
2. Jari Kurri — 32 — 80-81
3. Glenn Anderson — 30 — 80-81
4. Dave Lumley — 20 — 79-80
5. R. Summanen — 19 — 85-86

ASSISTS
1. Jari Kurri — 43 — 80-81
2. Dave Lumley — 38 — 79-80
3. Jason Arnott — 35 — 93-94
4. Glenn Anderson — 23 — 80-81
   Paul Coffey — 23 — 80-81

PENALTY MINUTES
1. Kelly Buchberger — 234 — 88-89
2. Steve Smith — 166 — 85-86
3. Dave Lumley — 138 — 79-80
4. Paul Coffey — 130 — 80-81
5. Jeff Beukeboom — 124 — 86-87

GOALTENDING RECORDS

GAMES PLAYED
1. Bill Ranford — 433
2. Grant Fuhr — 423
3. Andy Moog — 235
4. Curtis Joseph — 177
5. Eddie Mio — 77

WINS
1. Grant Fuhr — 226
2. Bill Ranford — 163
3. Andy Moog — 143
4. Curtis Joseph — 76
5. Ron Low — 30

LOSSES
1. Bill Ranford — 187
2. Grant Fuhr — 117
3. Curtis Joseph — 76
4. Andy Moog — 53
5. Eddie Mio — 28

SHUTOUTS
1. Curtis Joseph — 14
2. Grant Fuhr — 9
3. Bill Ranford — 8
4. Andy Moog — 4
5. Bob Essensa/Eddie Mio — 1

STANLEY CUP CHAMPIONS

YEAR	COACH
1990	John Muckler
1988	Glen Sather
1987	Glen Sather
1985	Glen Sather
1984	Glen Sather